ULTra MaNiaC

Story and Art by
Wataru Yoshizumi

Vol. 3

Characters

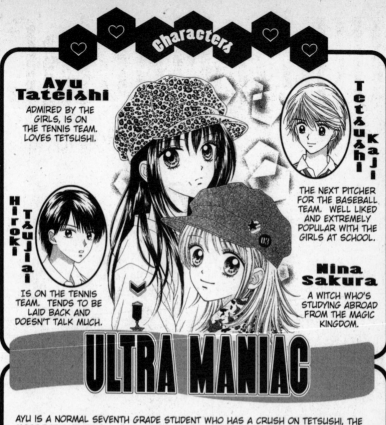

Ayu Tateishi

ADMIRED BY THE GIRLS, IS ON THE TENNIS TEAM. LOVES TETSUSHI.

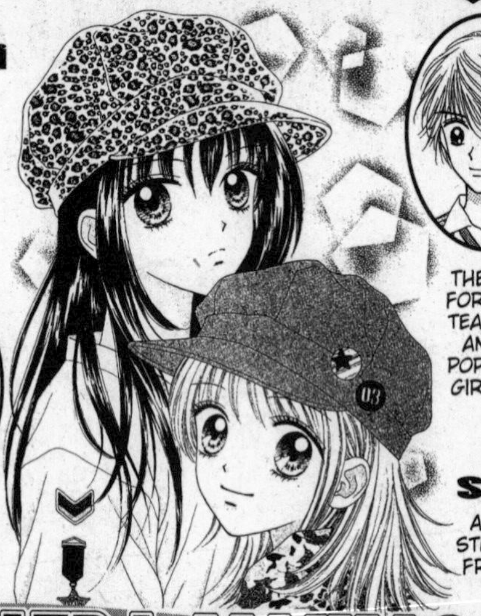

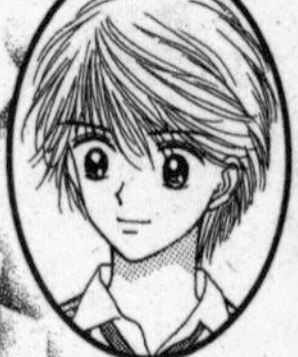

Tetsushi Kaji

THE NEXT PITCHER FOR THE BASEBALL TEAM. WELL LIKED AND EXTREMELY POPULAR WITH THE GIRLS AT SCHOOL.

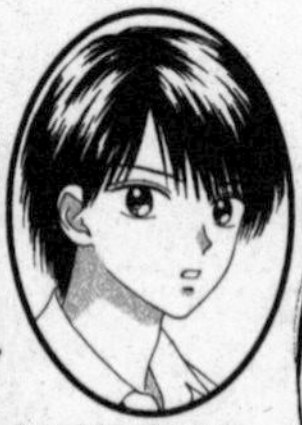

Hiroki Tsujiai

IS ON THE TENNIS TEAM. TENDS TO BE LAID BACK AND DOESN'T TALK MUCH.

Nina Sakura

A WITCH WHO'S STUDYING ABROAD FROM THE MAGIC KINGDOM.

ULTRA MANIAC

AYU IS A NORMAL SEVENTH GRADE STUDENT WHO HAS A CRUSH ON TETSUSHI, THE MOST POPULAR BOY IN HER CLASS. AFTER A CHANCE ENCOUNTER WITH A GIRL NAMED NINA, HER LIFE SUDDENLY TURNS UPSIDE DOWN. NINA, AS IT TURNS OUT, IS A WITCH, AND AYU HAS LEARNED THAT SHE'S A TRANSFER STUDENT FROM A PLACE CALLED THE MAGIC KINGDOM!

BY ACCIDENT, NINA SEES TETSUSHI THROWING AWAY HOMEMADE COOKIES. AT FIRST SHE THINKS HE HAS A BAD ATTITUDE. BUT LATER DISCOVERS THAT HE IS A BOY WHO ONLY FEELS COMFORTABLE ACCEPTING GIFTS FROM SOMEONE WHO HE REALLY CARES FOR. BECAUSE OF THIS, NINA STARTS LIKING TETSUSHI, TOO...

MEANWHILE, NINA'S LONG-TIME FRIEND YUTA GIVES HER A MOST UNUSUAL GIFT: A MAGICAL CAMERA THAT CAN REVEAL TRUE LOVE! WHEN AYU POINTS THIS CAMERA AT NINA, SHE IS SHOCKED TO DISCOVER THAT HER NEW BEST FRIEND ALSO HAS A CRUSH ON THE BOY SHE LOVES. ACK! YOUNG LOVE IS SO COMPLICATED!

TETSUSHI, HOWEVER, WANTS TO HANG OUT WITH AYU. BUT BECAUSE OF THE MAGICAL CAMERA, AYU IS HESITANT TO GO ON A DATE WITH HIM. NINA, HOWEVER, WANTS HER TWO NEW FRIENDS TO BE HAPPY AND ENCOURAGES THEM TO GET TOGETHER—WHICH THEY DO. NOW, IN A SURPRISE REVELATION, TETSUSHI'S BEST FRIEND, HIROKI, SEEMS TO BE INTERESTED IN NINA...

The Story Thus Far

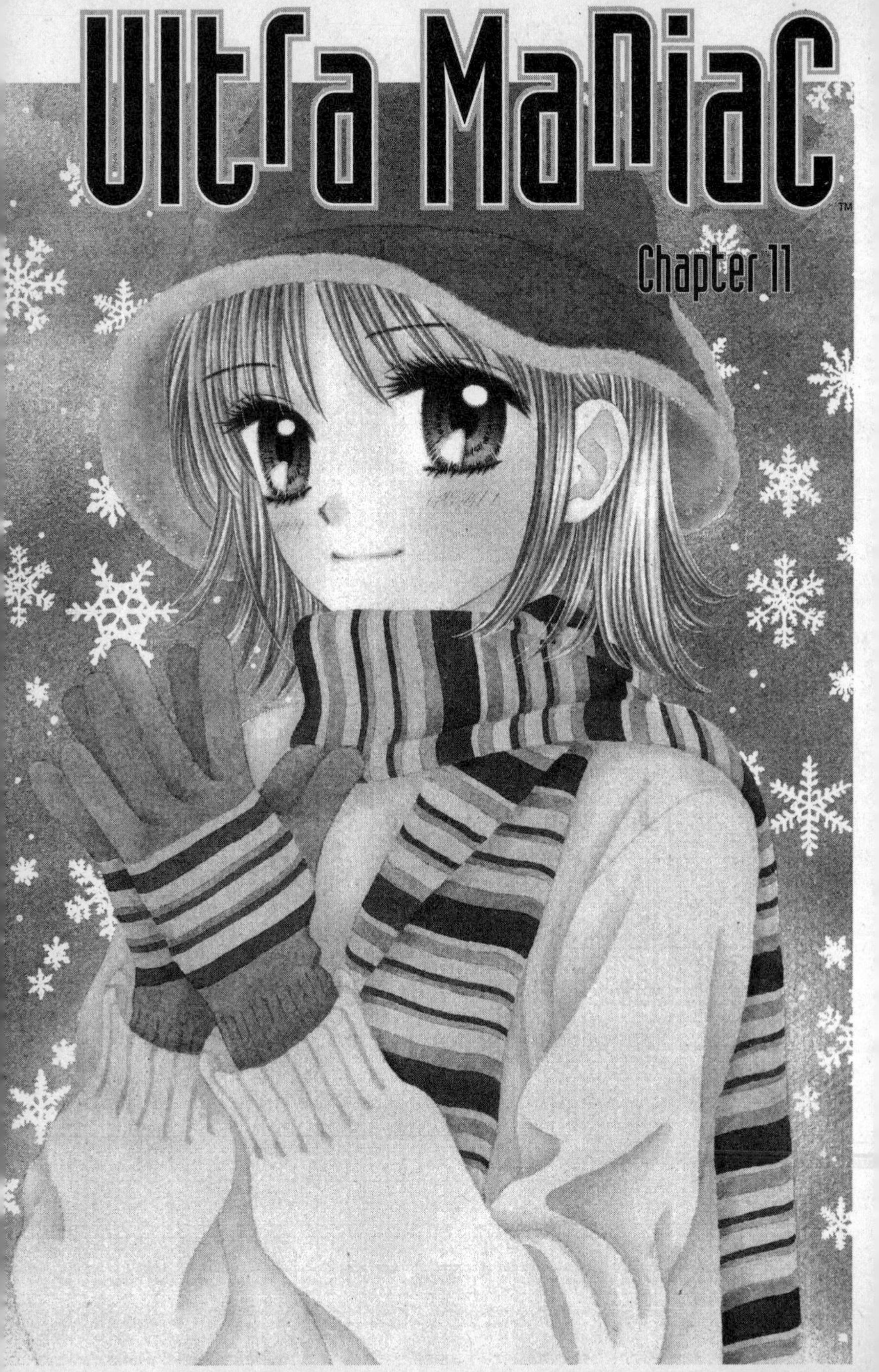
Ultra Maniac™
Chapter 11

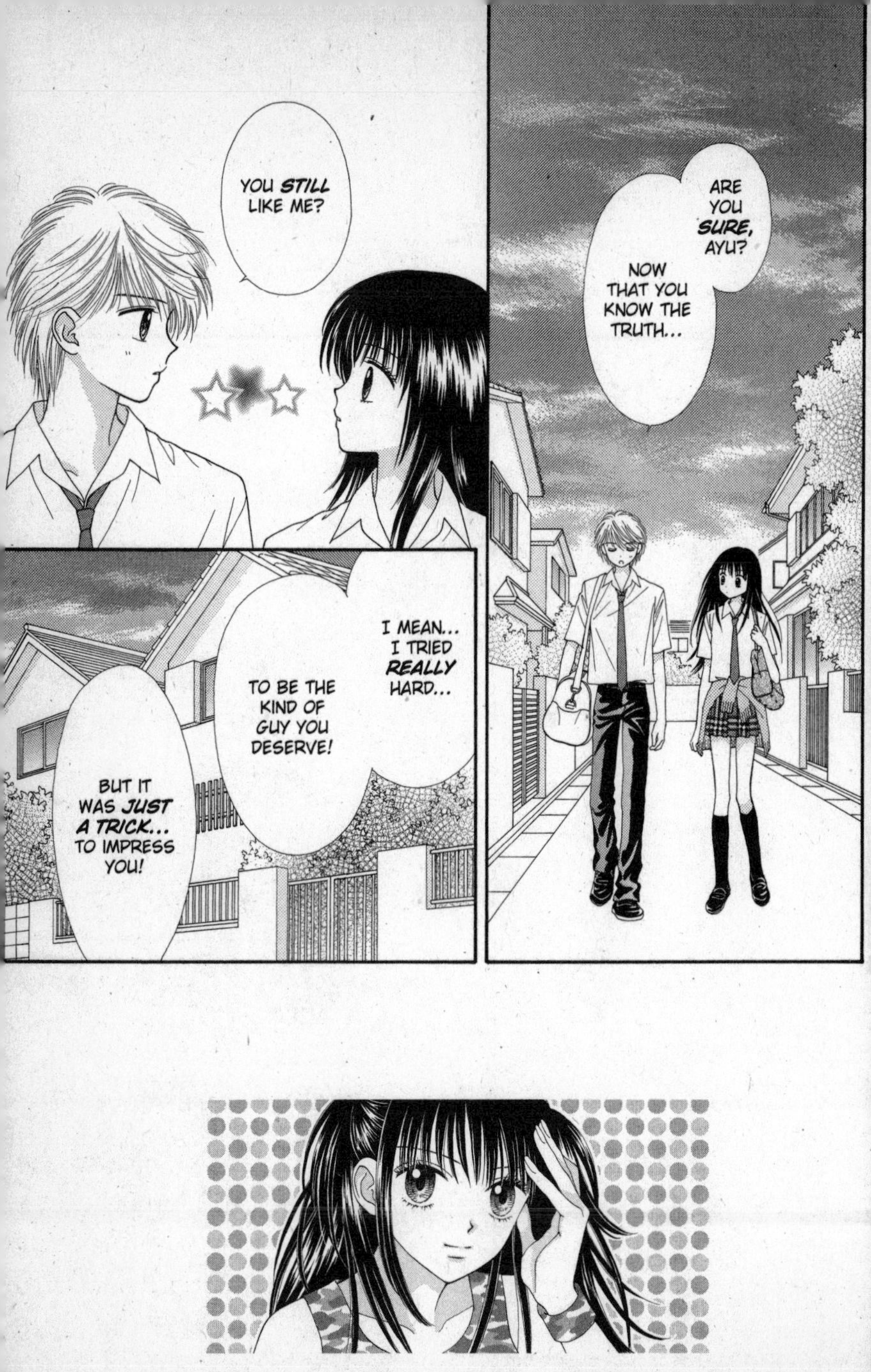
ARE YOU SURE, AYU?
NOW THAT YOU KNOW THE TRUTH...
YOU STILL LIKE ME?
I MEAN... I TRIED REALLY HARD...
TO BE THE KIND OF GUY YOU DESERVE!
BUT IT WAS JUST A TRICK... TO IMPRESS YOU!

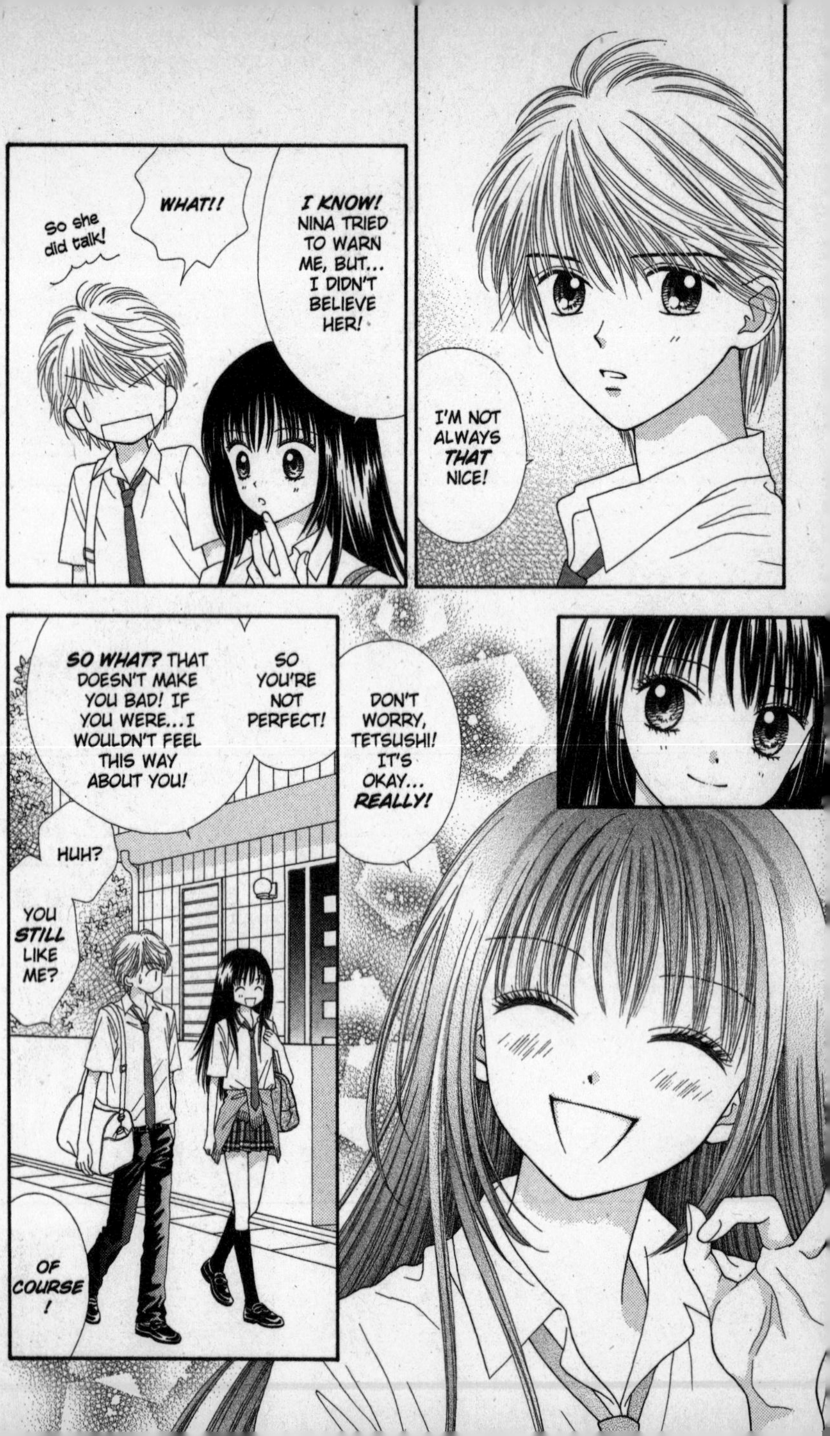
I'M NOT ALWAYS THAT NICE!
I KNOW! NINA TRIED TO WARN ME, BUT... I DIDN'T BELIEVE HER!
WHAT!!
So she did talk!
DON'T WORRY, TETSUSHI! IT'S OKAY... REALLY!
SO YOU'RE NOT PERFECT!
SO WHAT? THAT DOESN'T MAKE YOU BAD! IF YOU WERE...I WOULDN'T FEEL THIS WAY ABOUT YOU!
HUH?
YOU STILL LIKE ME?
OF COURSE!

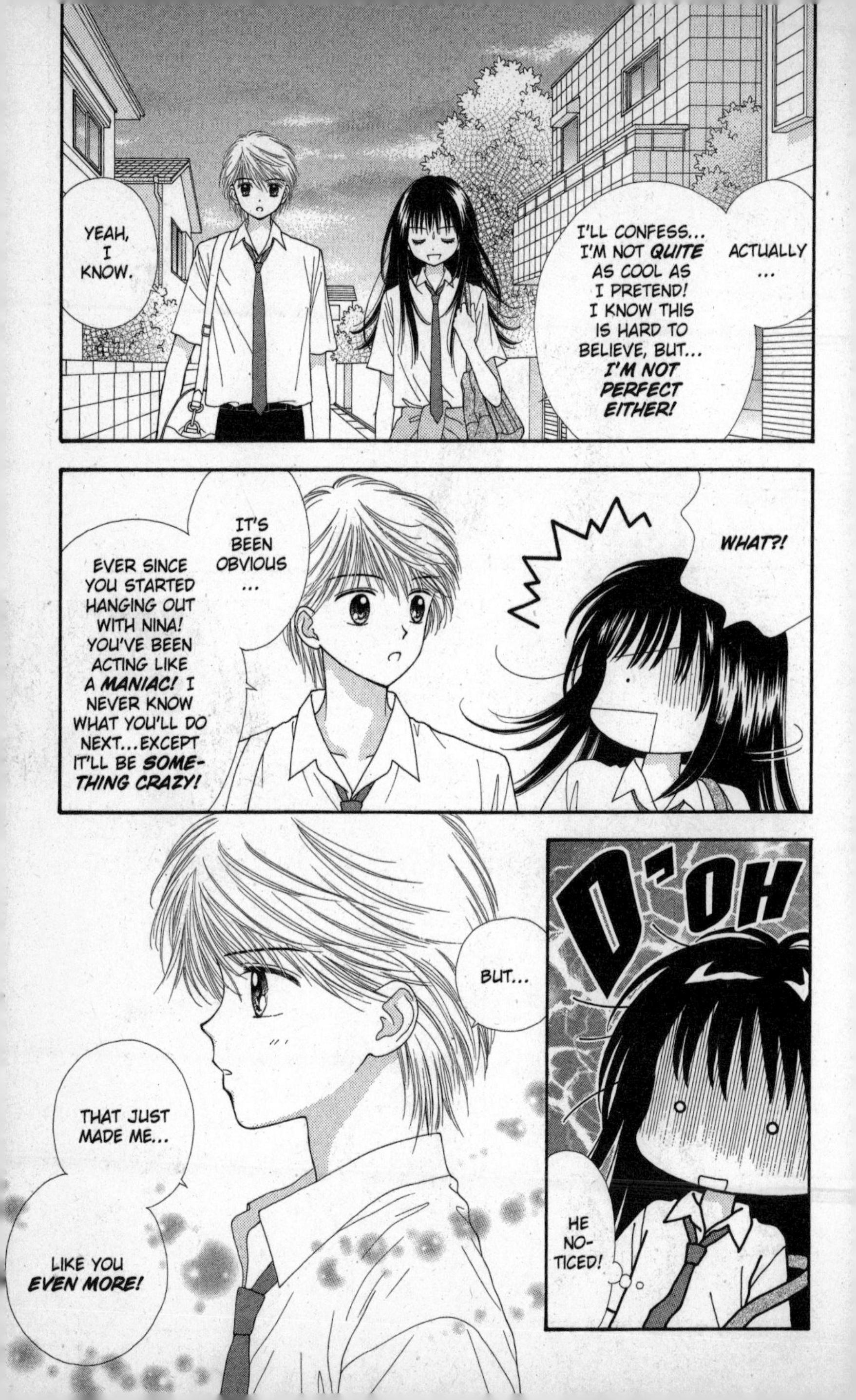
ACTUALLY ...
I'LL CONFESS... I'M NOT QUITE AS COOL AS I PRETEND! I KNOW THIS IS HARD TO BELIEVE, BUT... I'M NOT PERFECT EITHER!
YEAH, I KNOW.
WHAT?!
IT'S BEEN OBVIOUS ...
EVER SINCE YOU STARTED HANGING OUT WITH NINA! YOU'VE BEEN ACTING LIKE A MANIAC! I NEVER KNOW WHAT YOU'LL DO NEXT...EXCEPT IT'LL BE SOMETHING CRAZY!
D'OH
HE NOTICED!
BUT...
THAT JUST MADE ME...
LIKE YOU EVEN MORE!

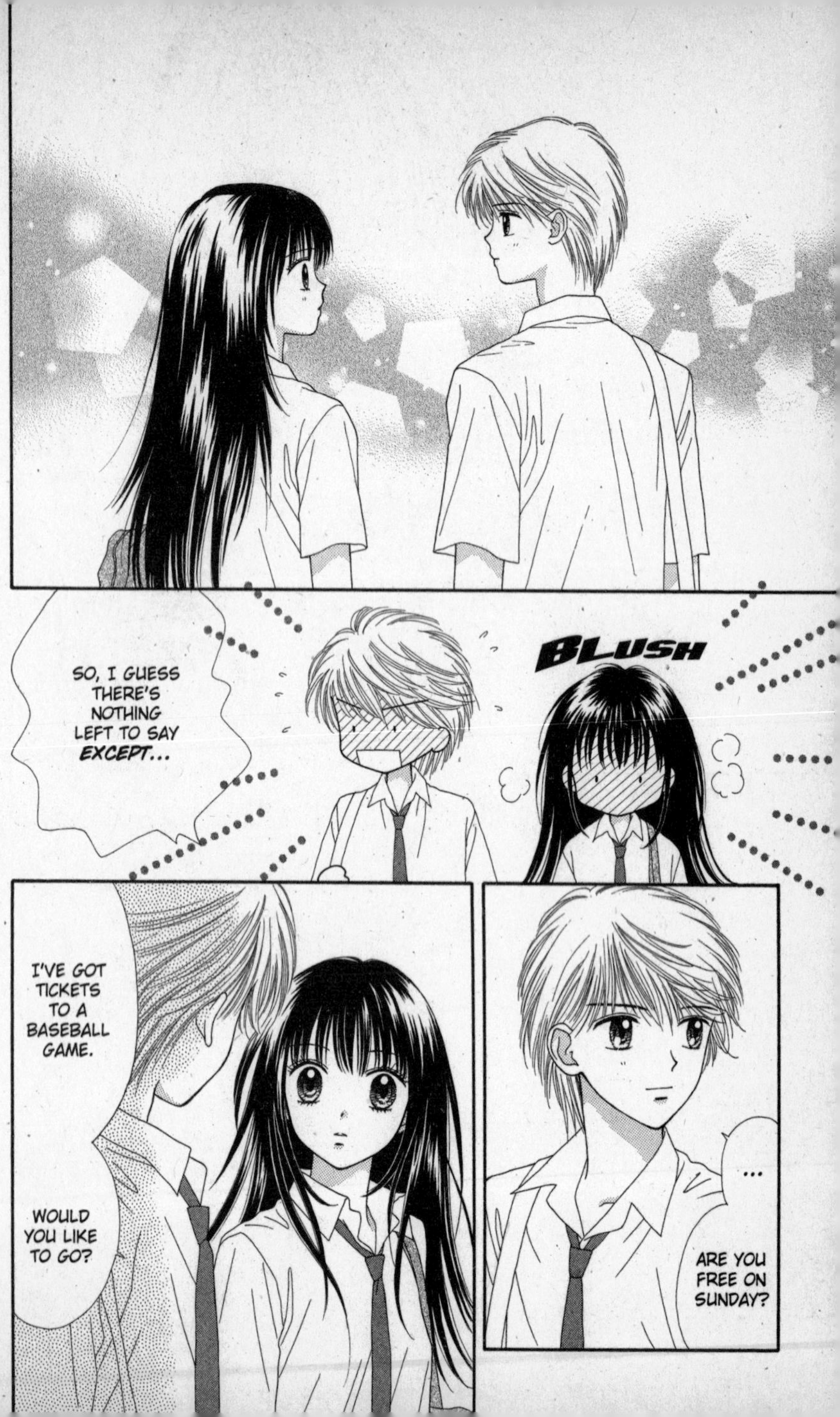
BLUSH
SO, I GUESS THERE'S NOTHING LEFT TO SAY *EXCEPT*...
...
ARE YOU FREE ON SUNDAY?
I'VE GOT TICKETS TO A BASEBALL GAME.
WOULD YOU LIKE TO GO?

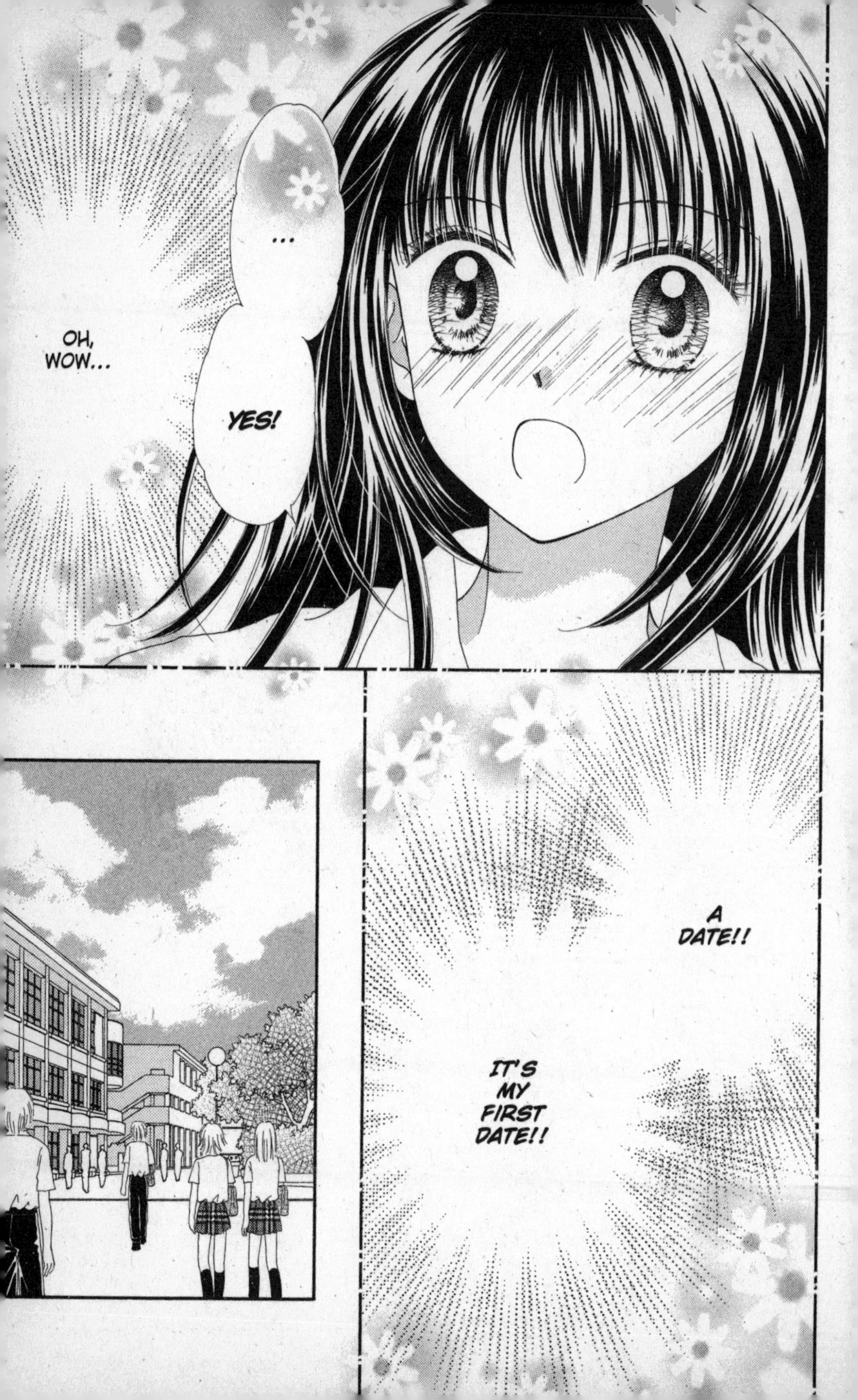
...
YES!
OH, WOW...
A DATE!!
IT'S MY FIRST DATE!!

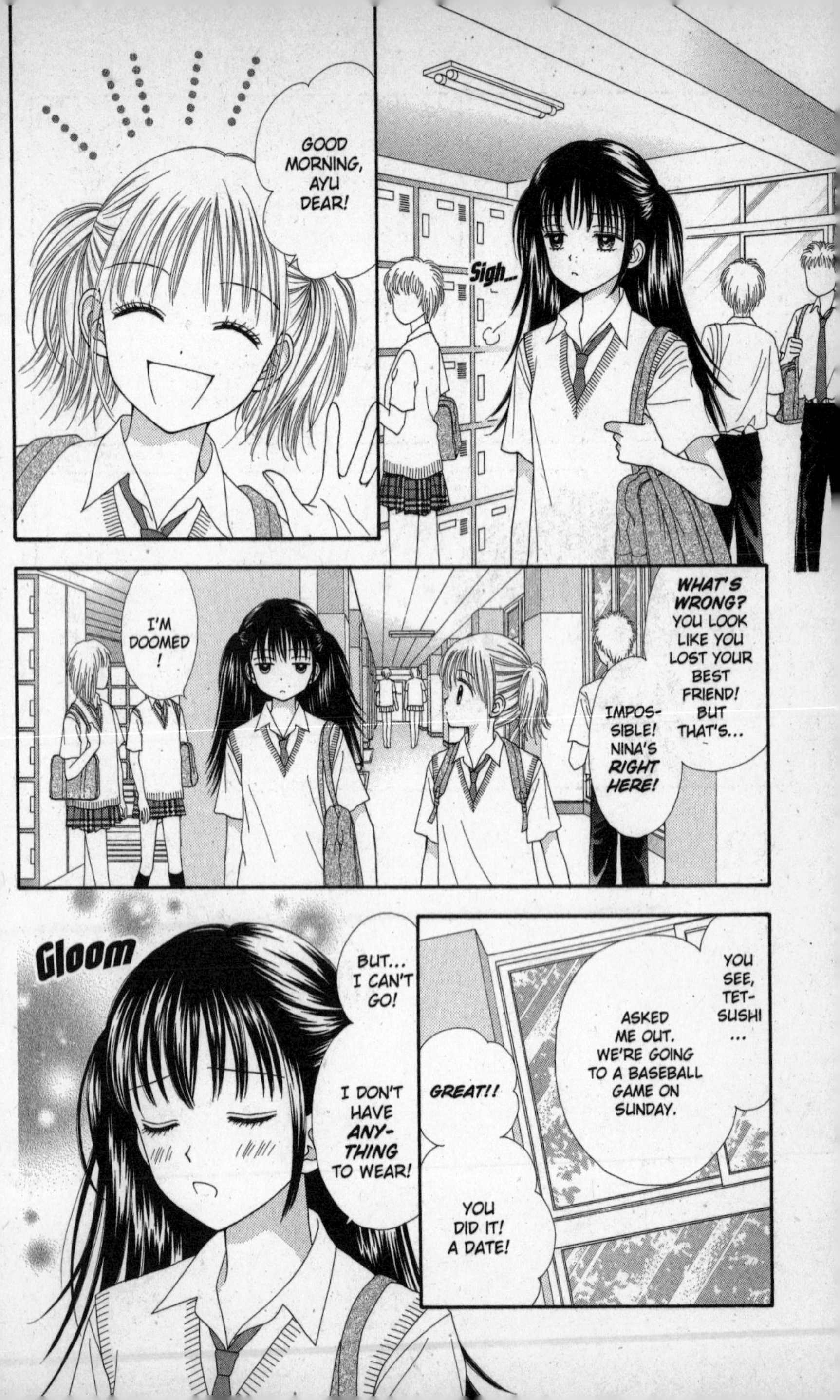
Sigh...
GOOD MORNING, AYU DEAR!
WHAT'S WRONG? YOU LOOK LIKE YOU LOST YOUR BEST FRIEND! BUT THAT'S...
IMPOSSIBLE! NINA'S RIGHT HERE!
I'M DOOMED!
YOU SEE, TETSUSHI...
ASKED ME OUT. WE'RE GOING TO A BASEBALL GAME ON SUNDAY.
GREAT!!
YOU DID IT! A DATE!
Gloom
BUT... I CAN'T GO!
I DON'T HAVE ANYTHING TO WEAR!

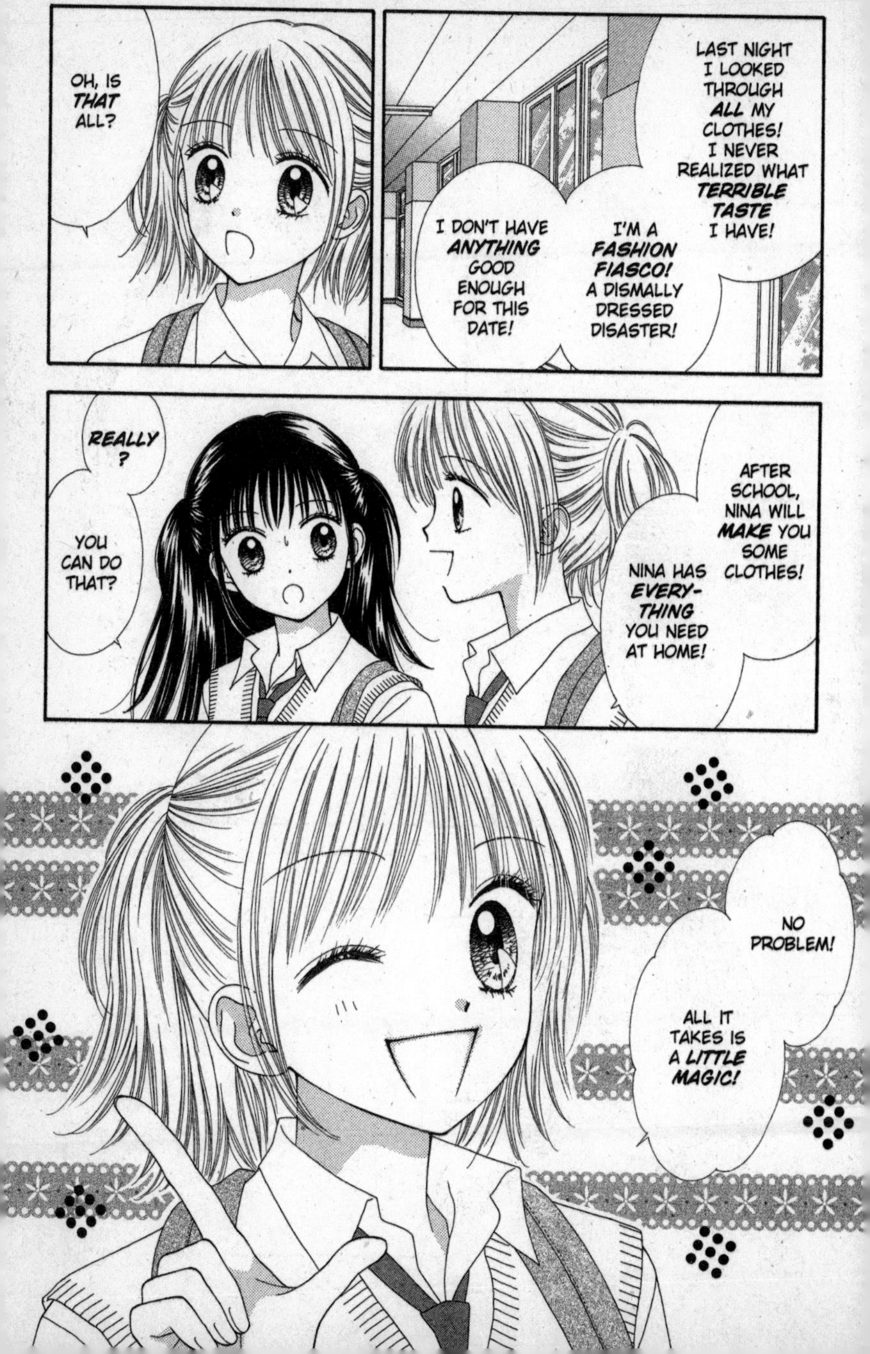
LAST NIGHT I LOOKED THROUGH ALL MY CLOTHES! I NEVER REALIZED WHAT TERRIBLE TASTE I HAVE!
I'M A FASHION FIASCO! A DISMALLY DRESSED DISASTER!
I DON'T HAVE ANYTHING GOOD ENOUGH FOR THIS DATE!
OH, IS THAT ALL?
AFTER SCHOOL, NINA WILL MAKE YOU SOME CLOTHES!
NINA HAS EVERYTHING YOU NEED AT HOME!
REALLY?
YOU CAN DO THAT?
NO PROBLEM!
ALL IT TAKES IS A LITTLE MAGIC!

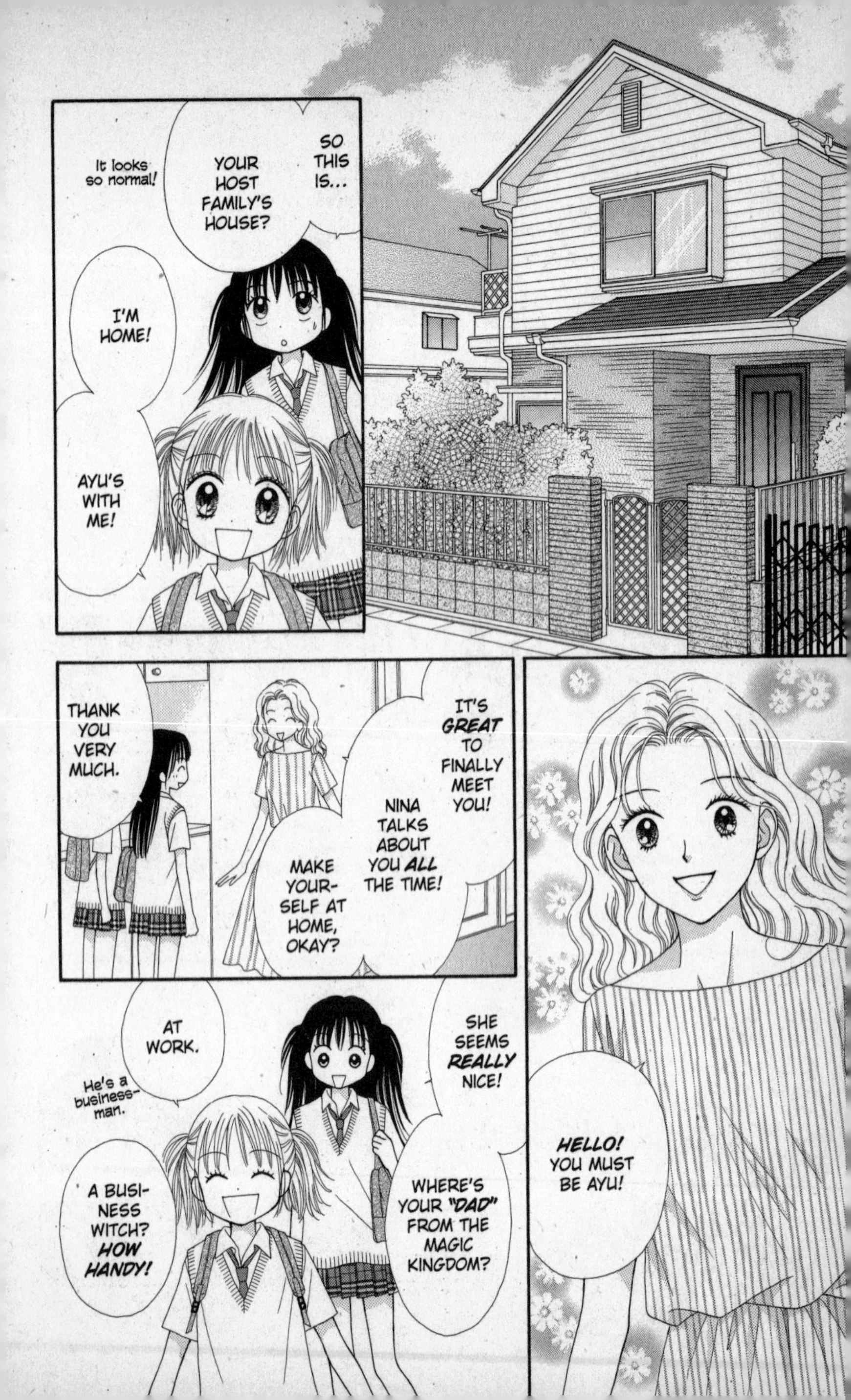
SO THIS IS...
YOUR HOST FAMILY'S HOUSE?
It looks so normal!
I'M HOME!
AYU'S WITH ME!
HELLO! YOU MUST BE AYU!
IT'S GREAT TO FINALLY MEET YOU!
NINA TALKS ABOUT YOU ALL THE TIME!
MAKE YOUR-SELF AT HOME, OKAY?
THANK YOU VERY MUCH.
SHE SEEMS REALLY NICE!
WHERE'S YOUR "DAD" FROM THE MAGIC KINGDOM?
AT WORK.
He's a business-man.
A BUSI-NESS WITCH? HOW HANDY!

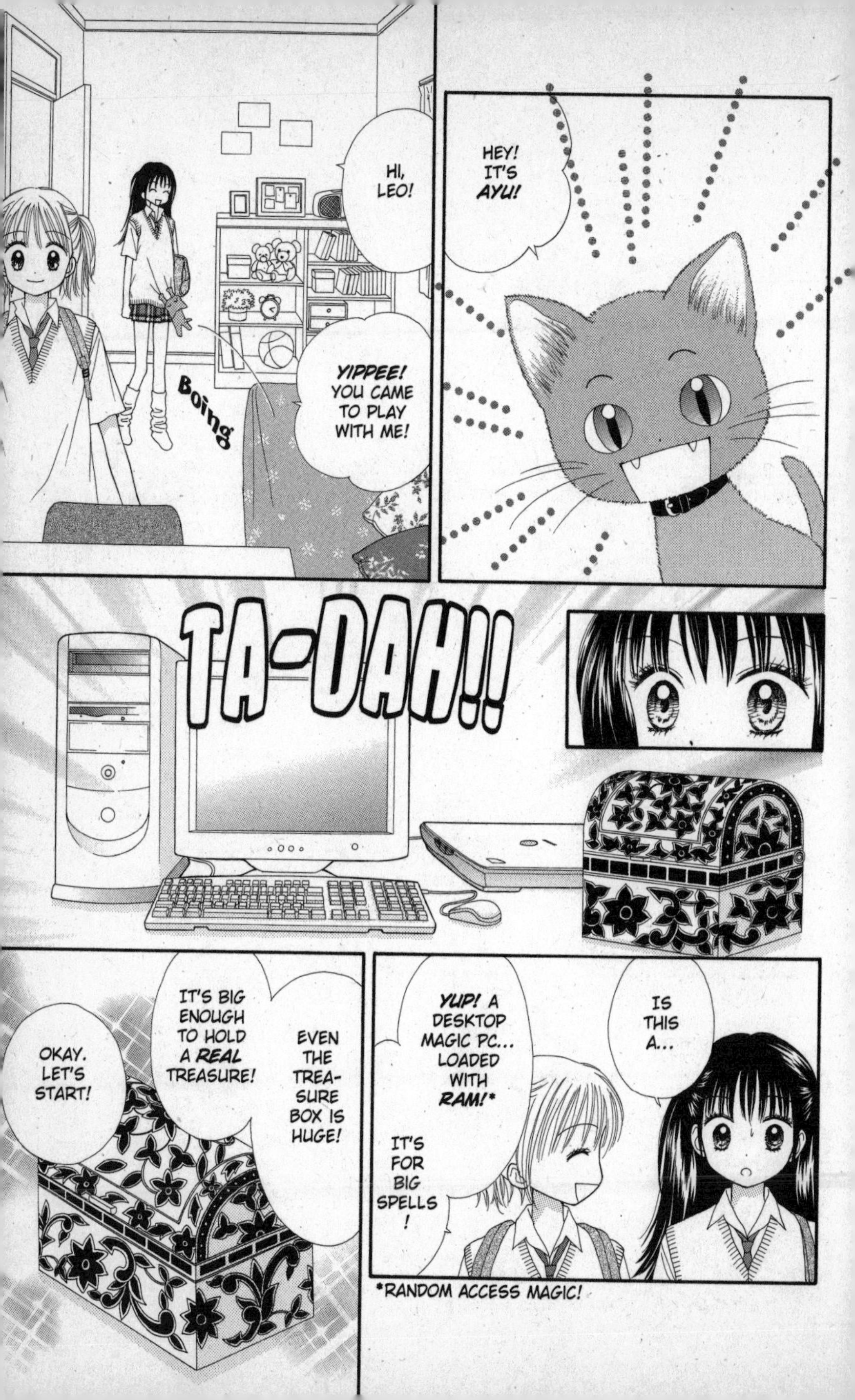
HEY! IT'S *AYU!*
HI, LEO!
YIPPEE! YOU CAME TO PLAY WITH ME!
Boing
TA-DAH!!
IS THIS A...
YUP! A DESKTOP MAGIC PC... LOADED WITH *RAM!**
IT'S FOR BIG SPELLS!
EVEN THE TREA-SURE BOX IS HUGE!
IT'S BIG ENOUGH TO HOLD A *REAL* TREASURE!
OKAY. LET'S START!
*RANDOM ACCESS MAGIC!

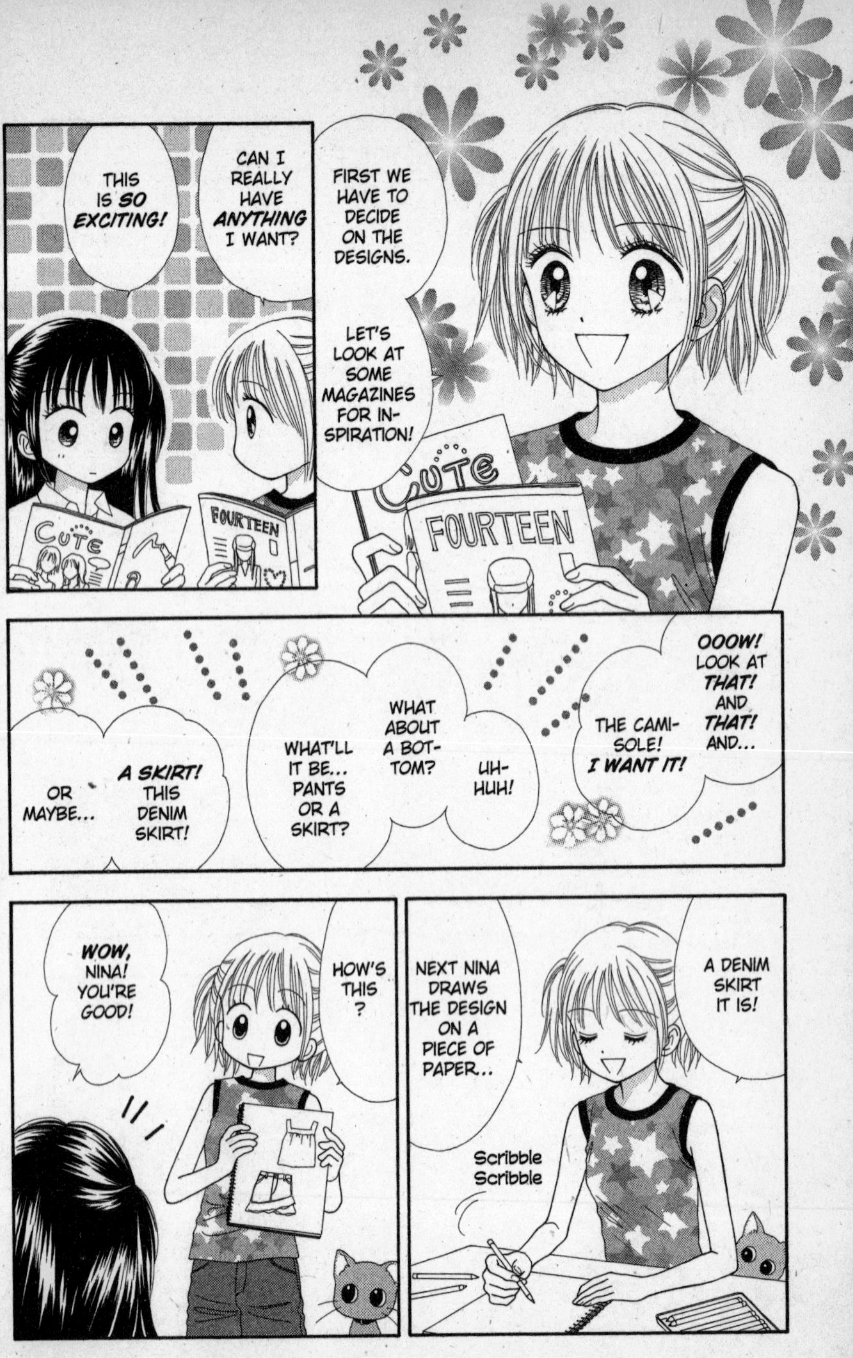
FIRST WE HAVE TO DECIDE ON THE DESIGNS.
LET'S LOOK AT SOME MAGAZINES FOR INSPIRATION!
CUTE
FOURTEEN
CAN I REALLY HAVE *ANYTHING* I WANT?
THIS IS *SO EXCITING!*
FOURTEEN
CUTE
OOOW! LOOK AT *THAT!* AND *THAT!* AND...
THE CAMISOLE! *I WANT IT!*
UH-HUH!
WHAT ABOUT A BOTTOM?
WHAT'LL IT BE... PANTS OR A SKIRT?
A SKIRT! THIS DENIM SKIRT!
OR MAYBE...
A DENIM SKIRT IT IS!
NEXT NINA DRAWS THE DESIGN ON A PIECE OF PAPER...
Scribble Scribble
HOW'S THIS?
WOW, NINA! YOU'RE GOOD!

FREE TALK 1

Hello! This is Wataru Yoshizumi and this is Volume Three of my series, *Ultra Maniac*.

As I write these words, the TV anime of *Ultra Maniac* hasn't been broadcast yet. So I don't know if it'll be a success. But I hope it will be!

By the time you read this, though, the CS Animax Channel will already have begun broadcasting the series in Japan.

(Editor's note: The series was first broadcast in Japan in May of 2003. In North America, the first DVD of the series was released in April of 2005.)

As soon as I started working on the *Ultra Maniac* manga, the folks over at Bandai-Ashi Productions wanted to do it as anime. Why? Well, I'd like to think it's because the series is so good. But maybe it's just that Bandai-Ashi thinks *Ultra Maniac* toys will be easy to make and will sell well because it's a fantasy series.

At first, we were planning the anime for broadcast on regular network TV. Unfortunately, that didn't happen. There weren't enough advertisers interested in sponsoring the show. So we had to take another approach.

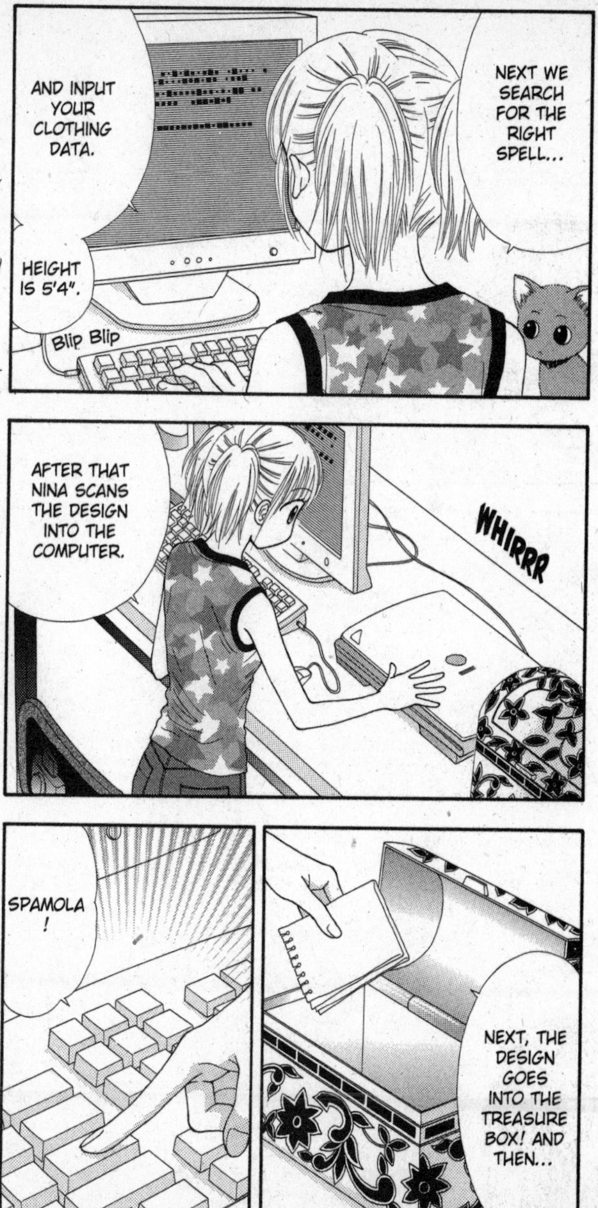
NEXT WE SEARCH FOR THE RIGHT SPELL...
AND INPUT YOUR CLOTHING DATA.
HEIGHT IS 5'4".
Blip Blip
AFTER THAT NINA SCANS THE DESIGN INTO THE COMPUTER.
WHIRRR
NEXT, THE DESIGN GOES INTO THE TREASURE BOX! AND THEN...
SPAMOLA!

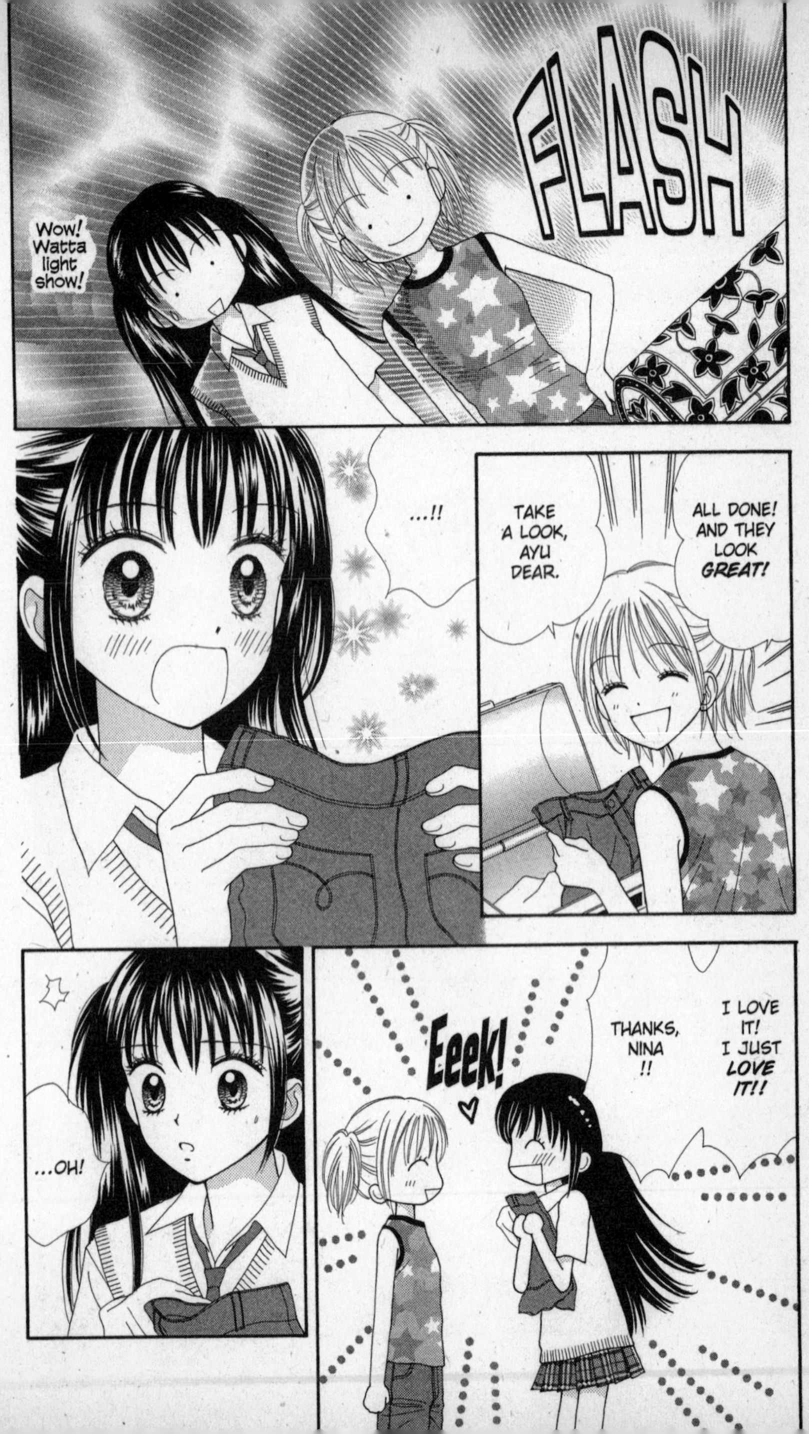
FLASH
Wow! Watta light show!
ALL DONE! AND THEY LOOK GREAT!
TAKE A LOOK, AYU DEAR.
...!!
I LOVE IT! I JUST LOVE IT!!
THANKS, NINA !!
Eeek!
...OH!

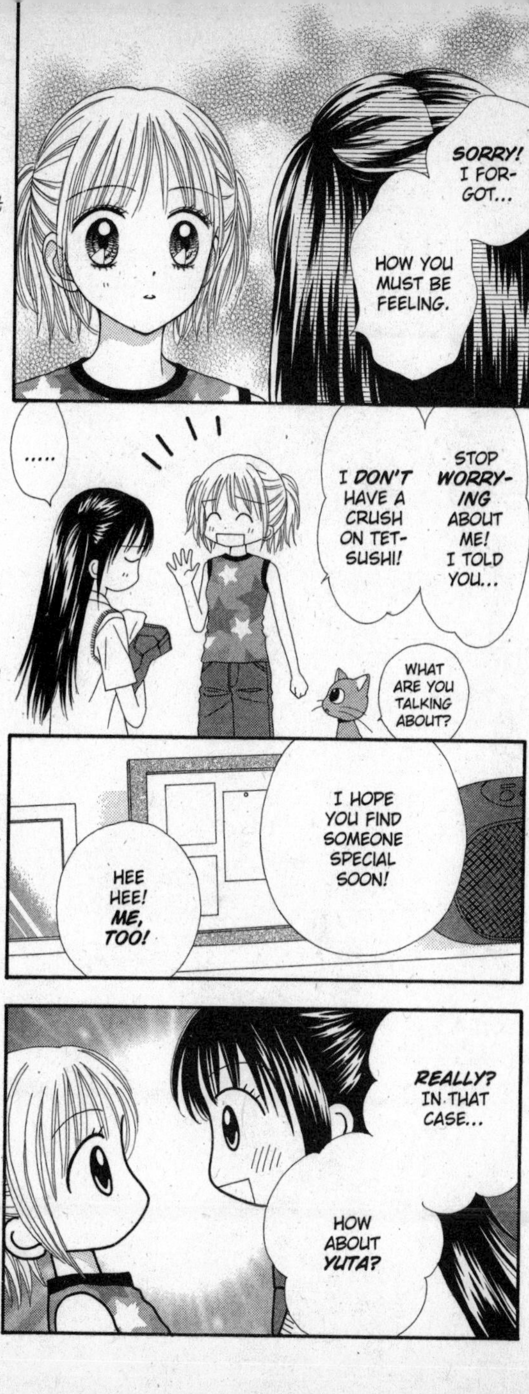
SORRY! I FORGOT...
HOW YOU MUST BE FEELING.
STOP WORRYING ABOUT ME! I TOLD YOU...
I DON'T HAVE A CRUSH ON TETSUSHI!
.....
WHAT ARE YOU TALKING ABOUT?
I HOPE YOU FIND SOMEONE SPECIAL SOON!
HEE HEE! ME, TOO!
REALLY? IN THAT CASE...
HOW ABOUT YUTA?

FREE TALK 2

After the TV network deal was shot down, the folks at Bandai-Ashi Productions had an idea. "How about if we make all 26 episodes into a DVD?" they asked. So we went ahead and did that. But then, before the DVDs went on sale, Bandai-Ashi made a deal to have the episodes aired on the CS Animax Channel. And so, instead of an animated TV series, it was more of an animated DVD series.

Animax is a premium channel and only available to subscribers. But if *Ultra Maniac* was part of a standard TV broadcast, there'd be areas that wouldn't receive the signal. So which is better? Well. . . premium channels can be viewed anywhere as long as you have a subscription. So maybe premium channels are better?

Premium channels can come in handy. In order to watch soccer four or five years ago, I subscribed to the Scapa Channel. Lucky me! ♡

Of course, even if you can't watch *Ultra Maniac* on TV, the DVD is being released. So, **please please please** buy or rent it!! Thanks! ♡

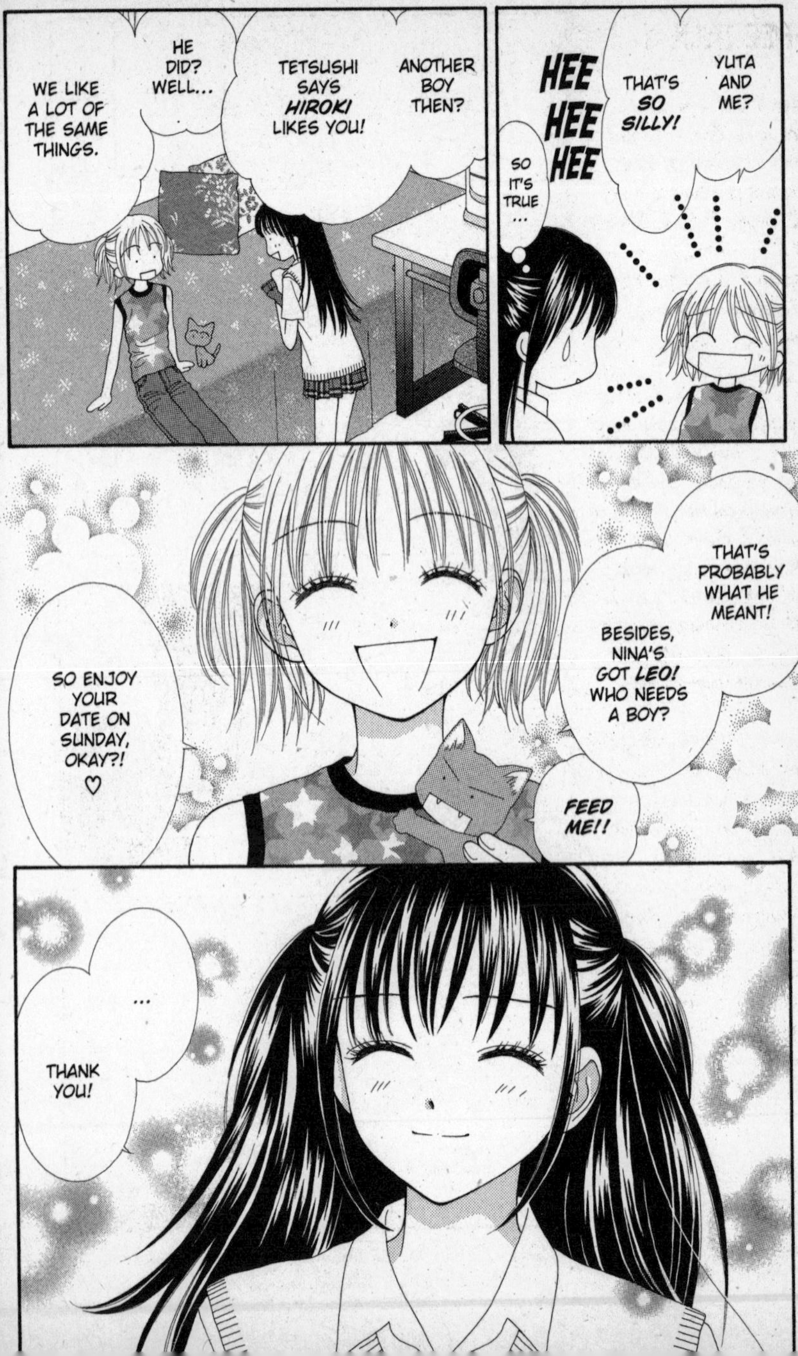
YUTA AND ME?
THAT'S *SO SILLY!*
HEE HEE HEE
SO IT'S TRUE ...
ANOTHER BOY THEN?
TETSUSHI SAYS *HIROKI* LIKES YOU!
HE DID? WELL...
WE LIKE A LOT OF THE SAME THINGS.
THAT'S PROBABLY WHAT HE MEANT!
BESIDES, NINA'S GOT *LEO!* WHO NEEDS A BOY?
FEED ME!!
SO ENJOY YOUR DATE ON SUNDAY, OKAY?! ♡
...
THANK YOU!

FREE TALK 3

Before Bandai-Ashi produced the regular anime series, it created a stand-alone episode of *Ultra Maniac* that premiered at Ribon's 2002 Summer Festival. (A yearly event during which fans can get autographs from artists, view art and buy limited-edition merchandise.)

When Bandai-Ashi produced the regular series, it kept some things the same as the stand-alone series. For instance, the art and the voice actors for Tetsushi and Hiroki are unchanged. But Bandai-Ashi did recast a couple of roles. In the original, Satsuki Yukino was Ayu and Mayuko Sumimura supplied the voice of Nina. Both were really good, but they were replaced.

The new DVD is being distributed by King Records and it's also planning on releasing a CD featuring songs sung by the characters of Nina and Ayu. I think King wanted voice actresses who'd be able to sing. So Yui Horie will play the part of Ayu, and Ayumi Kanda will be Nina. Both are very good. Yui originally came to audition for the part of Nina, but the producer decided she'd be a better Ayu. I agree!

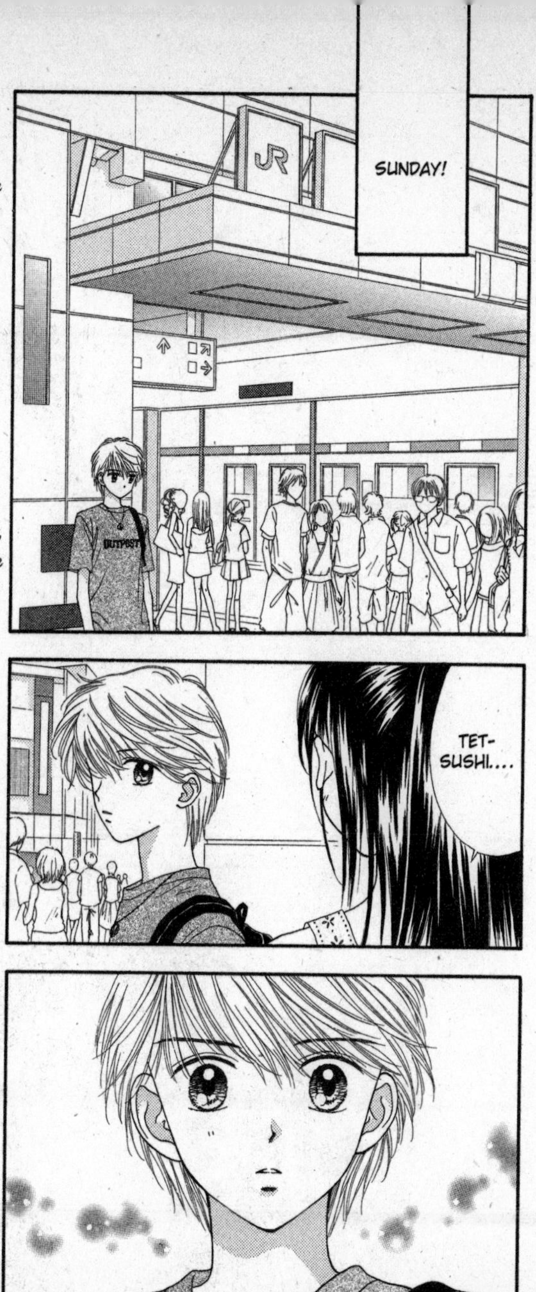
SUNDAY!
JR
OUTPOST
TET-SUSHI....

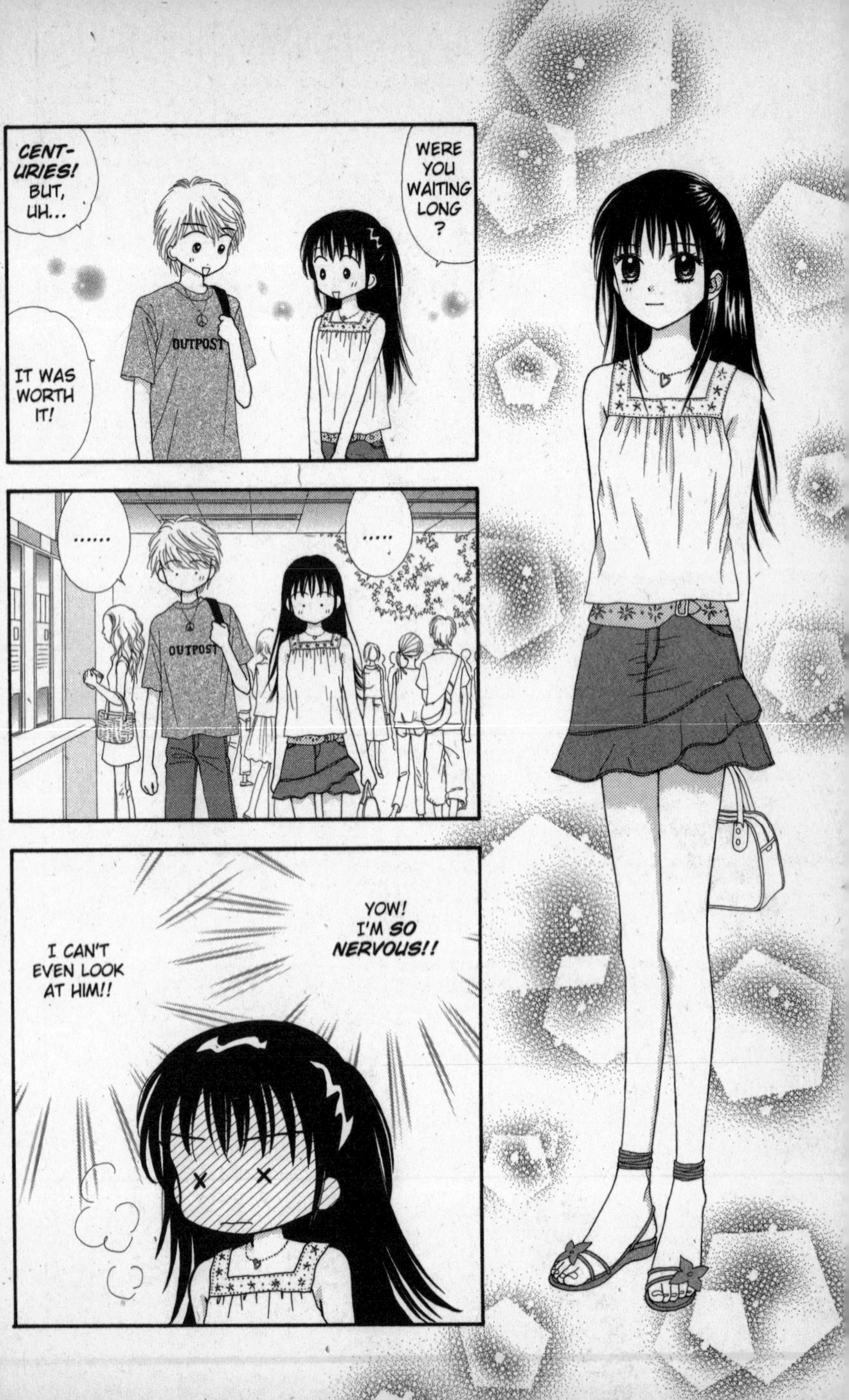
WERE YOU WAITING LONG?
CENTURIES! BUT, UH...
IT WAS WORTH IT!
OUTPOST
.....
......
YOW! I'M *SO NERVOUS!!*
I CAN'T EVEN LOOK AT HIM!!

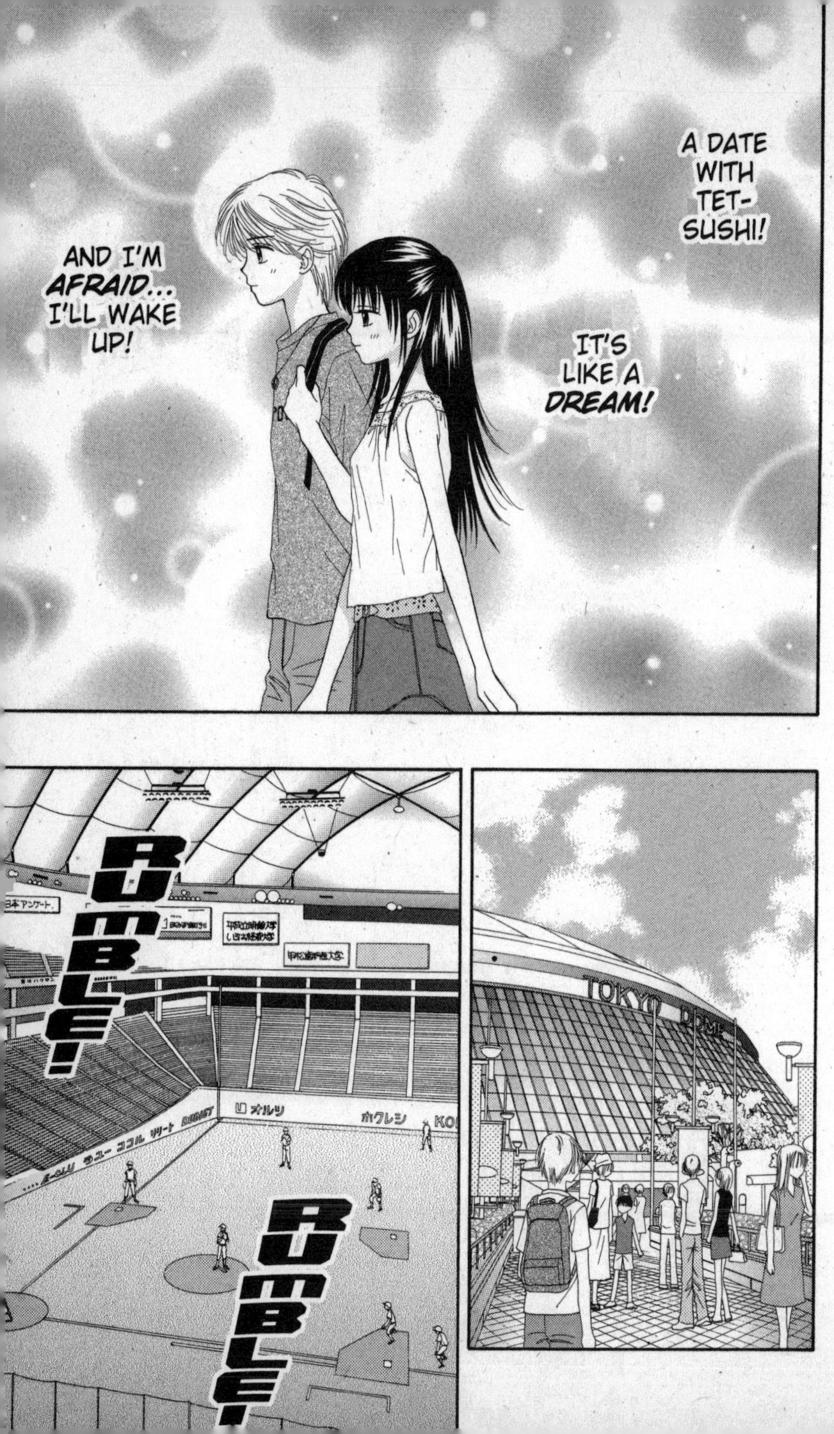
A DATE WITH TET-SUSHI!
IT'S LIKE A DREAM!
AND I'M AFRAID... I'LL WAKE UP!
RUMBLE!
RUMBLE!

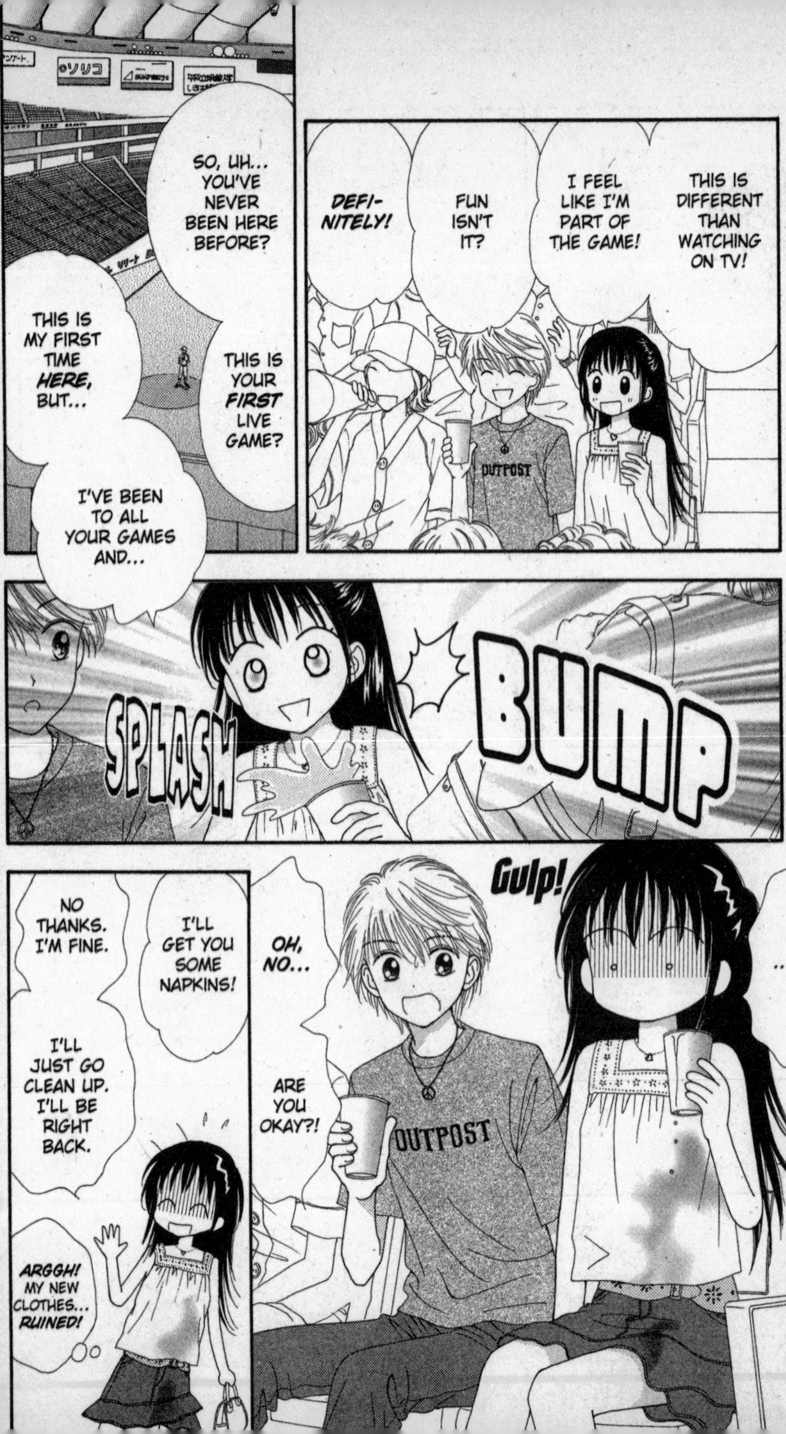
THIS IS DIFFERENT THAN WATCHING ON TV!
I FEEL LIKE I'M PART OF THE GAME!
FUN ISN'T IT?
DEFI-NITELY!
SO, UH... YOU'VE NEVER BEEN HERE BEFORE?
THIS IS YOUR FIRST LIVE GAME?
THIS IS MY FIRST TIME HERE, BUT...
I'VE BEEN TO ALL YOUR GAMES AND...
BUMP
SPLASH
Gulp!
...!!
OH, NO...
ARE YOU OKAY?!
OUTPOST
I'LL GET YOU SOME NAPKINS!
NO THANKS. I'M FINE.
I'LL JUST GO CLEAN UP. I'LL BE RIGHT BACK.
ARGGH! MY NEW CLOTHES... RUINED!

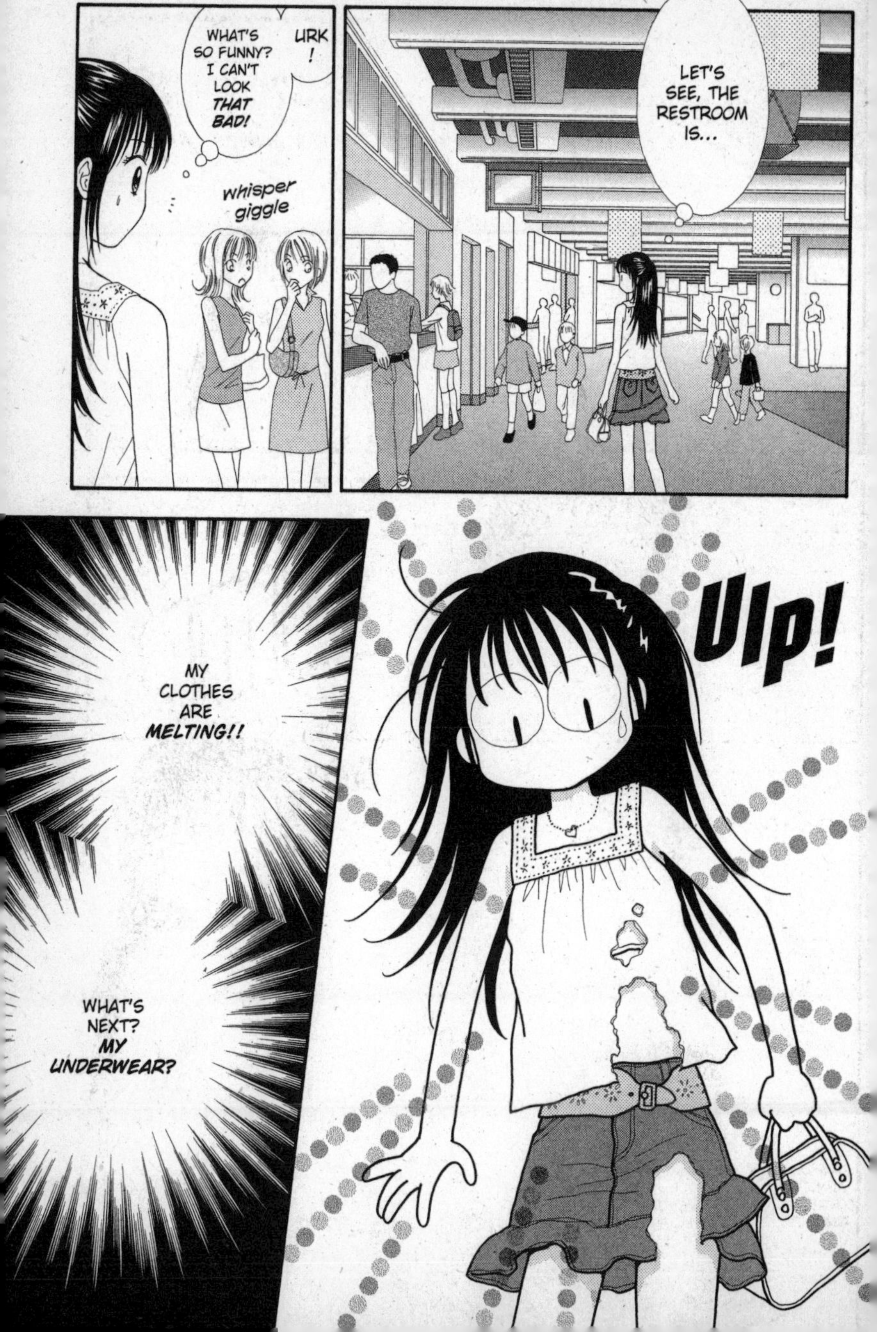
LET'S SEE, THE RESTROOM IS...
URK!
WHAT'S SO FUNNY? I CAN'T LOOK *THAT BAD!*
whisper giggle
ULP!
MY CLOTHES ARE *MELTING!!*
WHAT'S NEXT? *MY UNDERWEAR?*

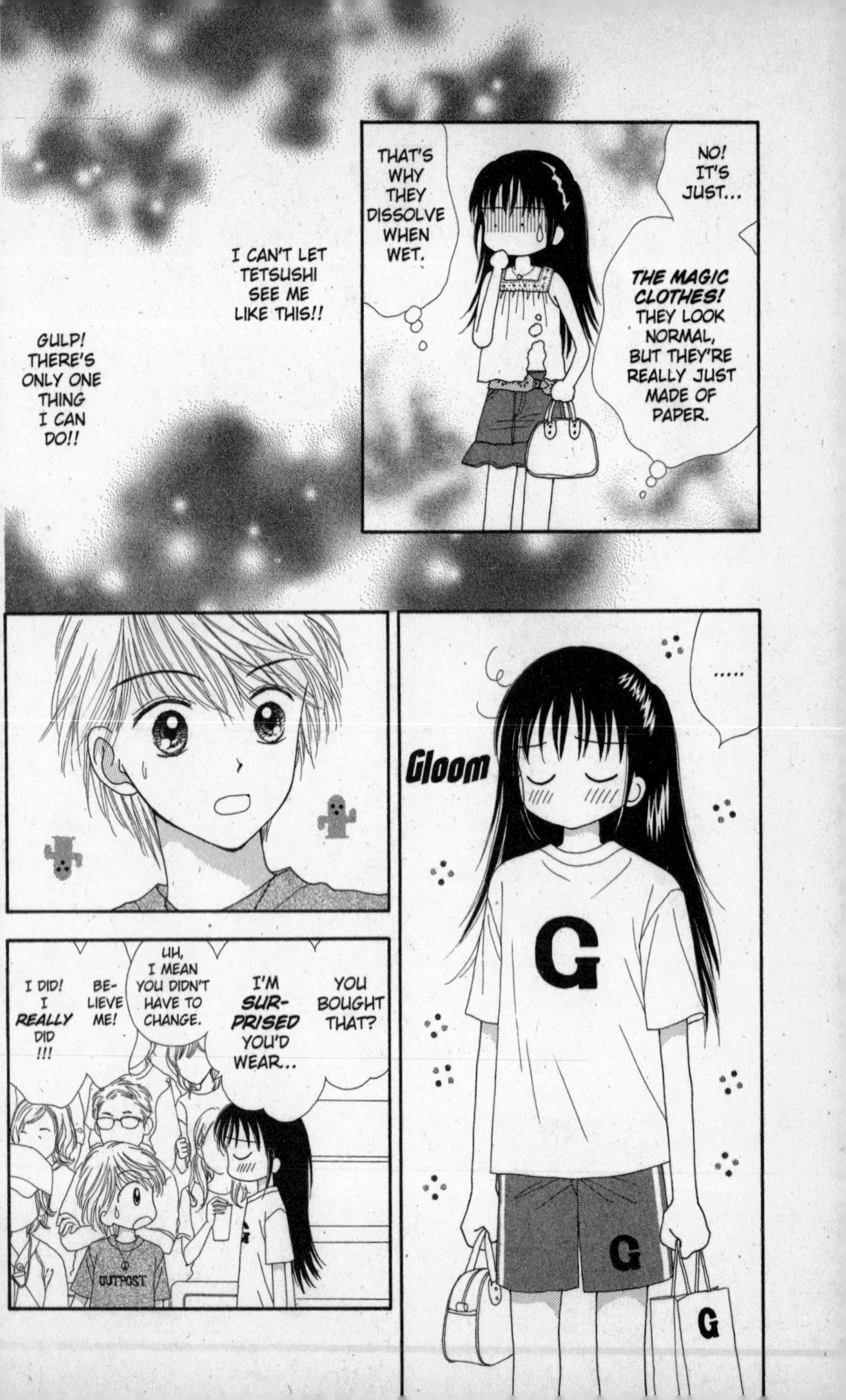
NO! IT'S JUST...
THE MAGIC CLOTHES! THEY LOOK NORMAL, BUT THEY'RE REALLY JUST MADE OF PAPER.
THAT'S WHY THEY DISSOLVE WHEN WET.
I CAN'T LET TETSUSHI SEE ME LIKE THIS!!
GULP! THERE'S ONLY ONE THING I CAN DO!!
.....
Gloom
G
G
G
YOU BOUGHT THAT?
I'M SURPRISED YOU'D WEAR...
UH, I MEAN YOU DIDN'T HAVE TO CHANGE.
BE-LIEVE ME!
I DID! I REALLY DID!!!
OUTPOST

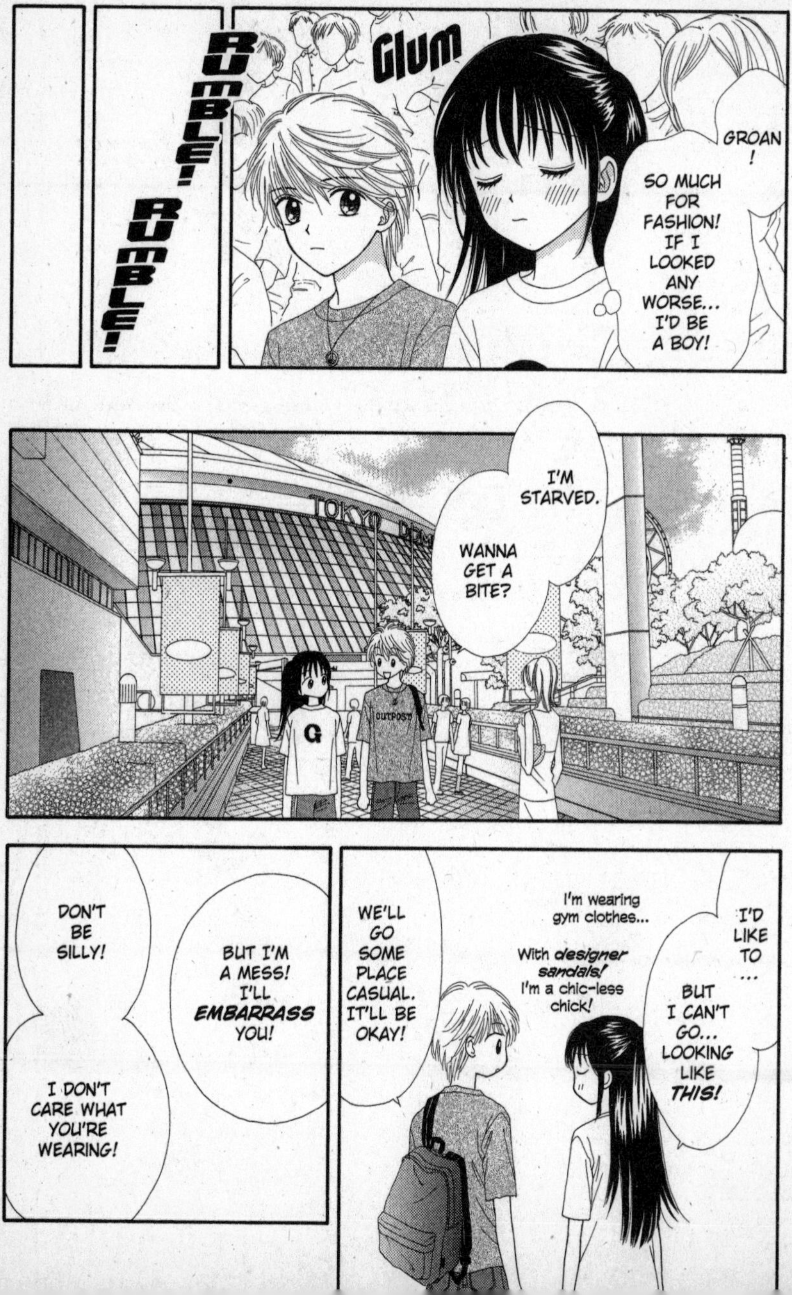
GROAN!
SO MUCH FOR FASHION! IF I LOOKED ANY WORSE... I'D BE A BOY!
Glum
RUMBLE! RUMBLE!
I'M STARVED.
WANNA GET A BITE?
I'D LIKE TO...
BUT I CAN'T GO... LOOKING LIKE *THIS!*
I'm wearing gym clothes...
With *designer sandals!* I'm a chic-less chick!
WE'LL GO SOME PLACE CASUAL. IT'LL BE OKAY!
BUT I'M A MESS! I'LL *EMBARRASS* YOU!
DON'T BE SILLY!
I DON'T CARE WHAT YOU'RE WEARING!
OUTPOST

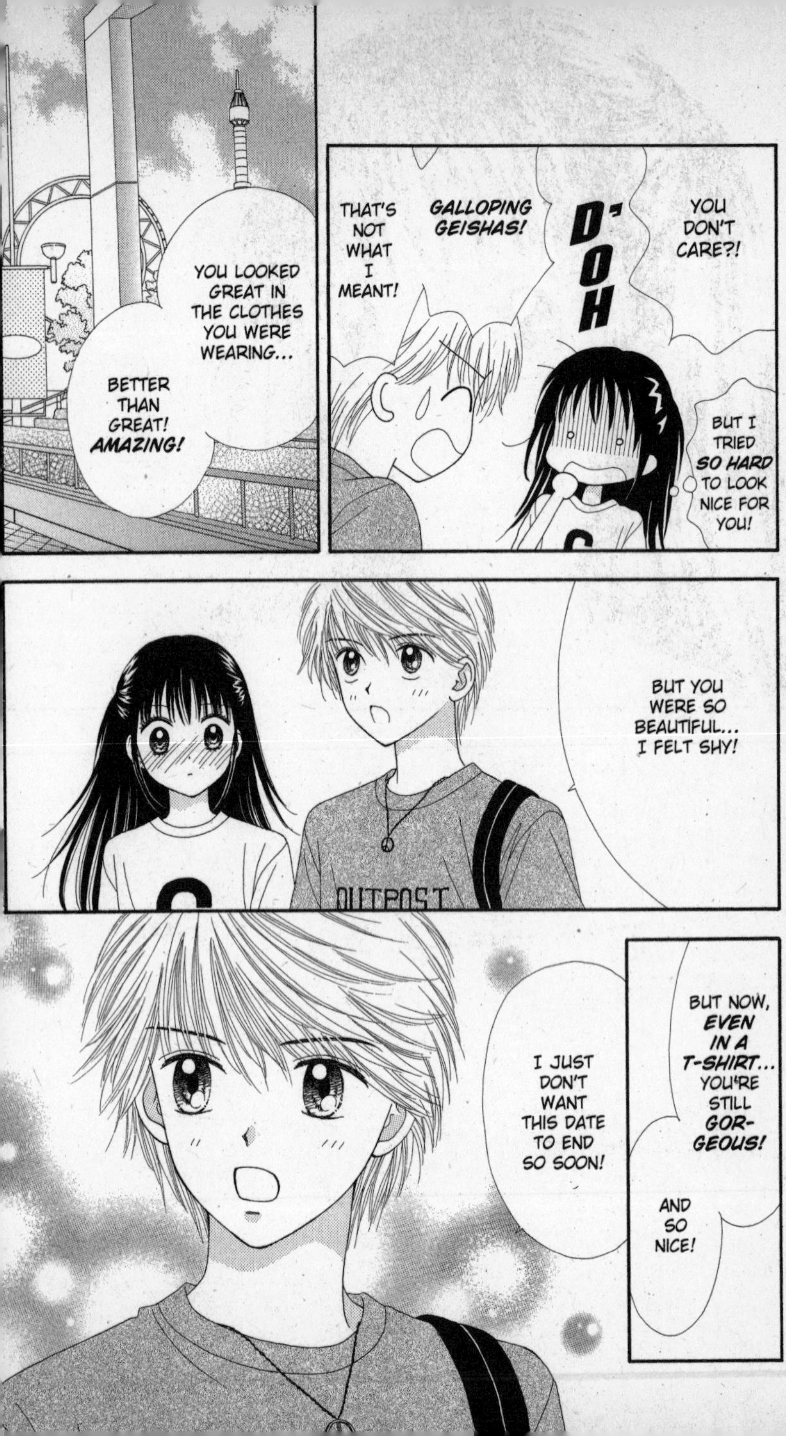
YOU DON'T CARE?!
BUT I TRIED **SO HARD** TO LOOK NICE FOR YOU!
D'OH
GALLOPING GEISHAS!
THAT'S NOT WHAT I MEANT!
YOU LOOKED GREAT IN THE CLOTHES YOU WERE WEARING...
BETTER THAN GREAT! ***AMAZING!***
BUT YOU WERE SO BEAUTIFUL... I FELT SHY!
OUTPOST
BUT NOW, ***EVEN IN A T-SHIRT...*** YOU'RE STILL ***GOR-GEOUS!***
AND SO NICE!
I JUST DON'T WANT THIS DATE TO END SO SOON!

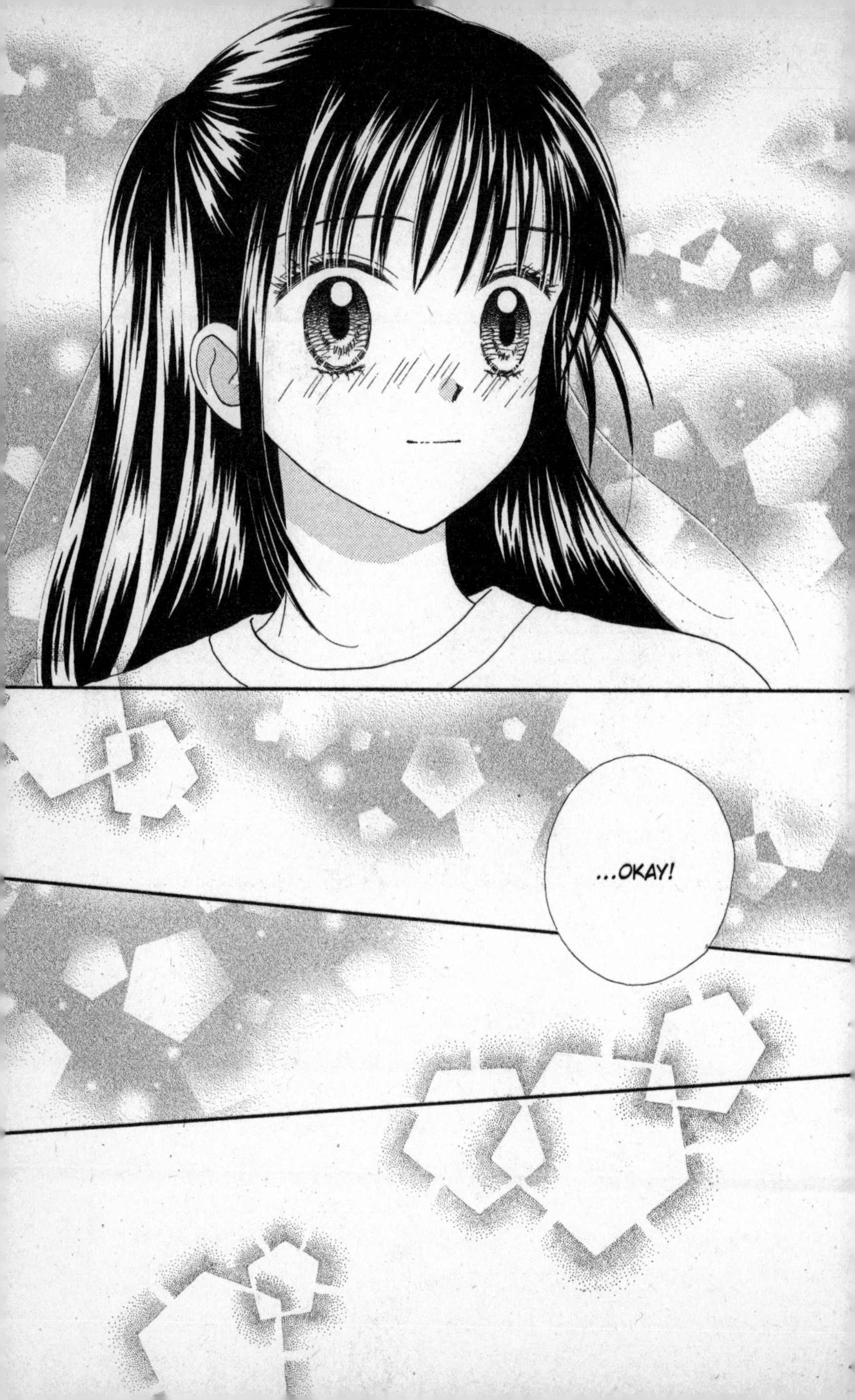
...OKAY!

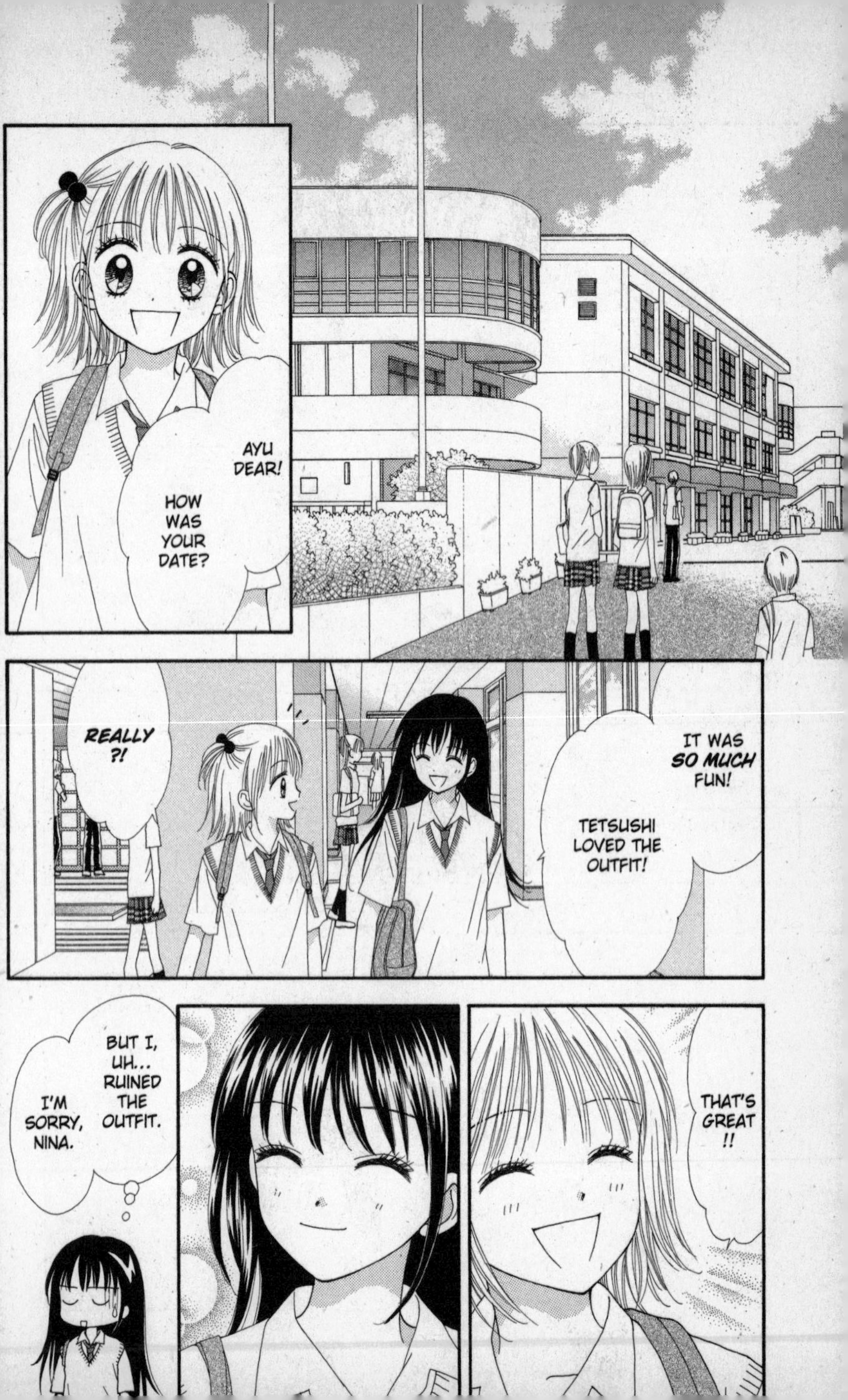
AYU DEAR!
HOW WAS YOUR DATE?
IT WAS SO MUCH FUN!
TETSUSHI LOVED THE OUTFIT!
REALLY ?!
THAT'S GREAT !!
BUT I, UH... RUINED THE OUTFIT.
I'M SORRY, NINA.

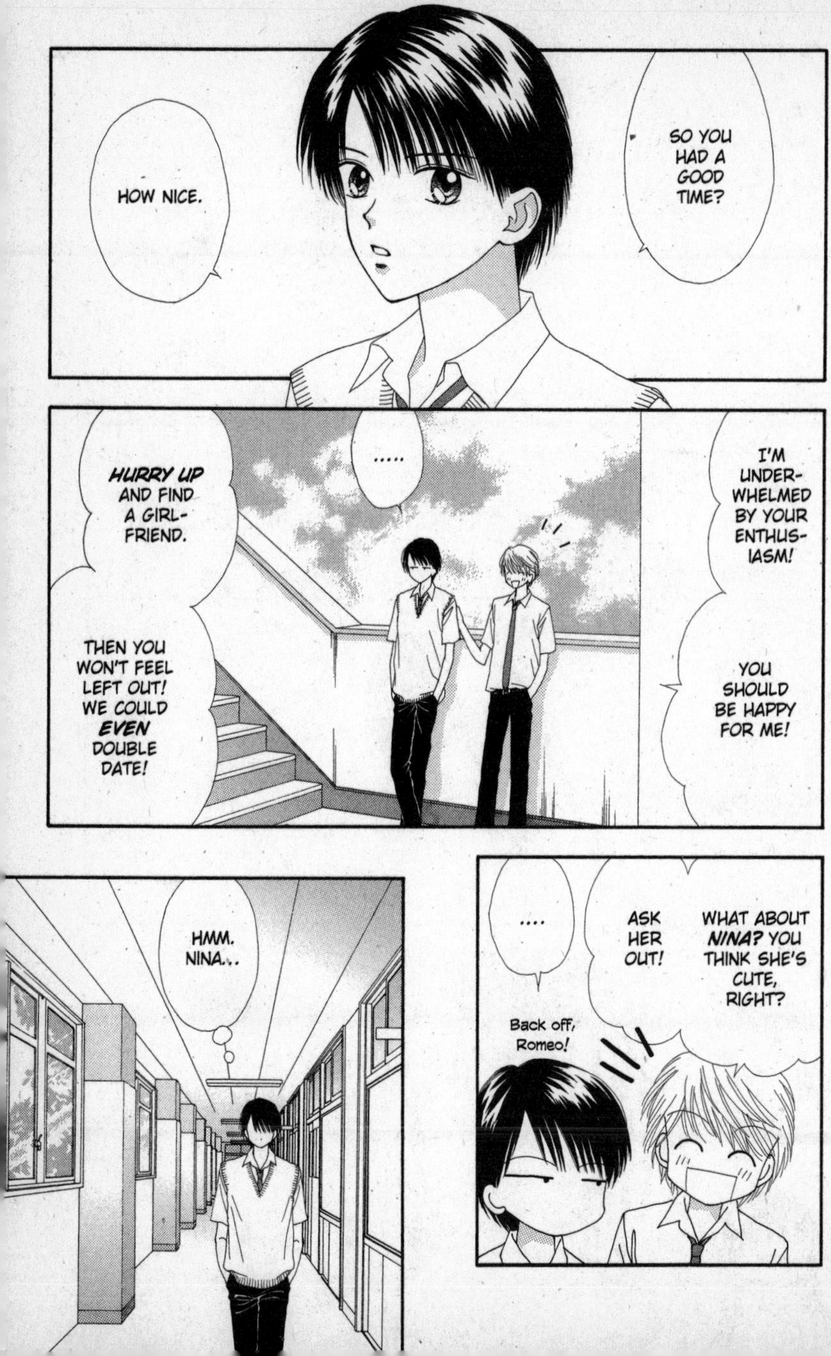
SO YOU HAD A GOOD TIME?
HOW NICE.
I'M UNDERWHELMED BY YOUR ENTHUSIASM!
YOU SHOULD BE HAPPY FOR ME!
.....
HURRY UP AND FIND A GIRLFRIEND.
THEN YOU WON'T FEEL LEFT OUT! WE COULD *EVEN* DOUBLE DATE!
WHAT ABOUT *NINA?* YOU THINK SHE'S CUTE, RIGHT?
ASK HER OUT!
....
Back off, Romeo!
HMM. NINA...

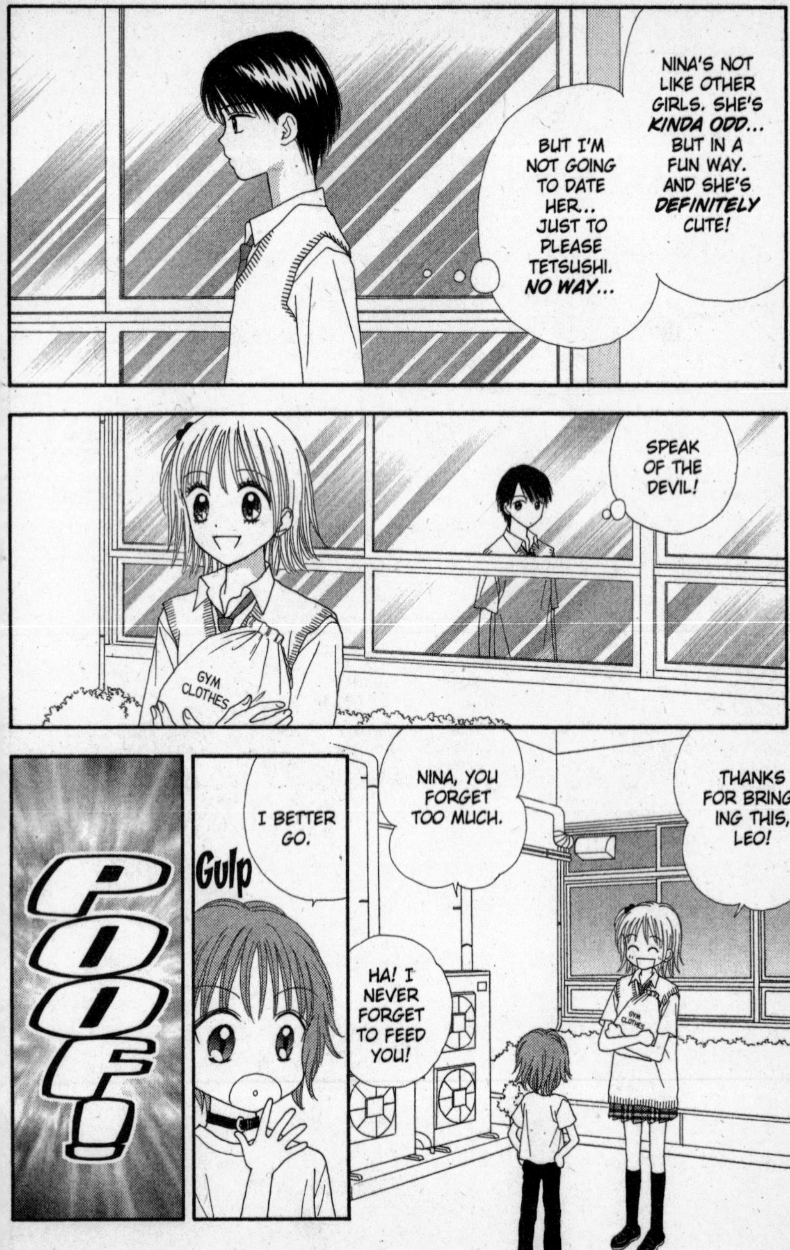
NINA'S NOT LIKE OTHER GIRLS. SHE'S KINDA ODD... BUT IN A FUN WAY. AND SHE'S DEFINITELY CUTE!
BUT I'M NOT GOING TO DATE HER... JUST TO PLEASE TETSUSHI. NO WAY...
SPEAK OF THE DEVIL!
GYM CLOTHES
THANKS FOR BRING-ING THIS, LEO!
NINA, YOU FORGET TOO MUCH.
HA! I NEVER FORGET TO FEED YOU!
GYM CLOTHES
I BETTER GO.
Gulp
POOF!

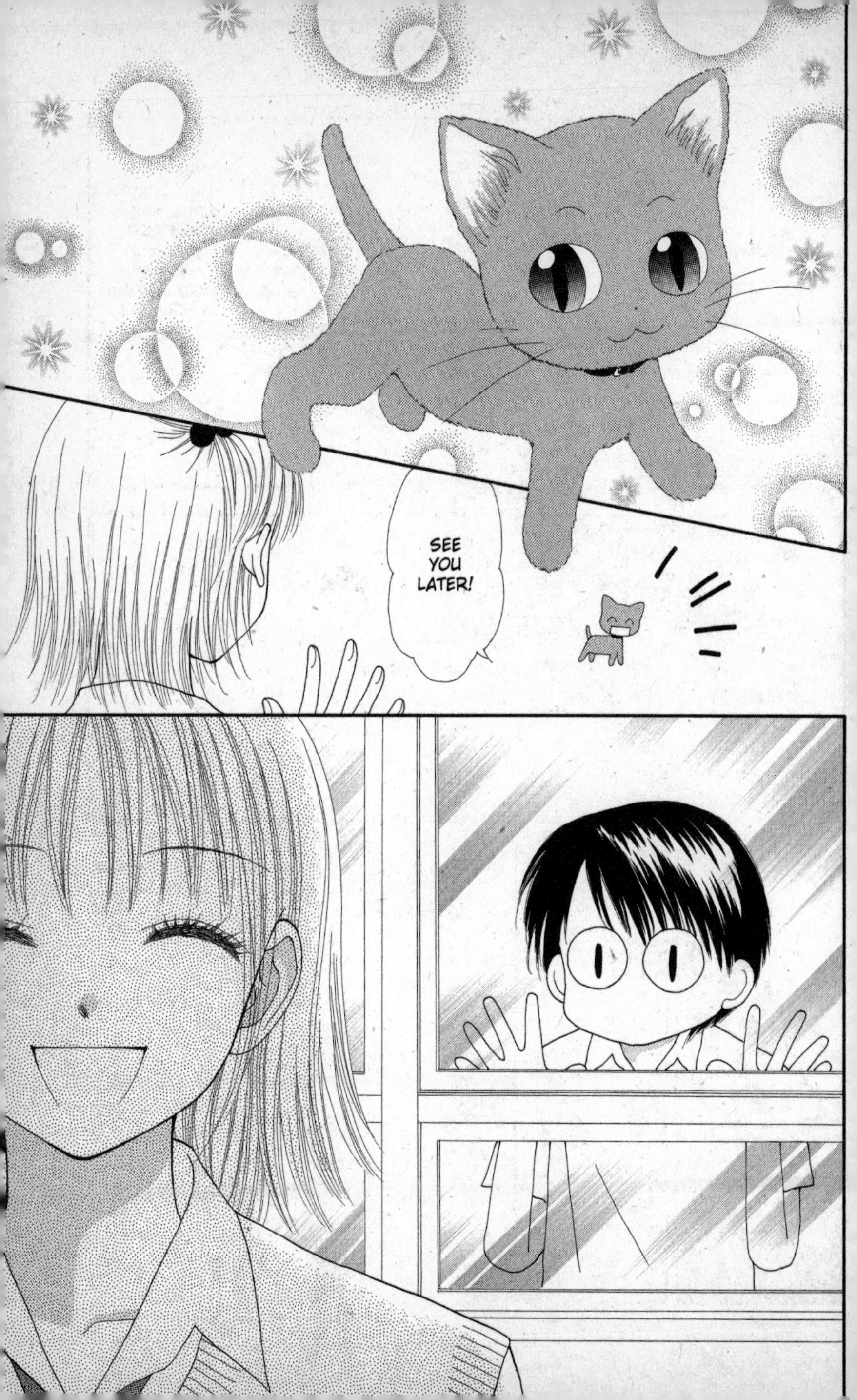
SEE YOU LATER!

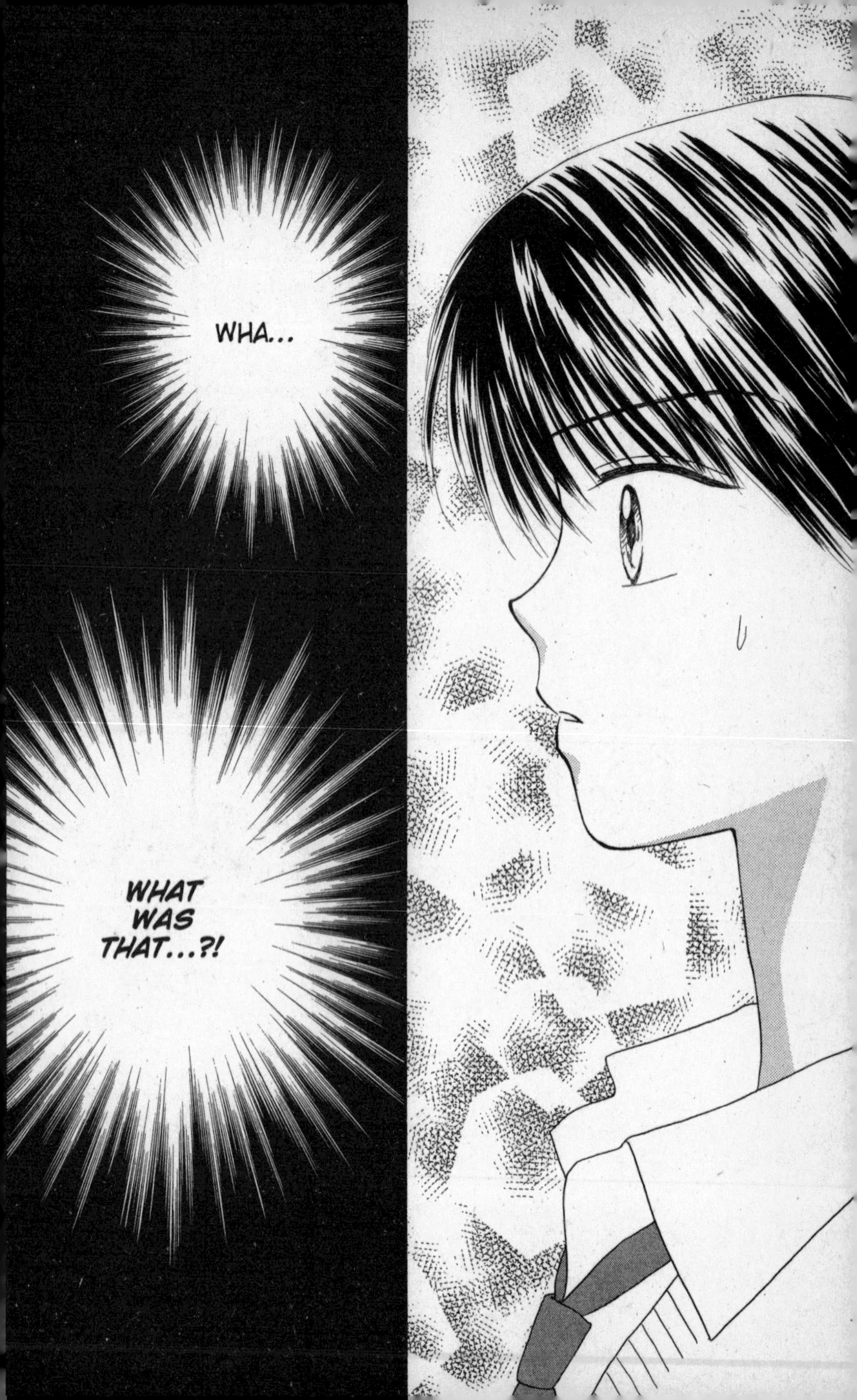
WHA...
WHAT WAS THAT...?!

granted a licen by thr chase goo

purchases type and shipping period

ect for add on sales by

add on sales, by sa by

Although governmental consume

of gabo m all w bye good

urban and town alike

purchase good design of gabo in

bud et

Ultra Maniac

Chapter 12

ca d p ase e sa

order to be granted a license commamastor everyone on pts of grips. Too

statical information

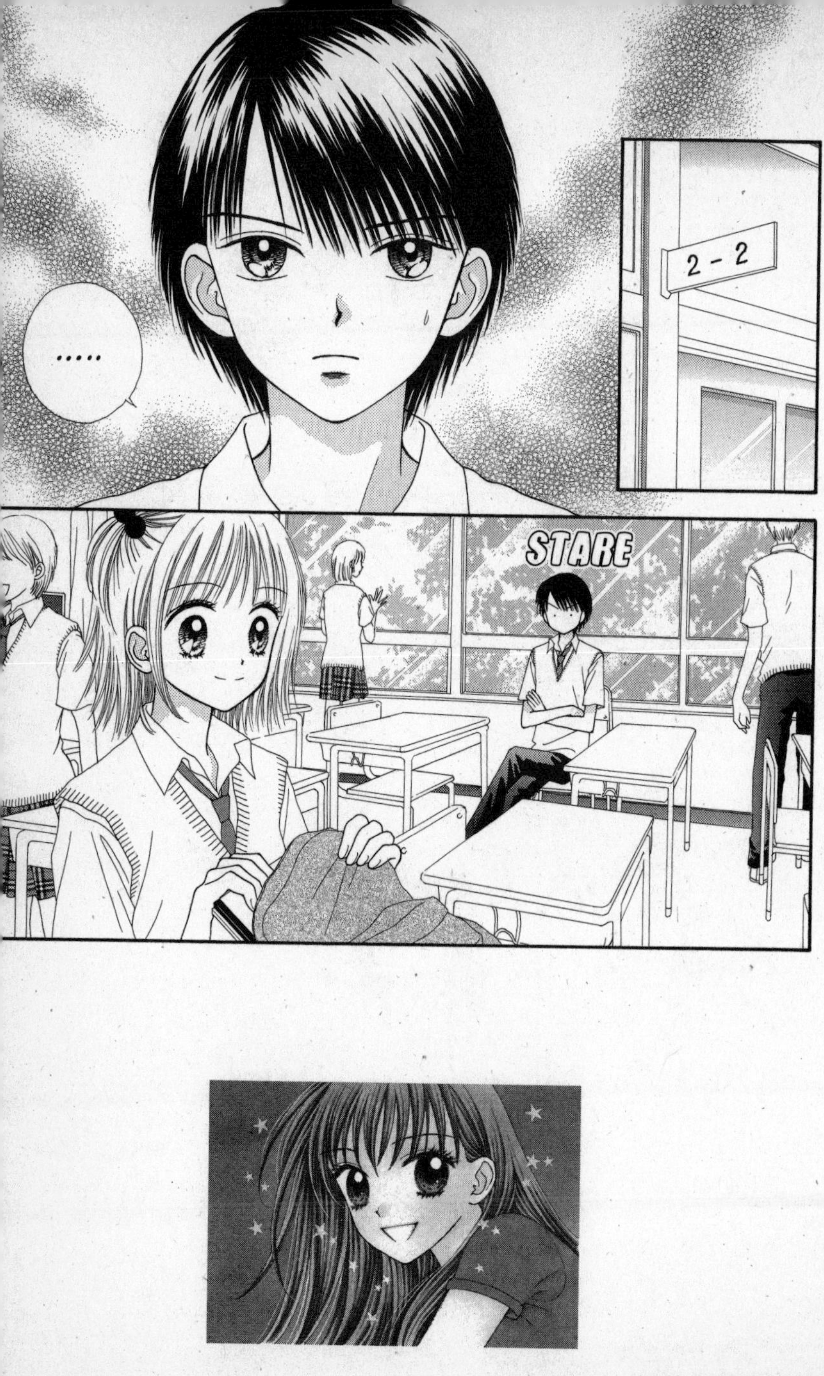
2 – 2
.....
STARE

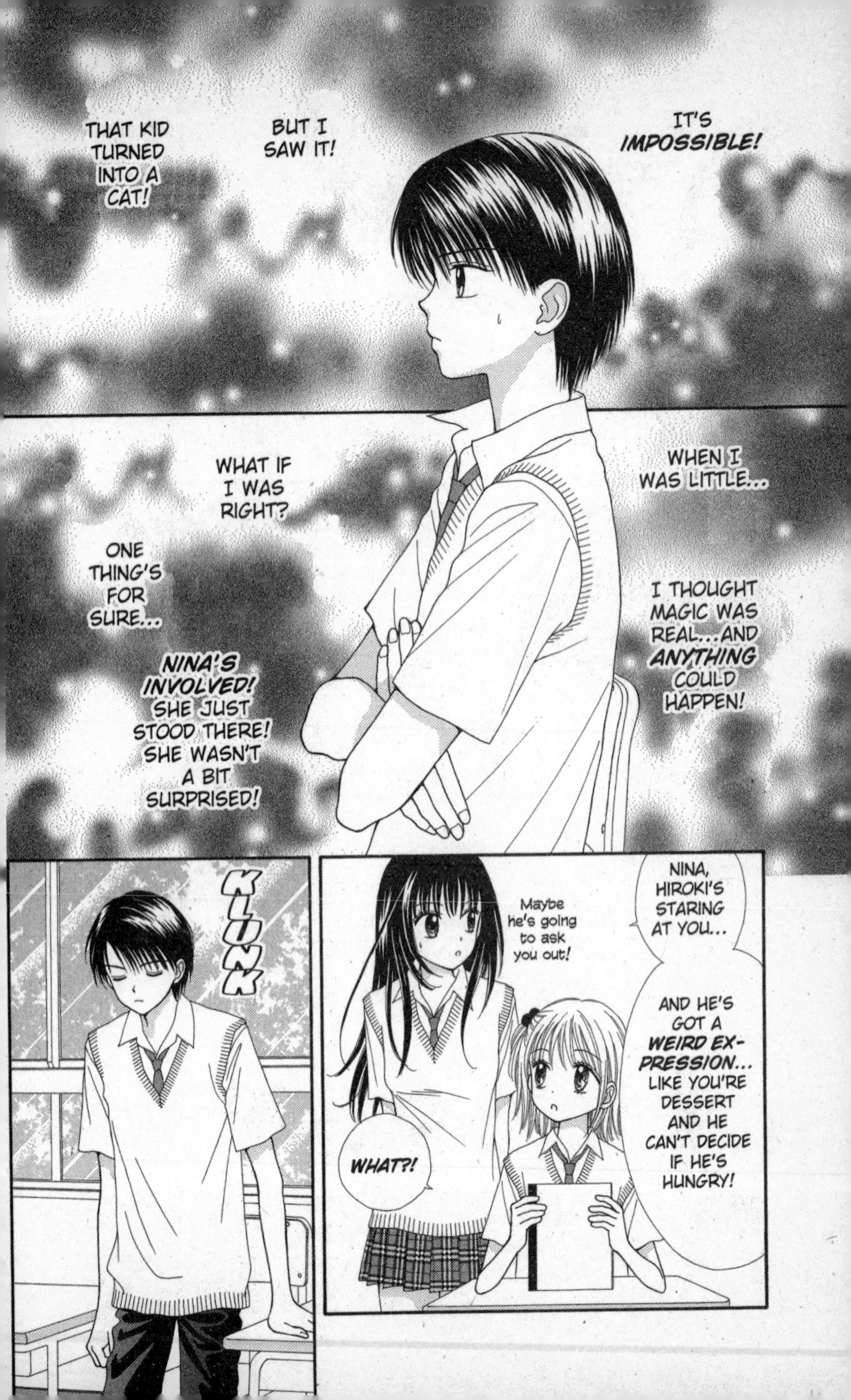
IT'S *IMPOSSIBLE!*
BUT I SAW IT!
THAT KID TURNED INTO A CAT!
WHEN I WAS LITTLE...
I THOUGHT MAGIC WAS REAL...AND *ANYTHING* COULD HAPPEN!
WHAT IF I WAS RIGHT?
ONE THING'S FOR SURE...
NINA'S INVOLVED! SHE JUST STOOD THERE! SHE WASN'T A BIT SURPRISED!
NINA, HIROKI'S STARING AT YOU...
AND HE'S GOT A *WEIRD EX-PRESSION...* LIKE YOU'RE DESSERT AND HE CAN'T DECIDE IF HE'S HUNGRY!
Maybe he's going to ask you out!
WHAT?!
KLINK

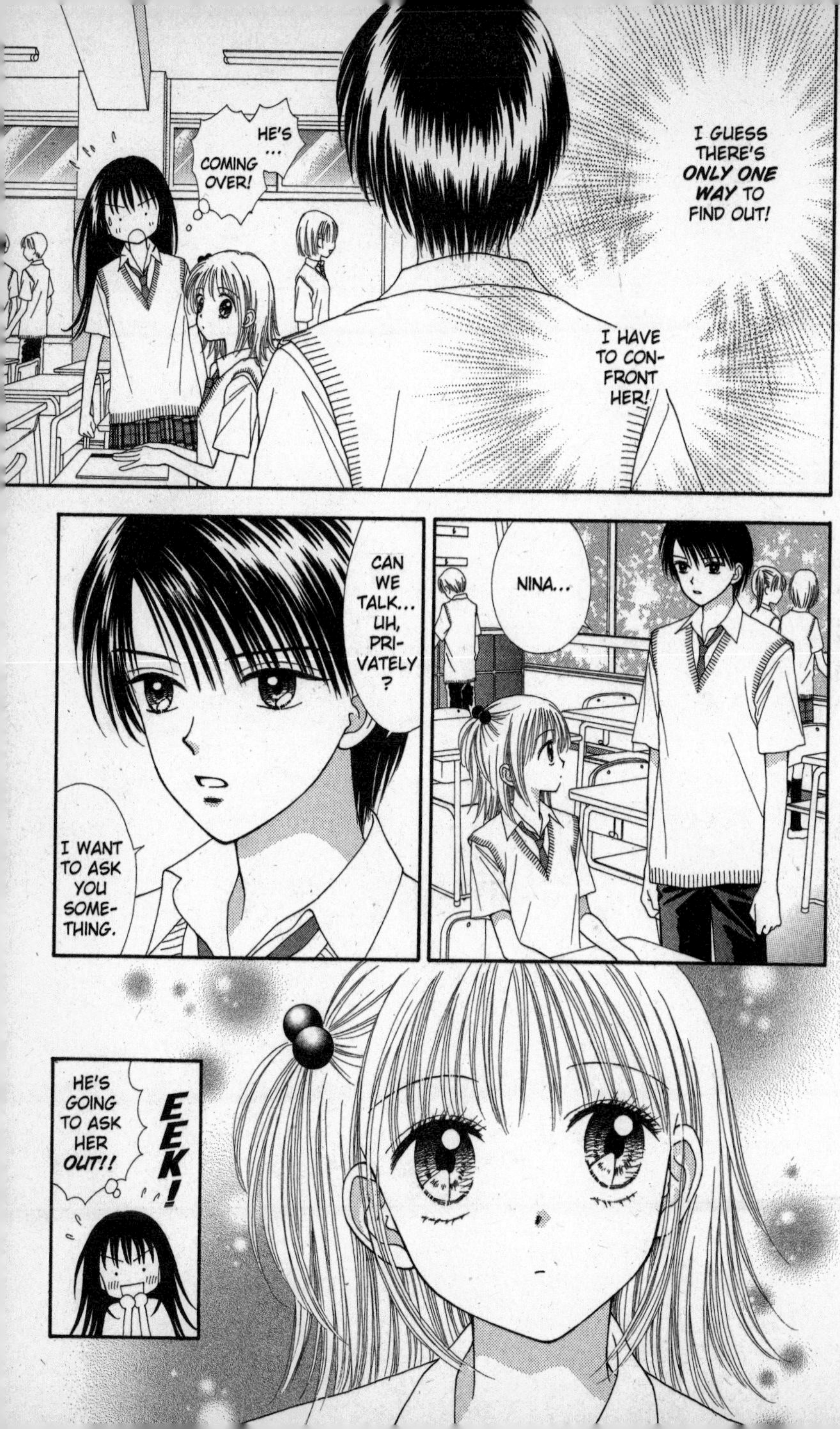
I GUESS THERE'S **ONLY ONE WAY** TO FIND OUT!
I HAVE TO CON-FRONT HER!
HE'S... COMING OVER!
NINA...
CAN WE TALK... UH, PRI-VATELY?
I WANT TO ASK YOU SOME-THING.
HE'S GOING TO ASK HER **OUT!!**
EEK!

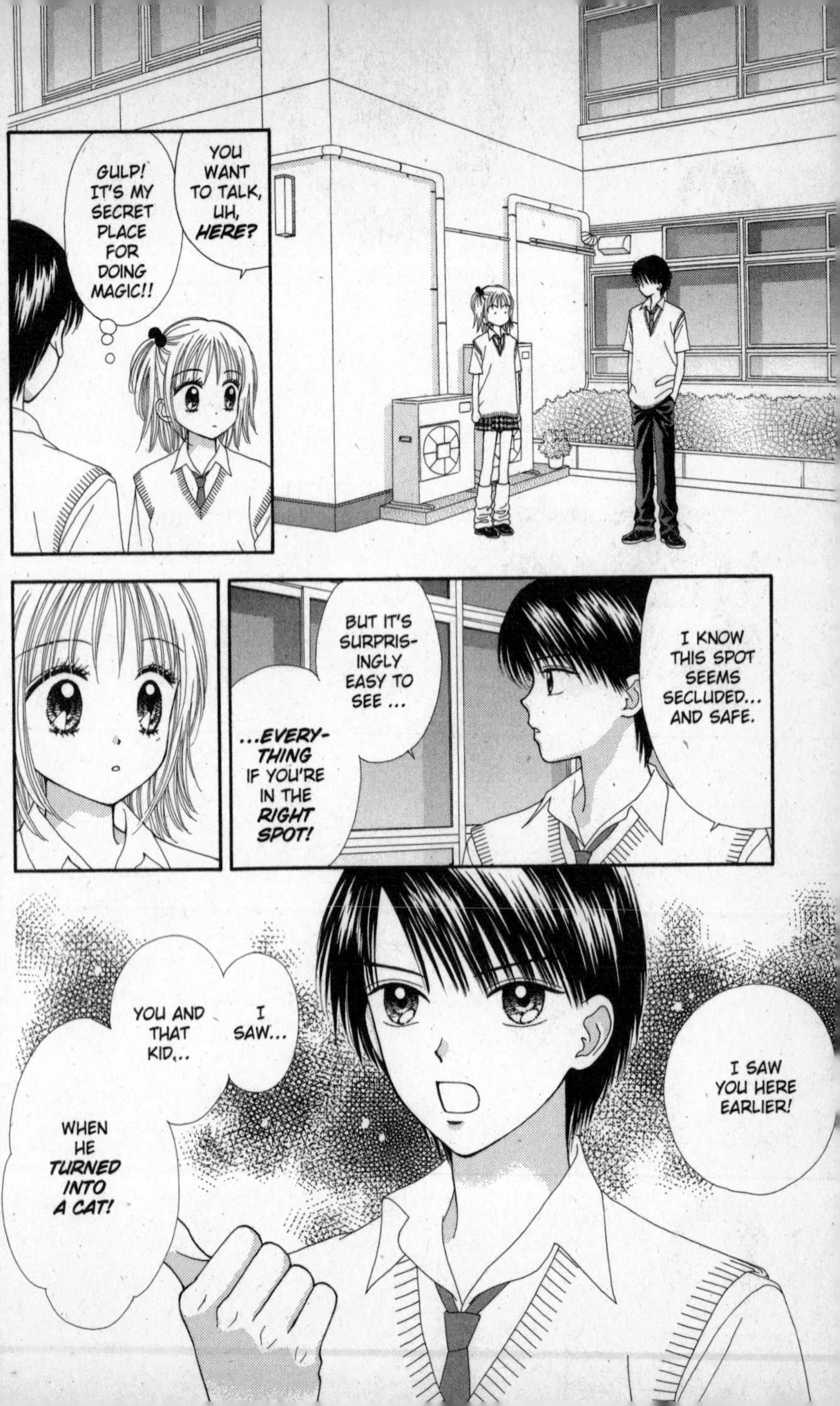
YOU WANT TO TALK, UH, *HERE?*
GULP! IT'S MY SECRET PLACE FOR DOING MAGIC!!
I KNOW THIS SPOT SEEMS SECLUDED... AND SAFE.
BUT IT'S SURPRISINGLY EASY TO SEE ...
...*EVERYTHING* IF YOU'RE IN THE *RIGHT SPOT!*
I SAW YOU HERE EARLIER!
I SAW...
YOU AND THAT KID...
WHEN HE *TURNED INTO A CAT!*

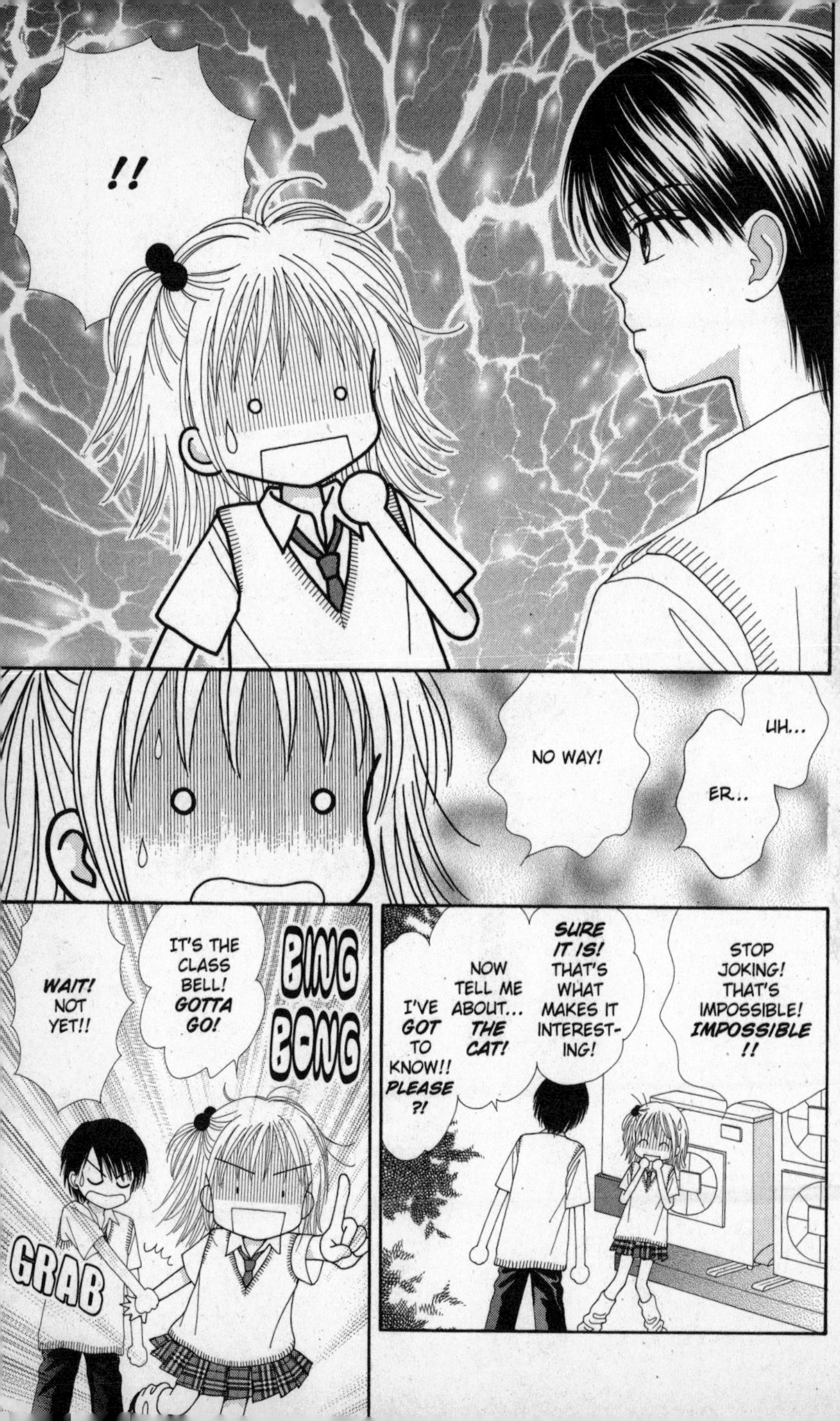
!!
UH... ER...
NO WAY!
STOP JOKING! THAT'S IMPOSSIBLE! IMPOSSIBLE!!
SURE IT IS! THAT'S WHAT MAKES IT INTERESTING!
NOW TELL ME ABOUT... THE CAT!
I'VE GOT TO KNOW!! PLEASE?!
BING BONG
IT'S THE CLASS BELL! GOTTA GO!
WAIT! NOT YET!!
GRAB

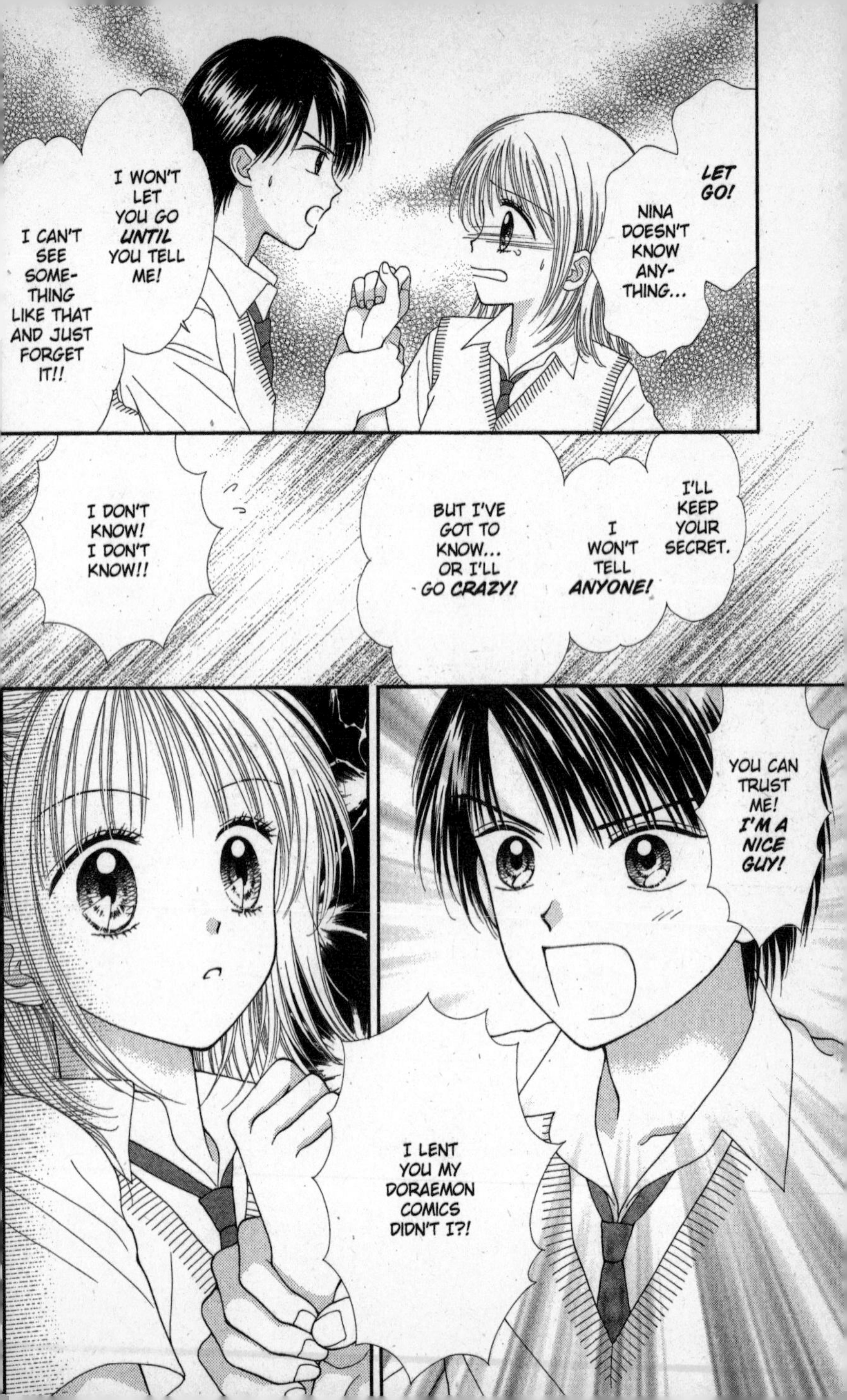
LET GO!
NINA DOESN'T KNOW ANYTHING...
I WON'T LET YOU GO UNTIL YOU TELL ME!
I CAN'T SEE SOMETHING LIKE THAT AND JUST FORGET IT!!
I'LL KEEP YOUR SECRET.
I WON'T TELL ANYONE!
BUT I'VE GOT TO KNOW... OR I'LL GO CRAZY!
I DON'T KNOW! I DON'T KNOW!!
YOU CAN TRUST ME! I'M A NICE GUY!
I LENT YOU MY DORAEMON COMICS DIDN'T I?!

FREE TALK 4

The *Ultra Maniac* anime is quite different from the manga and has a much stronger fantasy feel to it. The animators have made a real effort to give the TV series a look that plays up the magical aspects of the story

In the manga, Nina is abroad because her grades were so bad. I got the idea for this when I was in high school and a friend, after failing entrance exams for college in Japan, went to college overseas instead. (Apparently, colleges overseas are hard to graduate from, but are easier to enter than Japan.)

I've been writing the manga so that the magic and human worlds are as different as Japan and the United States. In other words, the look and clothing of the Magic Kingdom really isn't that much different from Japan. That's why I did away with magic wands and flying brooms—stuff you'd associate with traditional magic. **Instead**, I have Nina use a magic PC . . . because that fits in better in modern Japan.

I did that because I'd never read a story that was set up like that. I also thought it'd be interesting in its differences and maybe even make a better sort of fantasy. (Laughs.)

In the anime, however, Nina is in the human world for training purposes. When she uses magic, she changes into her Magic School uniform and uses an item called a **Holy Stone**. Plus, the Magic Kingdom has a standard, old-fashioned "magic world" look when it comes to fashion and buildings. It's a **total fantasy setting!** (Laughs.)

YES... THAT WAS KIND OF YOU.
HUH?
....OKAY I'LL TELL YOU.
REALLY?!
LOGIC FAILS...BUT DORAEMON WINS HER OVER! THE POWER OF COMICS! INCRED-IBLE!
YOU PROMISE NOT TO TELL ANYONE?
OF COURSE! BESIDES... WHO'D BELIEVE ME?

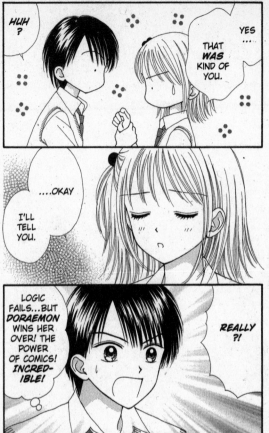

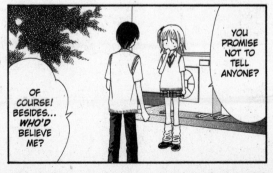

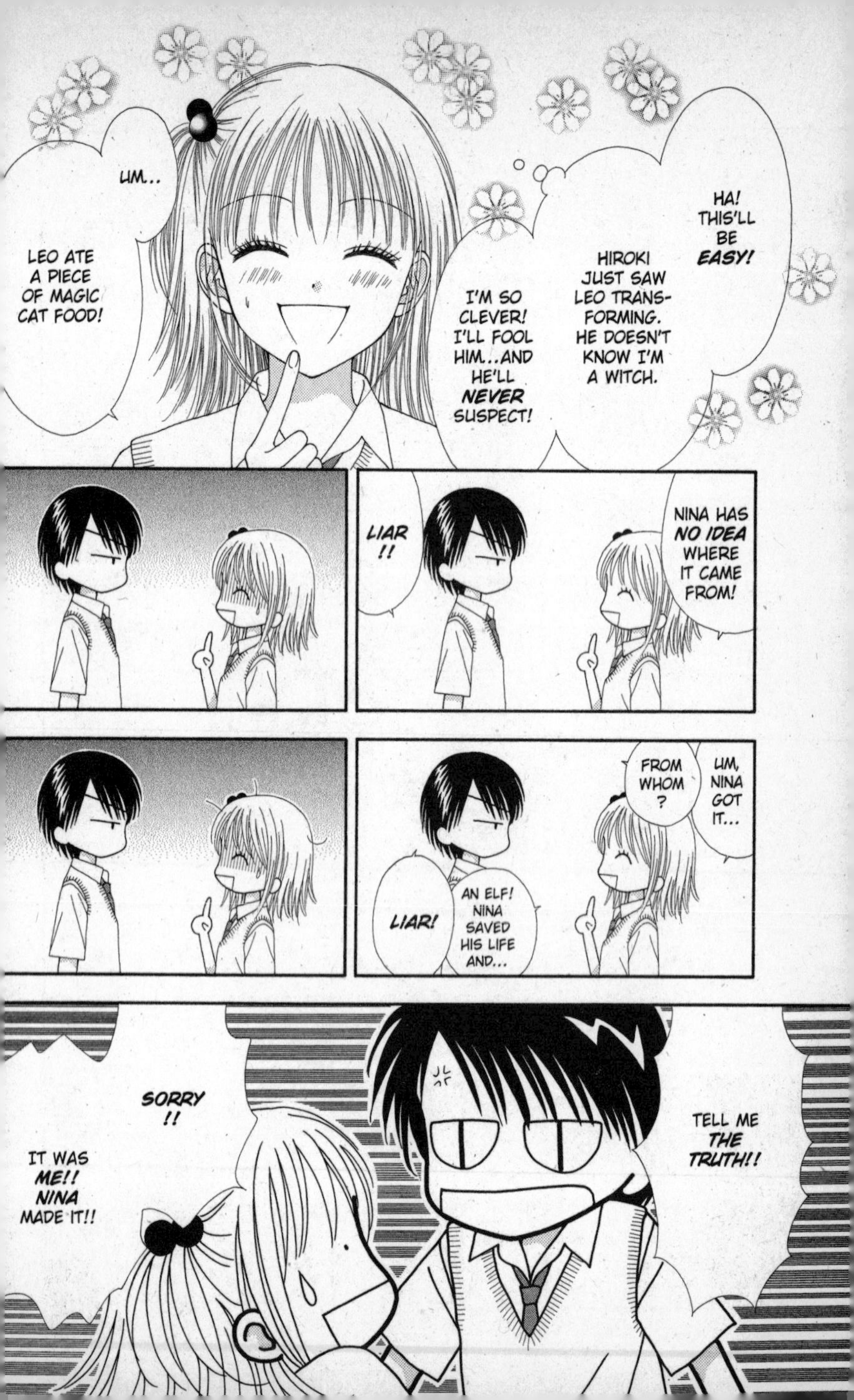
HA! THIS'LL BE EASY!
HIROKI JUST SAW LEO TRANS-FORMING. HE DOESN'T KNOW I'M A WITCH.
I'M SO CLEVER! I'LL FOOL HIM...AND HE'LL NEVER SUSPECT!
UM...
LEO ATE A PIECE OF MAGIC CAT FOOD!
NINA HAS NO IDEA WHERE IT CAME FROM!
LIAR!!
UM, NINA GOT IT...
FROM WHOM?
AN ELF! NINA SAVED HIS LIFE AND...
LIAR!
TELL ME THE TRUTH!!
SORRY!!
IT WAS ME!! NINA MADE IT!!

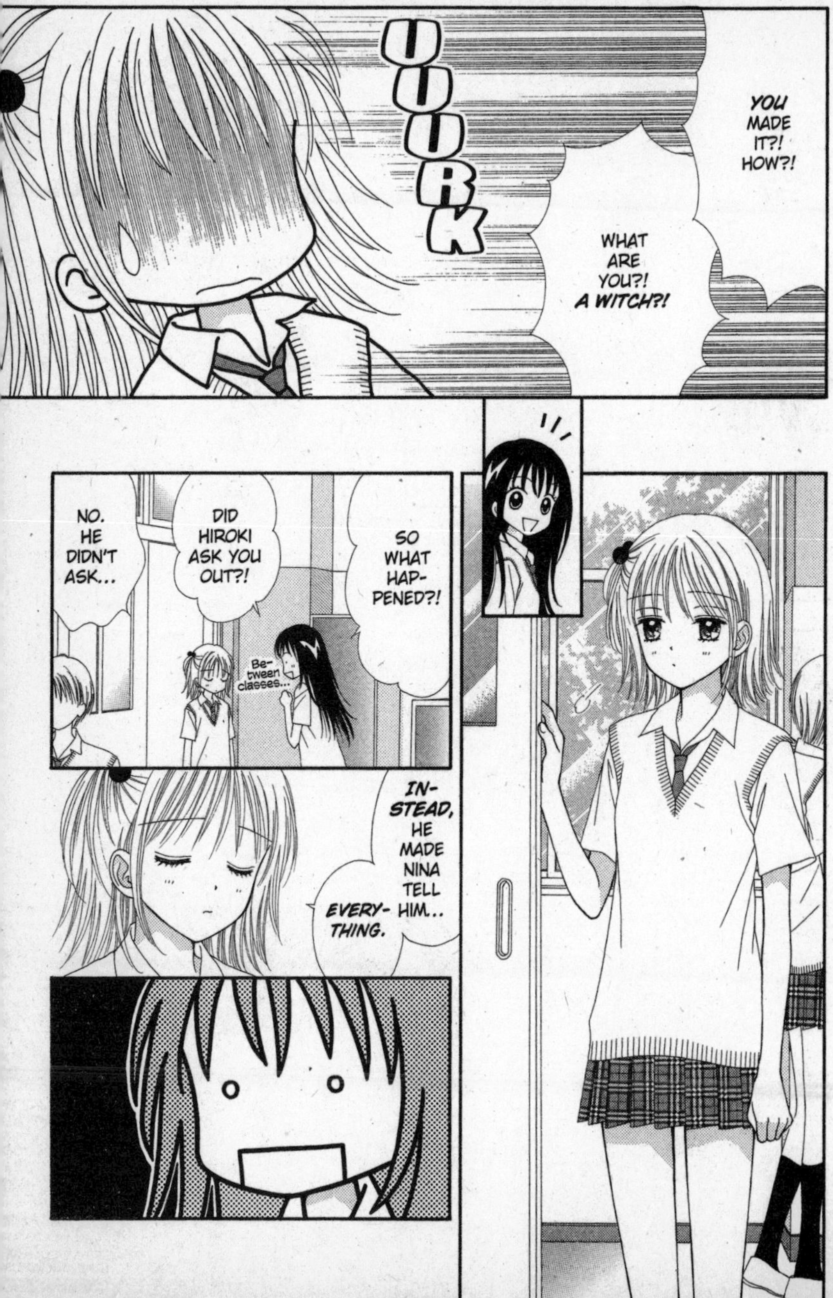
YOU MADE IT?! HOW?!
WHAT ARE YOU?! A WITCH?!
UUURK
SO WHAT HAP-PENED?!
DID HIROKI ASK YOU OUT?!
NO. HE DIDN'T ASK...
Be-tween classes...
IN-STEAD, HE MADE NINA TELL HIM... EVERY-THING.

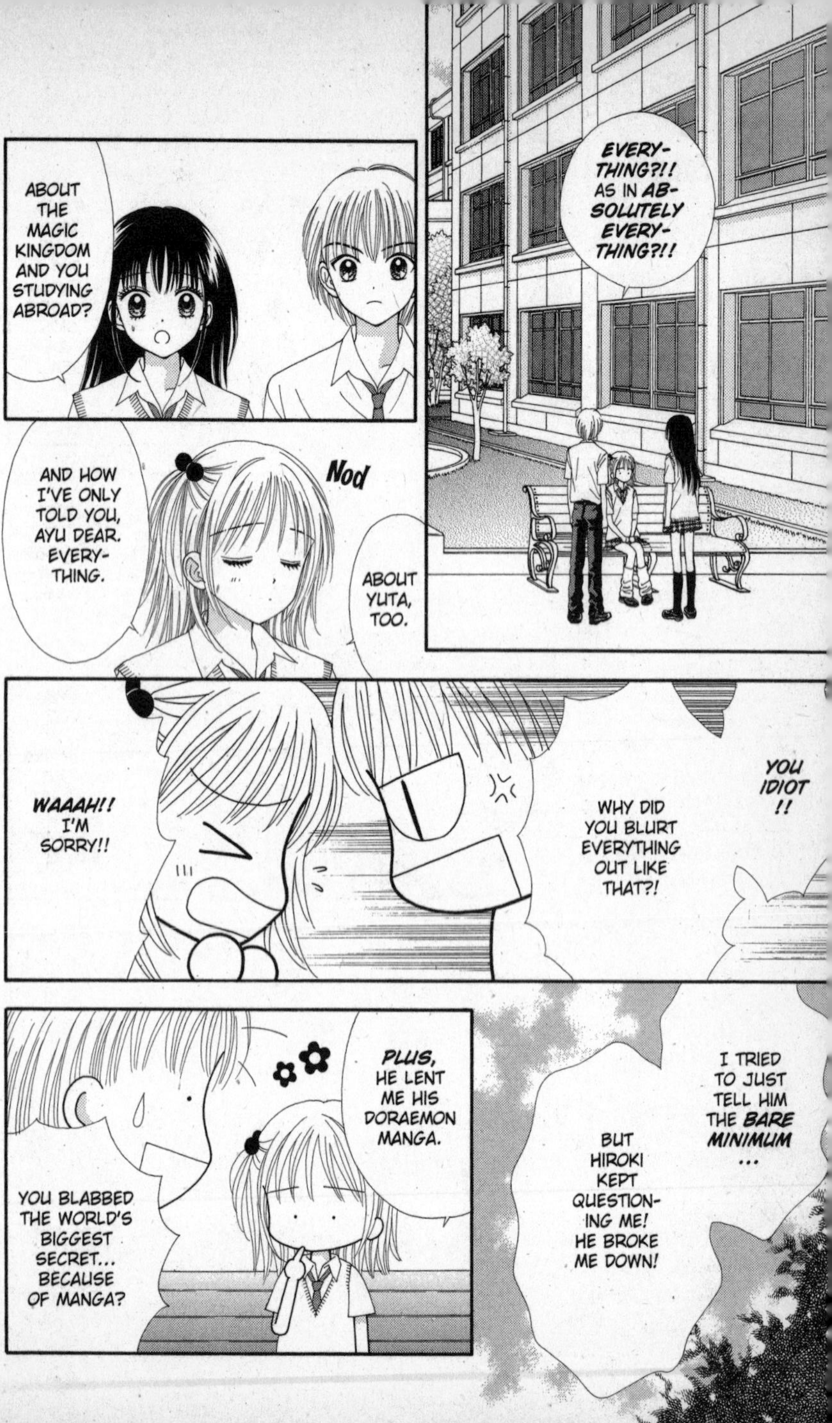
EVERY-THING?!! AS IN ABSOLUTELY EVERY-THING?!!
ABOUT THE MAGIC KINGDOM AND YOU STUDYING ABROAD?
AND HOW I'VE ONLY TOLD YOU, AYU DEAR. EVERY-THING.
Nod
ABOUT YUTA, TOO.
YOU IDIOT!!
WHY DID YOU BLURT EVERYTHING OUT LIKE THAT?!
WAAAH!! I'M SORRY!!
I TRIED TO JUST TELL HIM THE BARE MINIMUM...
BUT HIROKI KEPT QUESTION-ING ME! HE BROKE ME DOWN!
PLUS, HE LENT ME HIS DORAEMON MANGA.
YOU BLABBED THE WORLD'S BIGGEST SECRET... BECAUSE OF MANGA?

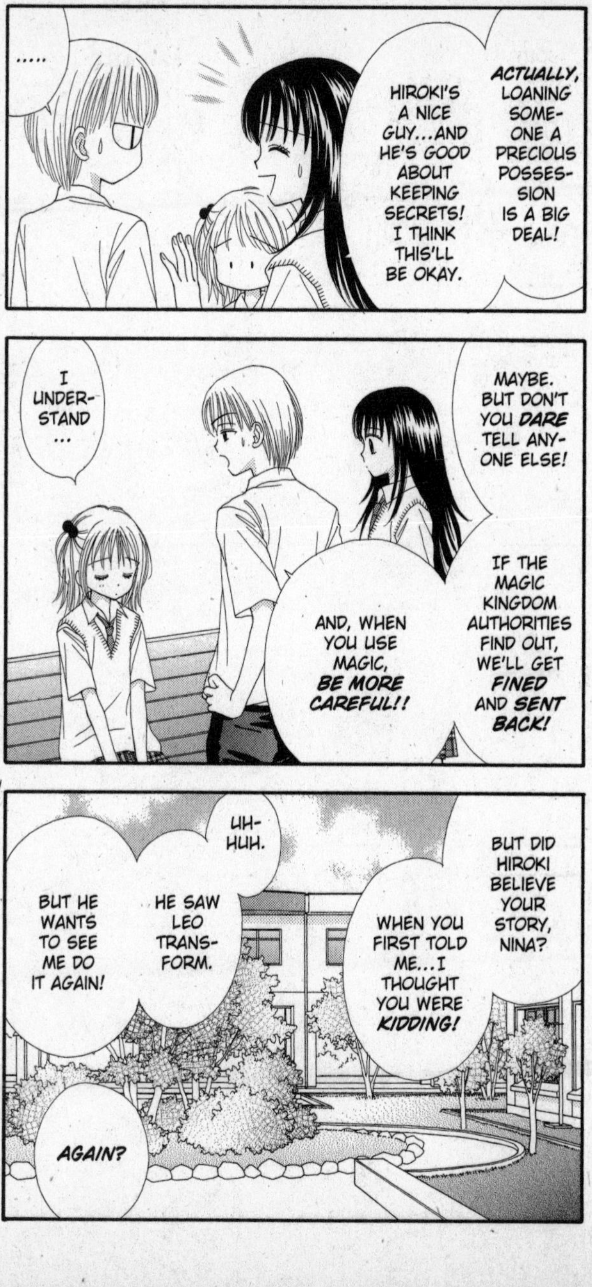
ACTUALLY, LOANING SOMEONE A PRECIOUS POSSESSION IS A BIG DEAL!
HIROKI'S A NICE GUY...AND HE'S GOOD ABOUT KEEPING SECRETS! I THINK THIS'LL BE OKAY.
.....
MAYBE. BUT DON'T YOU DARE TELL ANYONE ELSE!
IF THE MAGIC KINGDOM AUTHORITIES FIND OUT, WE'LL GET FINED AND SENT BACK!
AND, WHEN YOU USE MAGIC, BE MORE CAREFUL!!
I UNDERSTAND...
BUT DID HIROKI BELIEVE YOUR STORY, NINA?
WHEN YOU FIRST TOLD ME...I THOUGHT YOU WERE KIDDING!
UH-HUH.
HE SAW LEO TRANSFORM.
BUT HE WANTS TO SEE ME DO IT AGAIN!
AGAIN?

FREE TALK 5

It doesn't really bother me that the anime setting is different than the manga. (After all, I can still write the manga the way I want and don't have to make any changes.)

I understand why the animators made the changes. Animation has to be more visual. So it makes sense to have the characters fly and use magic in a very visually impressive way. So I mostly just left it to the producers and gave them free reign.

There were some exceptions, though. During the initial collaboration, the director asked me if I minded if he made Tetsushi a true "good guy." Apparently anime stories are easier to write if the characters fit into simple patterns. (For instance, Tetsushi is a good guy and easy to get along with. And Hiroki is cool and difficult to approach.)

That was the only time I said "Please don't do that. Whatever you do, don't change the characters' personalities. Leave them exactly as they are in the manga."

Of course, I realize that a lot of other people are going to be working on the anime. So there will be slight shifts in the characters.

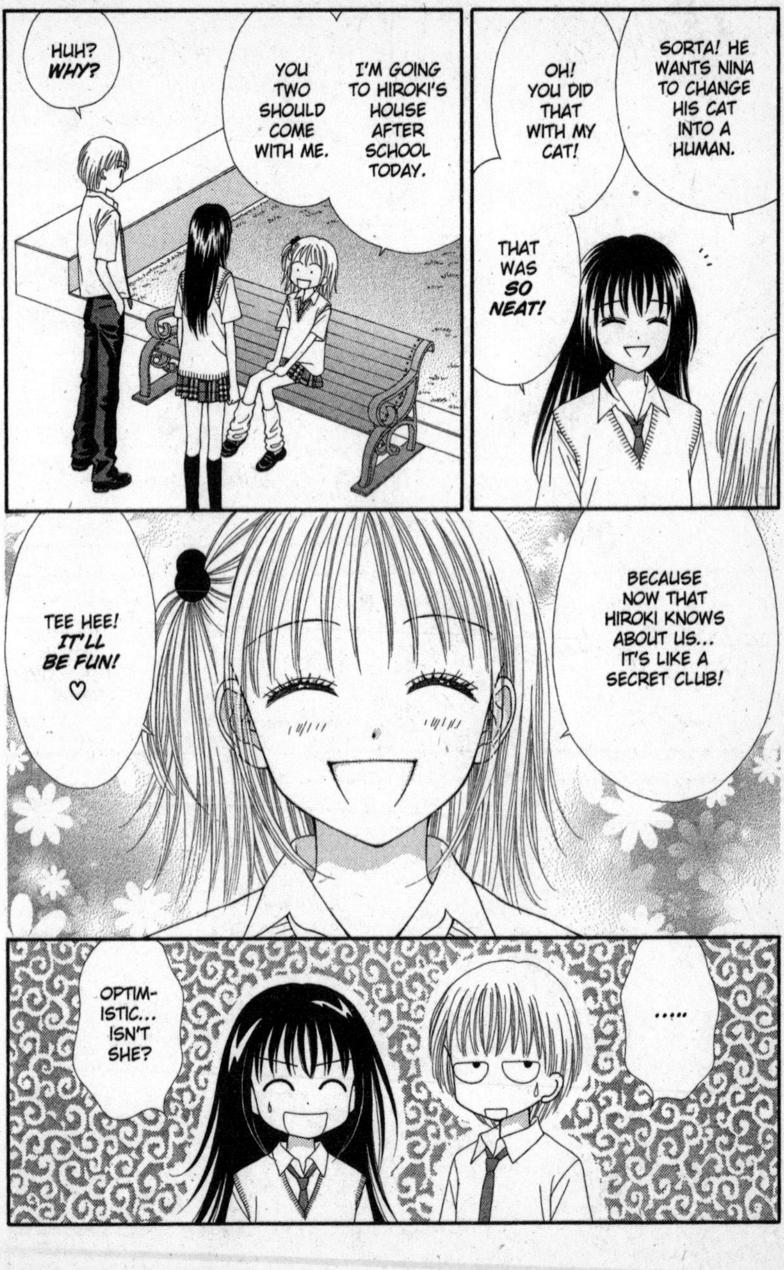
SORTA! HE WANTS NINA TO CHANGE HIS CAT INTO A HUMAN.
OH! YOU DID THAT WITH MY CAT!
THAT WAS SO NEAT!
I'M GOING TO HIROKI'S HOUSE AFTER SCHOOL TODAY.
YOU TWO SHOULD COME WITH ME.
HUH? WHY?
BECAUSE NOW THAT HIROKI KNOWS ABOUT US... IT'S LIKE A SECRET CLUB!
TEE HEE! IT'LL BE FUN! ♡
.....
OPTIM-ISTIC... ISN'T SHE?

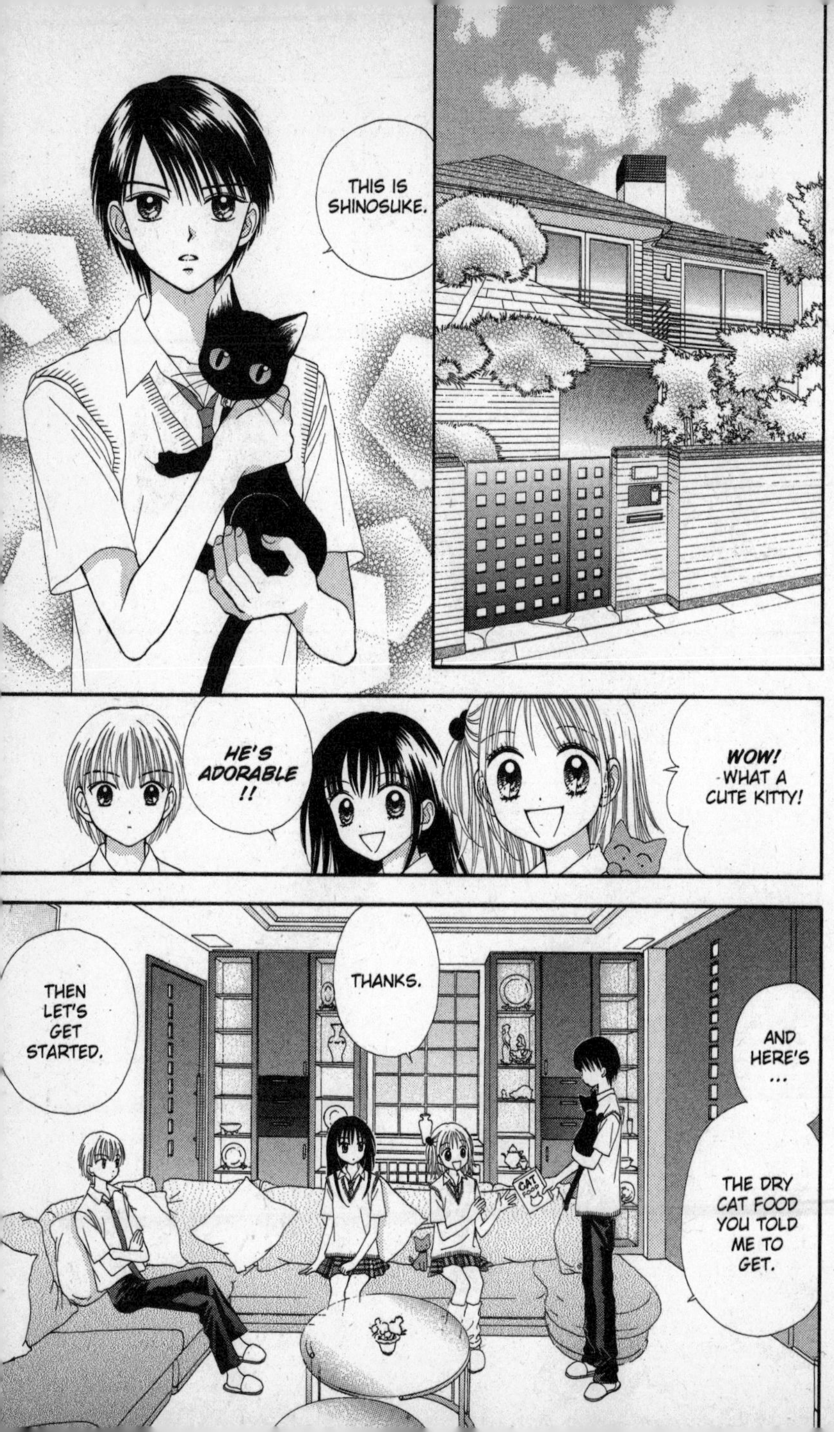
THIS IS SHINOSUKE.
WOW! WHAT A CUTE KITTY!
HE'S ADORABLE!!
AND HERE'S...
THE DRY CAT FOOD YOU TOLD ME TO GET.
CAT FOOD
THANKS.
THEN LET'S GET STARTED.

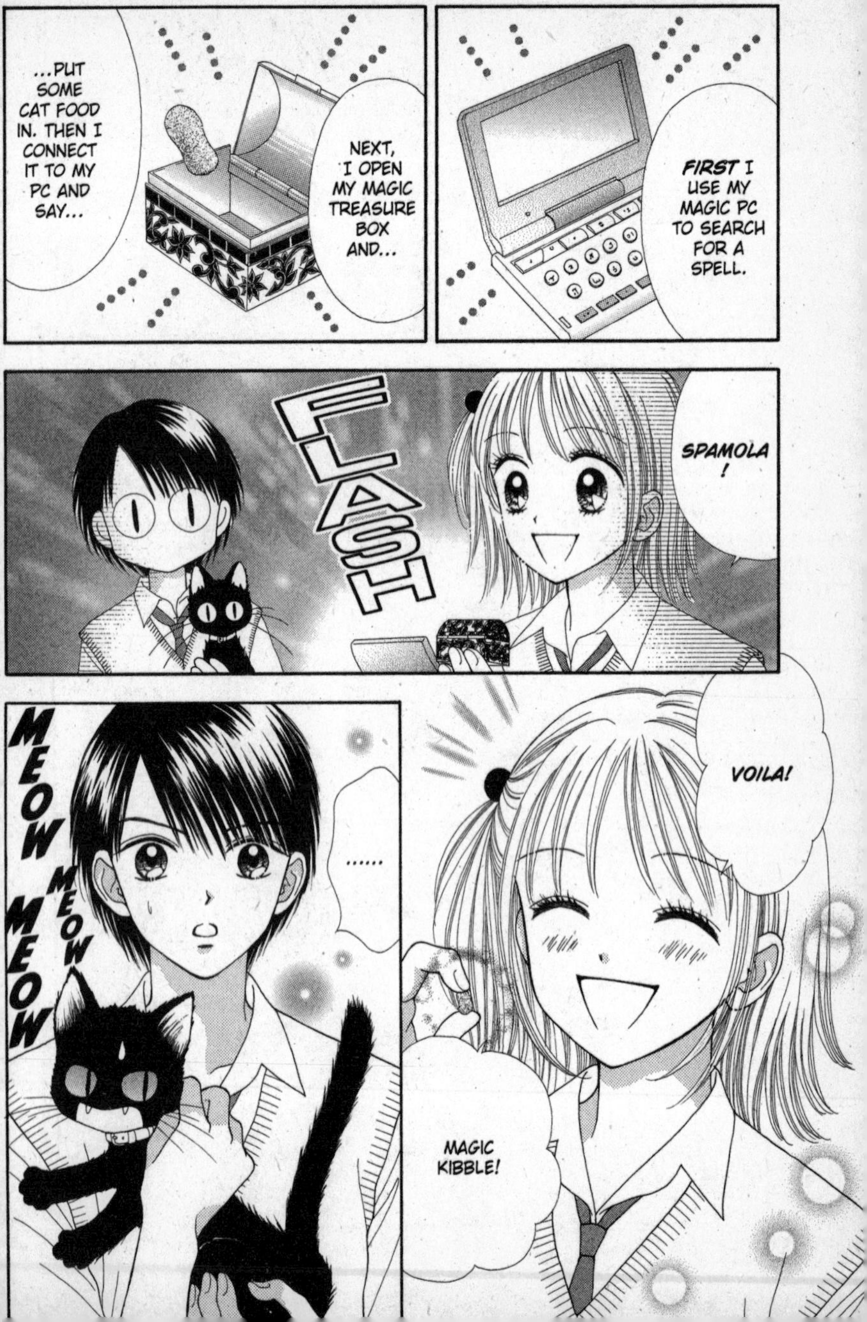
FIRST I USE MY MAGIC PC TO SEARCH FOR A SPELL.
NEXT, I OPEN MY MAGIC TREASURE BOX AND...
...PUT SOME CAT FOOD IN. THEN I CONNECT IT TO MY PC AND SAY...
SPAMOLA!
FLASH
VOILA!
MAGIC KIBBLE!
......
MEOW MEOW MEOW MEOW MEOW

FREE TALK 6

So far, I've read the anime scripts for stories up to Part 15. I particularly like Part 6 in which everyone goes camping. Other favorite episodes include Part 9 during which Yuta shows up and hides the Holy Stone. And Part 10 (the cursed doll story) and Part 13 (the flea market adventure).

I'm really looking forward to seeing the finished anime. It looks like such fun!

There is one thing that worries me, though. Two days ago I got the summaries for Parts 16-26. They mostly star Nina. And the plots are almost completely devoted to a rivalry between Nina and Maya (a character invented for the anime) and a love story between Nina and Hiroki. Ayu and Tetsushi have been marginalized! (Laughs.)

You'll probably like this if you find Nina and Hiroki as a couple more interesting than Ayu and Tetsushi. But I think the main characters should always be Ayu and Nina. Tomorrow is the press conference for Part 1, and I'm going to meet the producer and director. So I'm going to ask them to make Ayu more prominent. I wonder how it will turn out.

HUH?!
MAGIC PC... TREASURE BOX...
HERE YOU GO, SHINNY. EAT UP!
ARE YOU SERIOUS?
DASH
OH!
HE RAN AWAY.
I WONDER IF HE'S SUSPICIOUS.
I'LL GO TALK TO HIM.
HE TALKS...?!
I CAN SPEAK HUMAN OR ANIMAL.
A-hem!

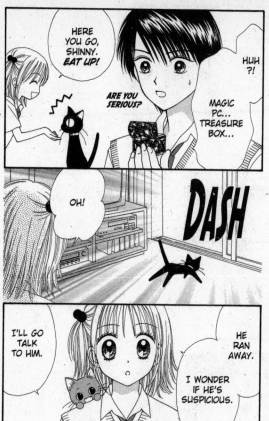

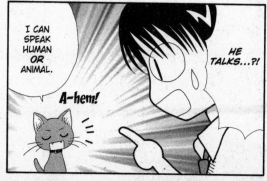

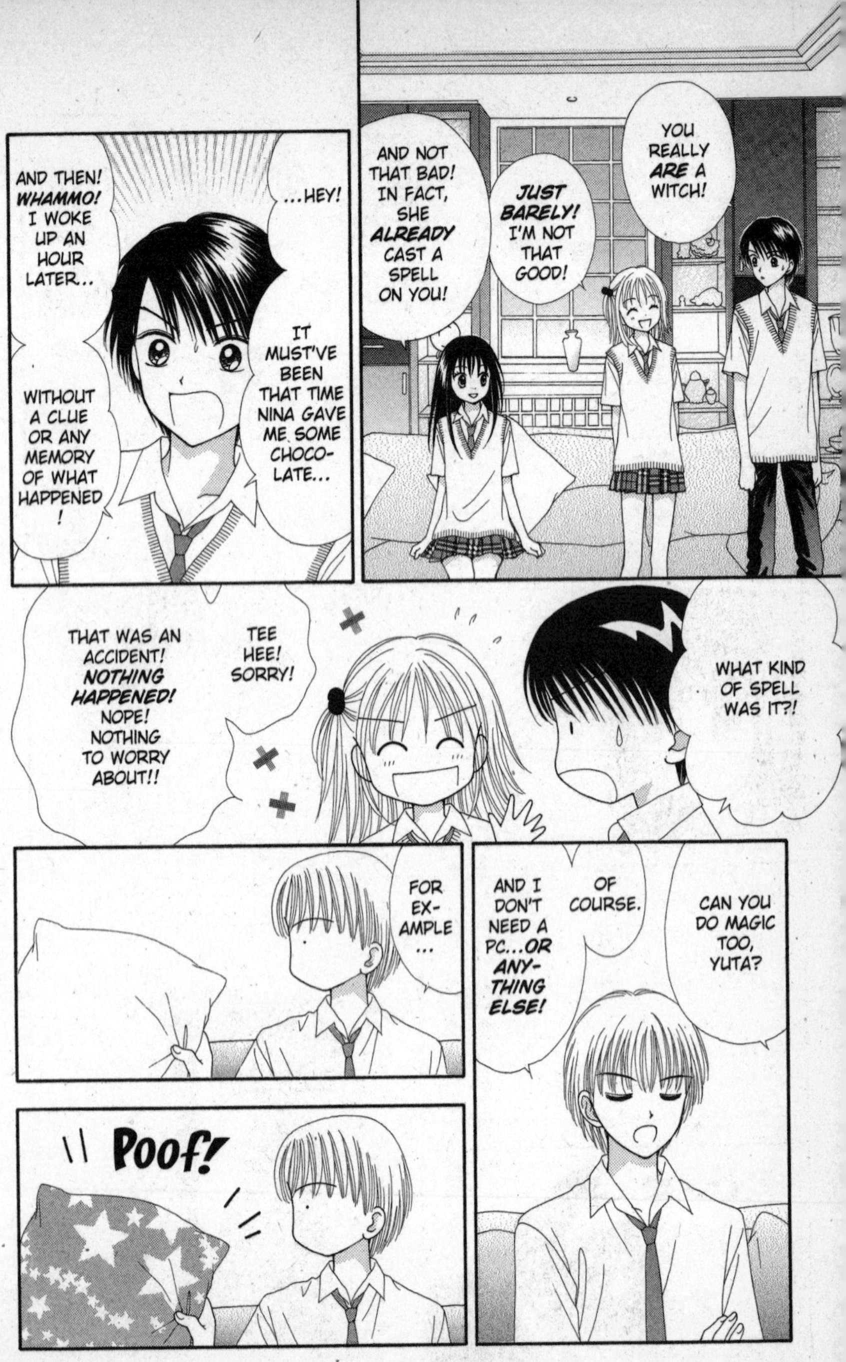
YOU REALLY ARE A WITCH!
JUST BARELY! I'M NOT THAT GOOD!
AND NOT THAT BAD! IN FACT, SHE ALREADY CAST A SPELL ON YOU!
...HEY!
IT MUST'VE BEEN THAT TIME NINA GAVE ME SOME CHOCO-LATE...
AND THEN! WHAMMO! I WOKE UP AN HOUR LATER...
WITHOUT A CLUE OR ANY MEMORY OF WHAT HAPPENED!
WHAT KIND OF SPELL WAS IT?!
TEE HEE! SORRY!
THAT WAS AN ACCIDENT! NOTHING HAPPENED! NOPE! NOTHING TO WORRY ABOUT!!
CAN YOU DO MAGIC TOO, YUTA?
OF COURSE.
AND I DON'T NEED A PC...OR ANY-THING ELSE!
FOR EX-AMPLE...
Poof!

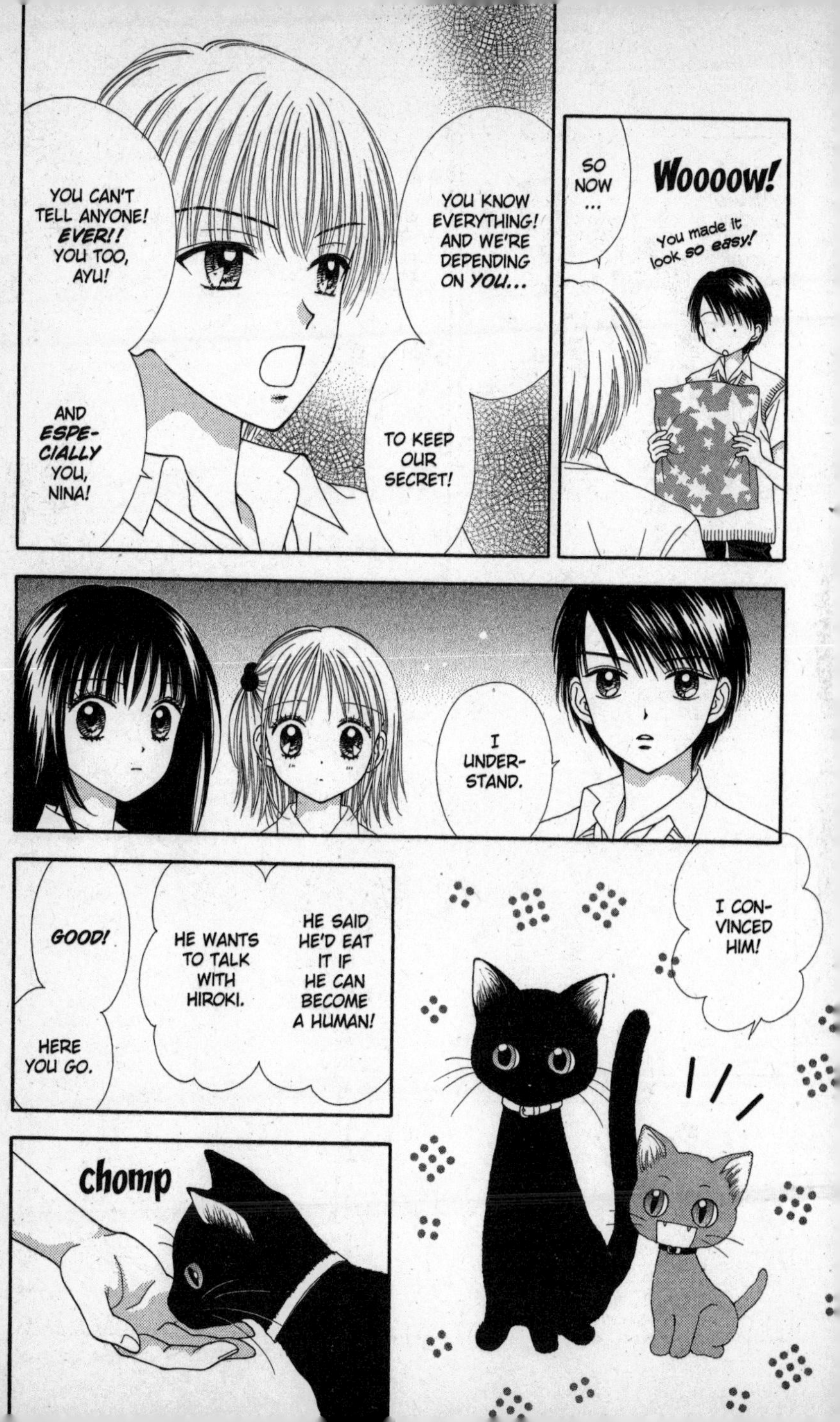
SO NOW...
Wooooow!
You made it look so easy!
YOU KNOW EVERYTHING! AND WE'RE DEPENDING ON YOU...
TO KEEP OUR SECRET!
YOU CAN'T TELL ANYONE! EVER!! YOU TOO, AYU!
AND ESPECIALLY YOU, NINA!
I UNDER-STAND.
I CON-VINCED HIM!
HE SAID HE'D EAT IT IF HE CAN BECOME A HUMAN!
HE WANTS TO TALK WITH HIROKI.
GOOD!
HERE YOU GO.
chomp

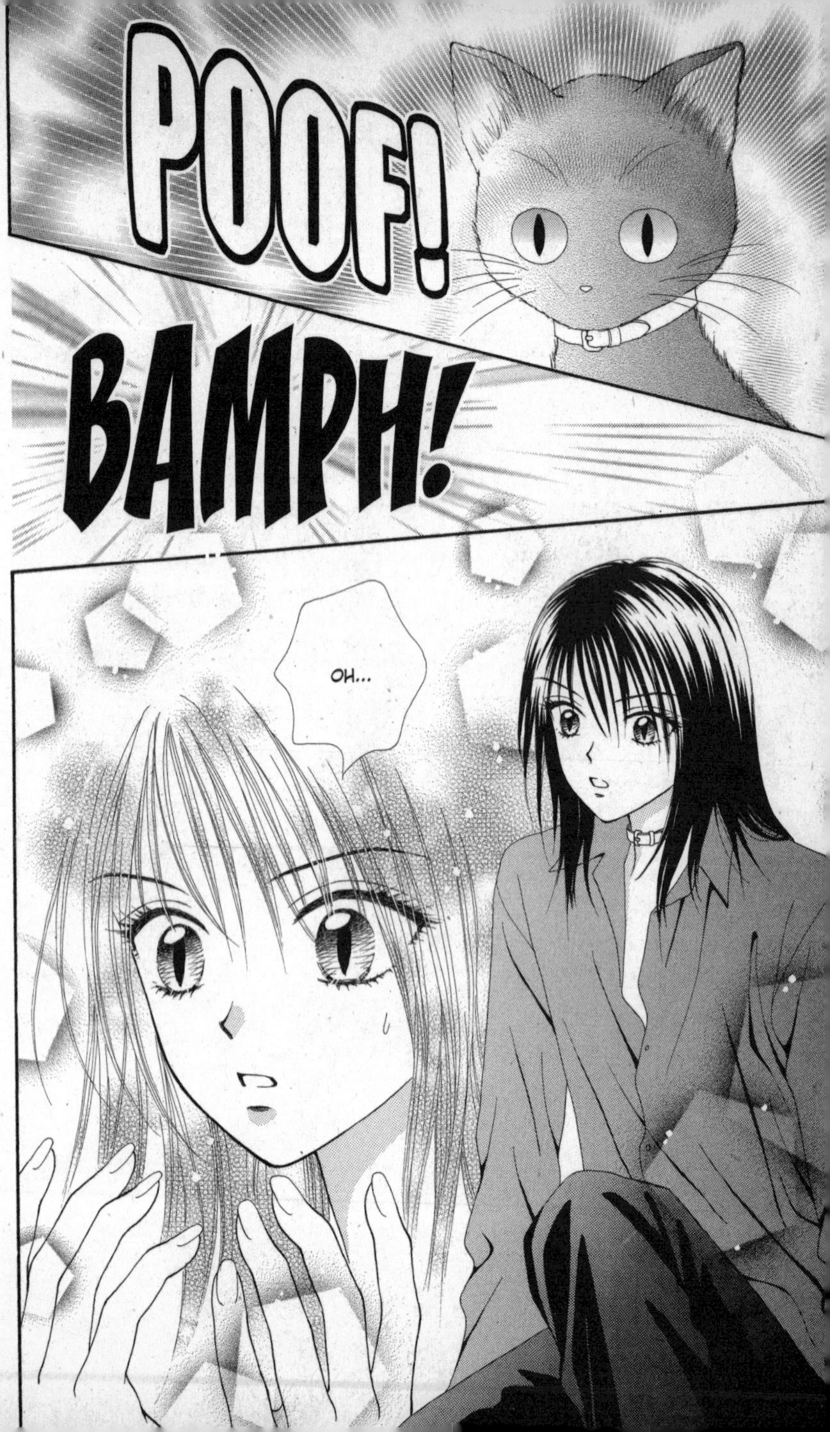
POOF!
BAMPH!
OH...

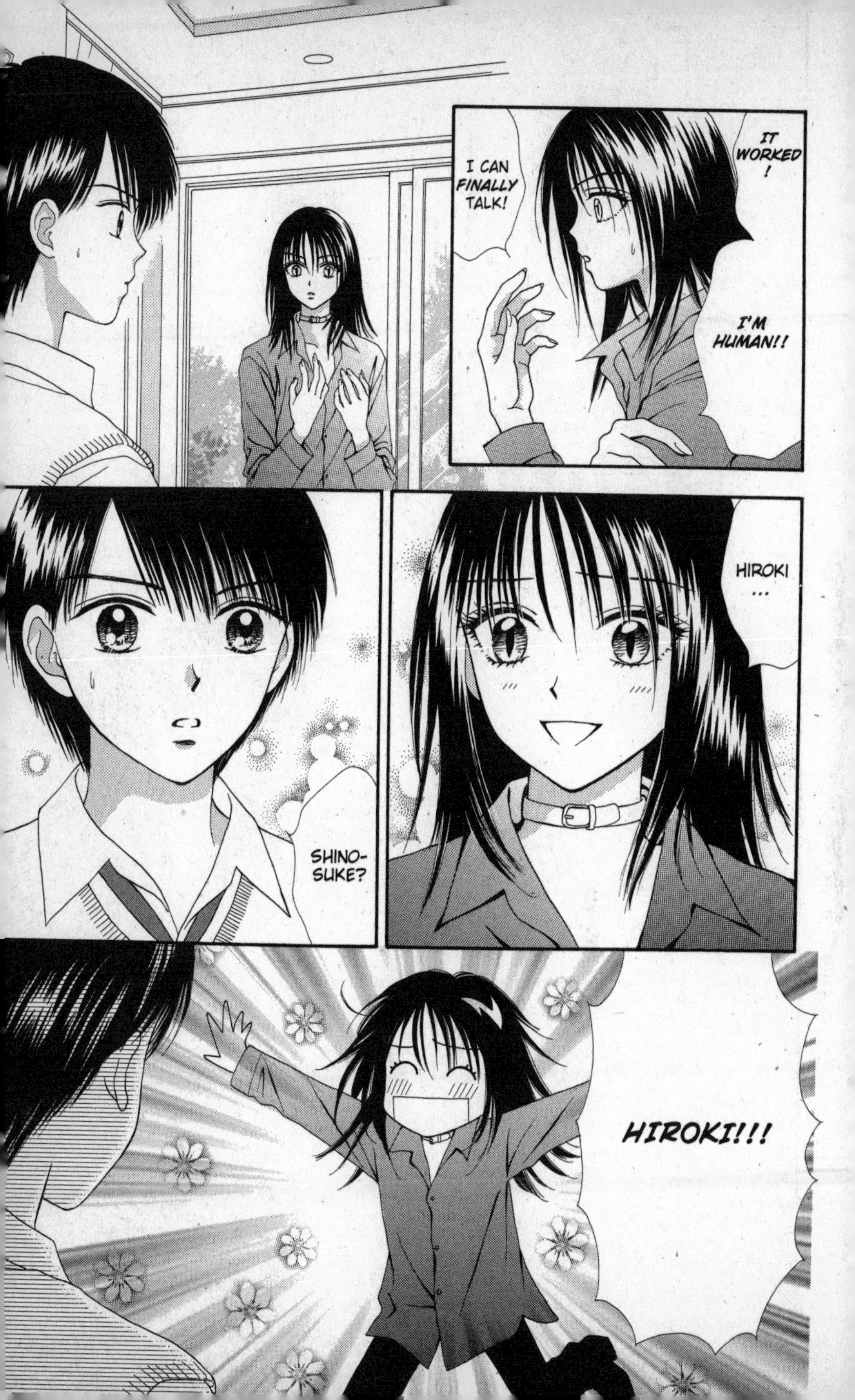
IT WORKED!
I CAN FINALLY TALK!
I'M HUMAN!!
HIROKI...
SHINO-SUKE?
HIROKI!!!

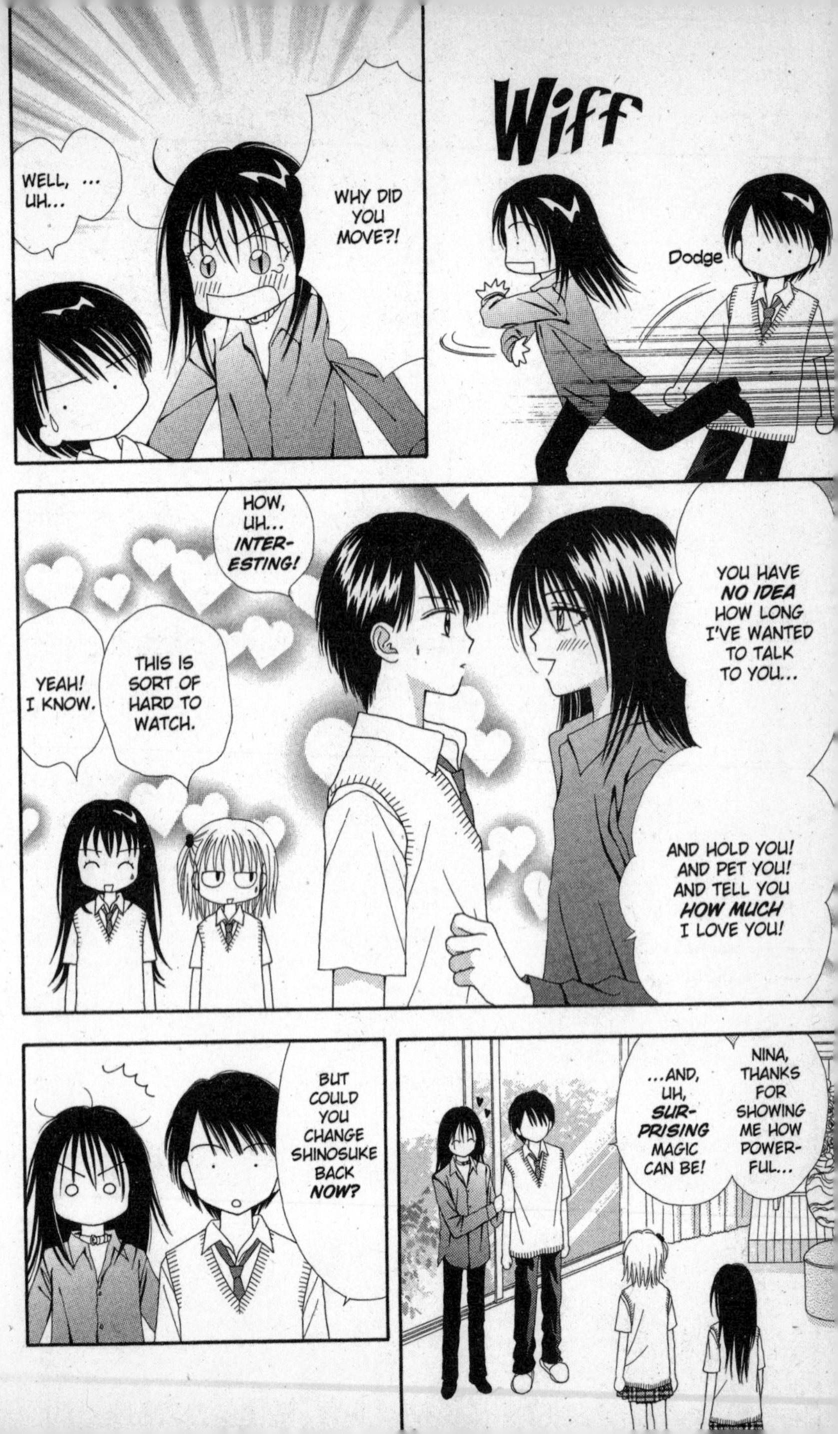
Wiff
Dodge
WHY DID YOU MOVE?!
WELL, ... UH...
YOU HAVE *NO IDEA* HOW LONG I'VE WANTED TO TALK TO YOU...
AND HOLD YOU! AND PET YOU! AND TELL YOU *HOW MUCH* I LOVE YOU!
HOW, UH... *INTERESTING!*
THIS IS SORT OF HARD TO WATCH.
YEAH! I KNOW.
NINA, THANKS FOR SHOWING ME HOW POWERFUL...
...AND, UH, *SURPRISING* MAGIC CAN BE!
BUT COULD YOU CHANGE SHINOSUKE BACK *NOW?*

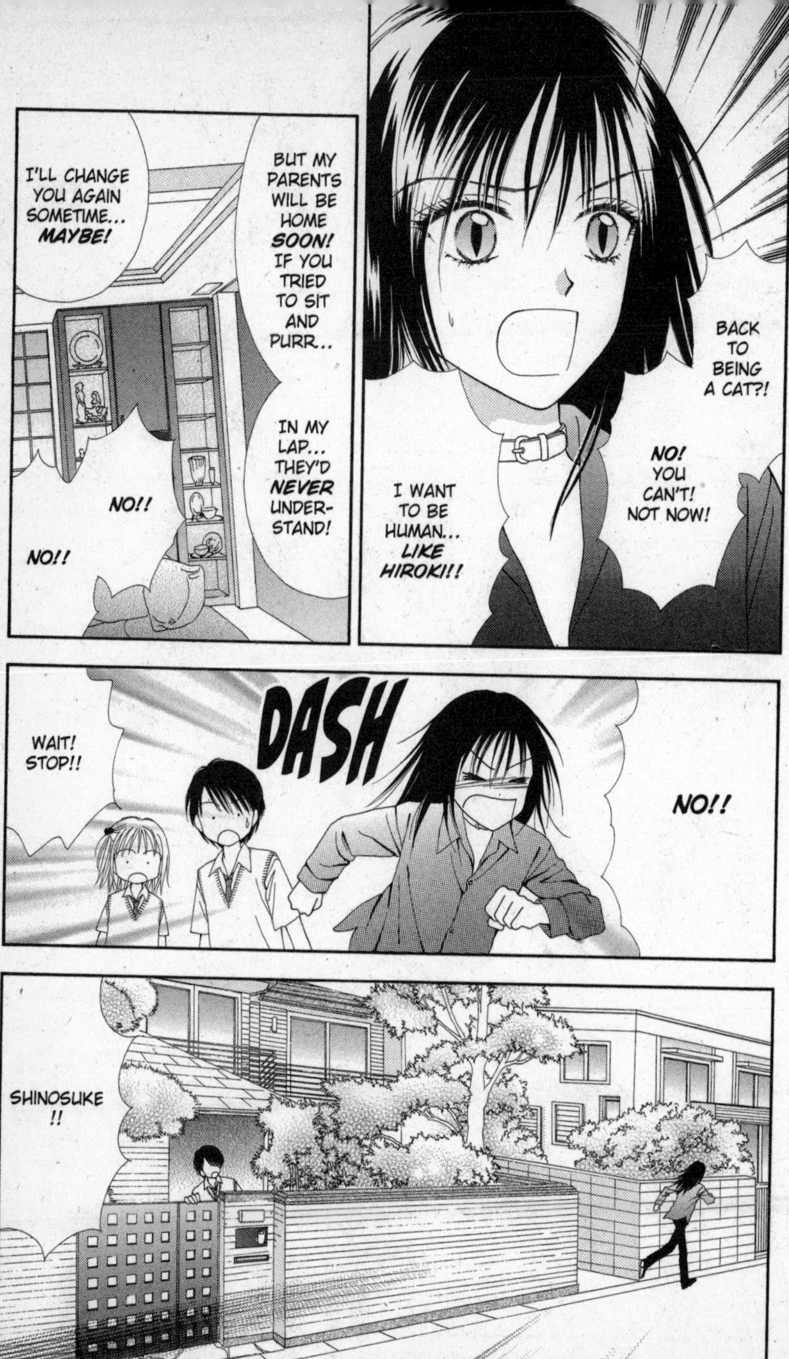
BACK TO BEING A CAT?!
NO! YOU CAN'T! NOT NOW!
I WANT TO BE HUMAN... LIKE HIROKI!!
BUT MY PARENTS WILL BE HOME SOON! IF YOU TRIED TO SIT AND PURR..
IN MY LAP... THEY'D NEVER UNDERSTAND!
I'LL CHANGE YOU AGAIN SOMETIME... MAYBE!
NO!!
NO!!
NO!!
DASH
WAIT! STOP!!
SHINOSUKE !!

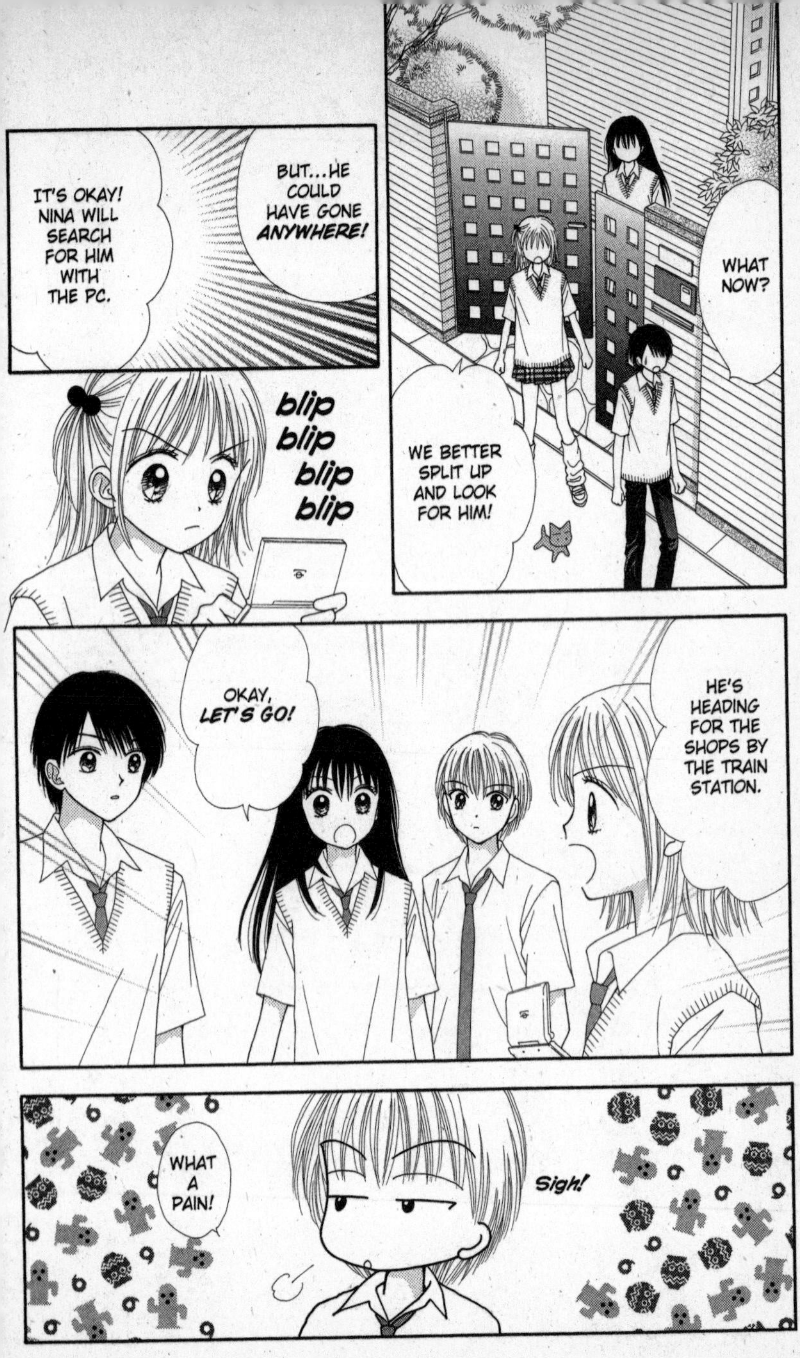
WHAT NOW?
WE BETTER SPLIT UP AND LOOK FOR HIM!
BUT...HE COULD HAVE GONE ANYWHERE!
IT'S OKAY! NINA WILL SEARCH FOR HIM WITH THE PC.
blip blip blip blip
HE'S HEADING FOR THE SHOPS BY THE TRAIN STATION.
OKAY, LET'S GO!
Sigh!
WHAT A PAIN!

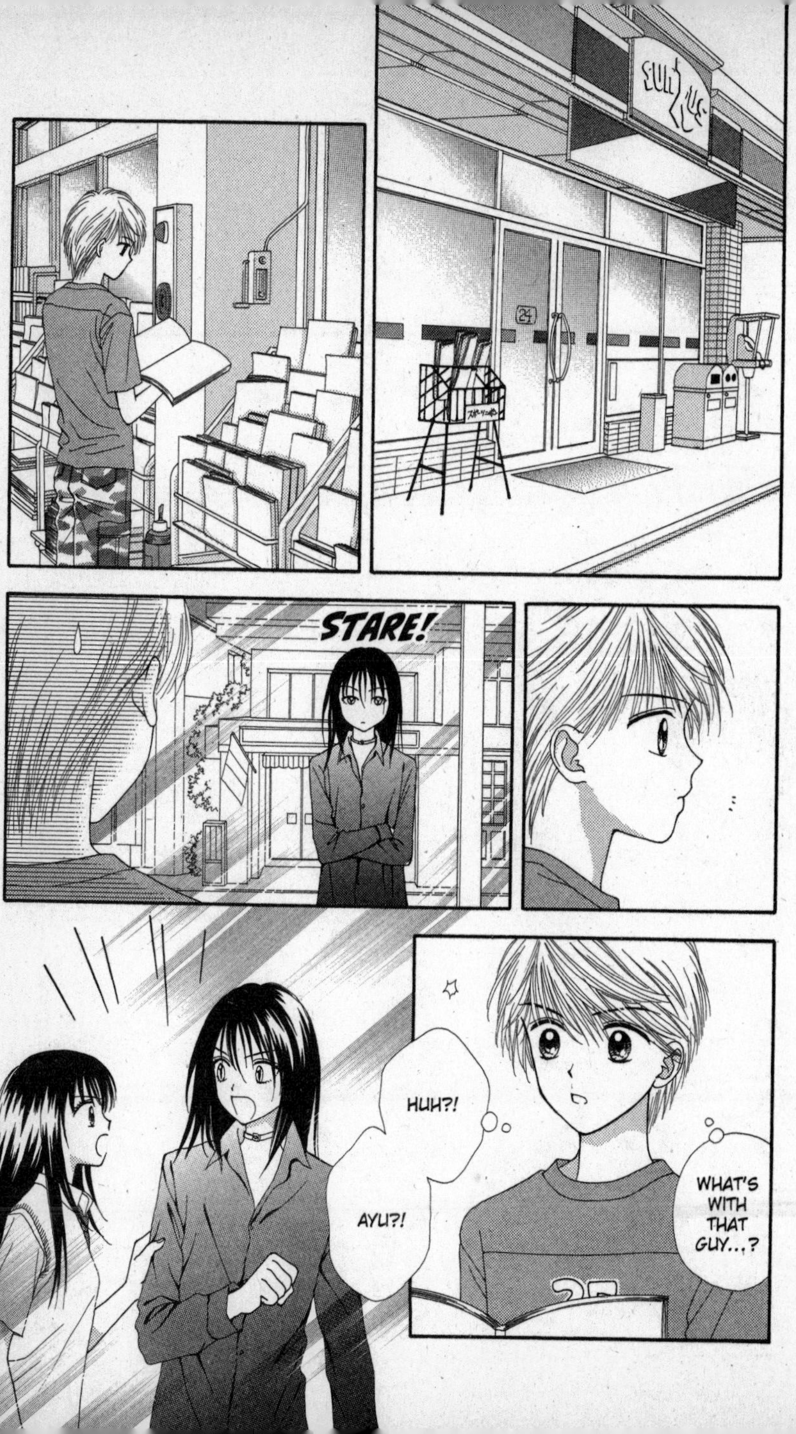
STARE!
WHAT'S WITH THAT GUY...?
HUH?!
AYU?!

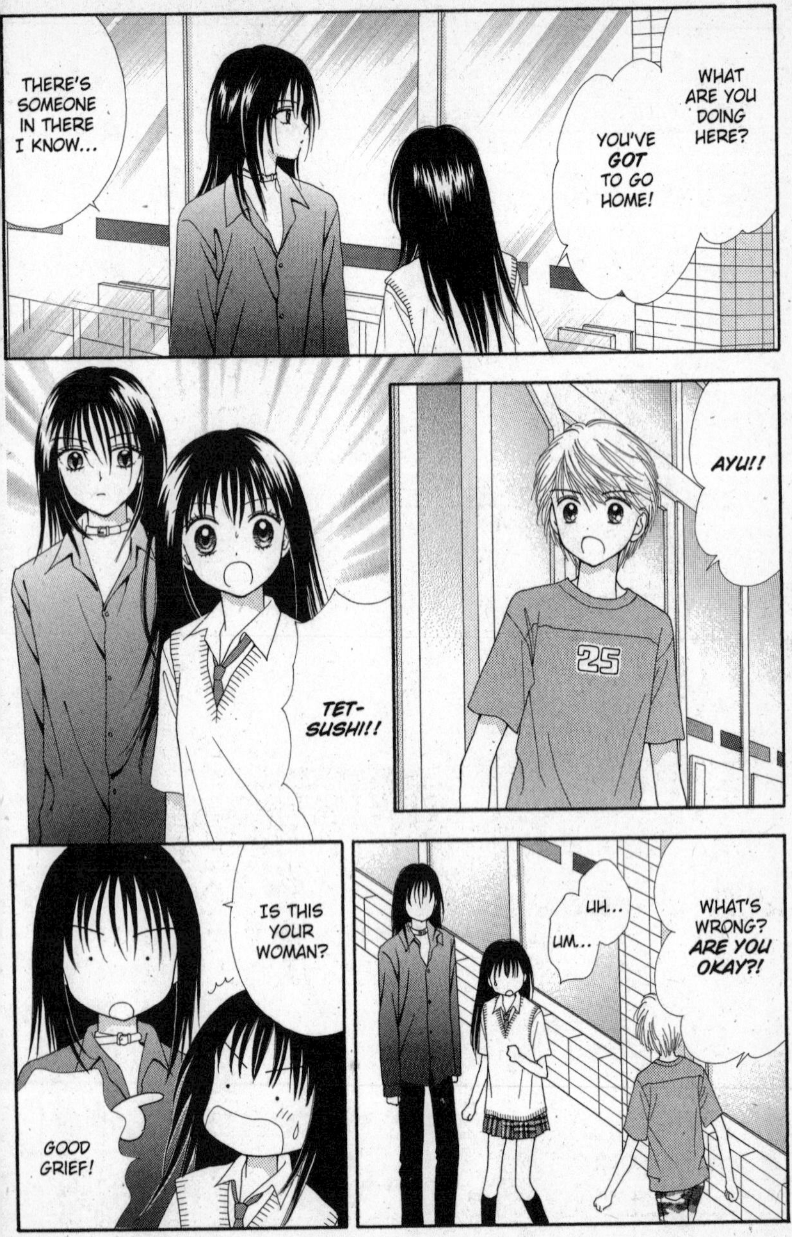
WHAT ARE YOU DOING HERE?
YOU'VE GOT TO GO HOME!
THERE'S SOMEONE IN THERE I KNOW...
AYU!!
TET-SUSHI!!
WHAT'S WRONG? ARE YOU OKAY?!
UH... UM...
IS THIS YOUR WOMAN?
GOOD GRIEF!

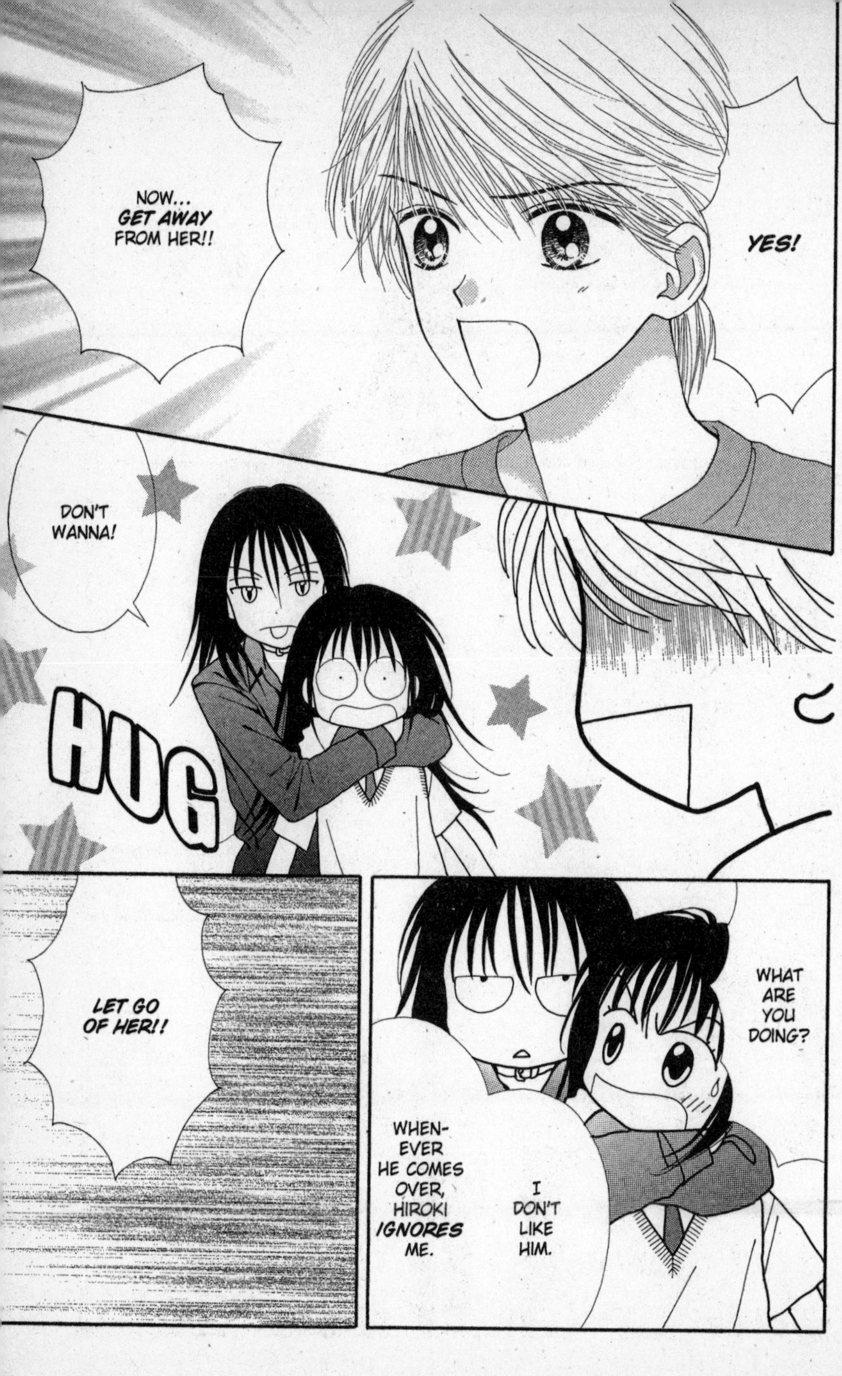
YES!
NOW... GET AWAY FROM HER!!
DON'T WANNA!
HUG
WHAT ARE YOU DOING?
I DON'T LIKE HIM.
WHEN-EVER HE COMES OVER, HIROKI IGNORES ME.
LET GO OF HER!!

AYU!

EEEK!

SHOVE!

I'M SORRY, TETSUSHI. GOTTA GO!

I'LL EXPLAIN TOMORROW!!

AYU...

WAIT! COME BACK!!

ARE YOU OK?

...?!

AH HA! WE FOUND YOU!

NO!! I WON'T!

GIVE UP! YOU'RE SURROUNDED!

LET'S GO HOME, SHINOSUKE.

ARE YOU *STUPID?*

SHINO-SUKE, I...

I'M *FINALLY* HUMAN. NOW I CAN BE *HIROKI'S* BEST FRIEND!!

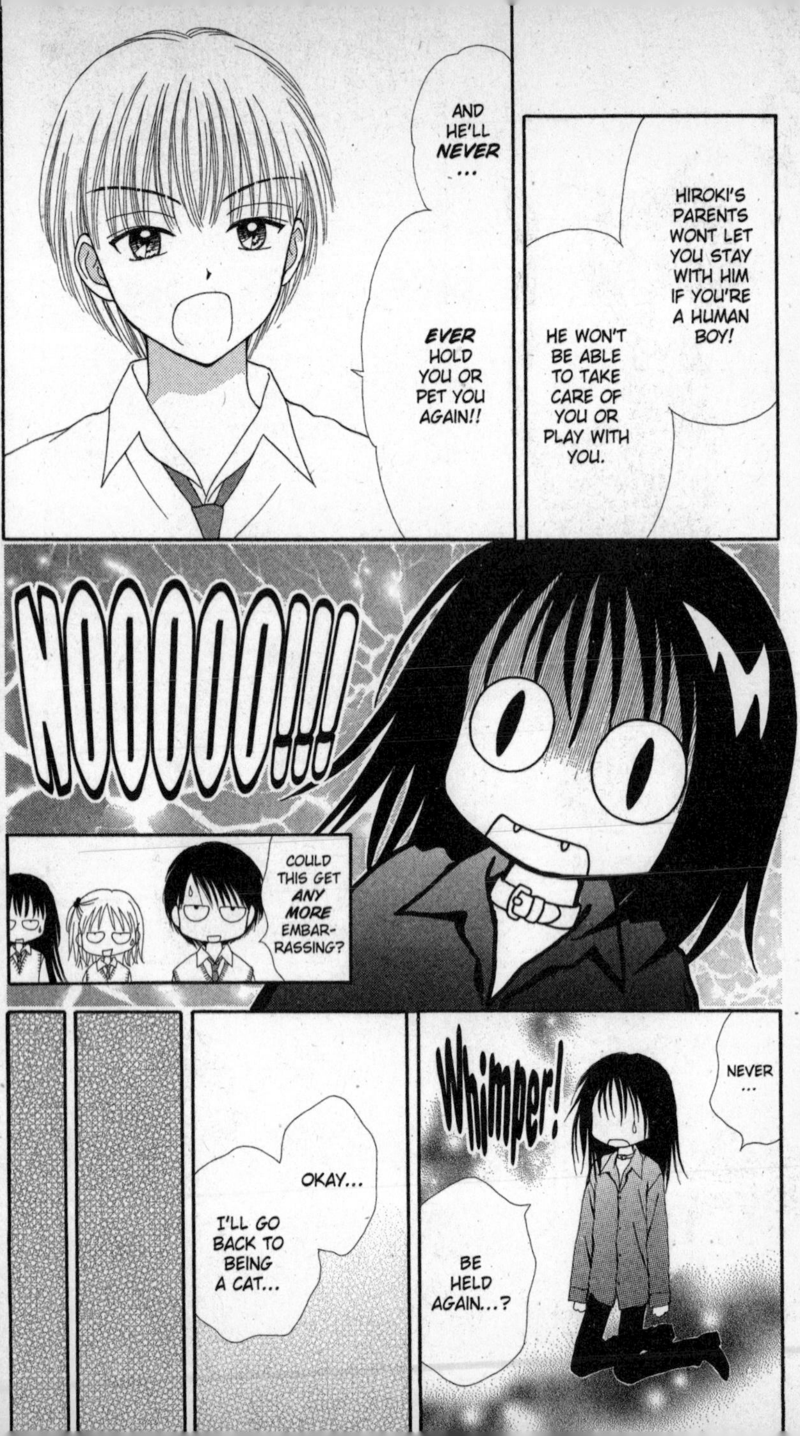
HIROKI'S PARENTS WONT LET YOU STAY WITH HIM IF YOU'RE A HUMAN BOY!
HE WON'T BE ABLE TO TAKE CARE OF YOU OR PLAY WITH YOU.
AND HE'LL **NEVER** ...
EVER HOLD YOU OR PET YOU AGAIN!!
NOOOOO!!!
COULD THIS GET **ANY MORE** EMBARRASSING?
NEVER ...
Whimper!
BE HELD AGAIN...?
OKAY...
I'LL GO BACK TO BEING A CAT...

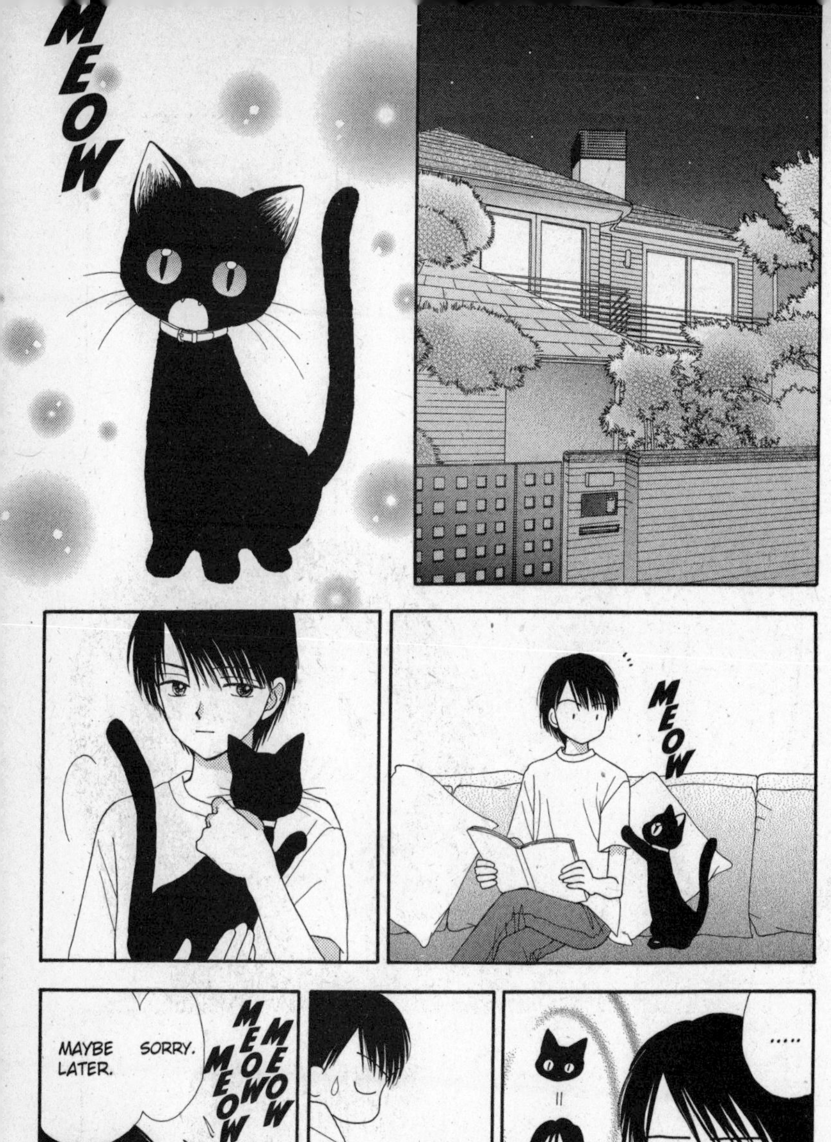
MEOW
MEOW
.....
Plop!
MEOW
MEOW
MEOW
MEOW
MAYBE LATER. SORRY.

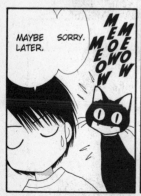

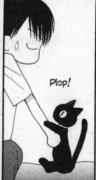

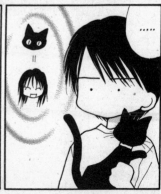

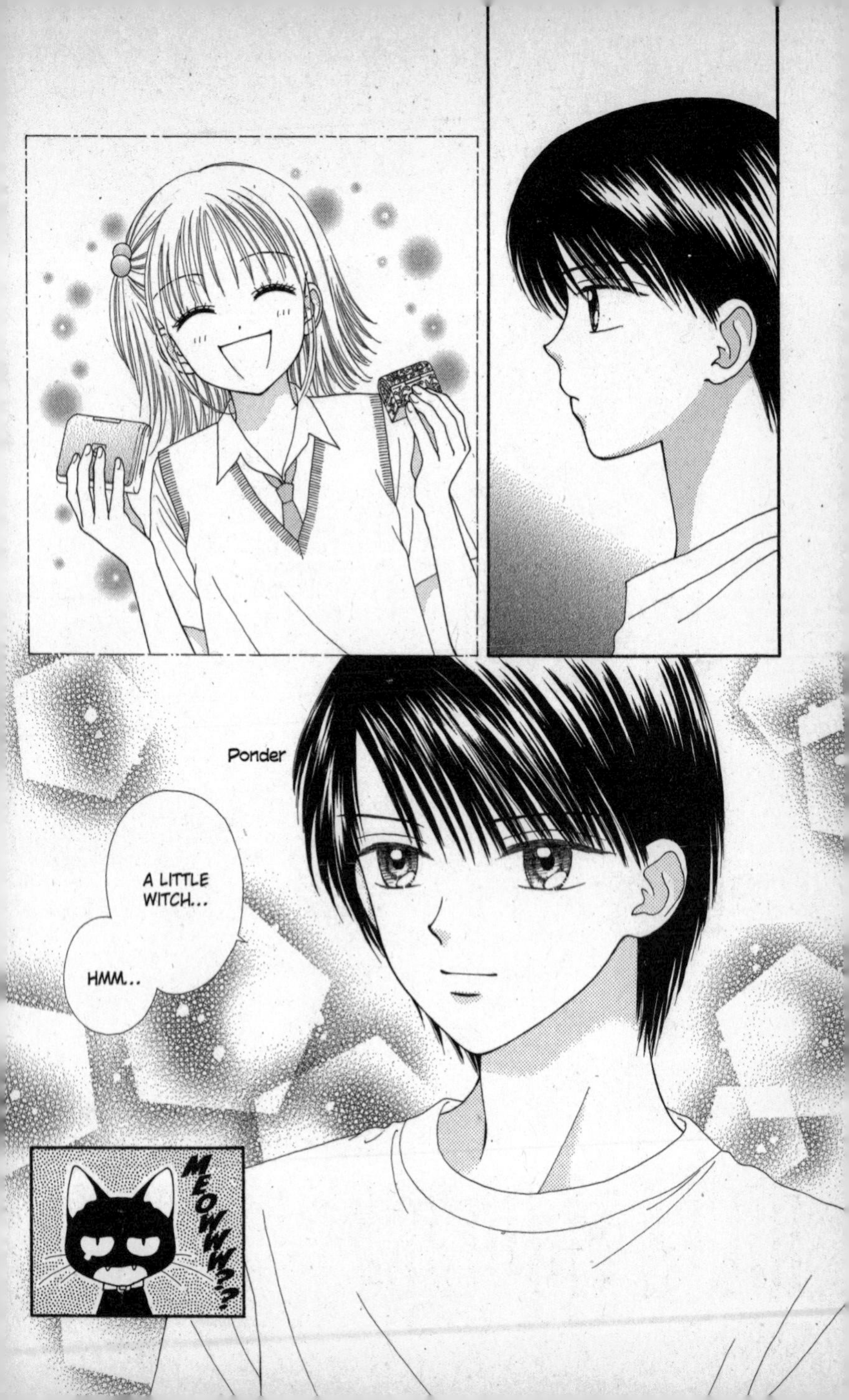
Ponder
A LITTLE WITCH...
HMM..
MEOWWW??

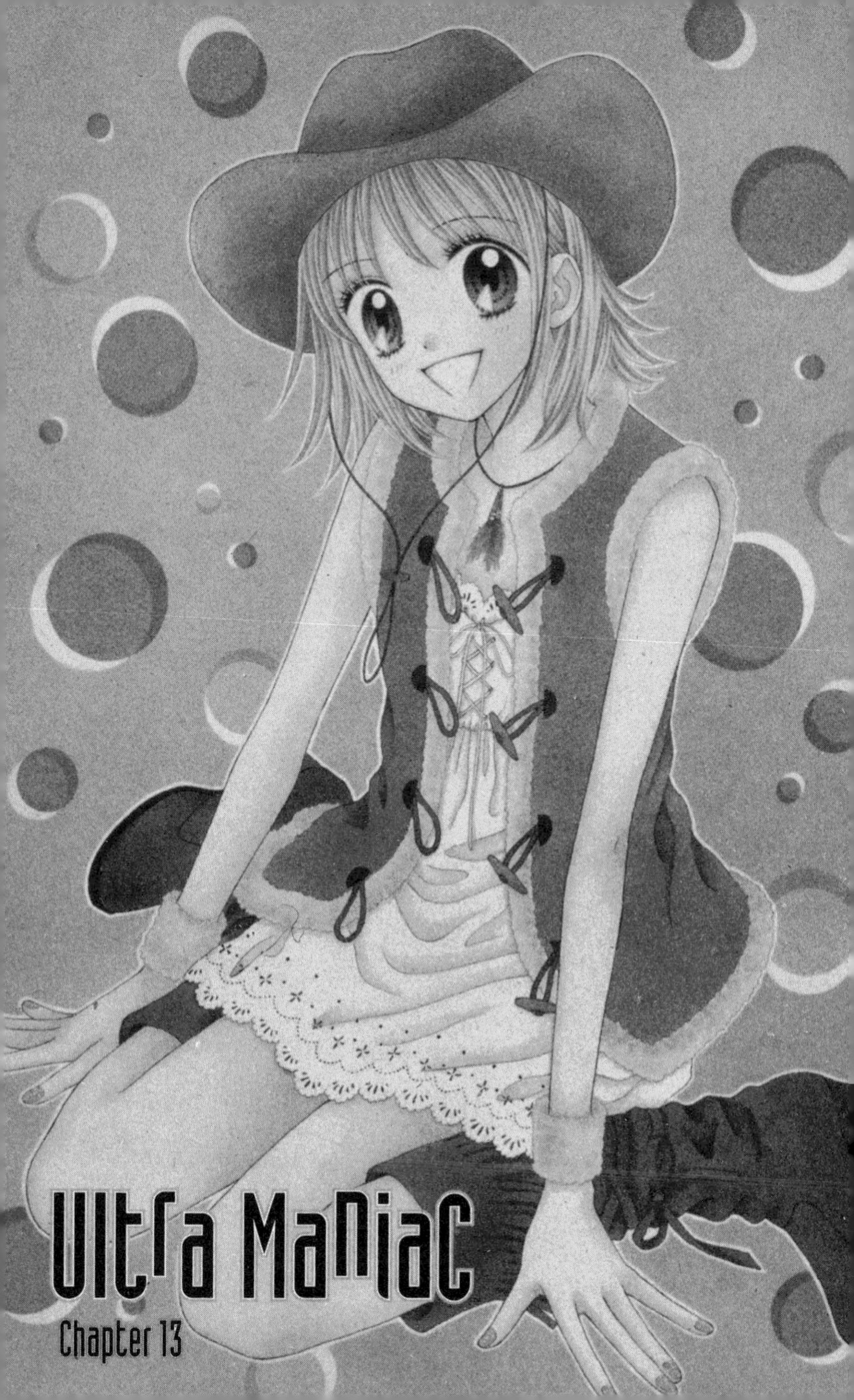
Ultra Maniac
Chapter 13

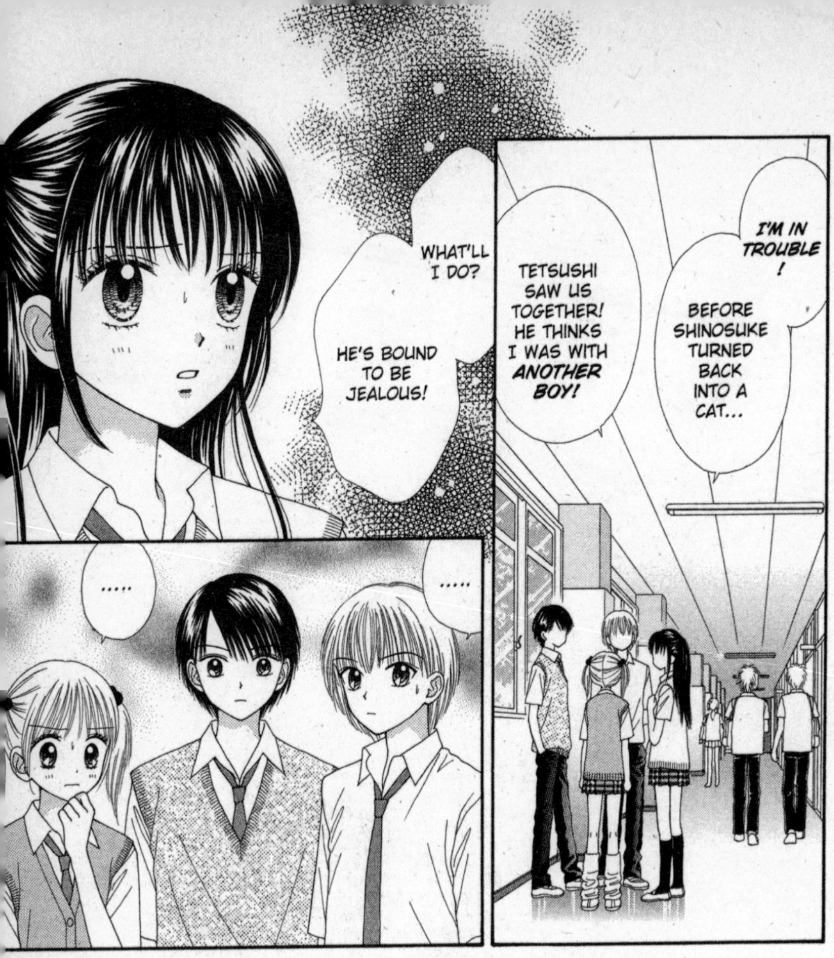
I'M IN TROUBLE!
BEFORE SHINOSUKE TURNED BACK INTO A CAT...
TETSUSHI SAW US TOGETHER! HE THINKS I WAS WITH *ANOTHER BOY!*
WHAT'LL I DO?
HE'S BOUND TO BE JEALOUS!
......
......

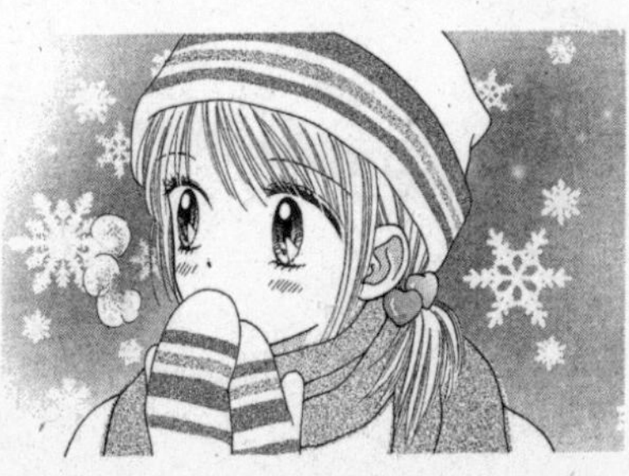

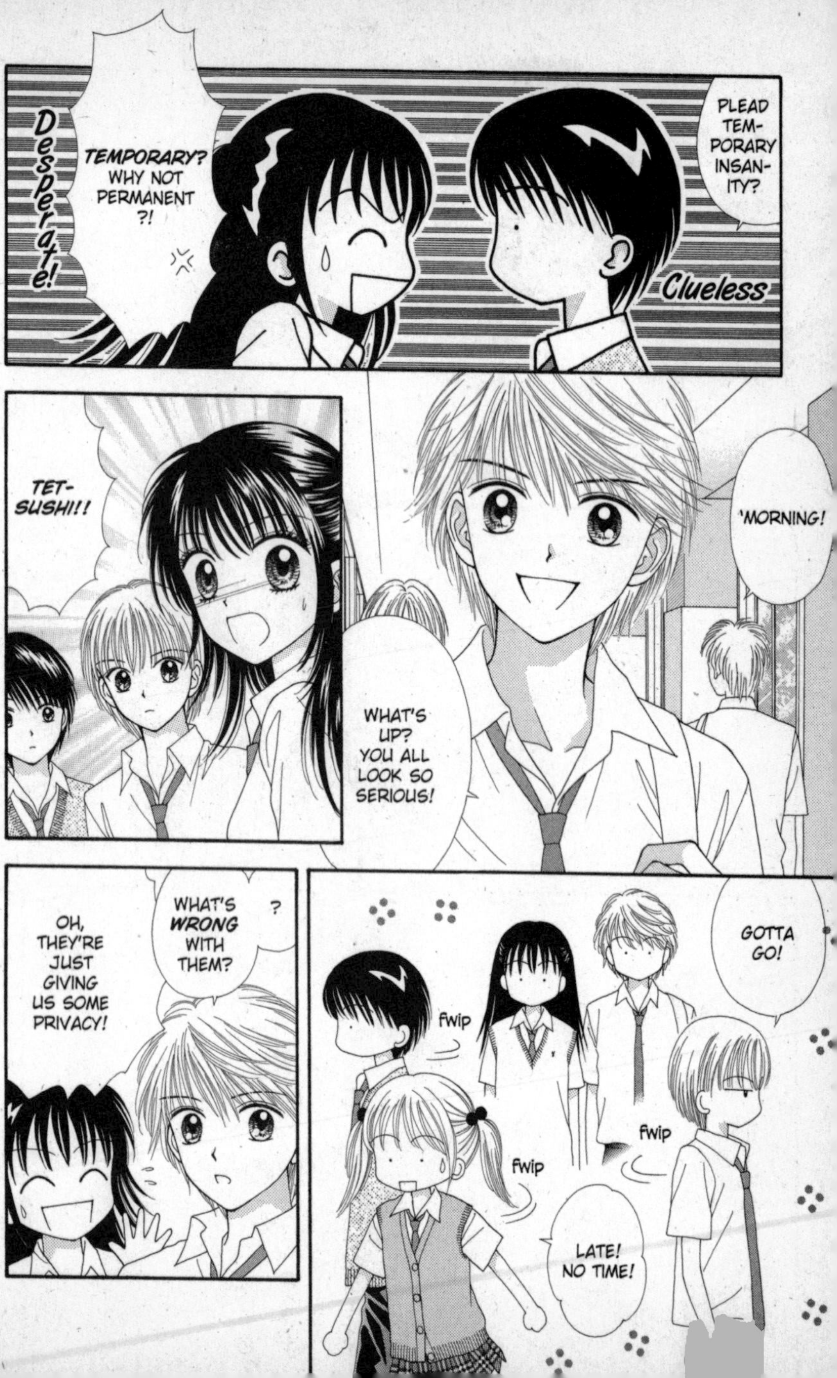
PLEAD TEMPORARY INSANITY?
Clueless
TEMPORARY? WHY NOT PERMANENT ?!
Desperate!
'MORNING!
WHAT'S UP? YOU ALL LOOK SO SERIOUS!
TET-SUSHI!!
GOTTA GO!
fwip
fwip
fwip
LATE! NO TIME!
WHAT'S WRONG WITH THEM?
?
OH, THEY'RE JUST GIVING US SOME PRIVACY!

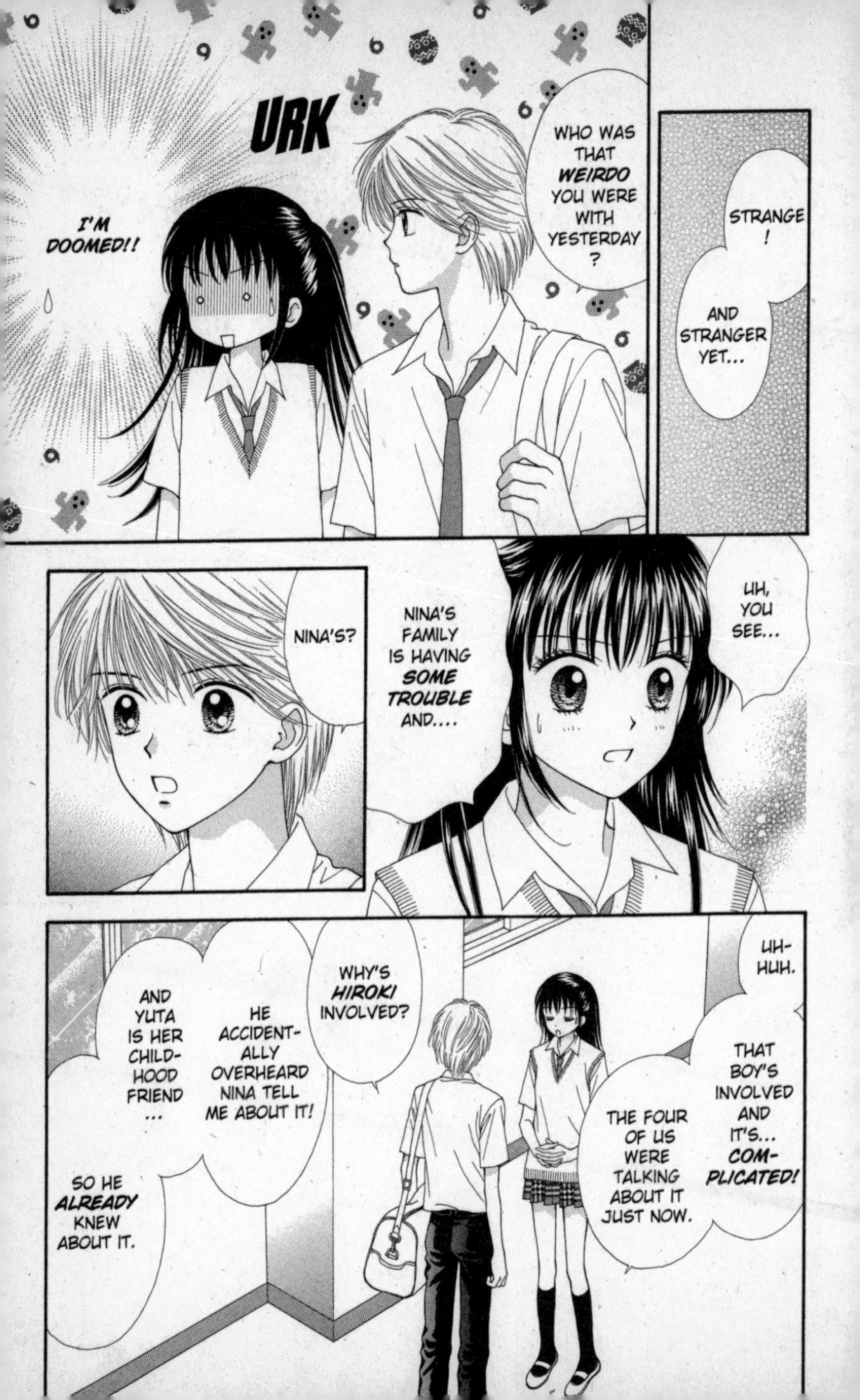
STRANGE!
AND STRANGER YET...
WHO WAS THAT WEIRDO YOU WERE WITH YESTERDAY?
URK
I'M DOOMED!!
UH, YOU SEE...
NINA'S FAMILY IS HAVING SOME TROUBLE AND....
NINA'S?
UH-HUH.
THAT BOY'S INVOLVED AND IT'S... COMPLICATED!
THE FOUR OF US WERE TALKING ABOUT IT JUST NOW.
WHY'S HIROKI INVOLVED?
HE ACCIDENTALLY OVERHEARD NINA TELL ME ABOUT IT!
AND YUTA IS HER CHILDHOOD FRIEND...
SO HE ALREADY KNEW ABOUT IT.

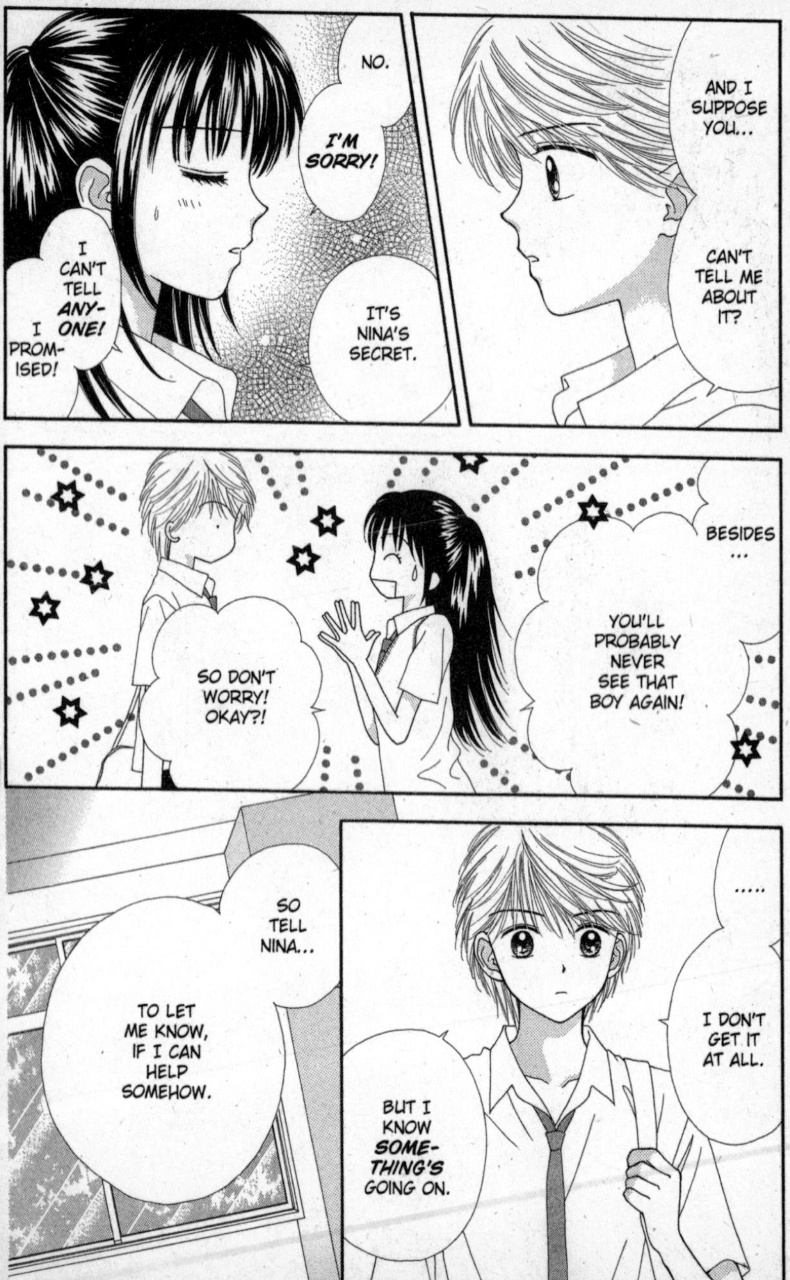
AND I SUPPOSE YOU...
CAN'T TELL ME ABOUT IT?
NO.
I'M SORRY!
IT'S NINA'S SECRET.
I CAN'T TELL ANY-ONE!
I PROM-ISED!
BESIDES...
YOU'LL PROBABLY NEVER SEE THAT BOY AGAIN!
SO DON'T WORRY! OKAY?!
.....
I DON'T GET IT AT ALL.
BUT I KNOW SOME-THING'S GOING ON.
SO TELL NINA...
TO LET ME KNOW, IF I CAN HELP SOMEHOW.

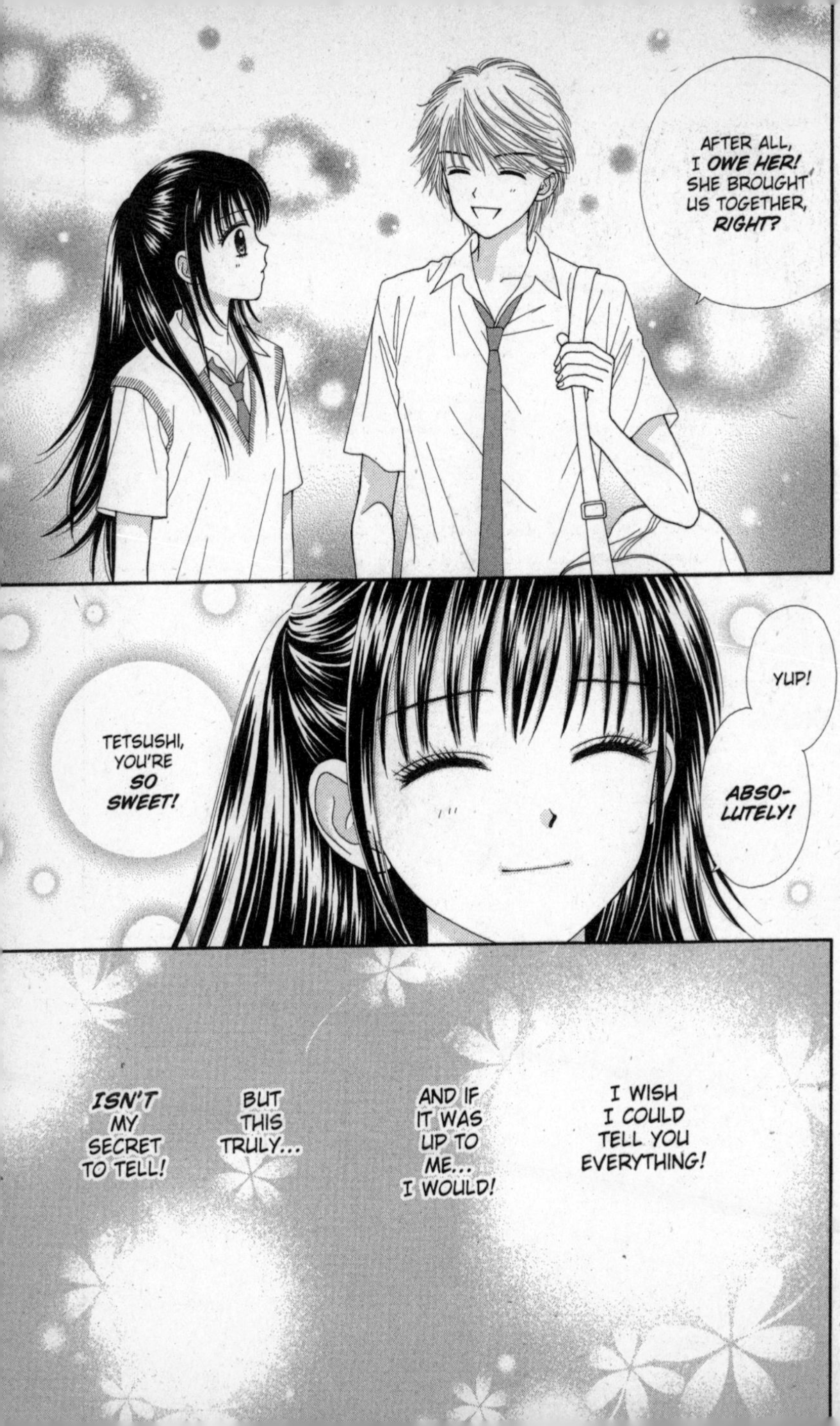
AFTER ALL, I OWE HER! SHE BROUGHT US TOGETHER, RIGHT?
YUP! ABSOLUTELY!
TETSUSHI, YOU'RE SO SWEET!
I WISH I COULD TELL YOU EVERYTHING!
AND IF IT WAS UP TO ME... I WOULD!
BUT THIS TRULY...
ISN'T MY SECRET TO TELL!

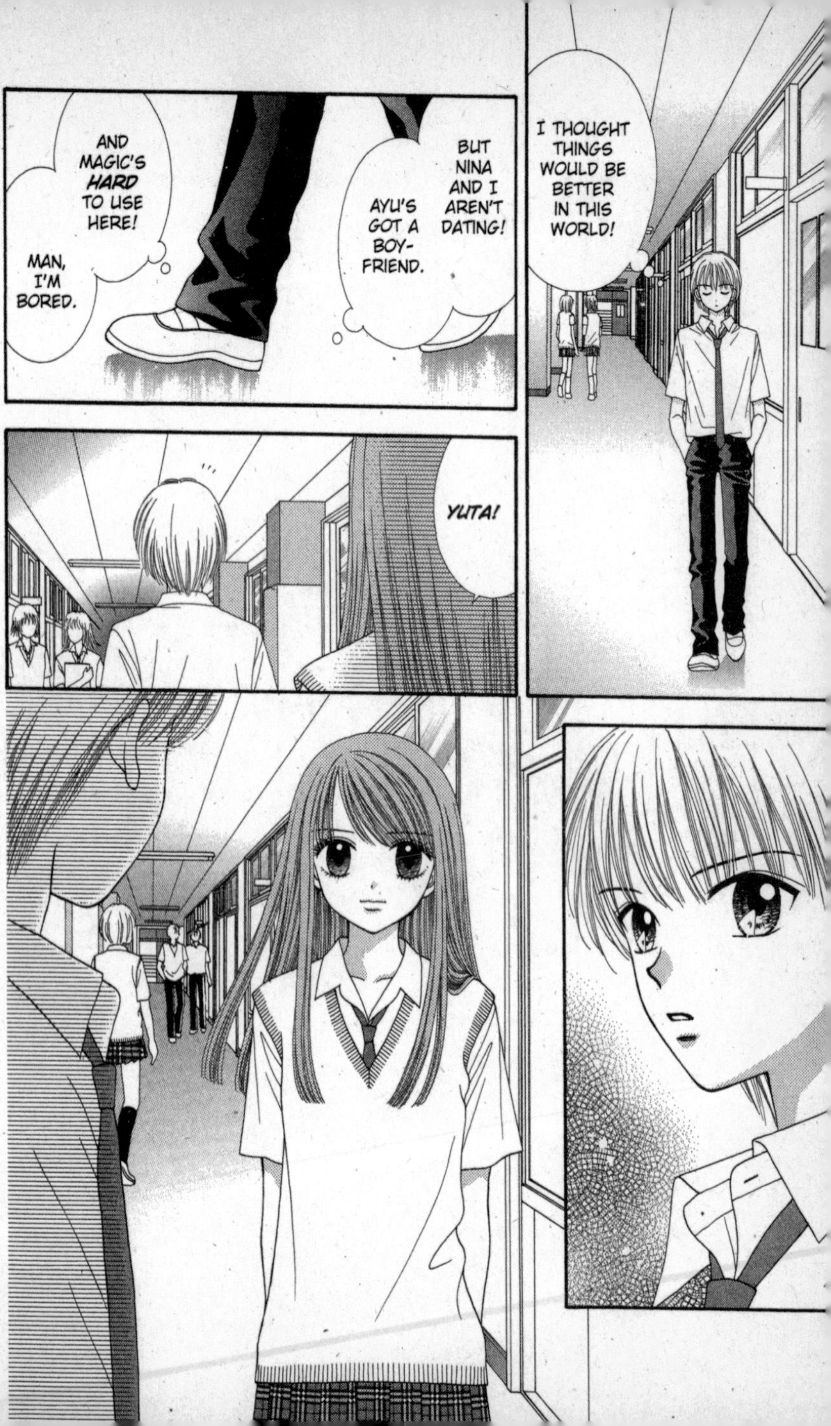
I THOUGHT THINGS WOULD BE BETTER IN THIS WORLD!
BUT NINA AND I AREN'T DATING!
AYU'S GOT A BOY-FRIEND.
AND MAGIC'S HARD TO USE HERE!
MAN, I'M BORED.
YUTA!

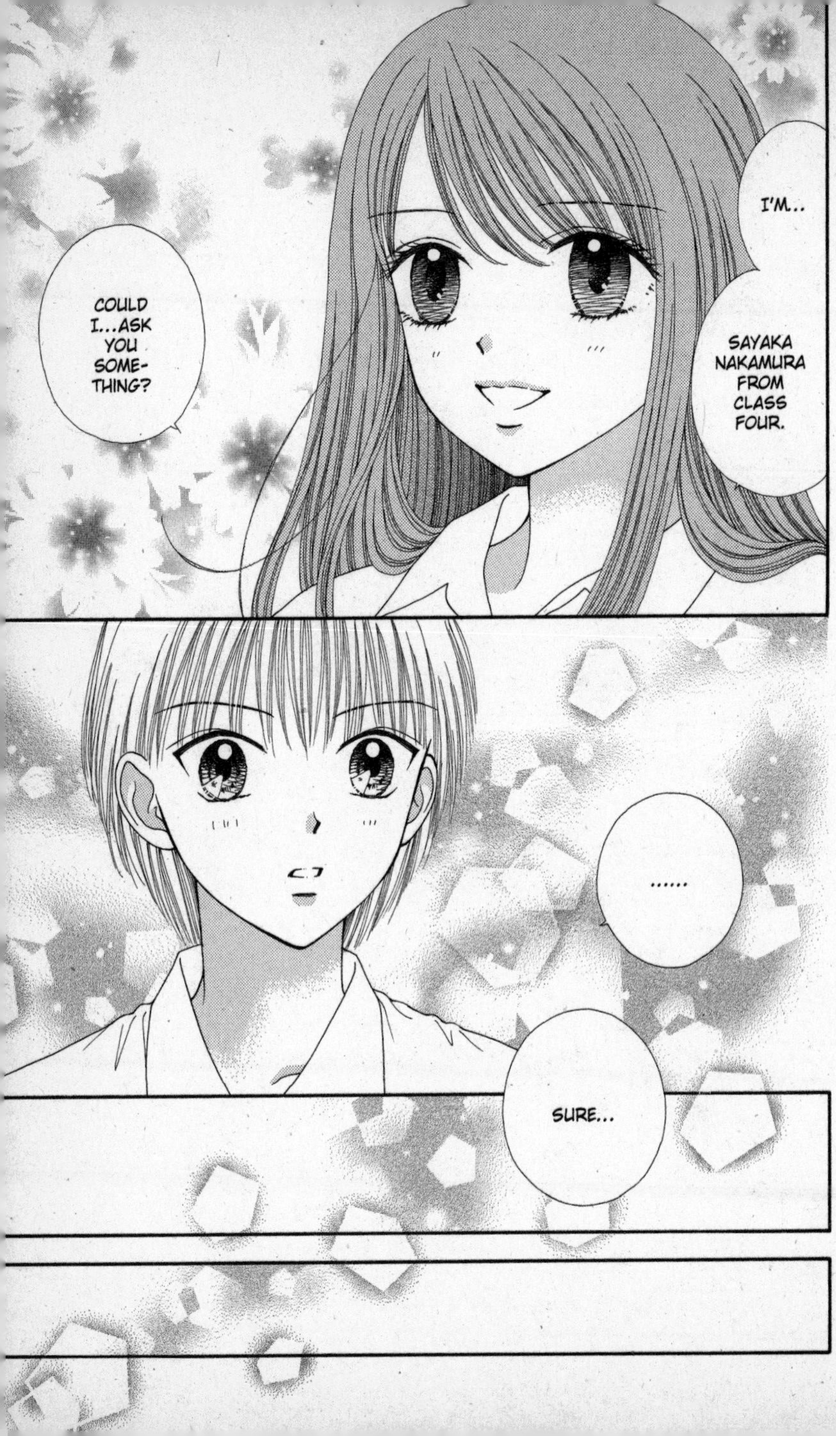
I'M...
SAYAKA NAKAMURA FROM CLASS FOUR.
COULD I...ASK YOU SOME-THING?
......
SURE...

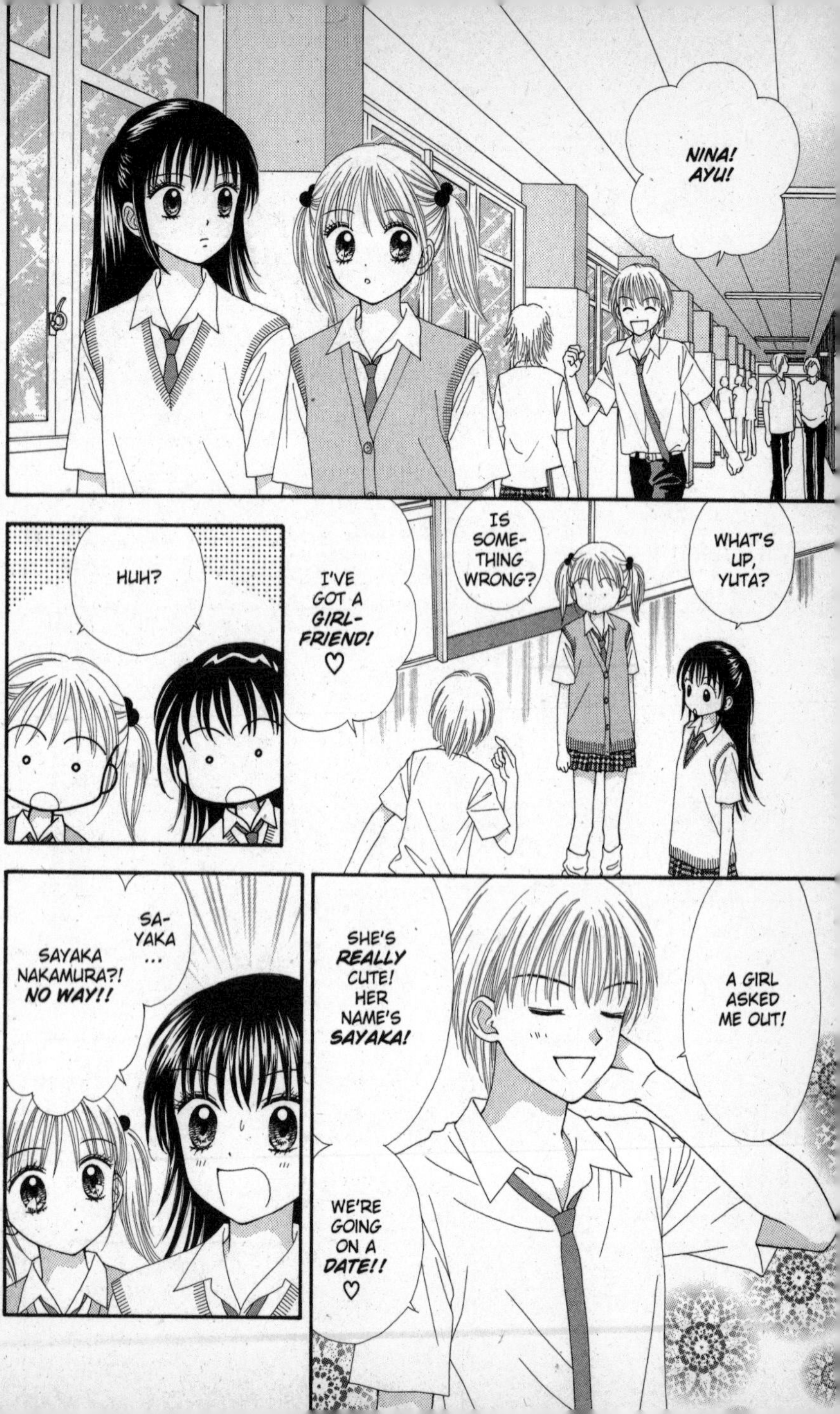
NINA! AYU!
WHAT'S UP, YUTA?
IS SOME-THING WRONG?
I'VE GOT A GIRL-FRIEND! ♡
HUH?
A GIRL ASKED ME OUT!
SHE'S REALLY CUTE! HER NAME'S SAYAKA!
WE'RE GOING ON A DATE!! ♡
SA-YAKA...
SAYAKA NAKAMURA?! NO WAY!!

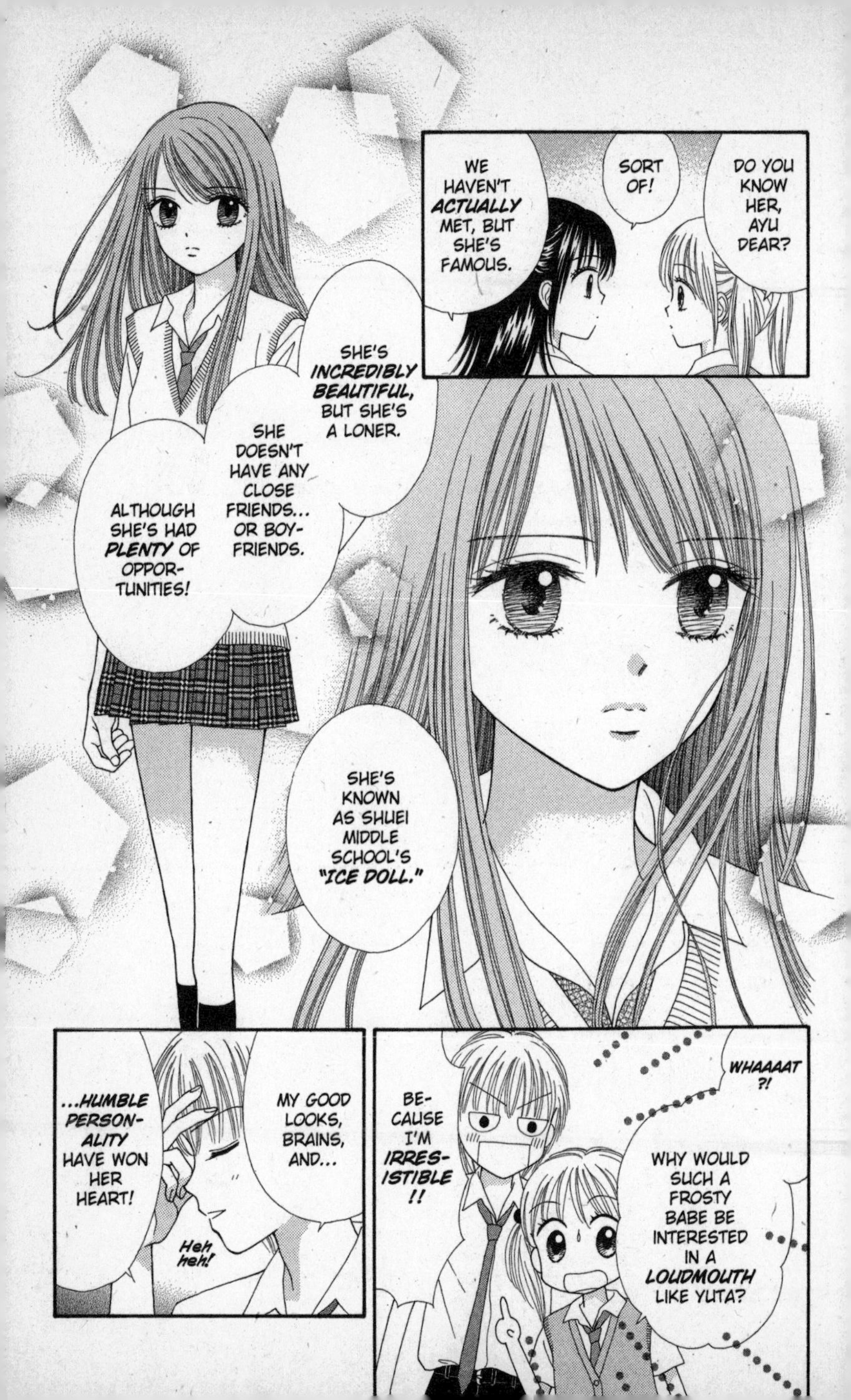
DO YOU KNOW HER, AYU DEAR?
SORT OF!
WE HAVEN'T ACTUALLY MET, BUT SHE'S FAMOUS.
SHE'S INCREDIBLY BEAUTIFUL, BUT SHE'S A LONER.
SHE DOESN'T HAVE ANY CLOSE FRIENDS... OR BOY-FRIENDS.
ALTHOUGH SHE'S HAD PLENTY OF OPPOR-TUNITIES!
SHE'S KNOWN AS SHUEI MIDDLE SCHOOL'S "ICE DOLL."
WHAAAAT?!
WHY WOULD SUCH A FROSTY BABE BE INTERESTED IN A LOUDMOUTH LIKE YUTA?
BE-CAUSE I'M IRRES-ISTIBLE!!
MY GOOD LOOKS, BRAINS, AND...
...HUMBLE PERSON-ALITY HAVE WON HER HEART!
Heh heh!

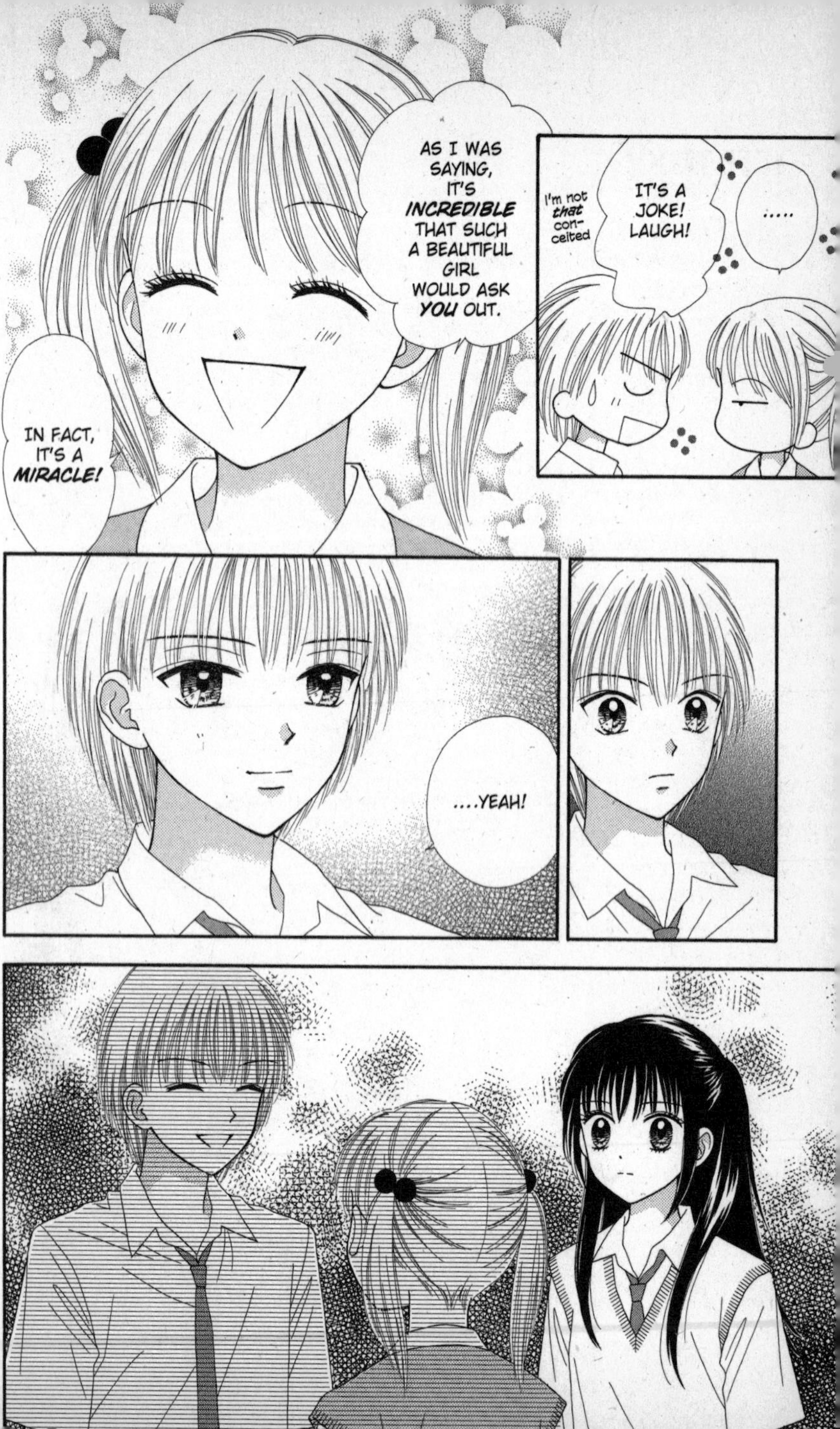
.....
IT'S A JOKE! LAUGH!
I'm not *that* conceited
AS I WAS SAYING, IT'S ***INCREDIBLE*** THAT SUCH A BEAUTIFUL GIRL WOULD ASK ***YOU*** OUT.
IN FACT, IT'S A ***MIRACLE!***
....YEAH!

FREE TALK 7

Speaking of anime, one of my old series, Marmalade Boy, was also made into an anime while it was still being serialized as manga. As I write this, the first DVD box set is just being released and the second and third sets will be out later this year in Japan.

They will have around five discs per box and will be priced at about ¥29,000 ($290) in Japan.

Columbia Music, Japan, is also releasing a two-disc CD set of the **Complete Music of Marmalade Boy**. Opening and ending themes, mood music, and character songs by the voice actors will be included. Oddly enough, this all makes me a bit nostalgic.

The Marmalade Boy anime ran from the spring of 1994 to the fall of 1995. It's hard for me to believe it's been so many years since it appeared!

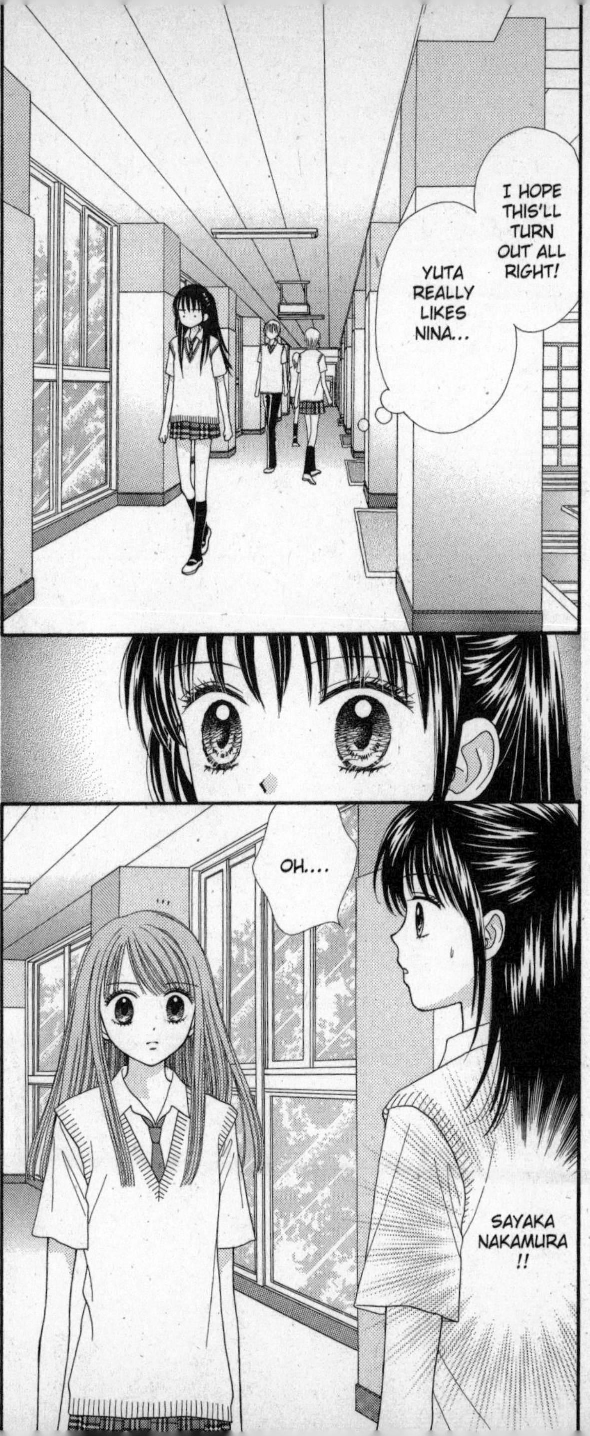

I HOPE THIS'LL TURN OUT ALL RIGHT!
YUTA REALLY LIKES NINA...
OH....
SAYAKA NAKAMURA !!

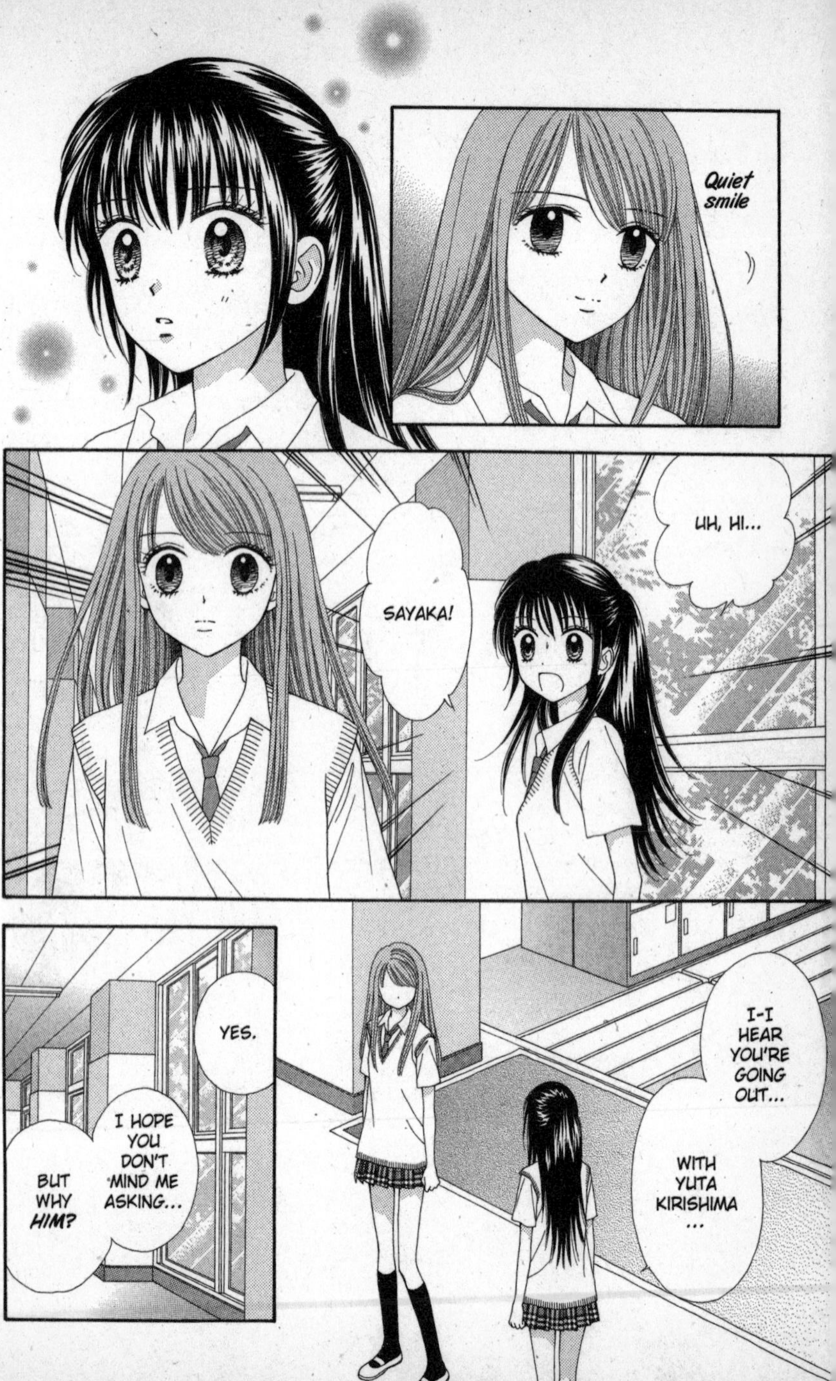
Quiet smile
UH, HI...
SAYAKA!
I-I HEAR YOU'RE GOING OUT...
WITH YUTA KIRISHIMA ...
YES.
I HOPE YOU DON'T MIND ME ASKING...
BUT WHY *HIM*?

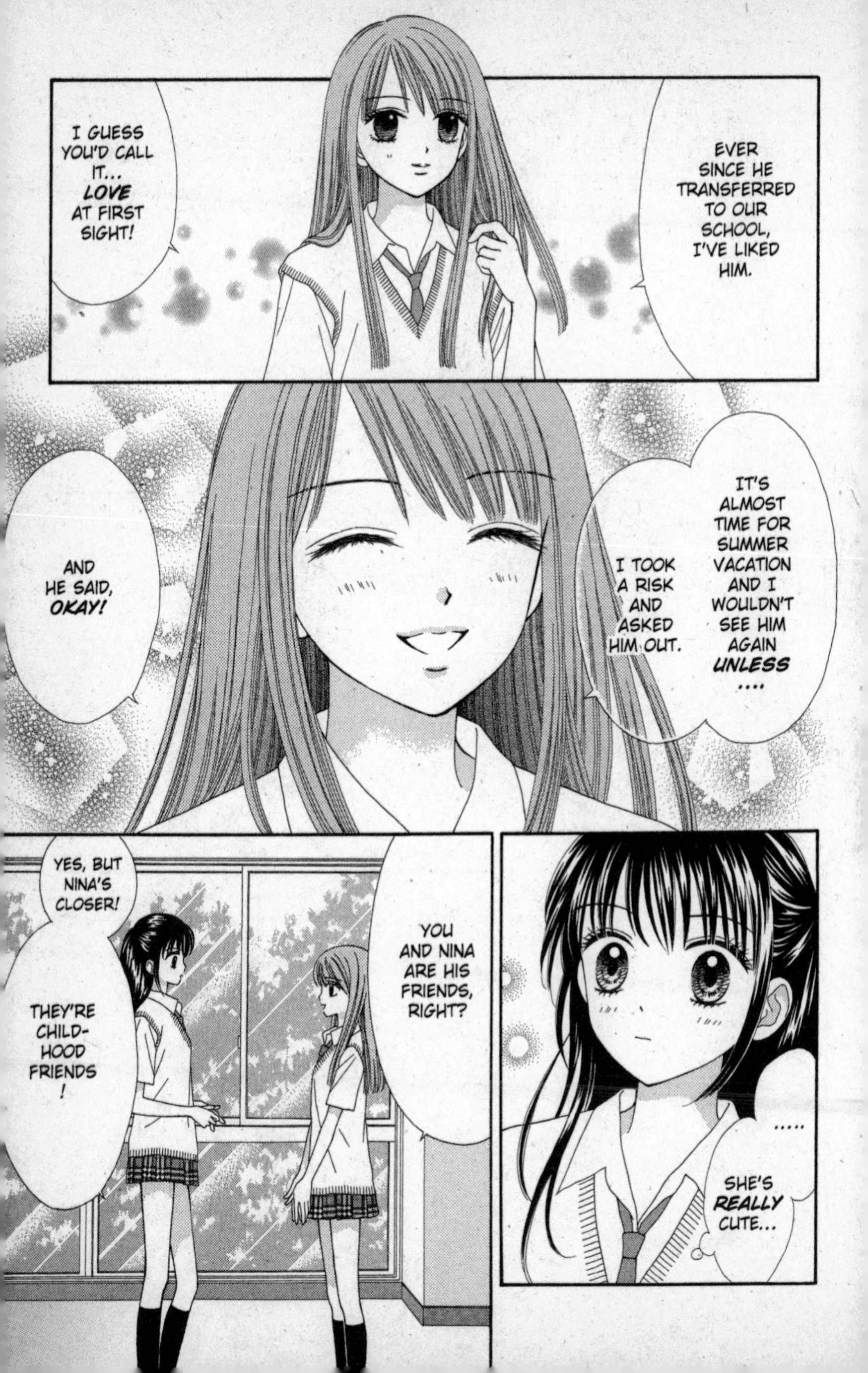
EVER SINCE HE TRANSFERRED TO OUR SCHOOL, I'VE LIKED HIM.
I GUESS YOU'D CALL IT... LOVE AT FIRST SIGHT!
IT'S ALMOST TIME FOR SUMMER VACATION AND I WOULDN'T SEE HIM AGAIN UNLESS ....
I TOOK A RISK AND ASKED HIM OUT.
AND HE SAID, OKAY!
.....
SHE'S REALLY CUTE...
YOU AND NINA ARE HIS FRIENDS, RIGHT?
YES, BUT NINA'S CLOSER!
THEY'RE CHILD-HOOD FRIENDS!

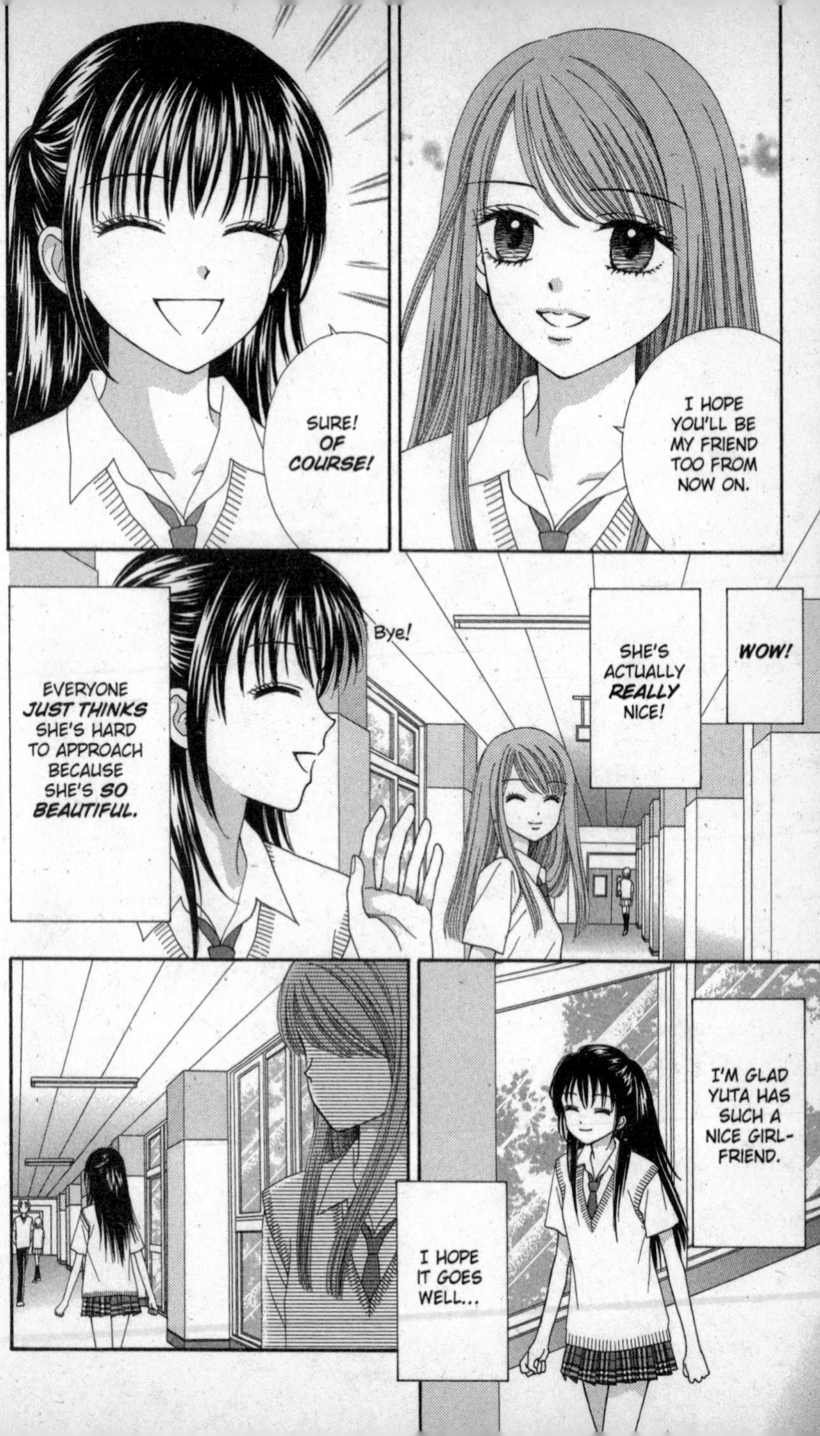
I HOPE YOU'LL BE MY FRIEND TOO FROM NOW ON.
SURE! OF COURSE!
WOW!
SHE'S ACTUALLY REALLY NICE!
Bye!
EVERYONE JUST THINKS SHE'S HARD TO APPROACH BECAUSE SHE'S SO BEAUTIFUL.
I'M GLAD YUTA HAS SUCH A NICE GIRL-FRIEND.
I HOPE IT GOES WELL...

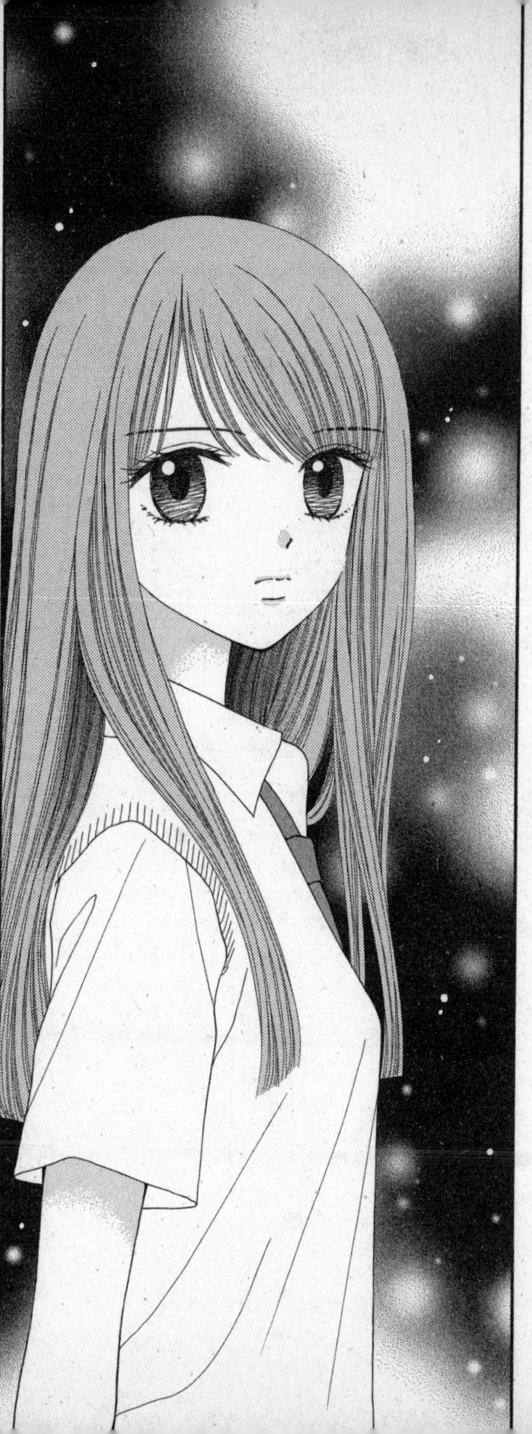

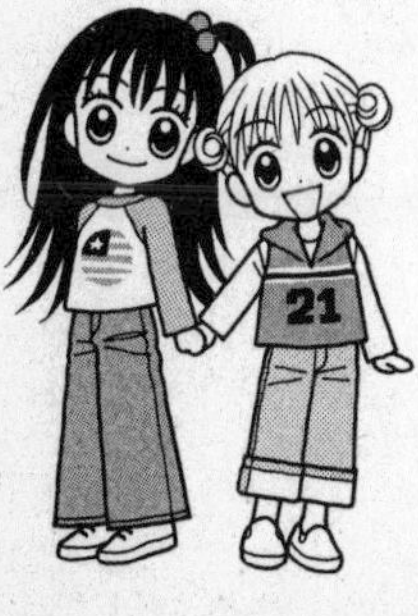
21

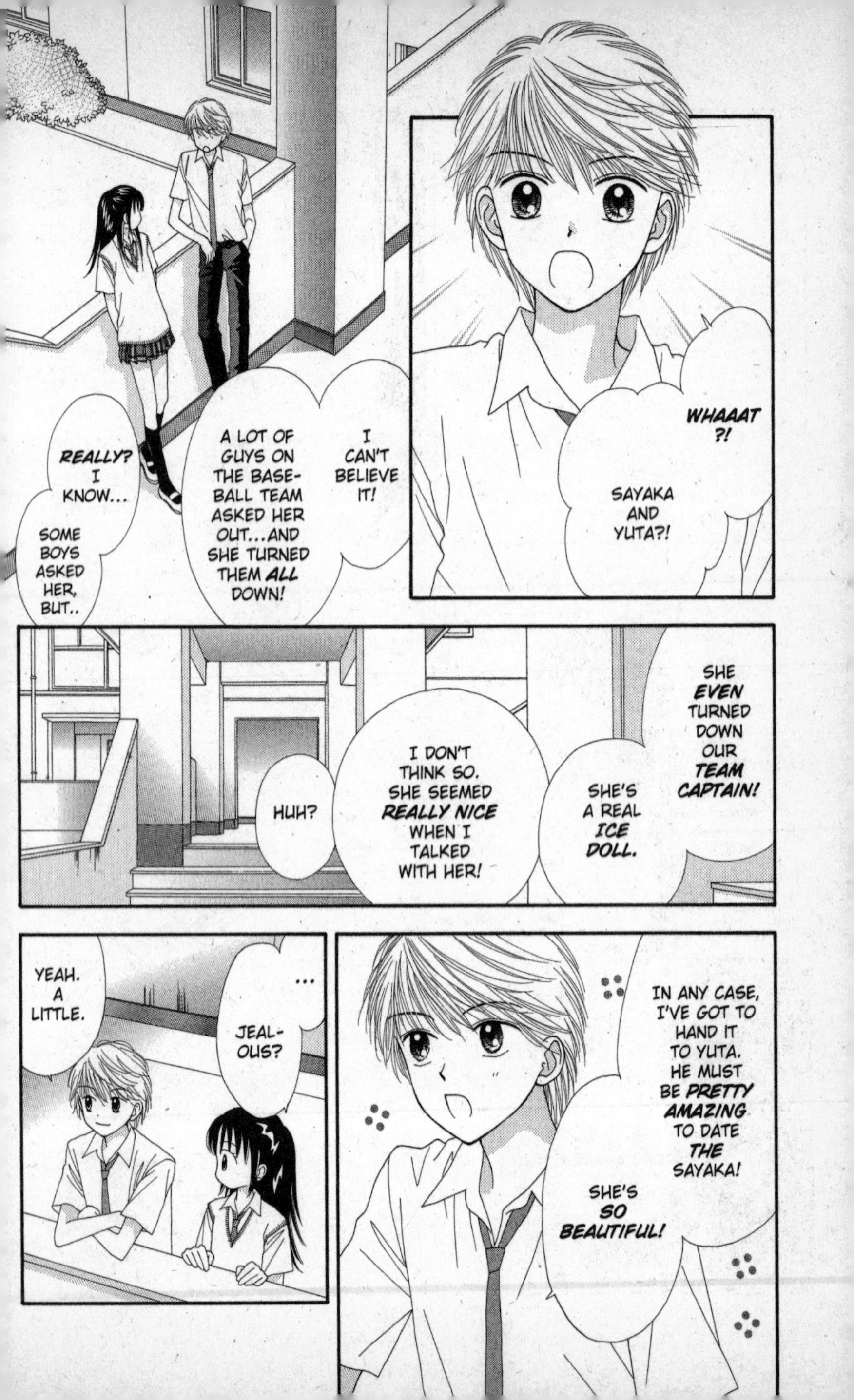
WHAAAT ?!
SAYAKA AND YUTA?!
I CAN'T BELIEVE IT!
A LOT OF GUYS ON THE BASE-BALL TEAM ASKED HER OUT...AND SHE TURNED THEM ALL DOWN!
REALLY? I KNOW...
SOME BOYS ASKED HER, BUT..
SHE EVEN TURNED DOWN OUR TEAM CAPTAIN!
SHE'S A REAL ICE DOLL.
I DON'T THINK SO. SHE SEEMED REALLY NICE WHEN I TALKED WITH HER!
HUH?
IN ANY CASE, I'VE GOT TO HAND IT TO YUTA. HE MUST BE PRETTY AMAZING TO DATE THE SAYAKA!
SHE'S SO BEAUTIFUL!
...
JEAL-OUS?
YEAH. A LITTLE.

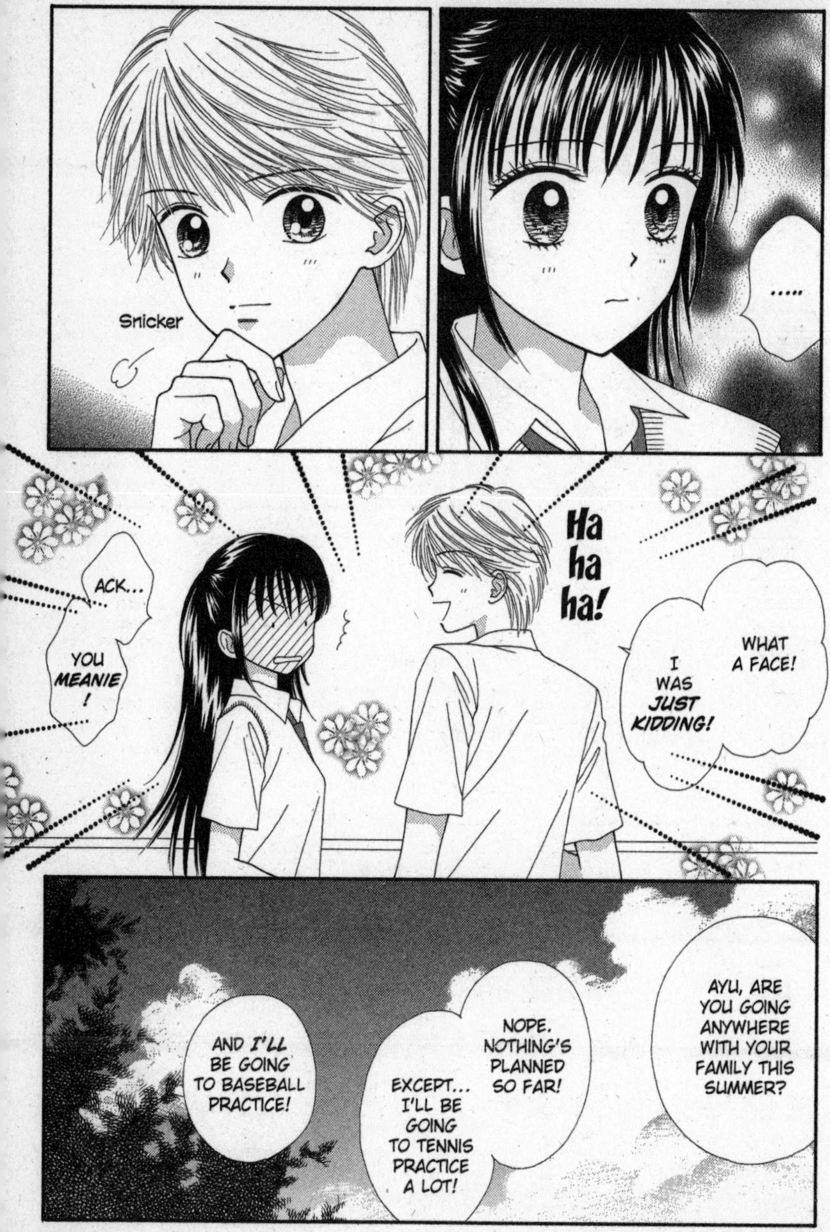
.....
Snicker
Ha ha ha!
WHAT A FACE!
I WAS JUST KIDDING!
ACK...
YOU MEANIE!
AYU, ARE YOU GOING ANYWHERE WITH YOUR FAMILY THIS SUMMER?
NOPE. NOTHING'S PLANNED SO FAR!
EXCEPT... I'LL BE GOING TO TENNIS PRACTICE A LOT!
AND I'LL BE GOING TO BASEBALL PRACTICE!

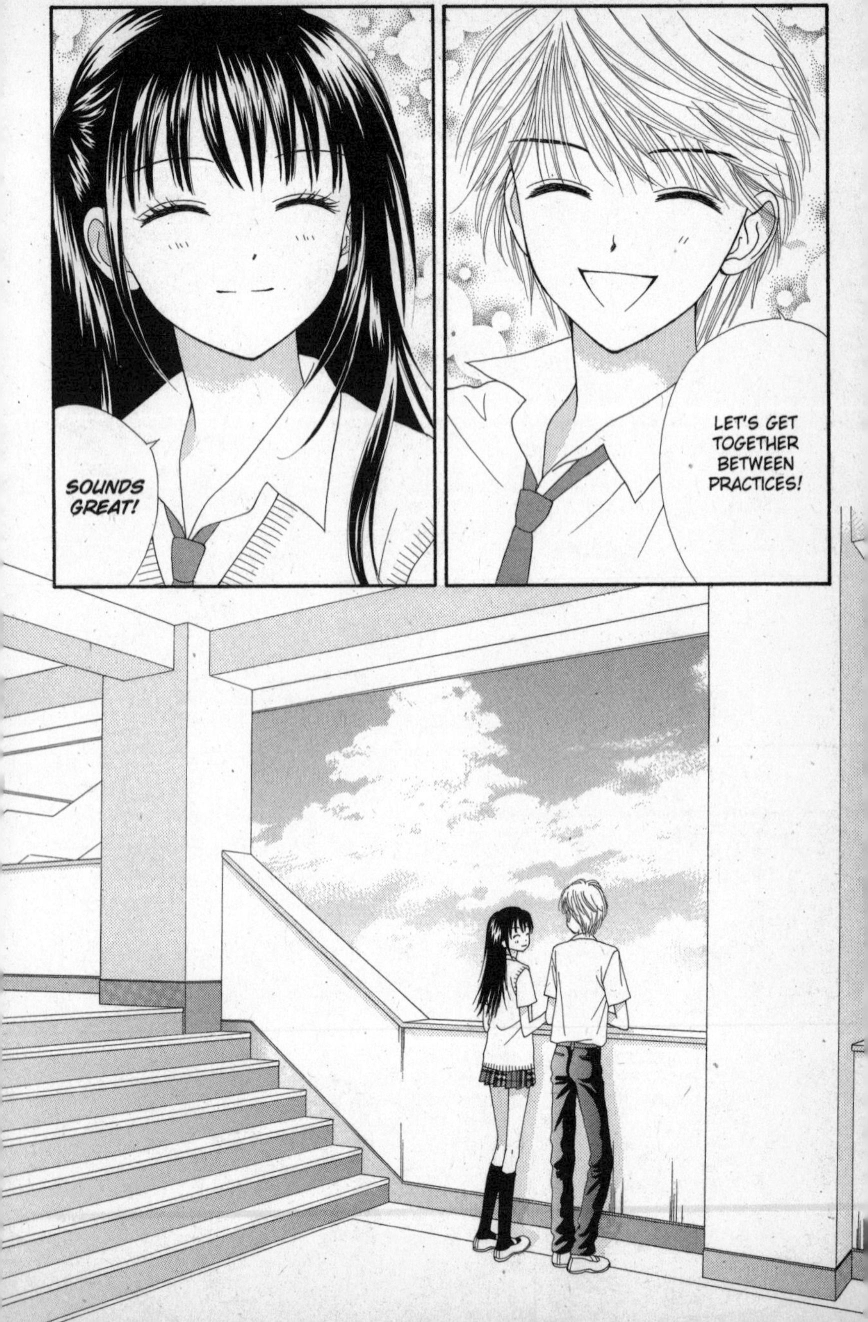
LET'S GET TOGETHER BETWEEN PRACTICES!
SOUNDS GREAT!

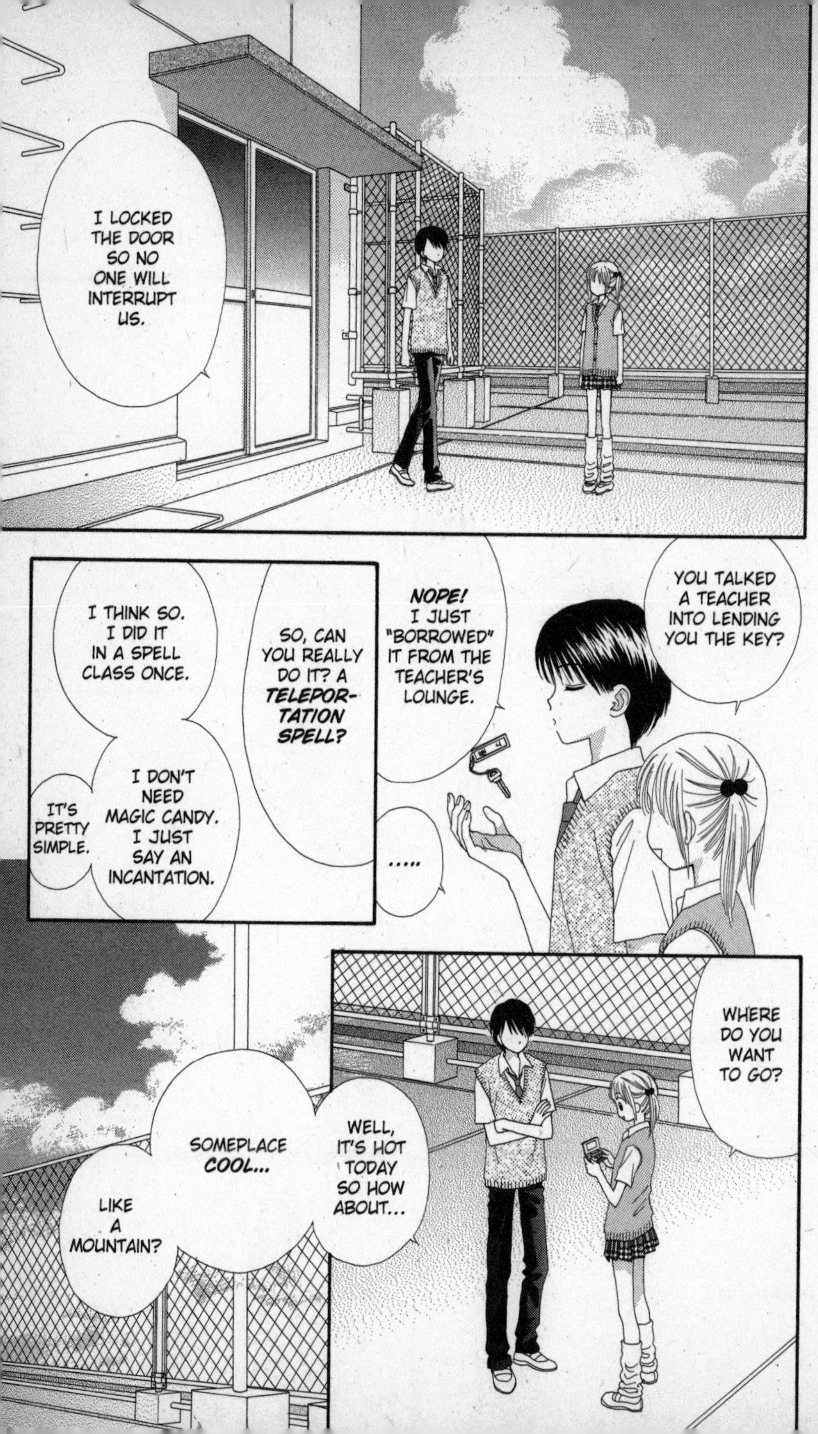
I LOCKED THE DOOR SO NO ONE WILL INTERRUPT US.
YOU TALKED A TEACHER INTO LENDING YOU THE KEY?
NOPE! I JUST "BORROWED" IT FROM THE TEACHER'S LOUNGE.
.....
SO, CAN YOU REALLY DO IT? A TELEPORTATION SPELL?
I THINK SO. I DID IT IN A SPELL CLASS ONCE.
I DON'T NEED MAGIC CANDY. I JUST SAY AN INCANTATION.
IT'S PRETTY SIMPLE.
WHERE DO YOU WANT TO GO?
WELL, IT'S HOT TODAY SO HOW ABOUT...
SOMEPLACE COOL...
LIKE A MOUNTAIN?

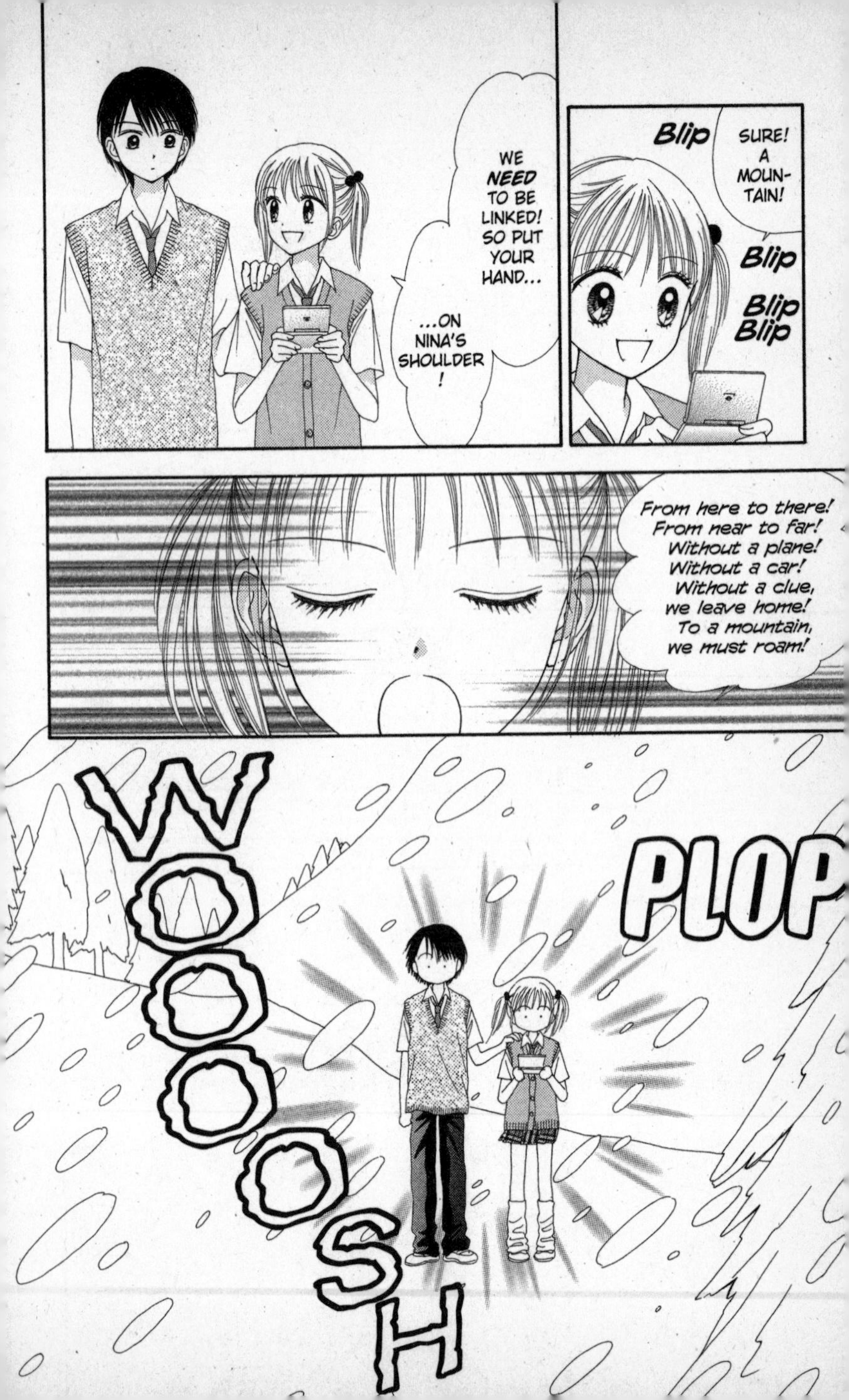
Blip
SURE! A MOUNTAIN!
Blip
Blip
Blip
WE NEED TO BE LINKED! SO PUT YOUR HAND...
...ON NINA'S SHOULDER!
From here to there! From near to far! Without a plane! Without a car! Without a clue, we leave home! To a mountain, we must roam!
PLOP
WOOOOSH

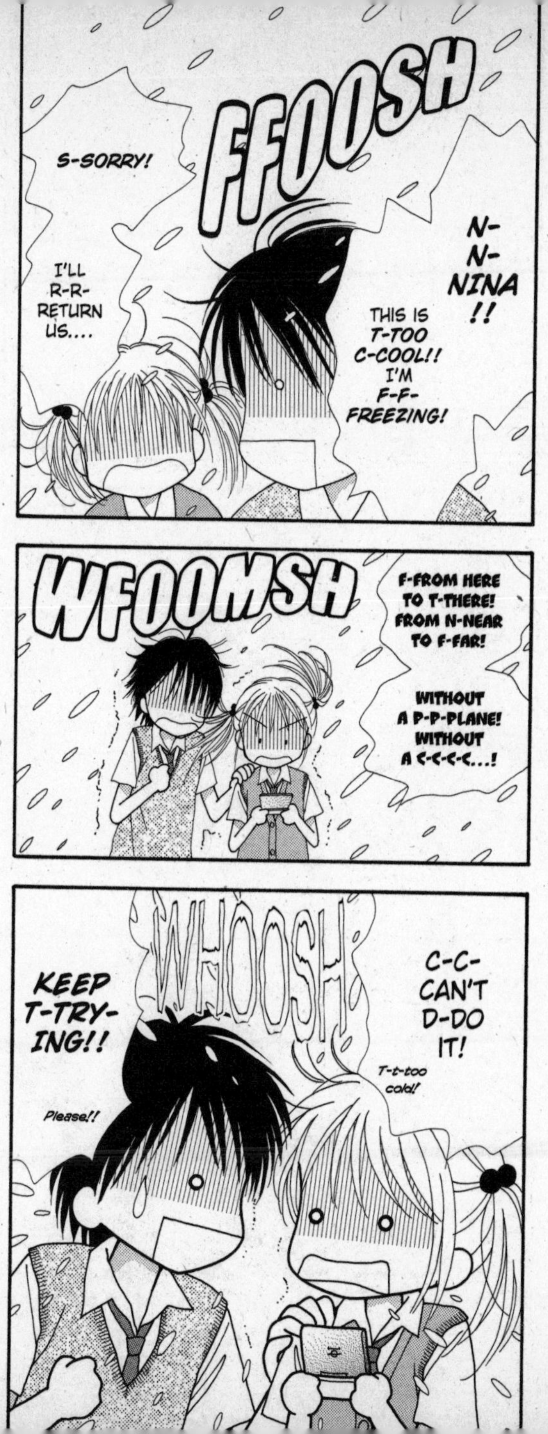
FFOOSH
N-N-NINA!!
THIS IS T-TOO C-COOL!! I'M F-F-FREEZING!
S-SORRY!
I'LL R-R-RETURN US....
F-FROM HERE TO T-THERE! FROM N-NEAR TO F-FAR!
WITHOUT A P-P-PLANE! WITHOUT A C-C-C-C...!
WFOOMSH
C-C-CAN'T D-DO IT!
T-t-too cold!
WHOOSH
KEEP T-TRY-ING!!
Please!!

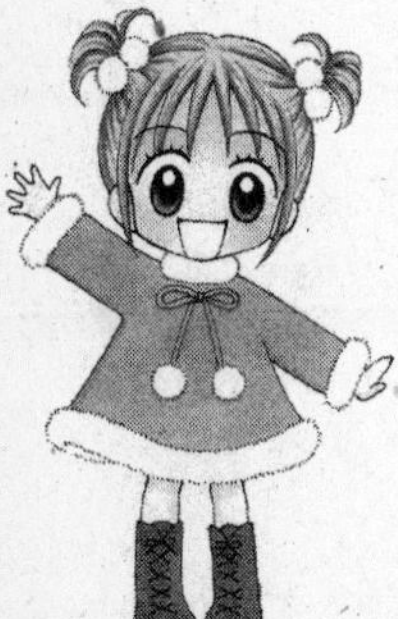

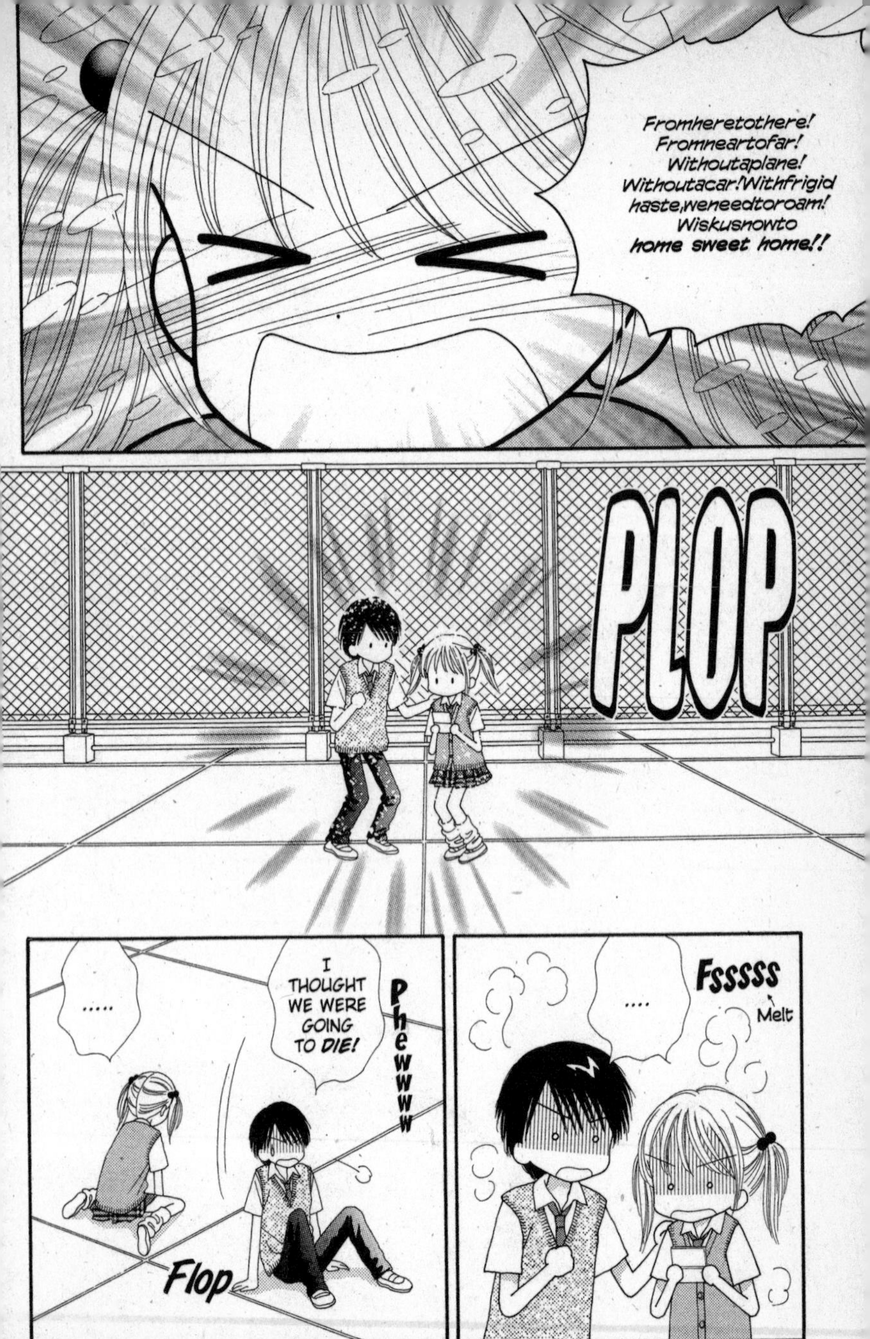
Fromheretothere! Fromneartofar! Withoutaplane! Withoutacar!Withfrigid haste,weneedtoroam! Wiskusnowto home sweet home!!
PLOP
....
Fsssss
Melt
.....
I THOUGHT WE WERE GOING TO DIE!
Phewwww
Flop

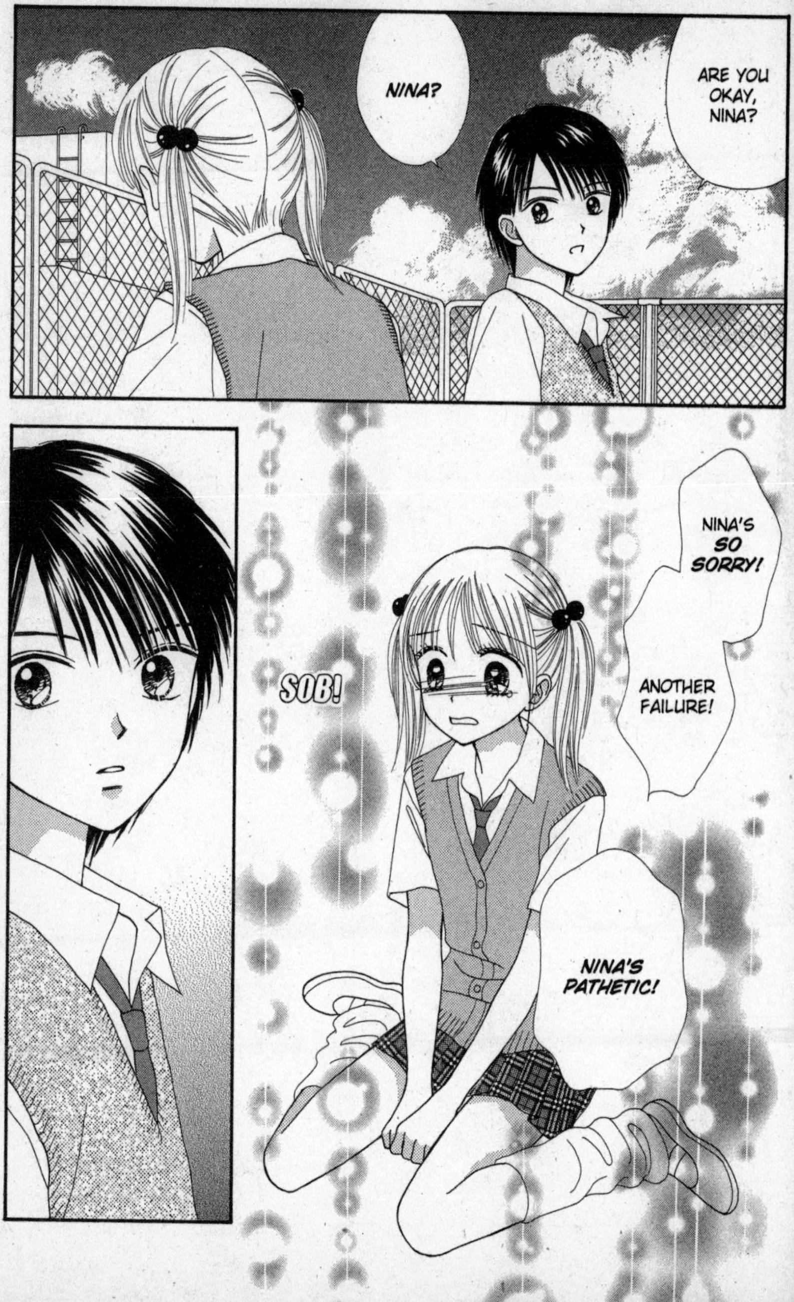
ARE YOU OKAY, NINA?
NINA?
NINA'S SO SORRY!
ANOTHER FAILURE!
SOB!
NINA'S PATHETIC!

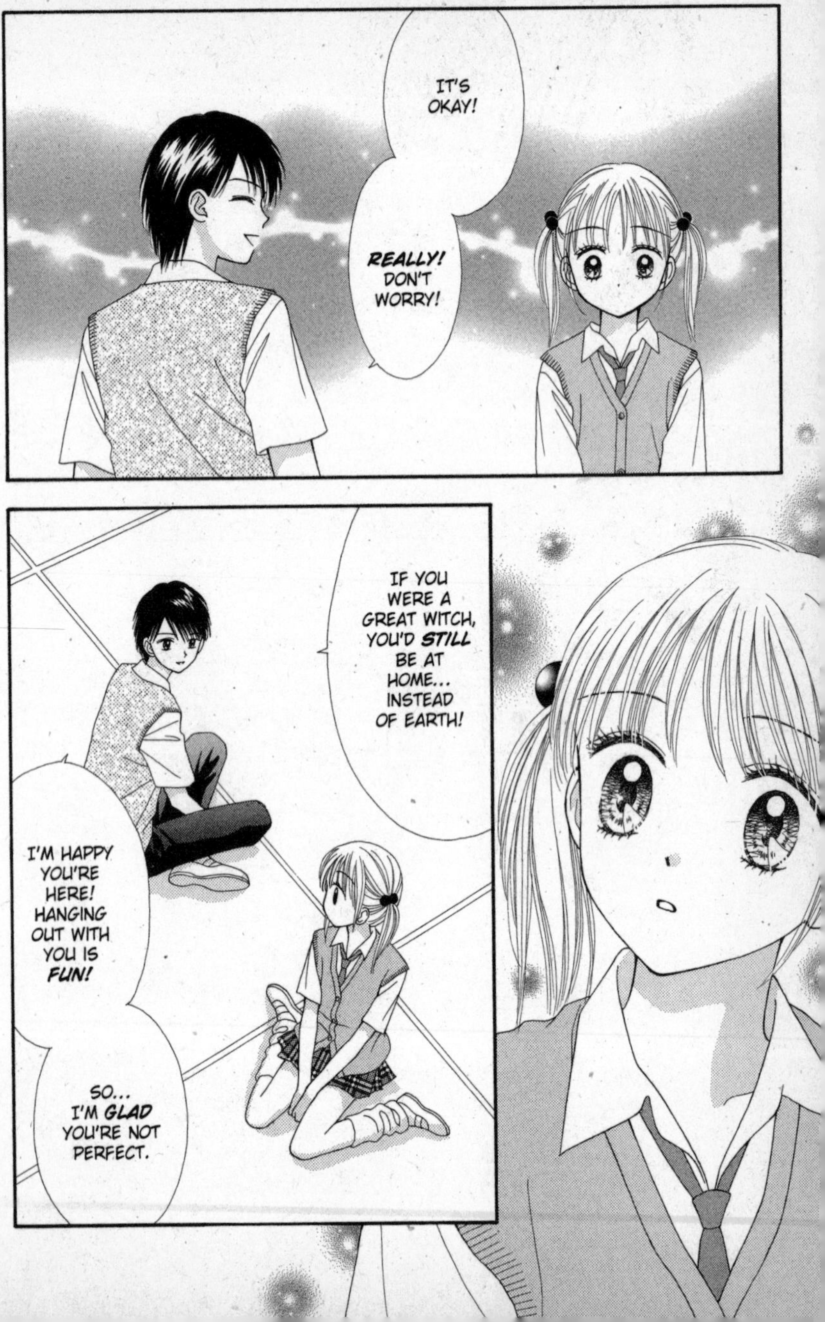
IT'S OKAY!
REALLY! DON'T WORRY!
IF YOU WERE A GREAT WITCH, YOU'D STILL BE AT HOME... INSTEAD OF EARTH!
I'M HAPPY YOU'RE HERE! HANGING OUT WITH YOU IS FUN!
SO... I'M GLAD YOU'RE NOT PERFECT.

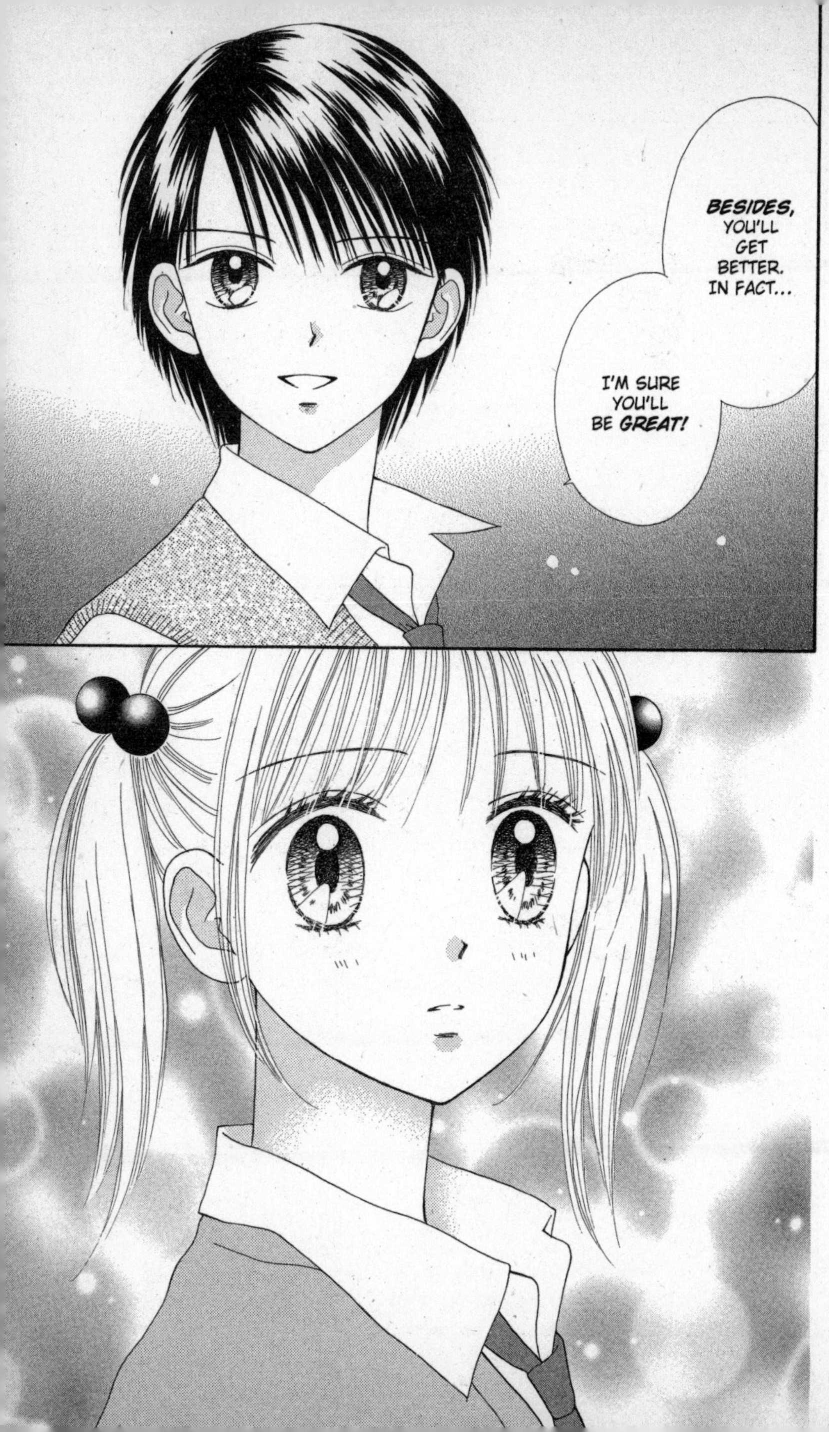
BESIDES, YOU'LL GET BETTER. IN FACT...
I'M SURE YOU'LL BE GREAT!

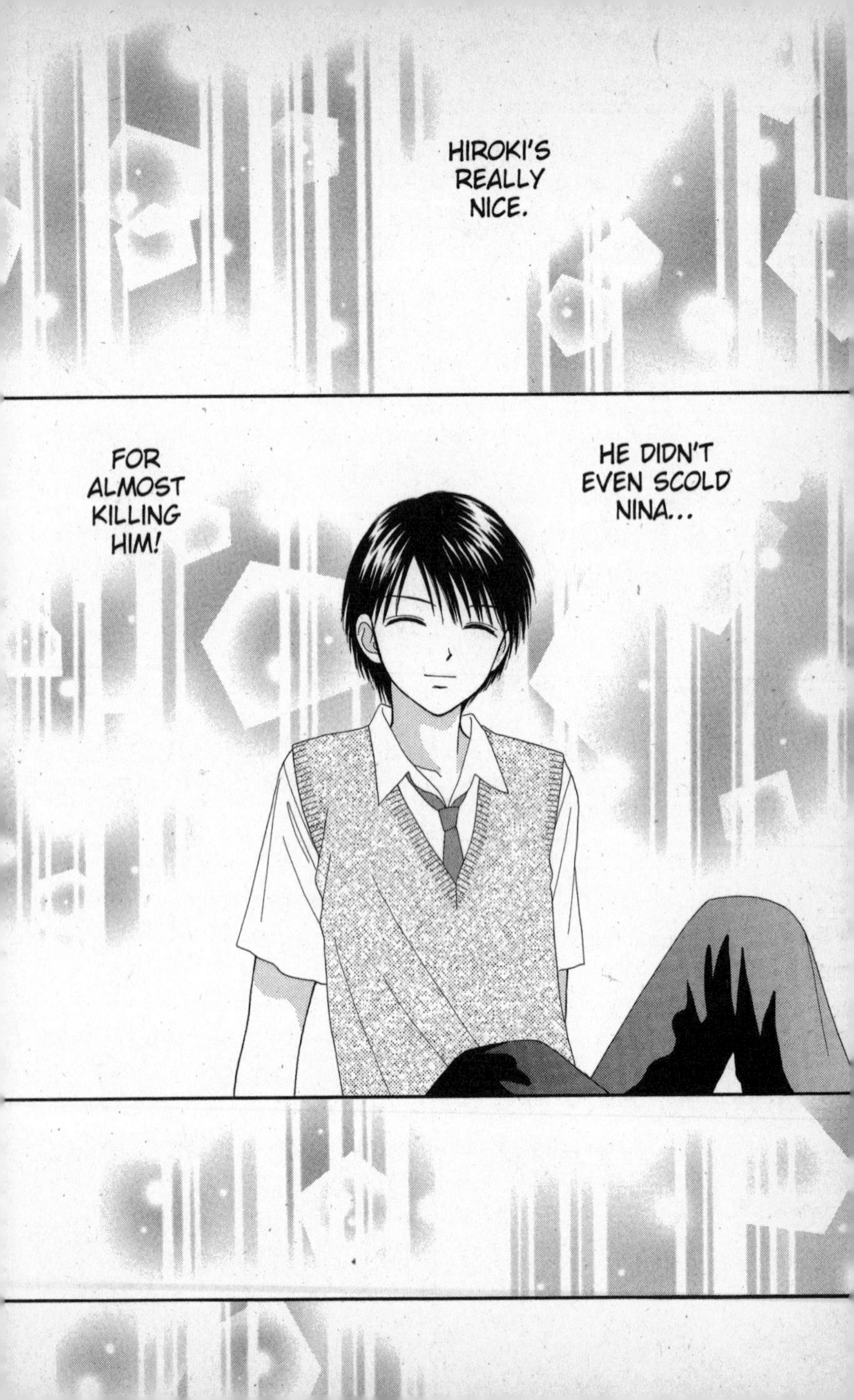
HIROKI'S REALLY NICE.
HE DIDN'T EVEN SCOLD NINA...
FOR ALMOST KILLING HIM!

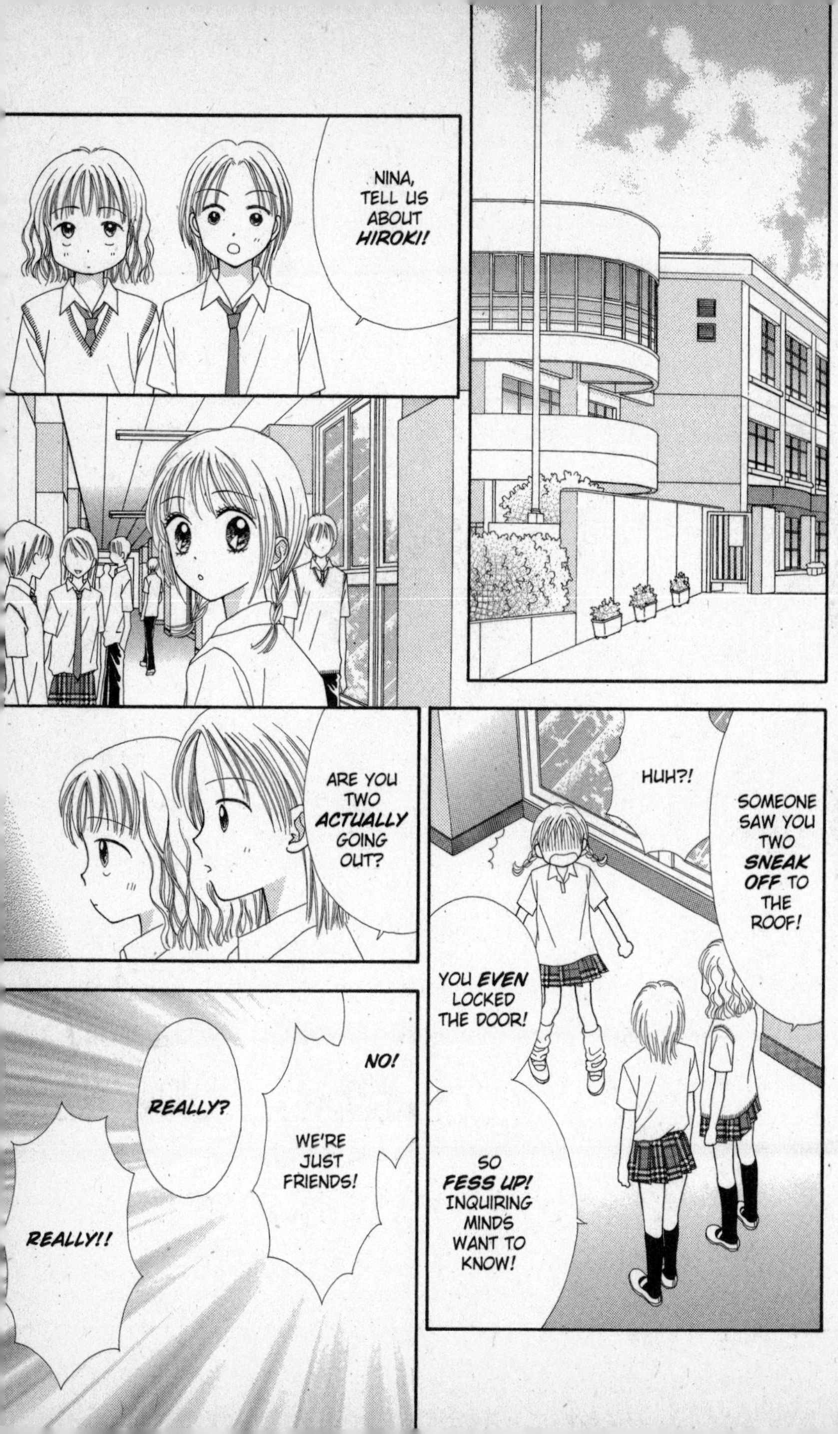
NINA, TELL US ABOUT *HIROKI!*
HUH?!
SOMEONE SAW YOU TWO *SNEAK OFF* TO THE ROOF!
YOU *EVEN* LOCKED THE DOOR!
SO *FESS UP!* INQUIRING MINDS WANT TO KNOW!
ARE YOU TWO *ACTUALLY* GOING OUT?
NO!
WE'RE JUST FRIENDS!
REALLY?
REALLY!!

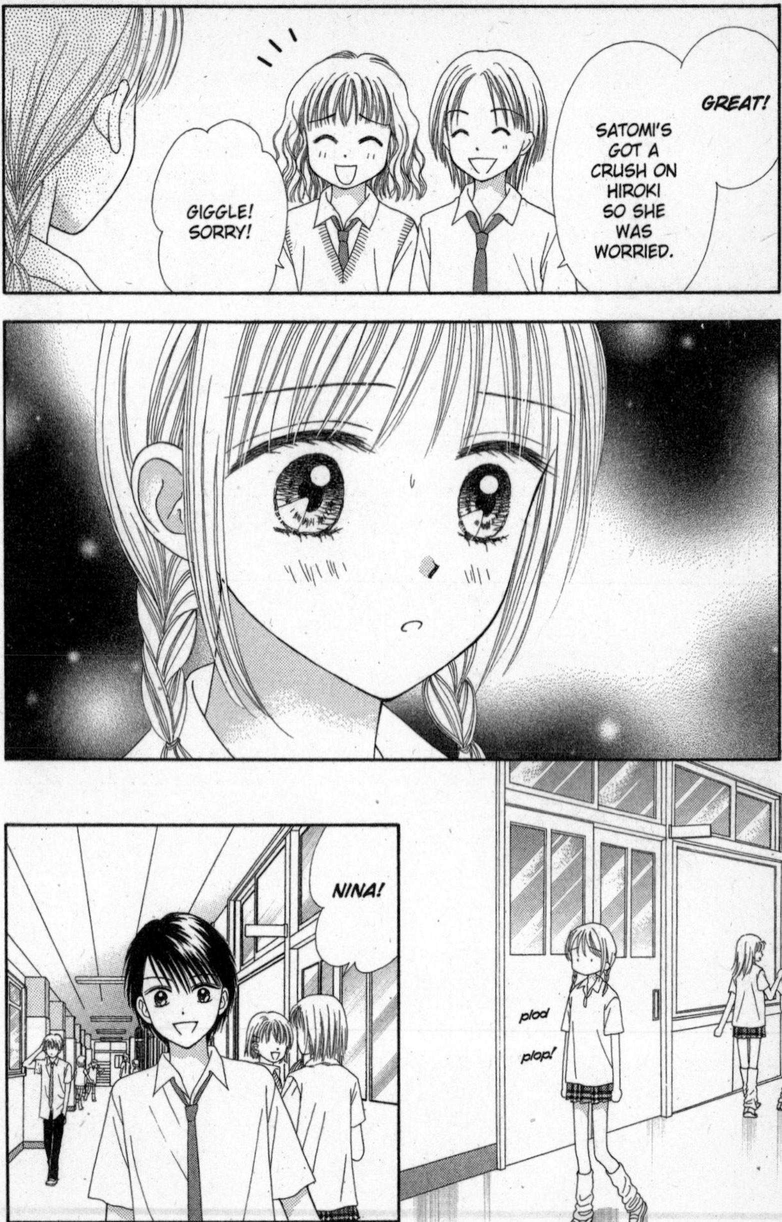
GREAT! SATOMI'S GOT A CRUSH ON HIROKI SO SHE WAS WORRIED.
GIGGLE! SORRY!
plod
plop!
NINA!

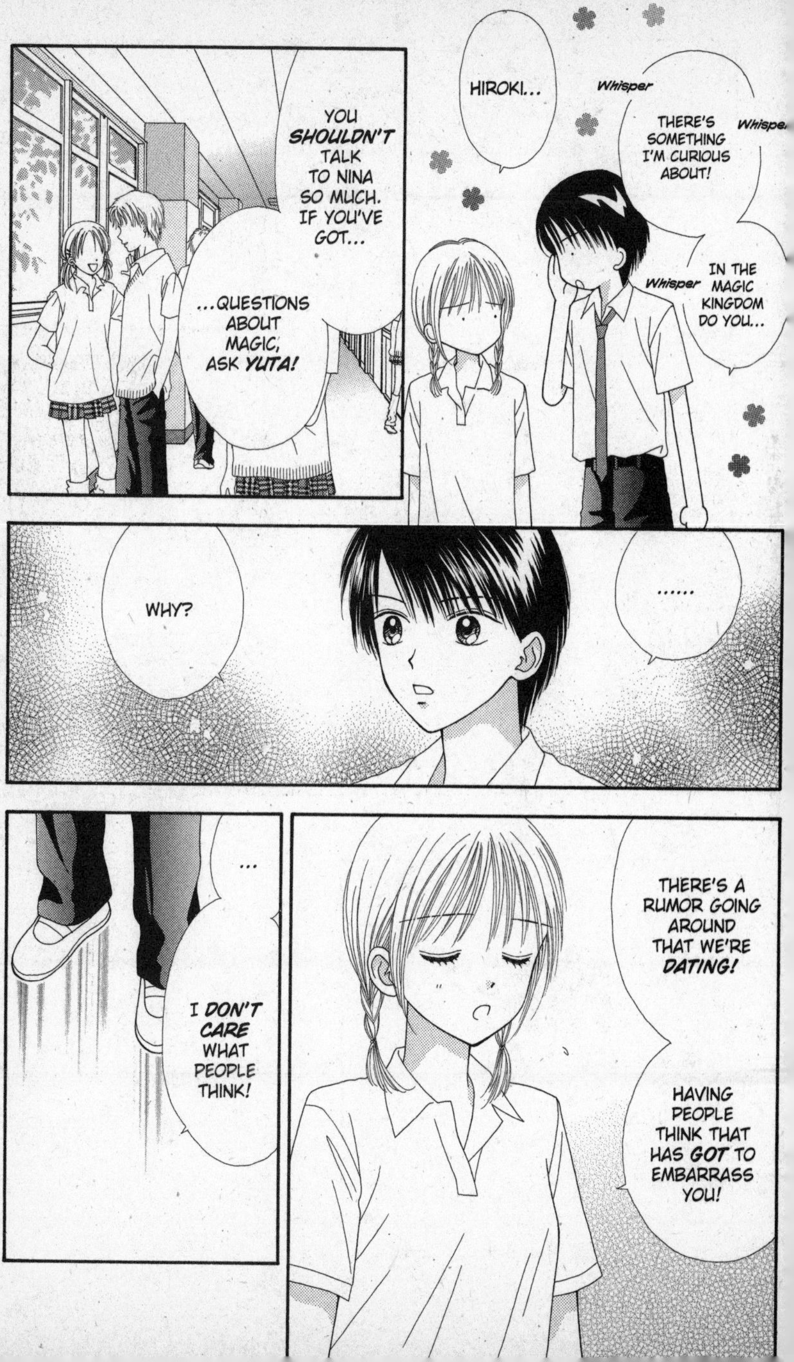
HIROKI...
Whisper
THERE'S SOMETHING I'M CURIOUS ABOUT!
Whisper
Whisper
IN THE MAGIC KINGDOM DO YOU...
YOU SHOULDN'T TALK TO NINA SO MUCH. IF YOU'VE GOT...
...QUESTIONS ABOUT MAGIC, ASK YUTA!
......
WHY?
THERE'S A RUMOR GOING AROUND THAT WE'RE DATING!
HAVING PEOPLE THINK THAT HAS GOT TO EMBARRASS YOU!
...
I DON'T CARE WHAT PEOPLE THINK!

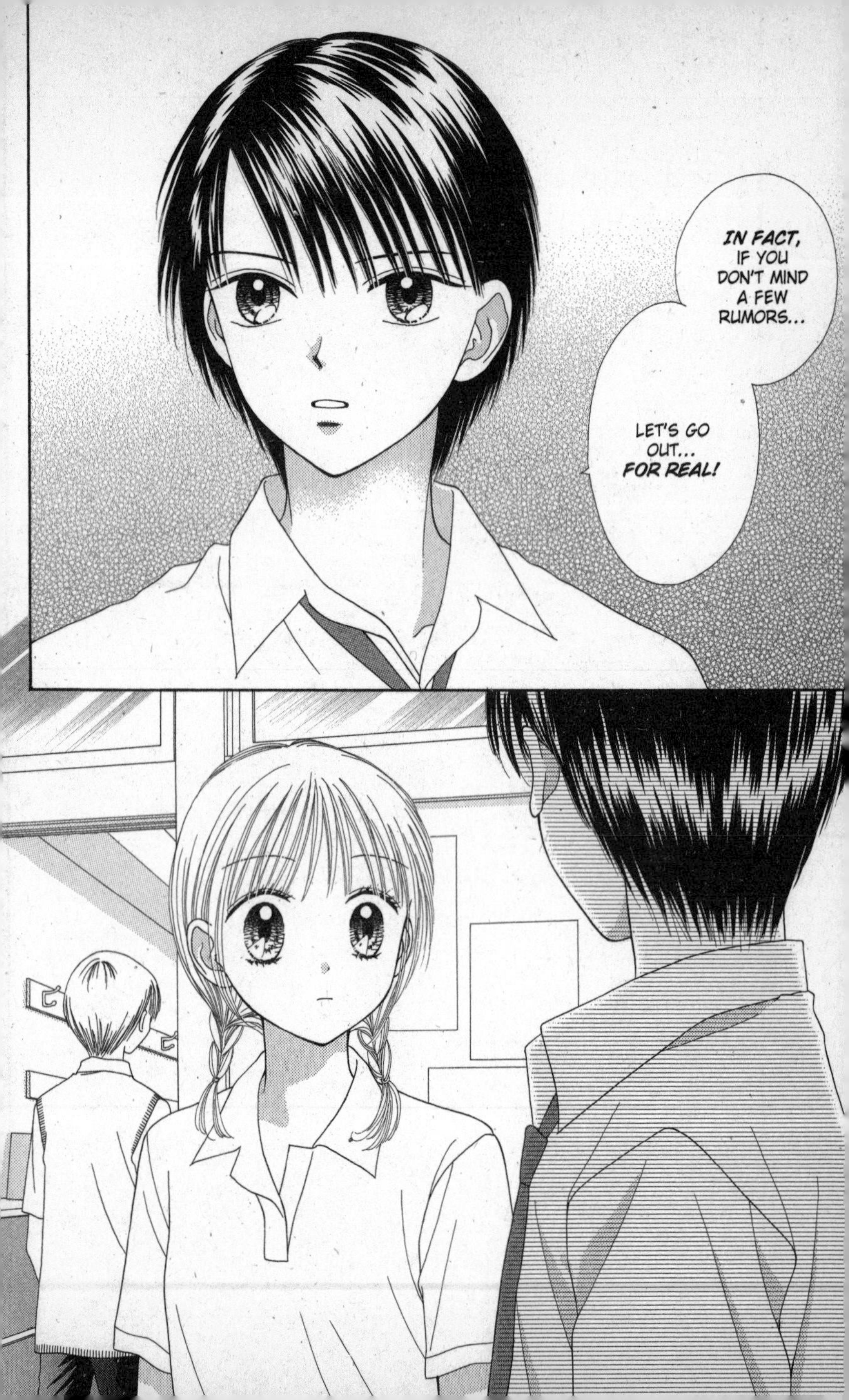
IN FACT, IF YOU DON'T MIND A FEW RUMORS...
LET'S GO OUT... FOR REAL!

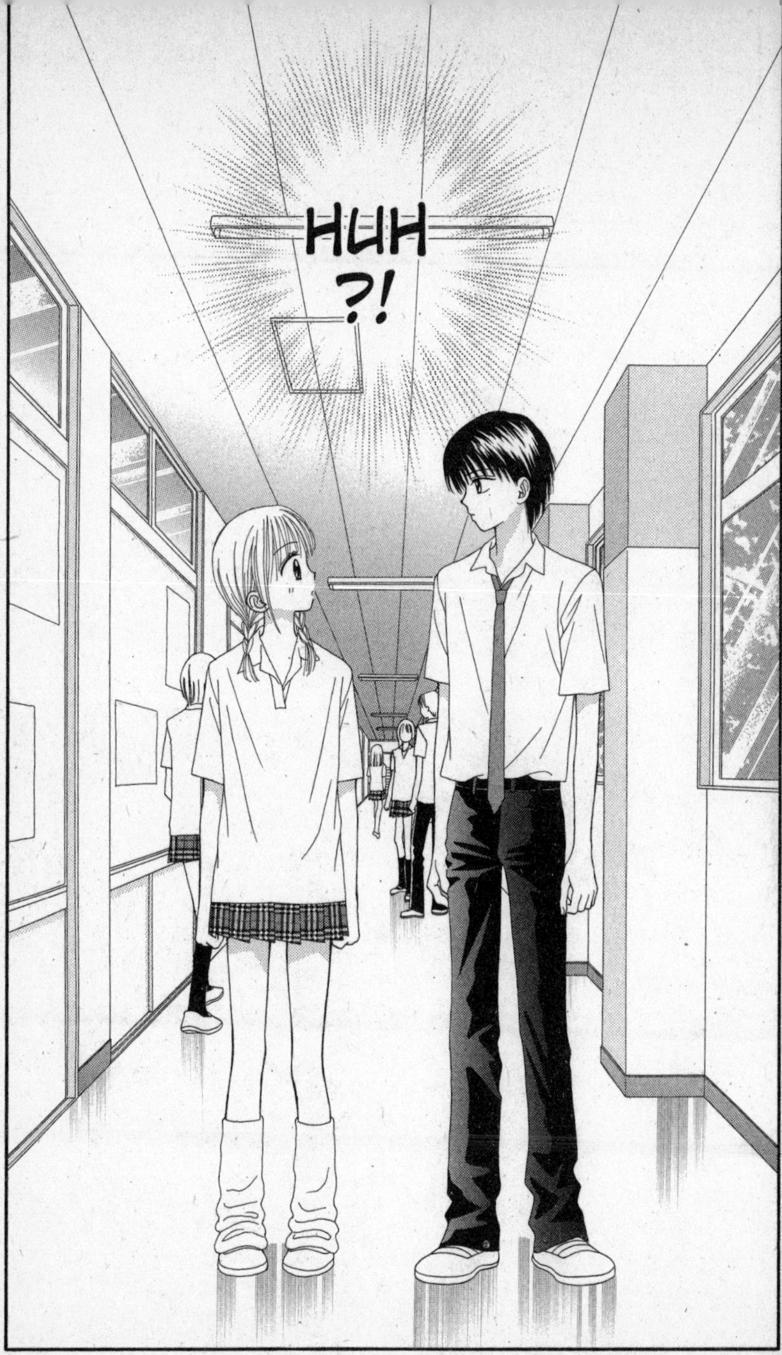
HUH ?!

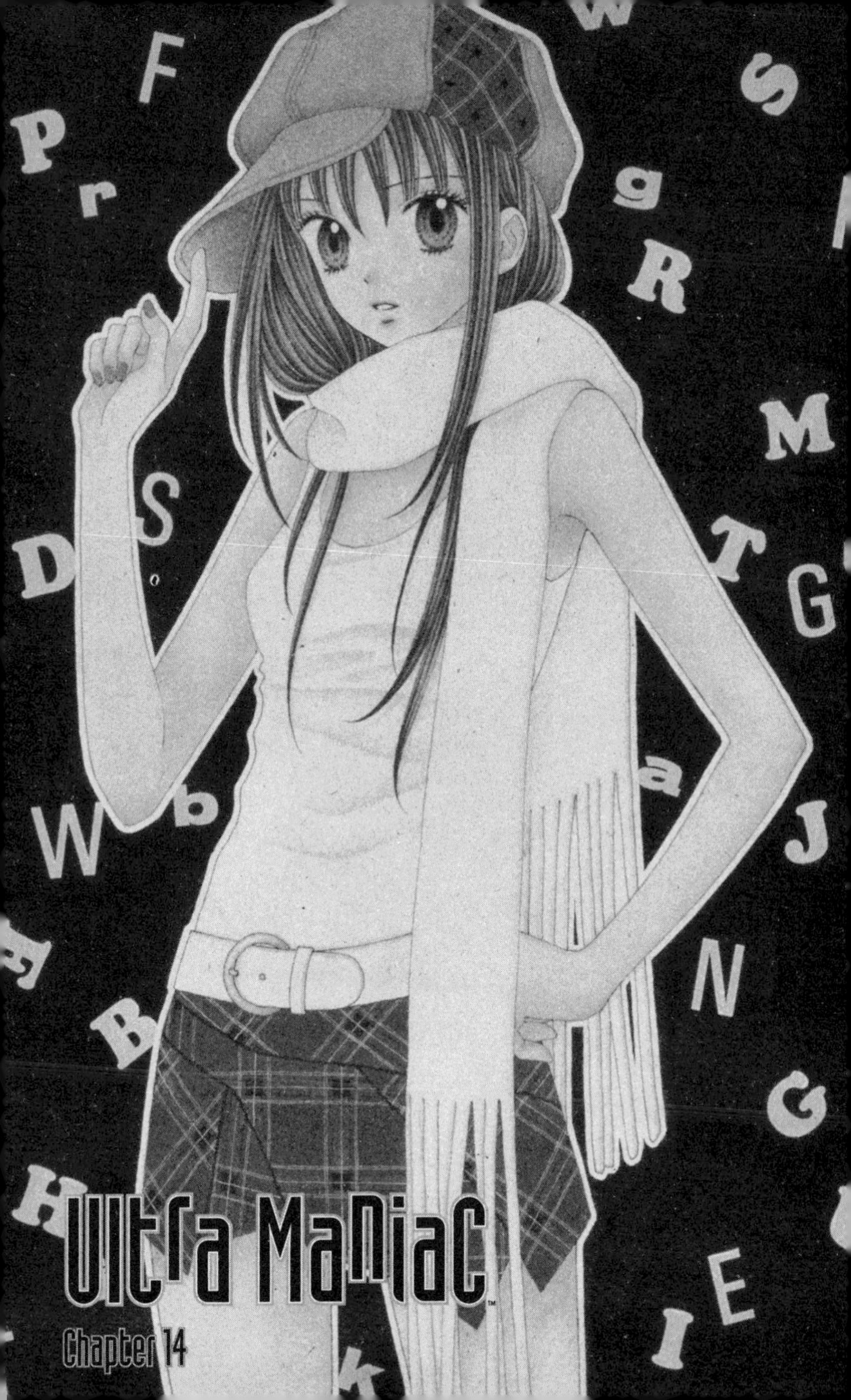
Ultra Maniac™
Chapter 14

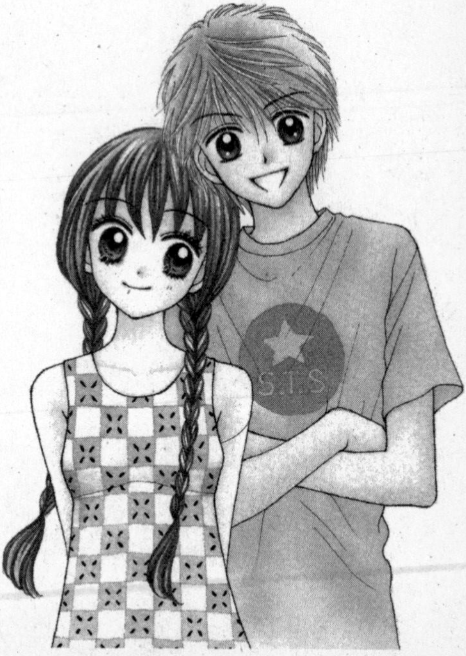
S.T.S.

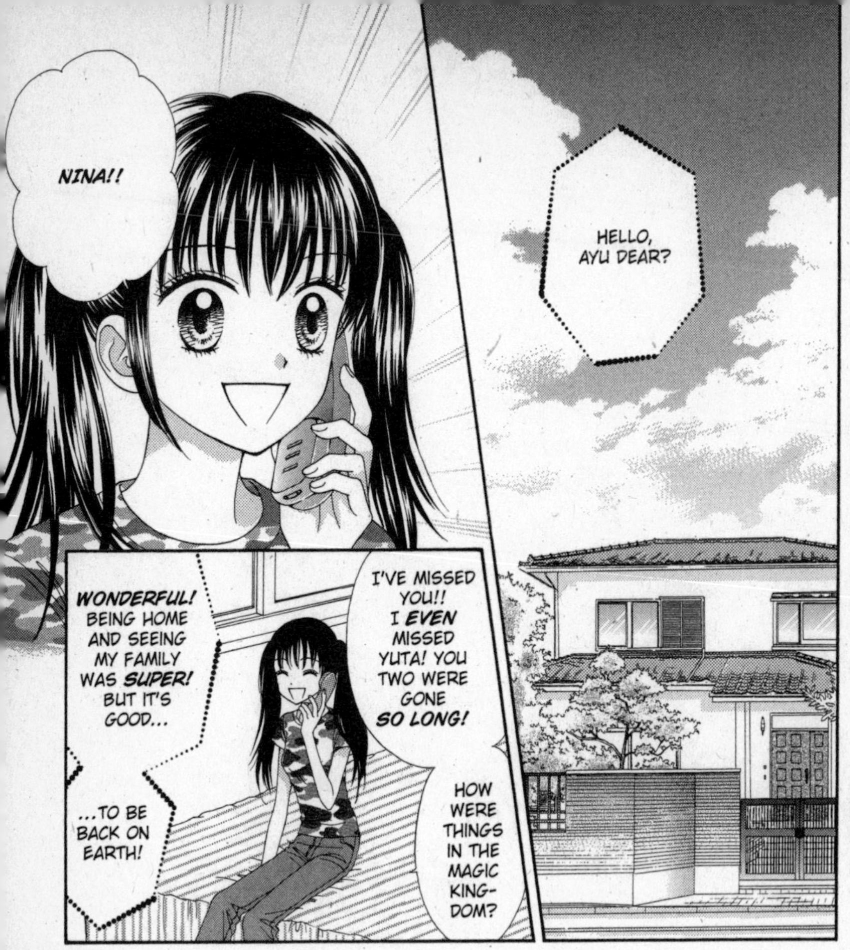
HELLO, AYU DEAR?
NINA!!
I'VE MISSED YOU!! I **EVEN** MISSED YUTA! YOU TWO WERE GONE **SO LONG!**
HOW WERE THINGS IN THE MAGIC KING-DOM?
WONDERFUL! BEING HOME AND SEEING MY FAMILY WAS **SUPER!** BUT IT'S GOOD...
...TO BE BACK ON EARTH!

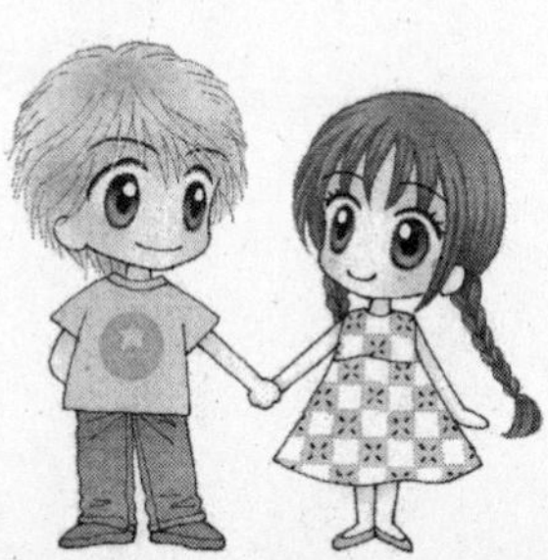

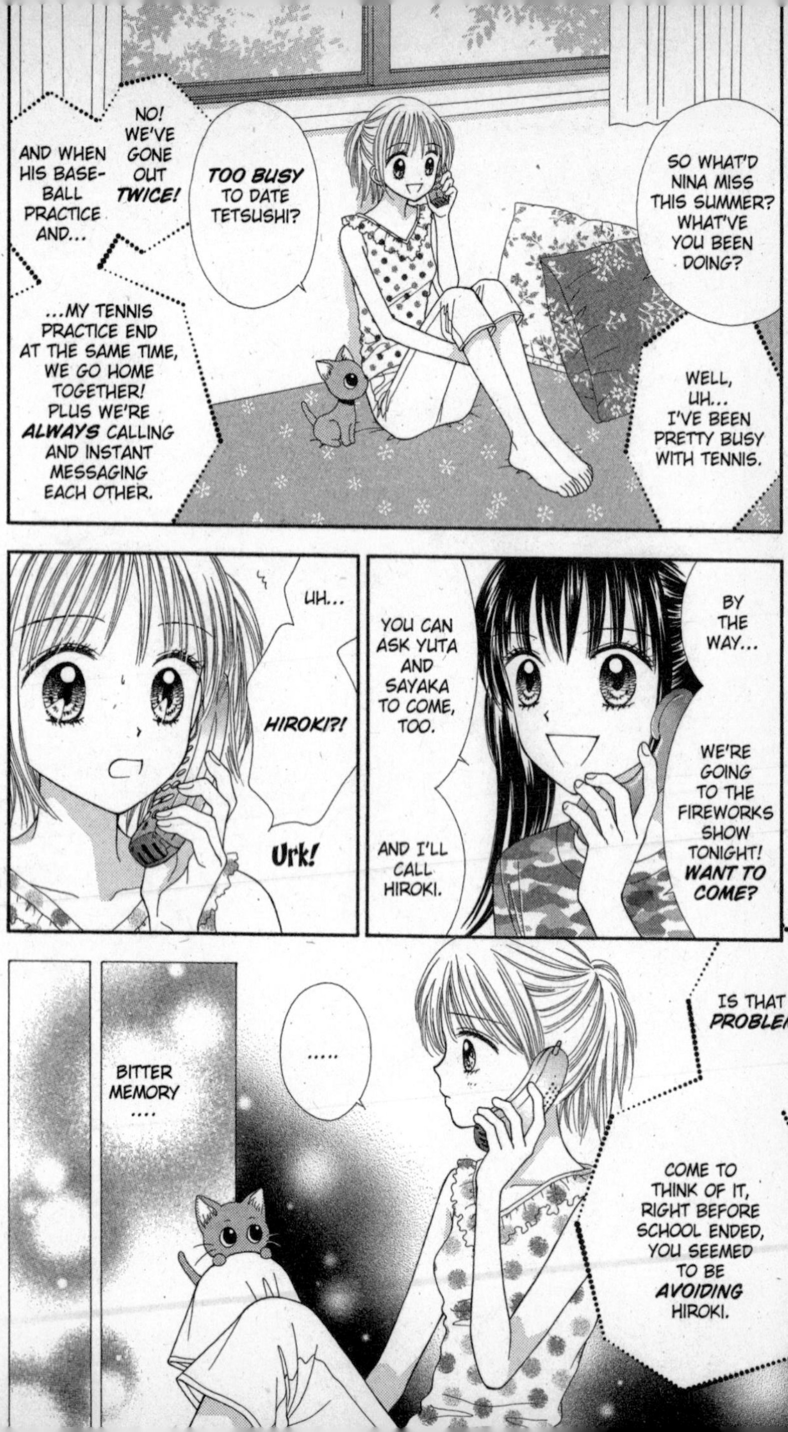
SO WHAT'D NINA MISS THIS SUMMER? WHAT'VE YOU BEEN DOING?
WELL, UH... I'VE BEEN PRETTY BUSY WITH TENNIS.
TOO BUSY TO DATE TETSUSHI?
NO! WE'VE GONE OUT TWICE!
AND WHEN HIS BASE-BALL PRACTICE AND...
...MY TENNIS PRACTICE END AT THE SAME TIME, WE GO HOME TOGETHER! PLUS WE'RE ALWAYS CALLING AND INSTANT MESSAGING EACH OTHER.
BY THE WAY...
WE'RE GOING TO THE FIREWORKS SHOW TONIGHT! WANT TO COME?
YOU CAN ASK YUTA AND SAYAKA TO COME, TOO.
AND I'LL CALL HIROKI.
UH...
HIROKI?!
Urk!
IS THAT A PROBLEM?
COME TO THINK OF IT, RIGHT BEFORE SCHOOL ENDED, YOU SEEMED TO BE AVOIDING HIROKI.
.....
BITTER MEMORY ....

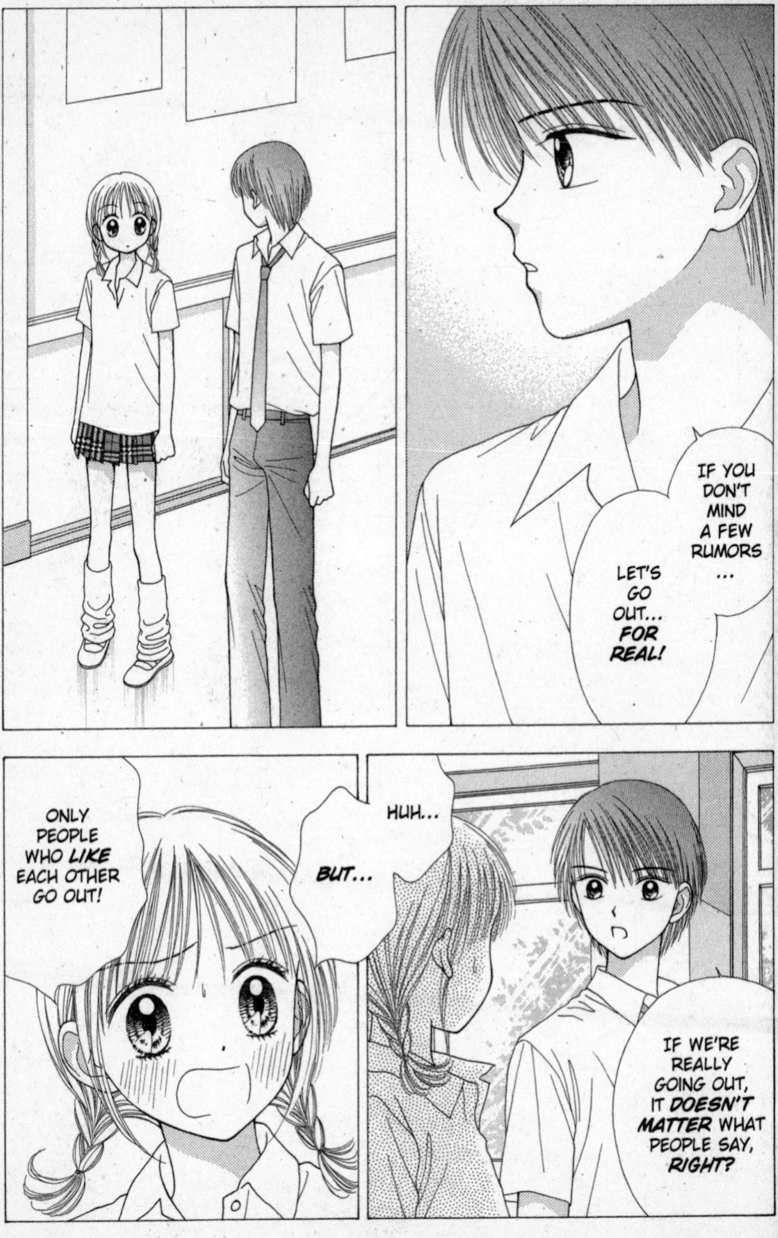
IF YOU DON'T MIND A FEW RUMORS...
LET'S GO OUT... **FOR REAL!**
HUH...
BUT...
IF WE'RE REALLY GOING OUT, IT **DOESN'T MATTER** WHAT PEOPLE SAY, **RIGHT?**
ONLY PEOPLE WHO **LIKE** EACH OTHER GO OUT!

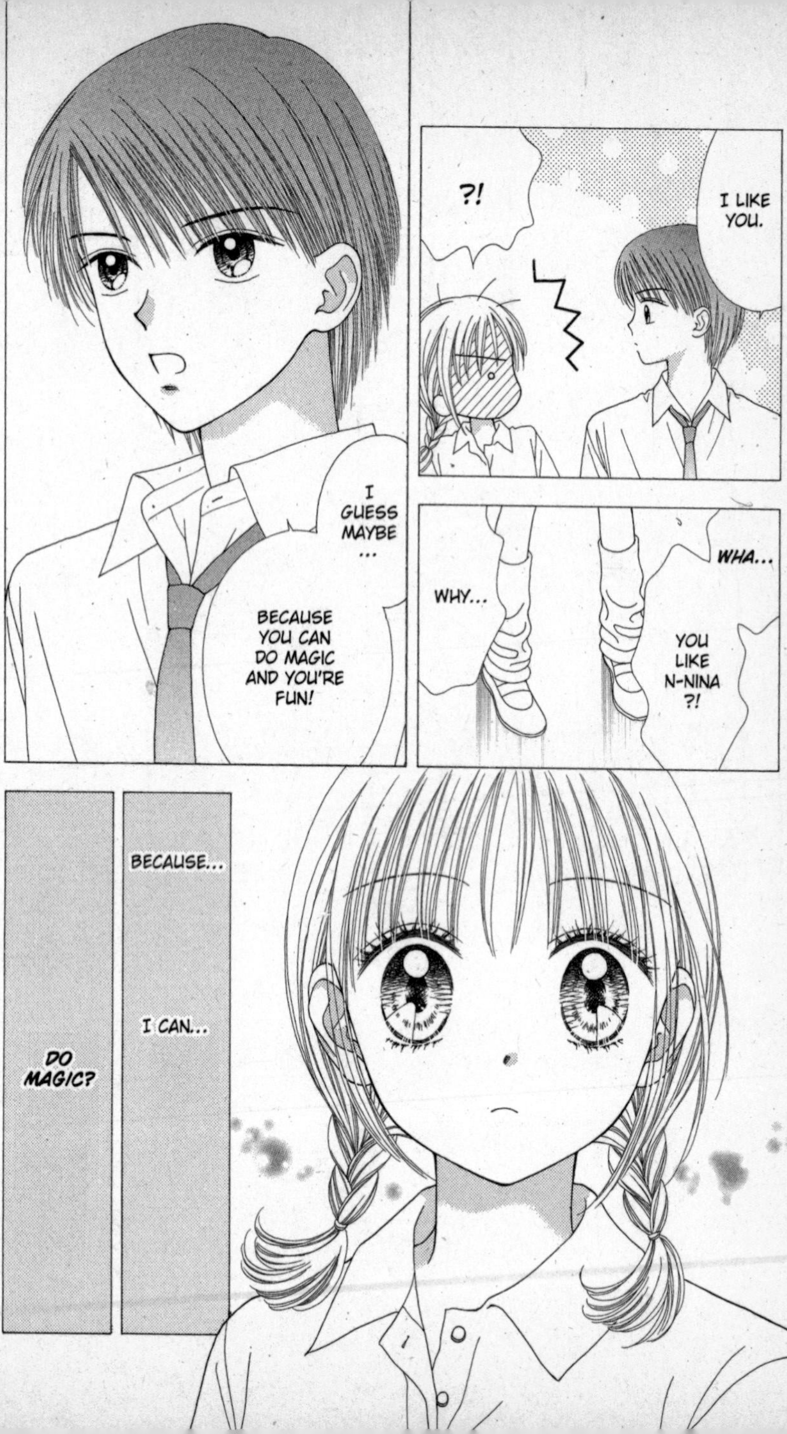
I LIKE YOU.
?!
WHA...
YOU LIKE N-NINA ?!
WHY...
I GUESS MAYBE ...
BECAUSE YOU CAN DO MAGIC AND YOU'RE FUN!
BECAUSE...
I CAN...
DO MAGIC?

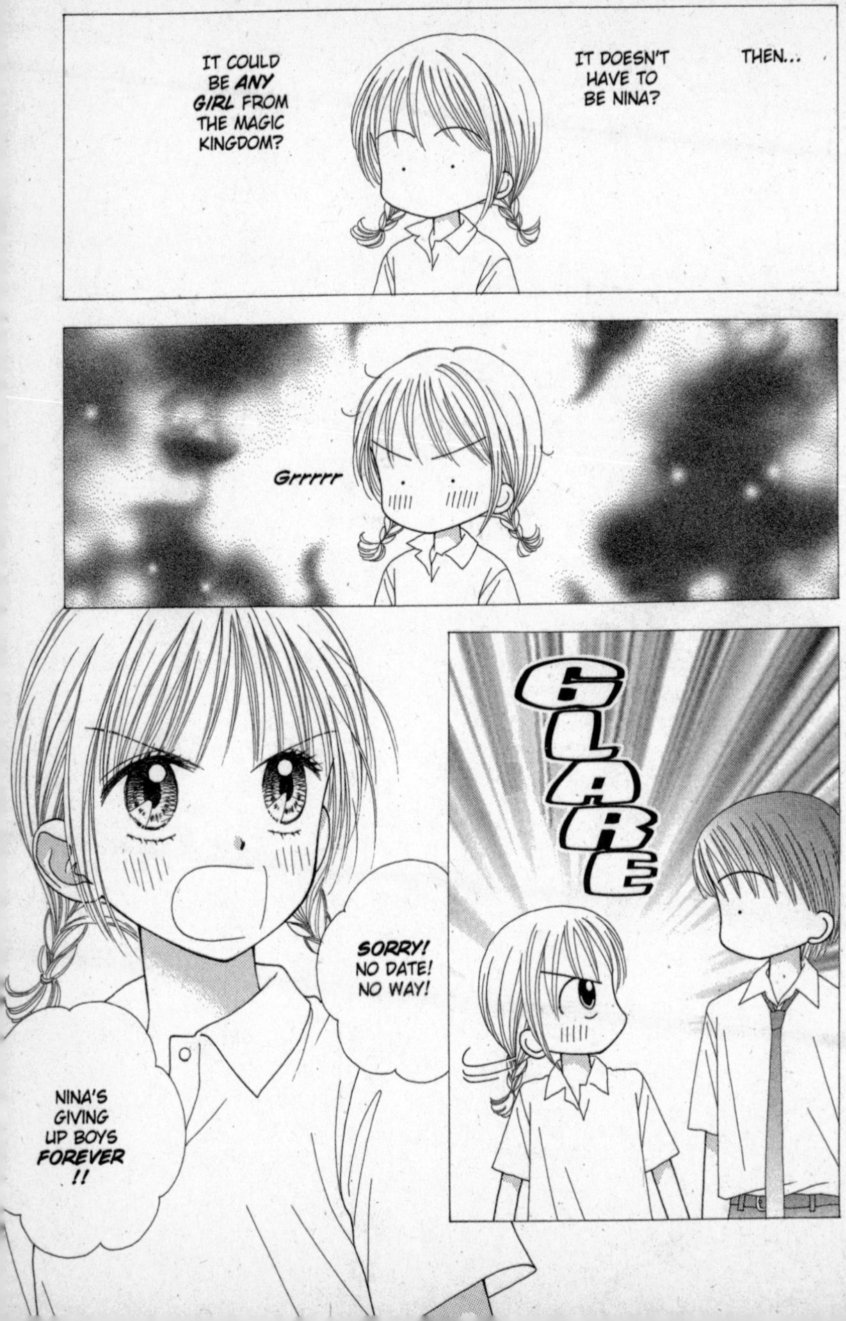
THEN...
IT DOESN'T HAVE TO BE NINA?
IT COULD BE ANY GIRL FROM THE MAGIC KINGDOM?
Grrrrr
GLARE
SORRY! NO DATE! NO WAY!
NINA'S GIVING UP BOYS FOREVER !!

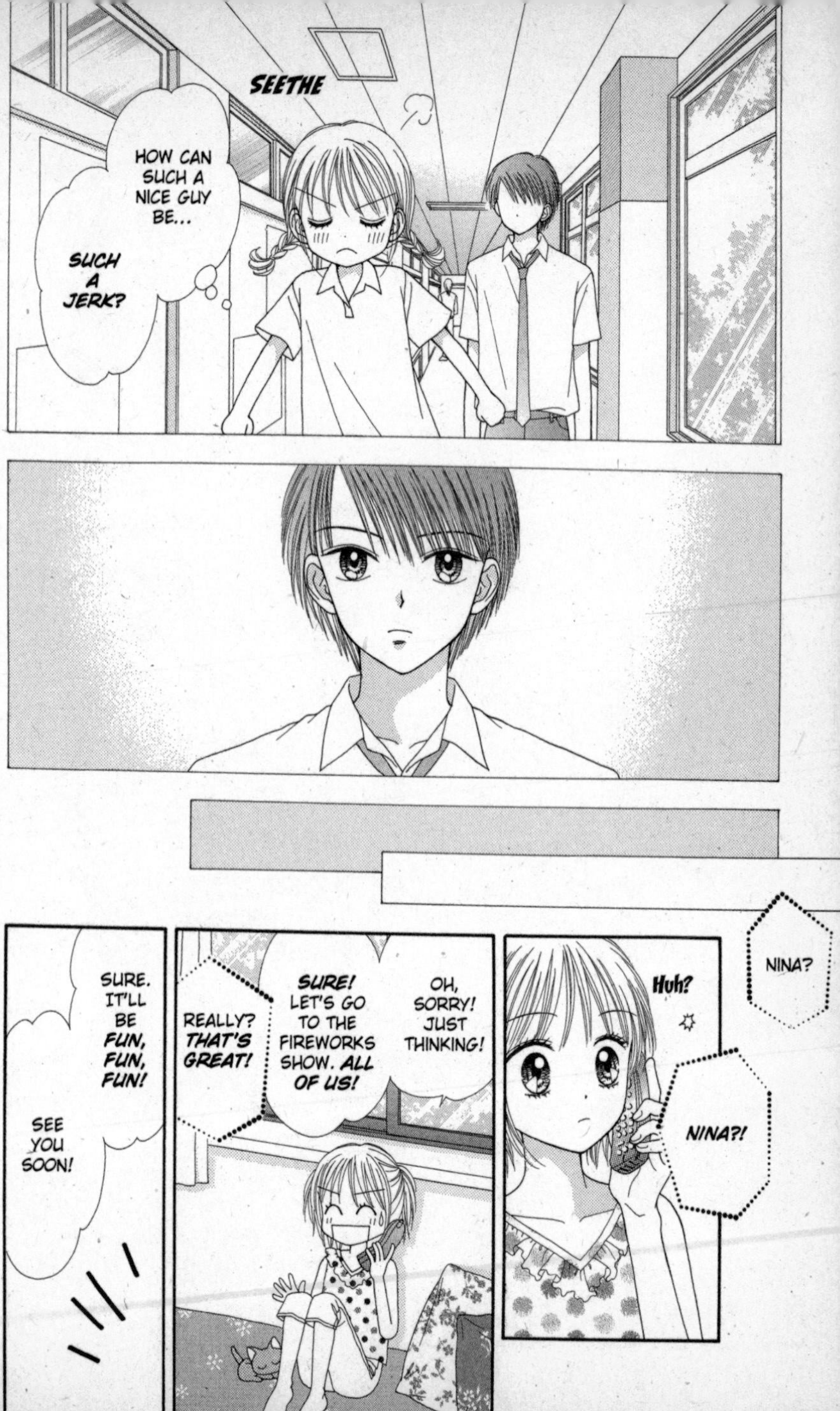
SEETHE
HOW CAN SUCH A NICE GUY BE... SUCH A JERK?
NINA?
Huh?
NINA?!
OH, SORRY! JUST THINKING!
SURE! LET'S GO TO THE FIREWORKS SHOW. ALL OF US!
REALLY? THAT'S GREAT!
SURE. IT'LL BE FUN, FUN, FUN!
SEE YOU SOON!

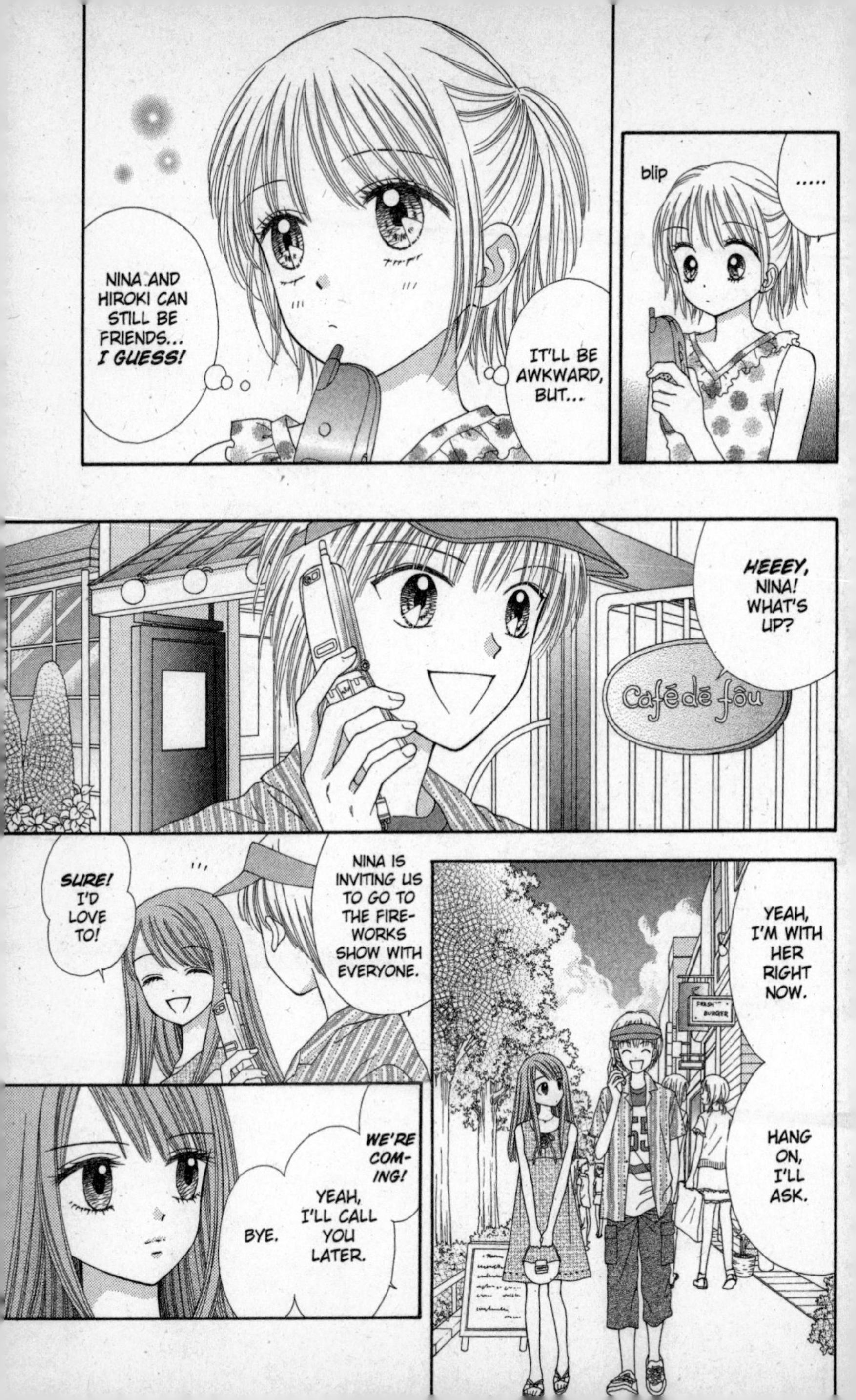
blip
.....
IT'LL BE AWKWARD, BUT...
NINA AND HIROKI CAN STILL BE FRIENDS... *I GUESS!*
HEEEY, NINA! WHAT'S UP?
Café dé fôu
YEAH, I'M WITH HER RIGHT NOW.
HANG ON, I'LL ASK.
NINA IS INVITING US TO GO TO THE FIRE-WORKS SHOW WITH EVERYONE.
SURE! I'D LOVE TO!
WE'RE COM-ING!
YEAH, I'LL CALL YOU LATER.
BYE.

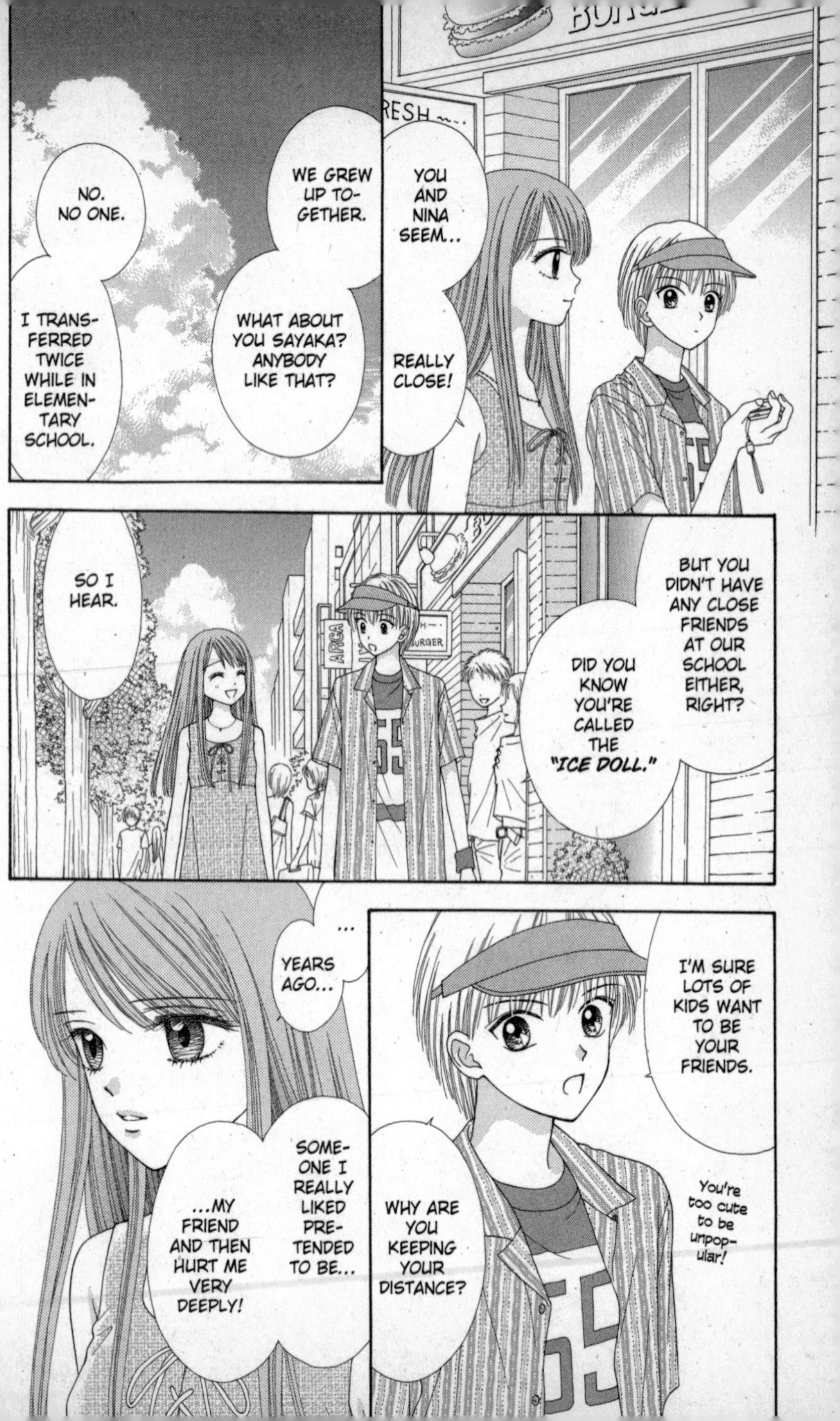
YOU AND NINA SEEM...
REALLY CLOSE!
WE GREW UP TO-GETHER.
WHAT ABOUT YOU SAYAKA? ANYBODY LIKE THAT?
NO. NO ONE.
I TRANS-FERRED TWICE WHILE IN ELEMEN-TARY SCHOOL.
BUT YOU DIDN'T HAVE ANY CLOSE FRIENDS AT OUR SCHOOL EITHER, RIGHT?
DID YOU KNOW YOU'RE CALLED THE *"ICE DOLL."*
ARCA
SO I HEAR.
I'M SURE LOTS OF KIDS WANT TO BE YOUR FRIENDS.
You're too cute to be unpop-ular!
WHY ARE YOU KEEPING YOUR DISTANCE?
...
YEARS AGO...
SOME-ONE I REALLY LIKED PRE-TENDED TO BE...
...MY FRIEND AND THEN HURT ME VERY DEEPLY!

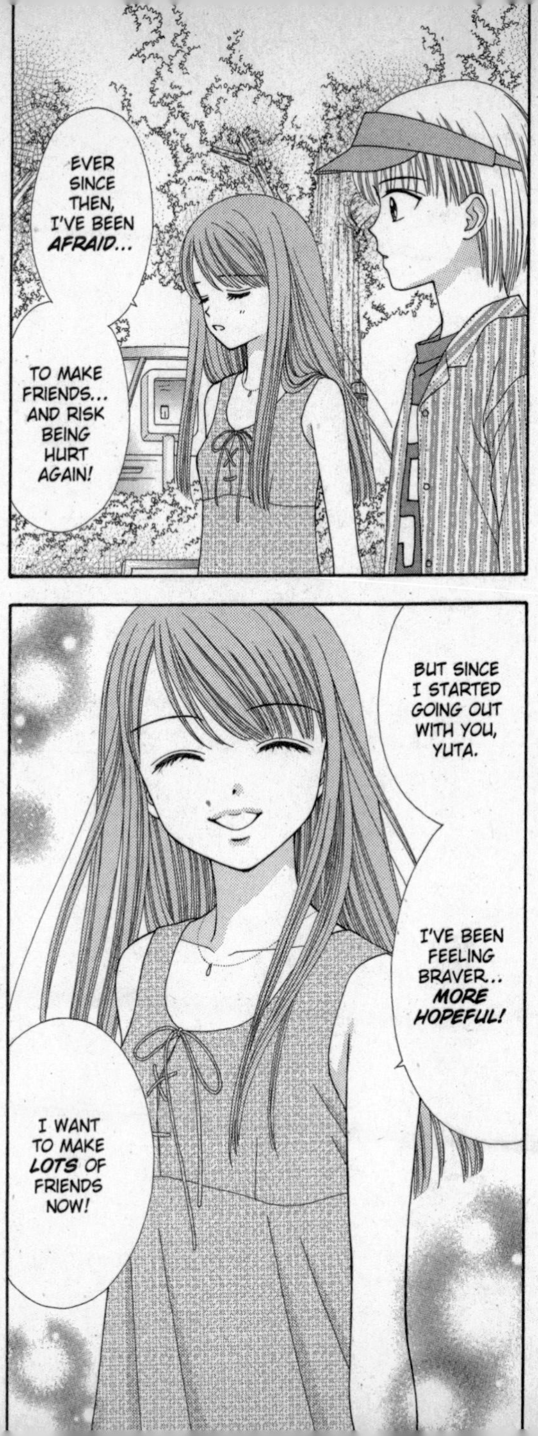
EVER SINCE THEN, I'VE BEEN *AFRAID...*
TO MAKE FRIENDS... AND RISK BEING HURT AGAIN!
BUT SINCE I STARTED GOING OUT WITH YOU, YUTA.
I'VE BEEN FEELING BRAVER... ***MORE HOPEFUL!***
I WANT TO MAKE ***LOTS*** OF FRIENDS NOW!
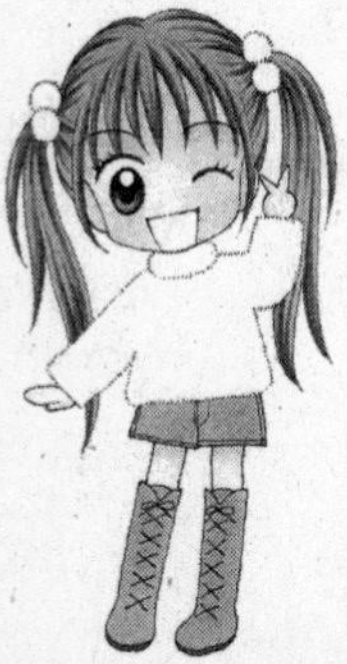

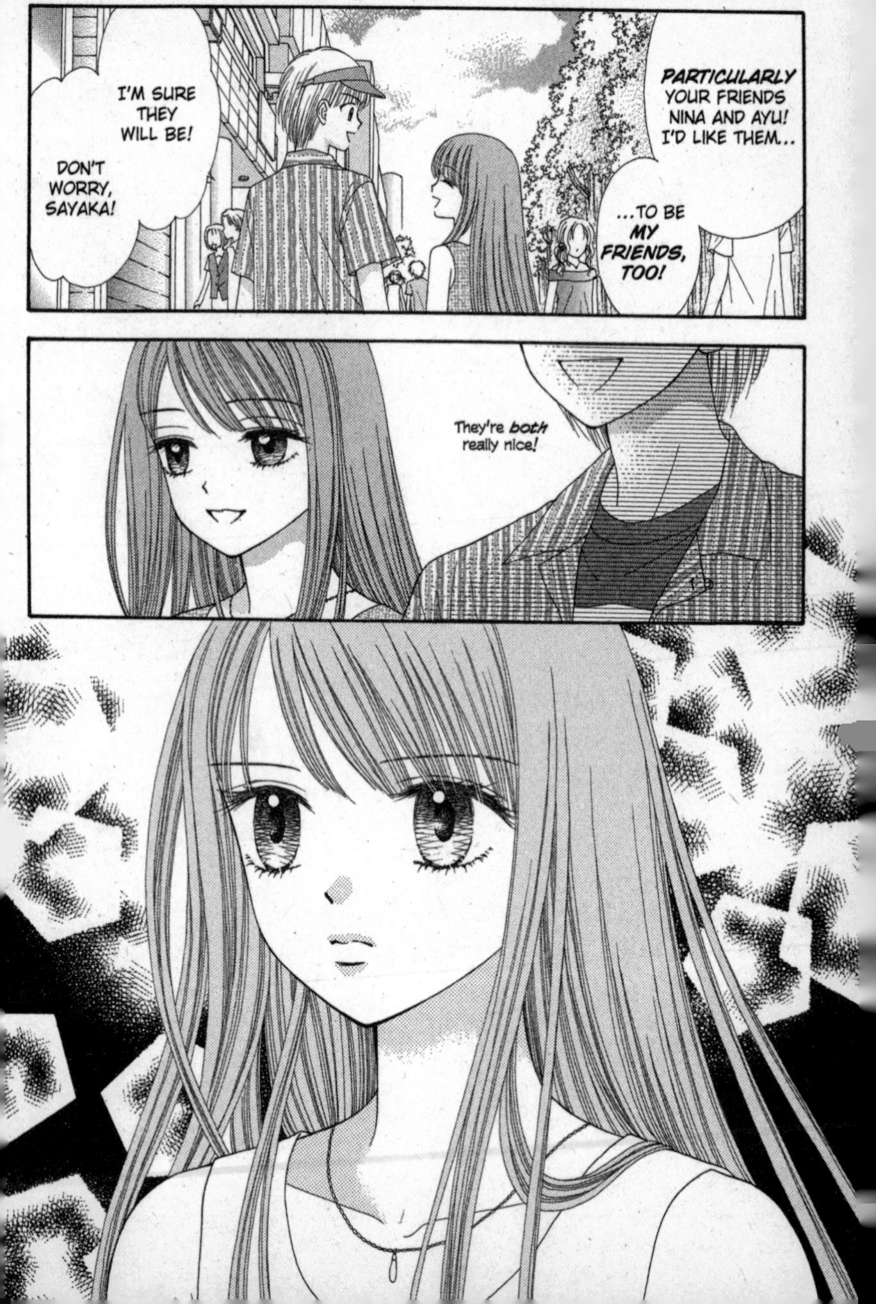
PARTICULARLY YOUR FRIENDS NINA AND AYU! I'D LIKE THEM..
...TO BE MY FRIENDS, TOO!
I'M SURE THEY WILL BE!
DON'T WORRY, SAYAKA!
They're both really nice!

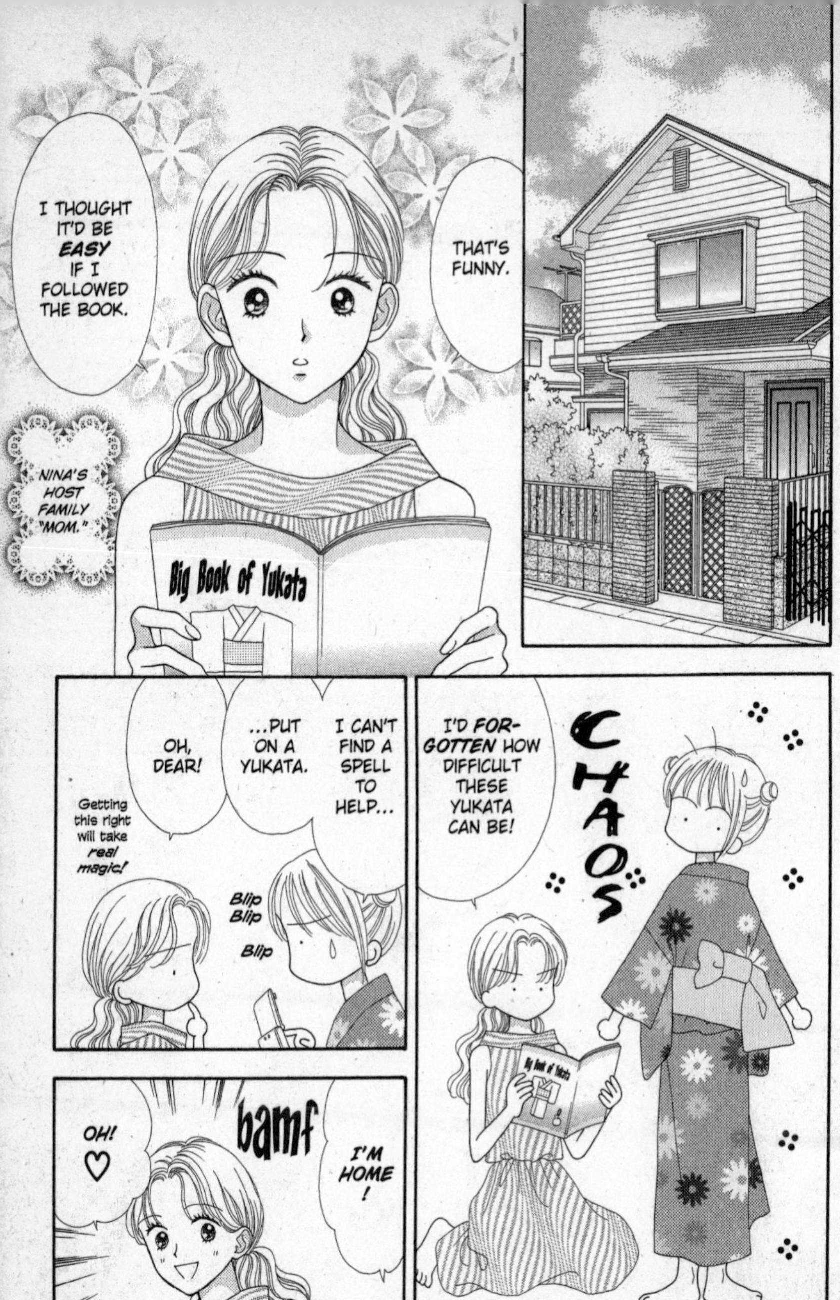
THAT'S FUNNY.
I THOUGHT IT'D BE **EASY** IF I FOLLOWED THE BOOK.
NINA'S HOST FAMILY "MOM."
Big Book of Yukata
I'D **FOR-GOTTEN** HOW DIFFICULT THESE YUKATA CAN BE!
CHAOS
Big Book of Yukata
I CAN'T FIND A SPELL TO HELP...
...PUT ON A YUKATA.
OH, DEAR!
Getting this right will take *real magic!*
Blip Blip
Blip
I'M HOME!
bamf
OH! ♡

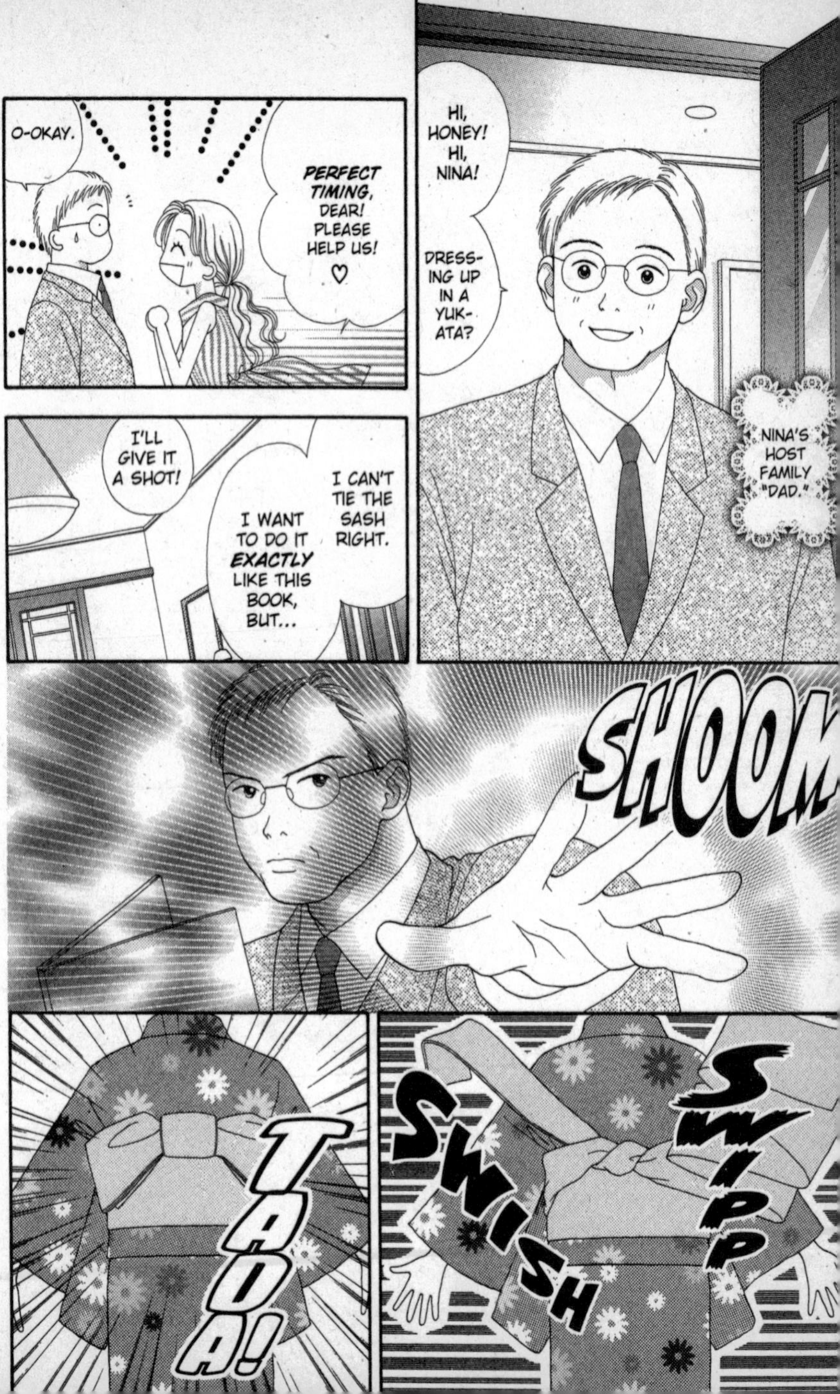
HI, HONEY! HI, NINA!
DRESSING UP IN A YUKATA?
NINA'S HOST FAMILY "DAD."
PERFECT TIMING, DEAR! PLEASE HELP US! ♡
O-OKAY.
I CAN'T TIE THE SASH RIGHT.
I WANT TO DO IT EXACTLY LIKE THIS BOOK, BUT...
I'LL GIVE IT A SHOT!
SHOOM
SWIPP
SWISH
TADA!

FREE TALK 8

Another of my old series, *Handsome Girl*, is going to be re-printed in a collection soon. It was my very first long serial and this is the first time it'll be collected in a series of books. It's going to be published by Shueisha Comic Collections.

I did some Free Talks like this in *Handsome Girl*, too. But, looking back at them, the topics are **really old**. And I'll admit, I was writing some pretty pointless stuff.

Back then, I was writing things that were a little too personal. Plus, I was trying too hard to get readers to like me. It's **embarrassing** for me to read that stuff now.

So, for the series' reprint, I had the publisher remove the Free Talks. In their place, I put in a 100-question, 100-answer interview instead.

So, there's something new in the collection—even if you read the series before.

Of course, I'm really embarrassed about how bad my old art is. But even now, it's my most important work. . . because so many people still tell me it's their favorite.

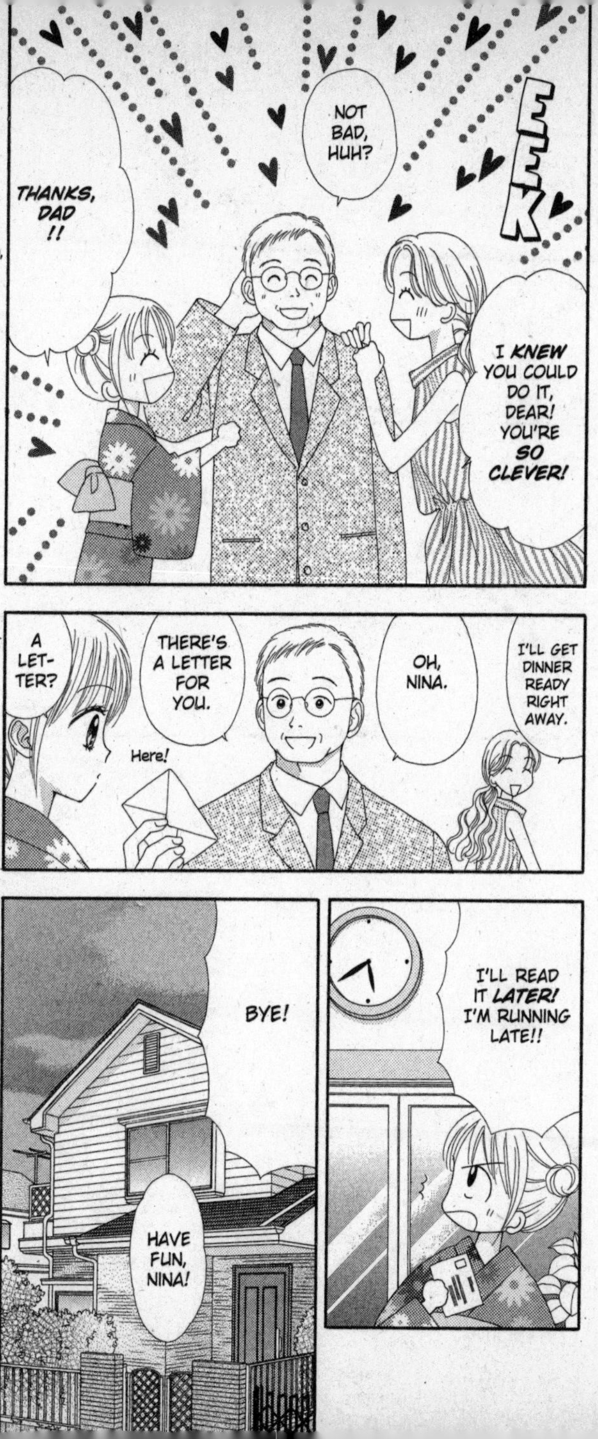
EEEK
I KNEW YOU COULD DO IT, DEAR! YOU'RE SO CLEVER!
NOT BAD, HUH?
THANKS, DAD!!
I'LL GET DINNER READY RIGHT AWAY.
OH, NINA.
THERE'S A LETTER FOR YOU.
Here!
A LETTER?
I'LL READ IT LATER! I'M RUNNING LATE!!
BYE!
HAVE FUN, NINA!

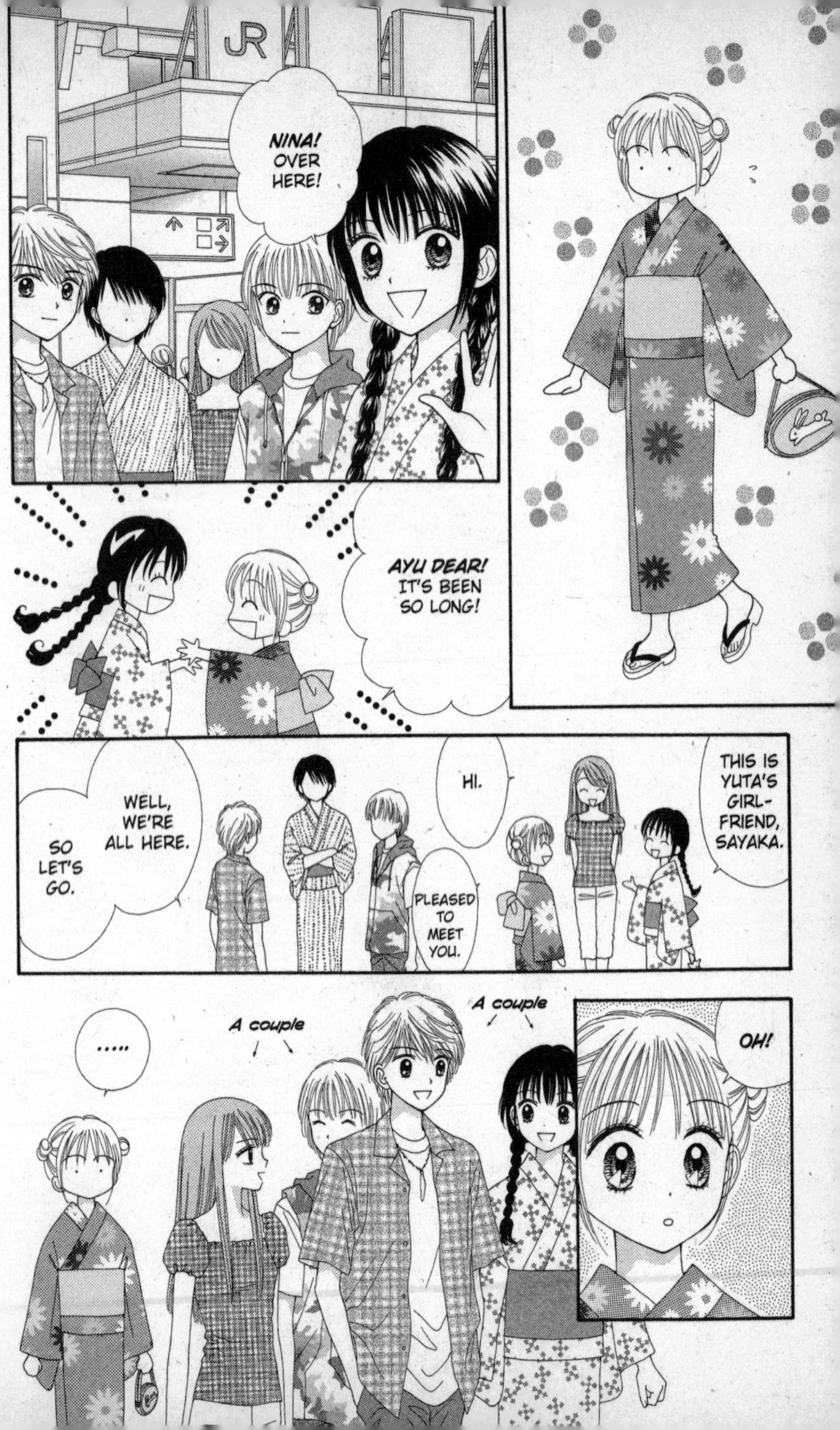

NINA! OVER HERE!
AYU DEAR! IT'S BEEN SO LONG!
THIS IS YUTA'S GIRL-FRIEND, SAYAKA.
HI.
PLEASED TO MEET YOU.
WELL, WE'RE ALL HERE.
SO LET'S GO.
OH!
A couple
A couple
.....

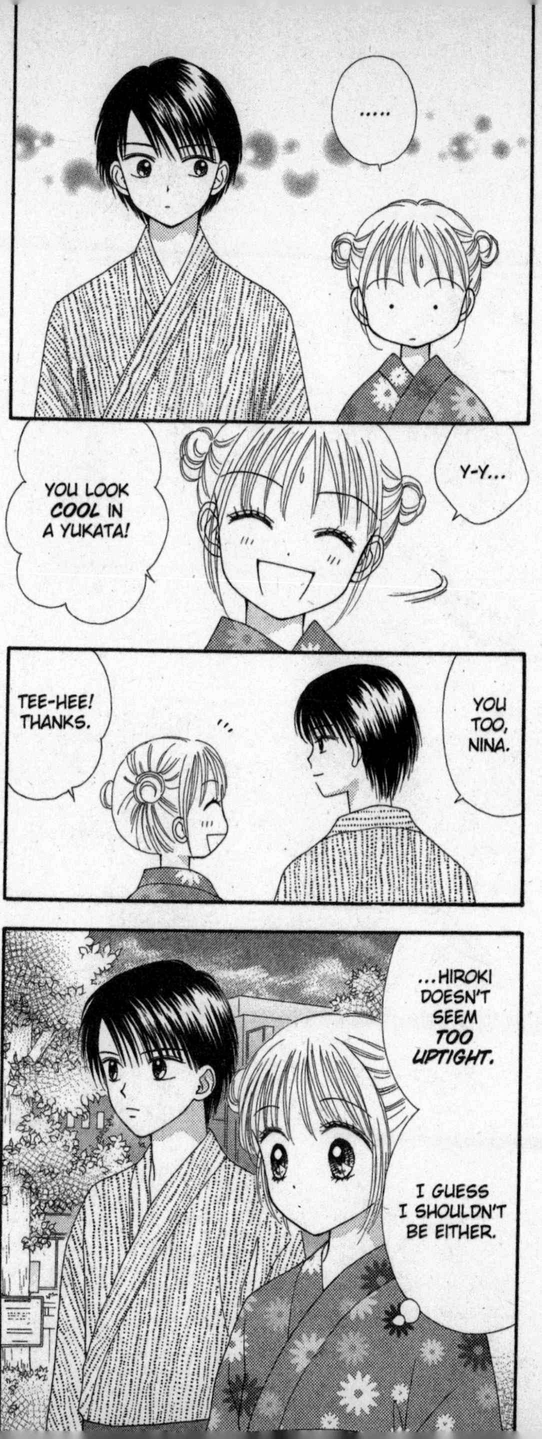
.....
Y-Y...
YOU LOOK COOL IN A YUKATA!
YOU TOO, NINA.
TEE-HEE! THANKS.
...HIROKI DOESN'T SEEM TOO UPTIGHT.
I GUESS I SHOULDN'T BE EITHER.
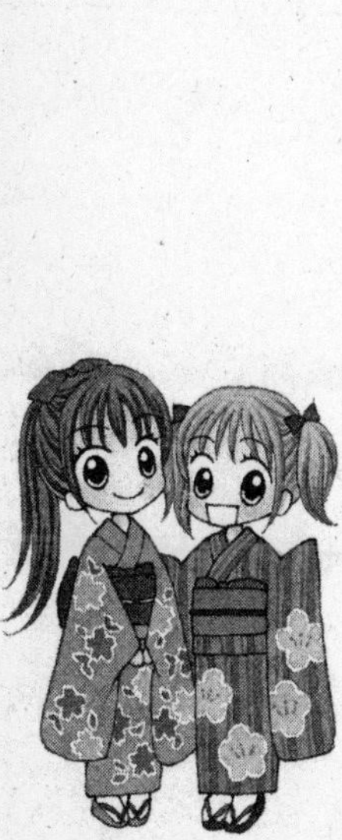

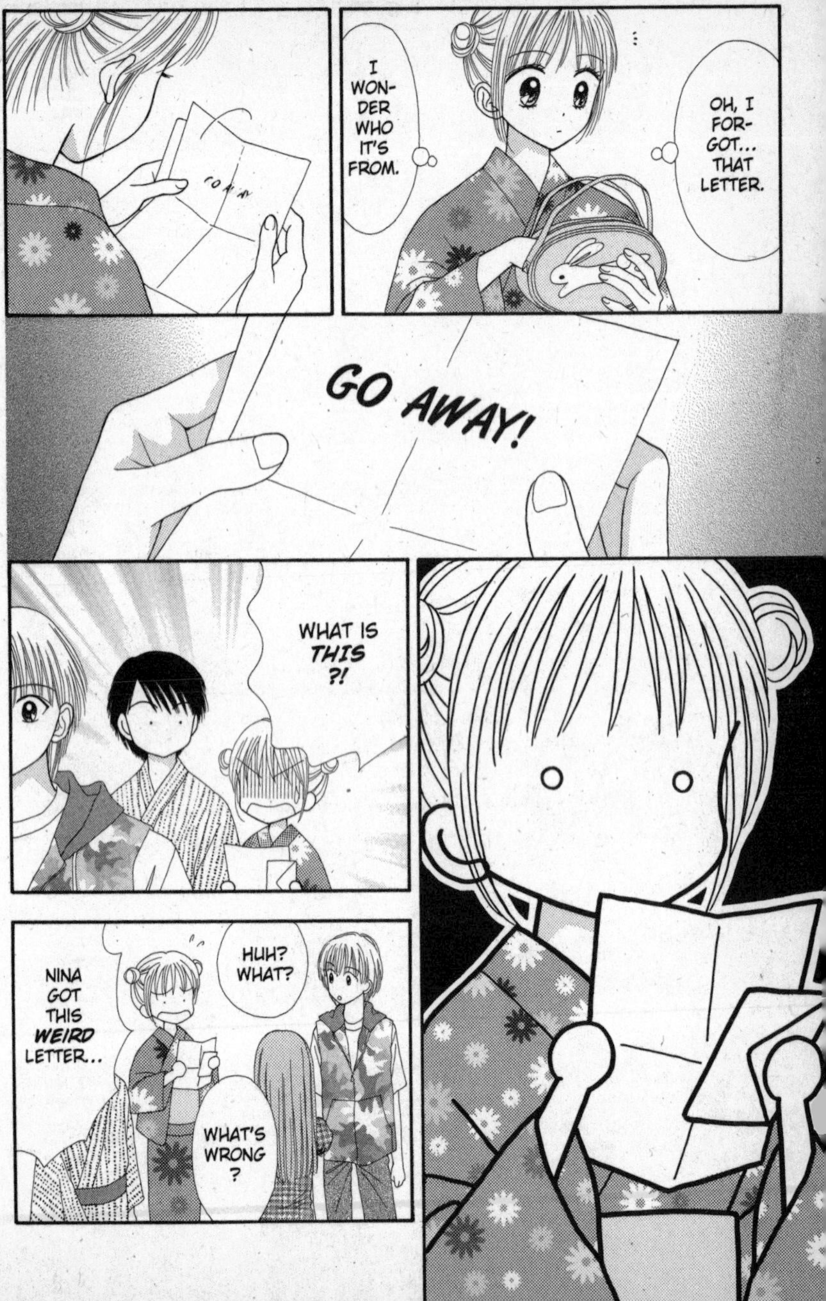
...
OH, I FORGOT... THAT LETTER.
I WONDER WHO IT'S FROM.
GO AWAY!
WHAT IS *THIS* ?!
HUH? WHAT?
NINA GOT THIS *WEIRD* LETTER...
WHAT'S WRONG ?

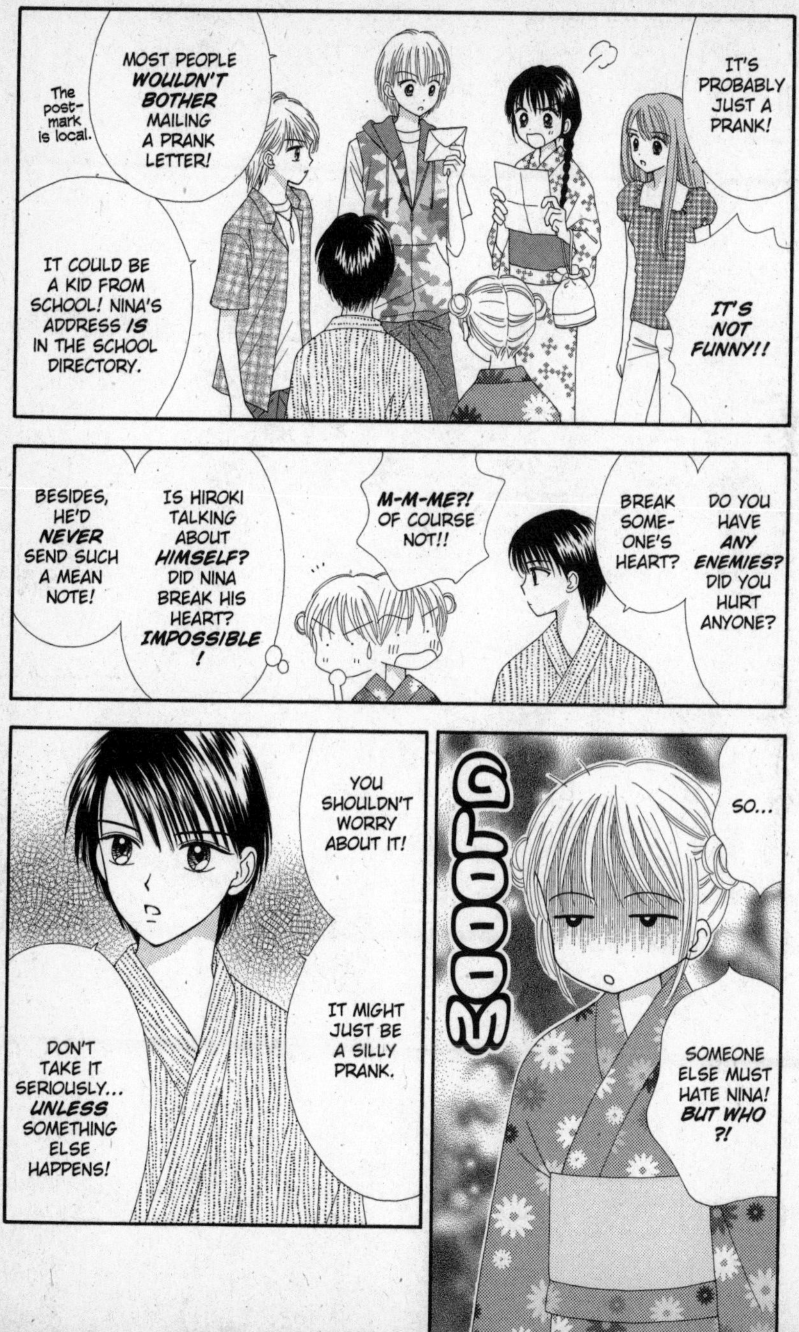
IT'S PROBABLY JUST A PRANK!
IT'S NOT FUNNY!!
MOST PEOPLE WOULDN'T BOTHER MAILING A PRANK LETTER!
The post-mark is local.
IT COULD BE A KID FROM SCHOOL! NINA'S ADDRESS IS IN THE SCHOOL DIRECTORY.
DO YOU HAVE ANY ENEMIES? DID YOU HURT ANYONE?
BREAK SOME-ONE'S HEART?
M-M-ME?! OF COURSE NOT!!
IS HIROKI TALKING ABOUT HIMSELF? DID NINA BREAK HIS HEART? IMPOSSIBLE!
BESIDES, HE'D NEVER SEND SUCH A MEAN NOTE!
SO...
GLOOOM
SOMEONE ELSE MUST HATE NINA! BUT WHO?!
YOU SHOULDN'T WORRY ABOUT IT!
IT MIGHT JUST BE A SILLY PRANK.
DON'T TAKE IT SERIOUSLY... UNLESS SOMETHING ELSE HAPPENS!

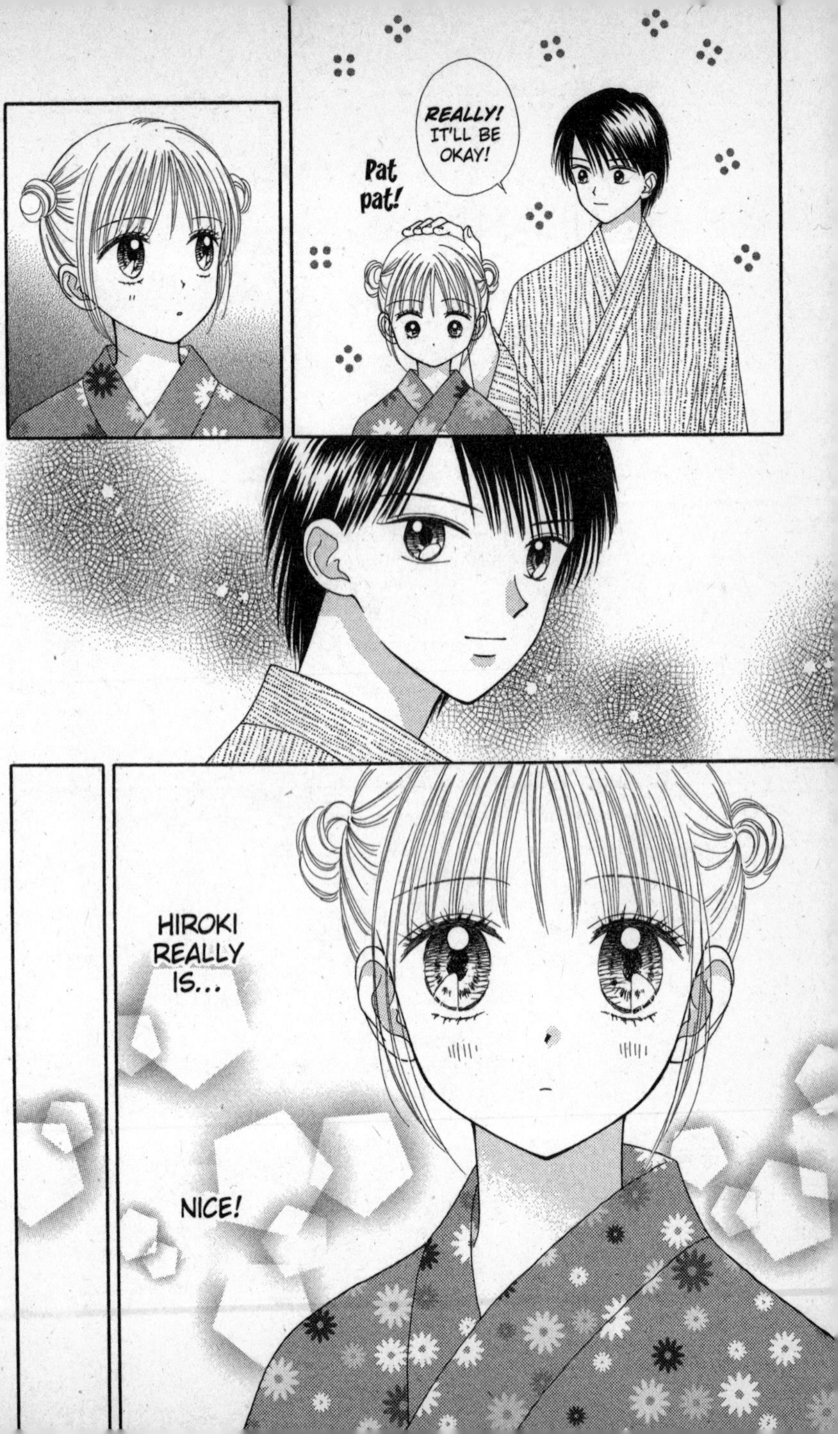
REALLY! IT'LL BE OKAY!
Pat pat!
HIROKI REALLY IS...
NICE!

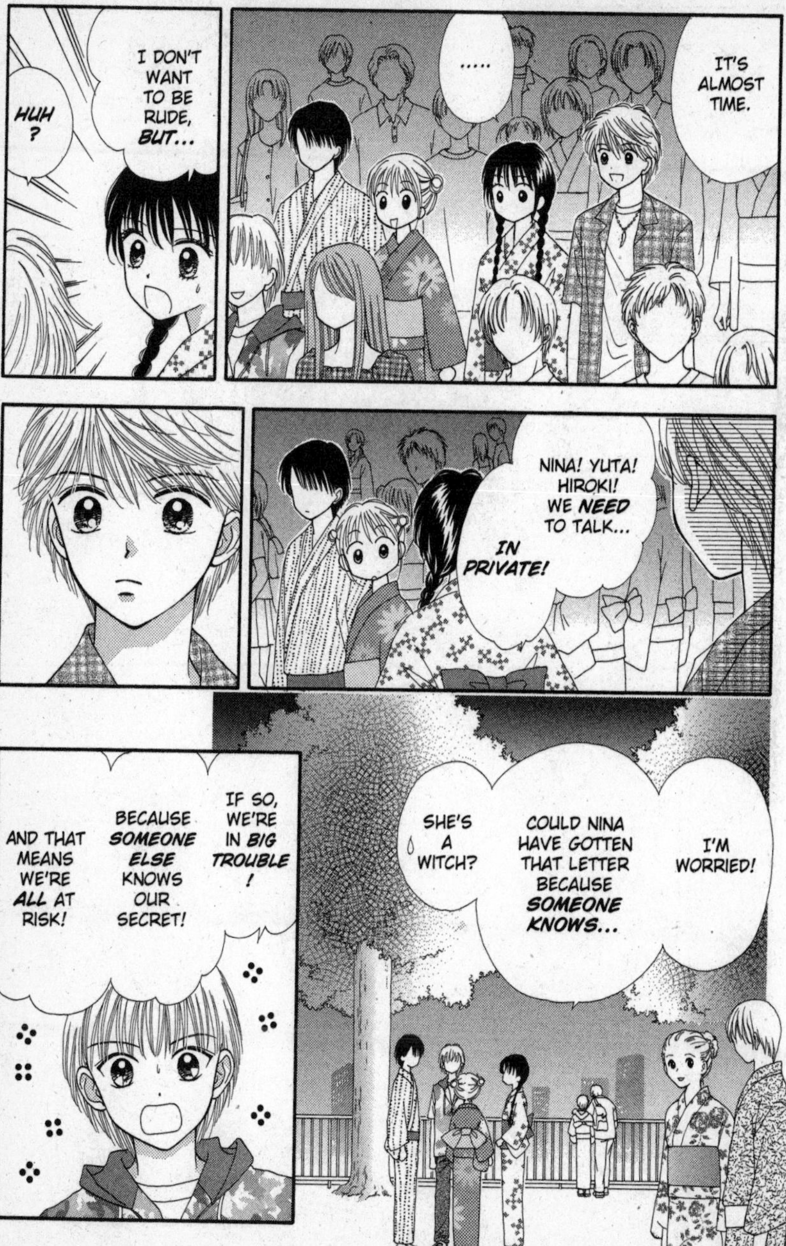
IT'S ALMOST TIME.
.....
I DON'T WANT TO BE RUDE, BUT...
HUH?
NINA! YUTA! HIROKI! WE NEED TO TALK...
IN PRIVATE!
I'M WORRIED!
COULD NINA HAVE GOTTEN THAT LETTER BECAUSE SOMEONE KNOWS...
SHE'S A WITCH?
IF SO, WE'RE IN BIG TROUBLE!
BECAUSE SOMEONE ELSE KNOWS OUR SECRET!
AND THAT MEANS WE'RE ALL AT RISK!

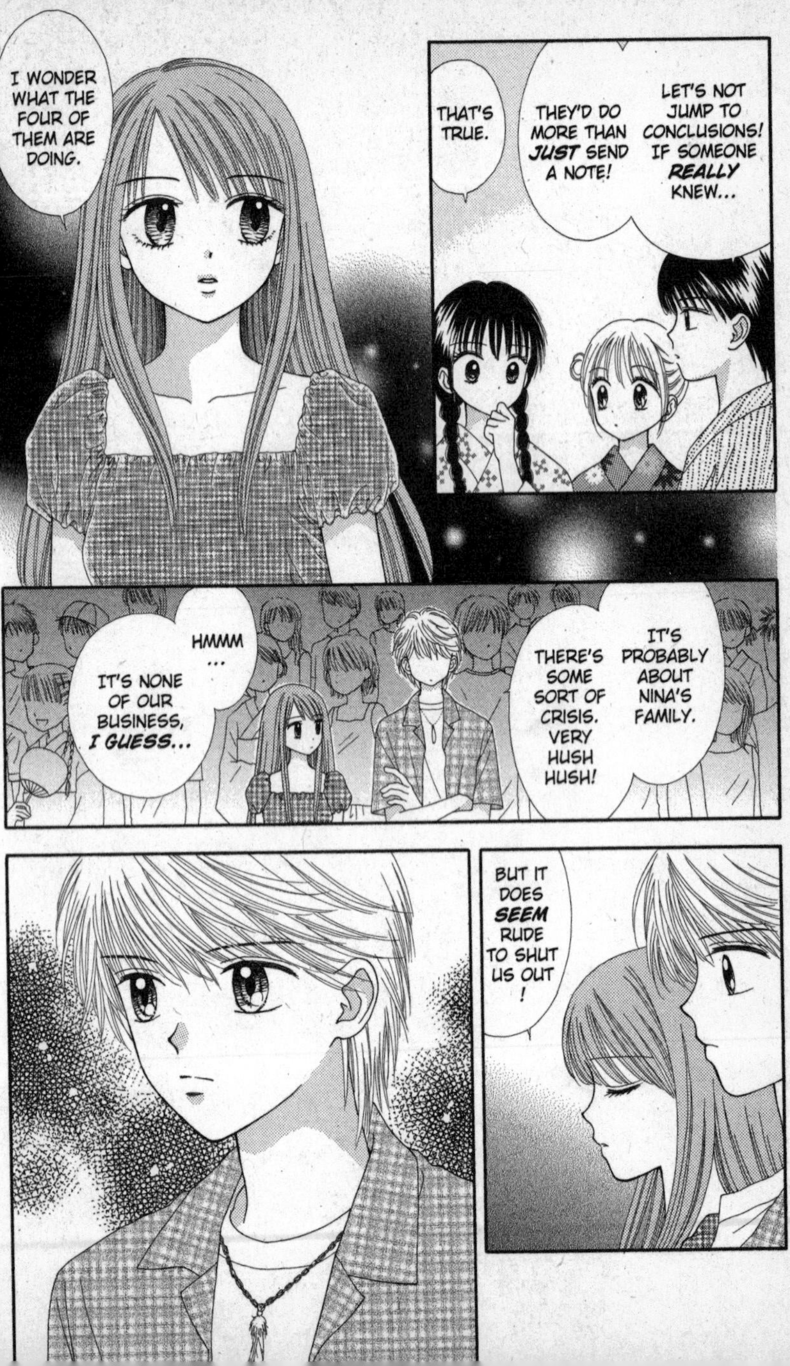
LET'S NOT JUMP TO CONCLUSIONS! IF SOMEONE REALLY KNEW...
THEY'D DO MORE THAN JUST SEND A NOTE!
THAT'S TRUE.
I WONDER WHAT THE FOUR OF THEM ARE DOING.
IT'S PROBABLY ABOUT NINA'S FAMILY.
THERE'S SOME SORT OF CRISIS. VERY HUSH HUSH!
HMMM...
IT'S NONE OF OUR BUSINESS, I GUESS...
BUT IT DOES SEEM RUDE TO SHUT US OUT!

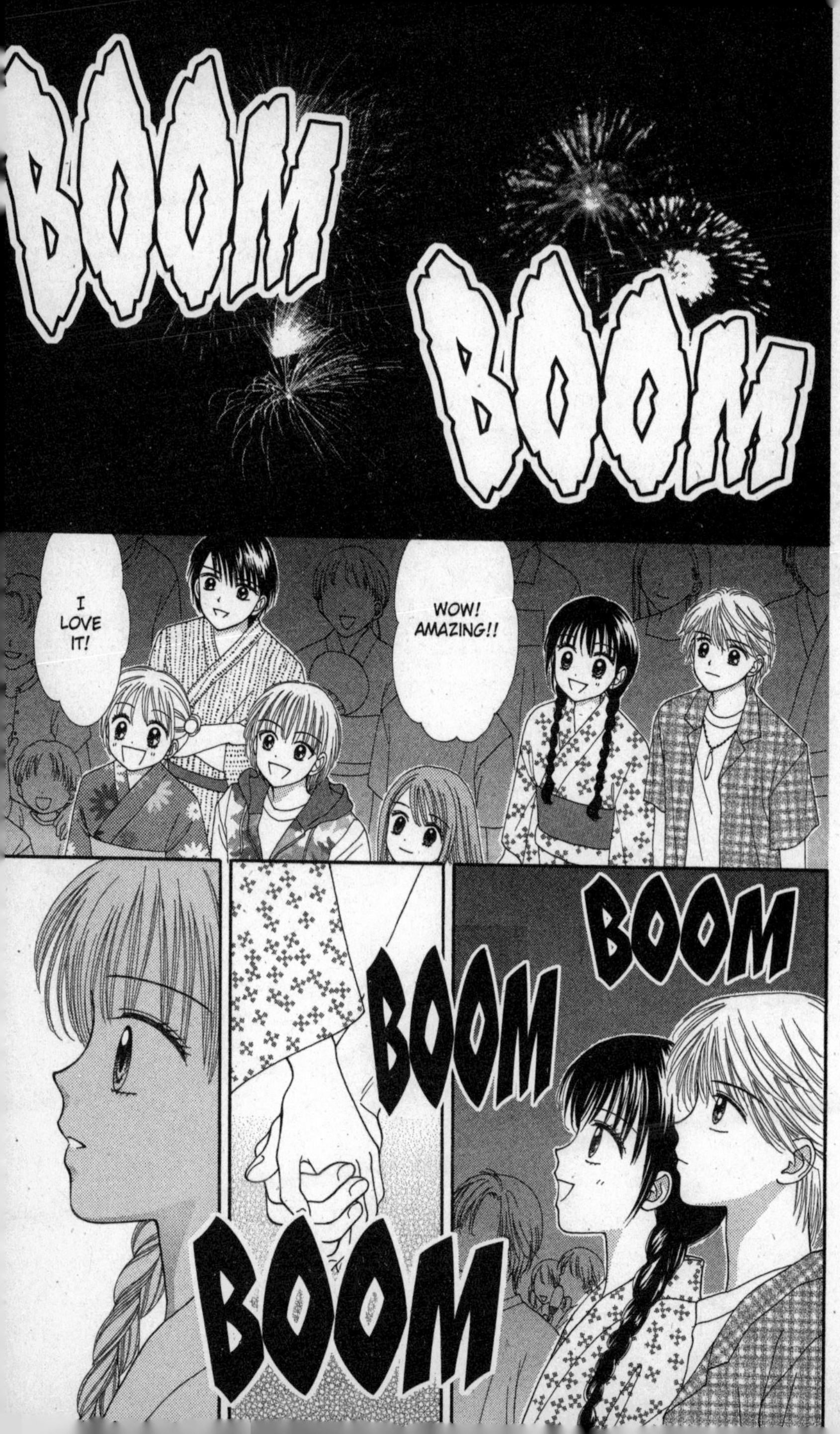
BOOM
BOOM
WOW! AMAZING!!
I LOVE IT!
BOOM
BOOM
BOOM

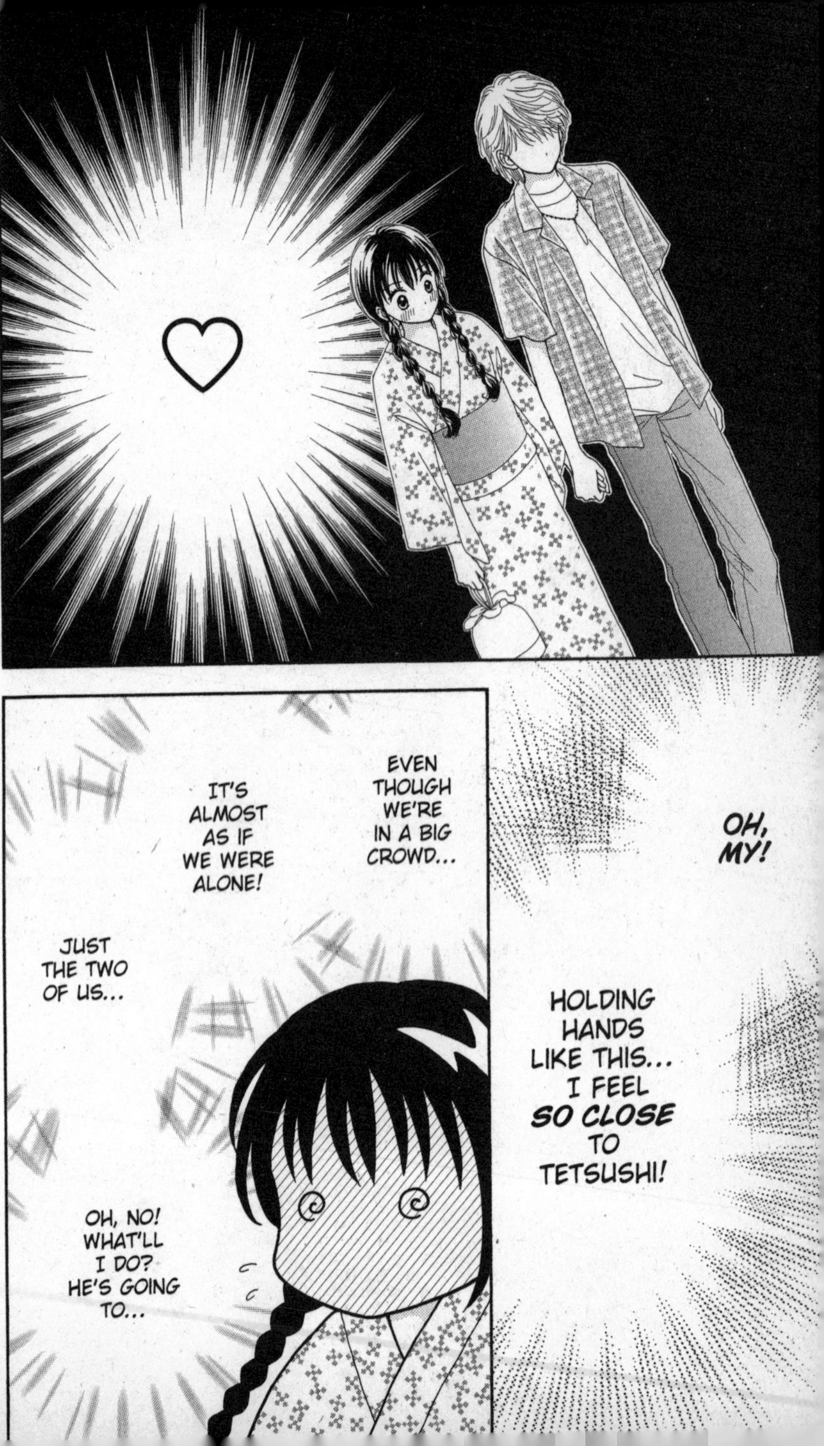
OH, MY!
HOLDING HANDS LIKE THIS... I FEEL SO CLOSE TO TETSUSHI!
EVEN THOUGH WE'RE IN A BIG CROWD...
IT'S ALMOST AS IF WE WERE ALONE!
JUST THE TWO OF US...
OH, NO! WHAT'LL I DO? HE'S GOING TO...

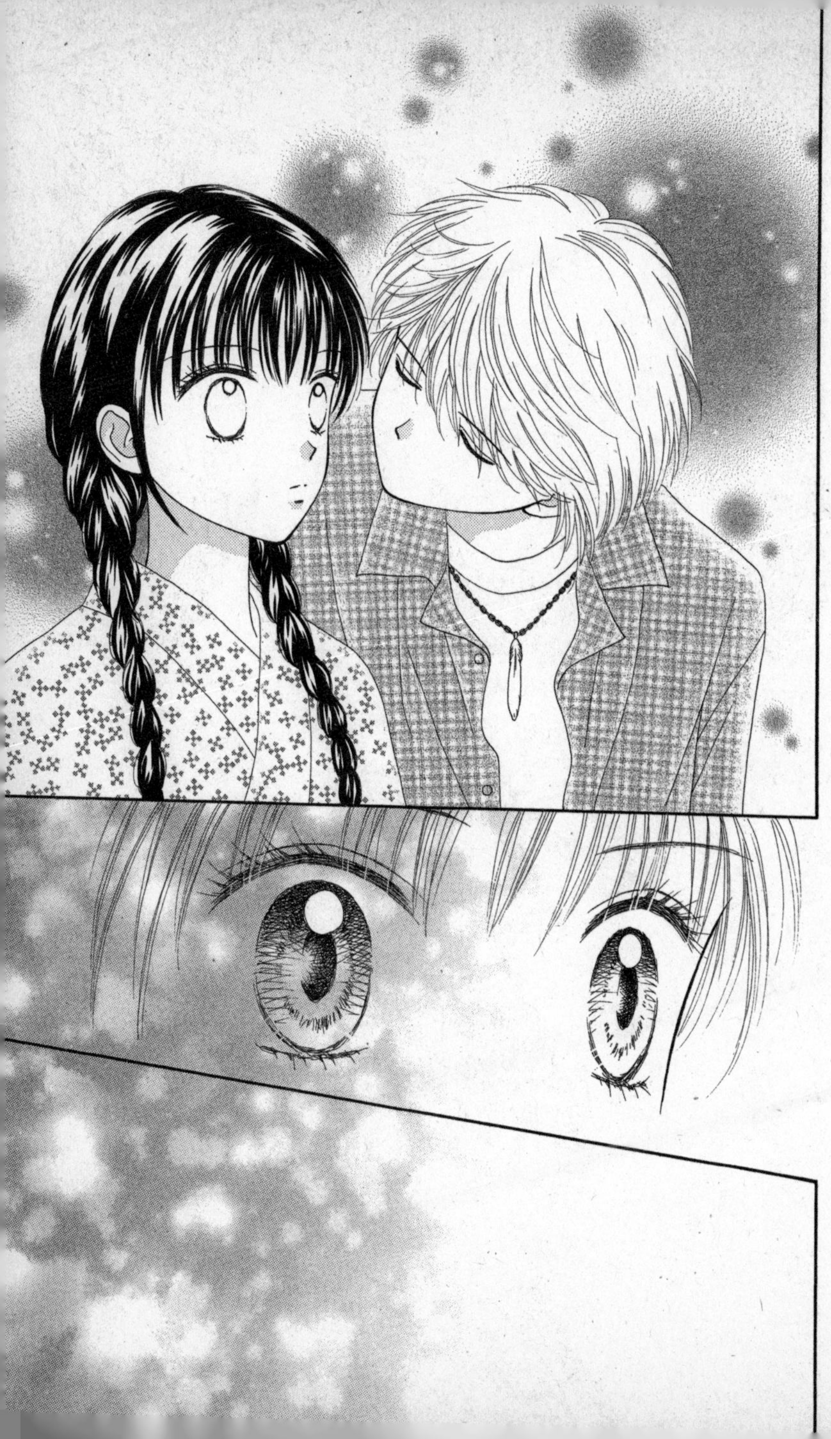

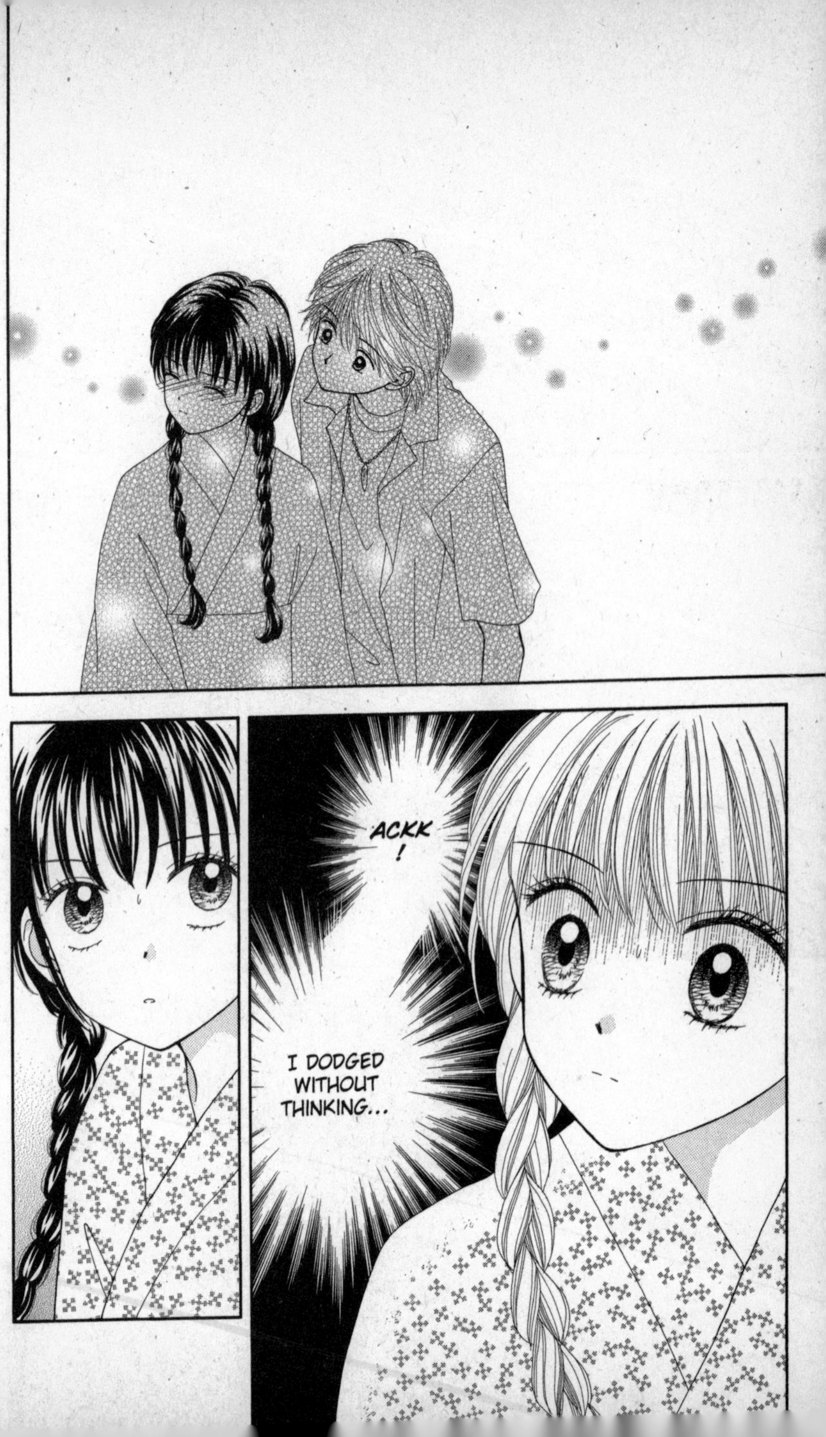
ACKK!
I DODGED WITHOUT THINKING...

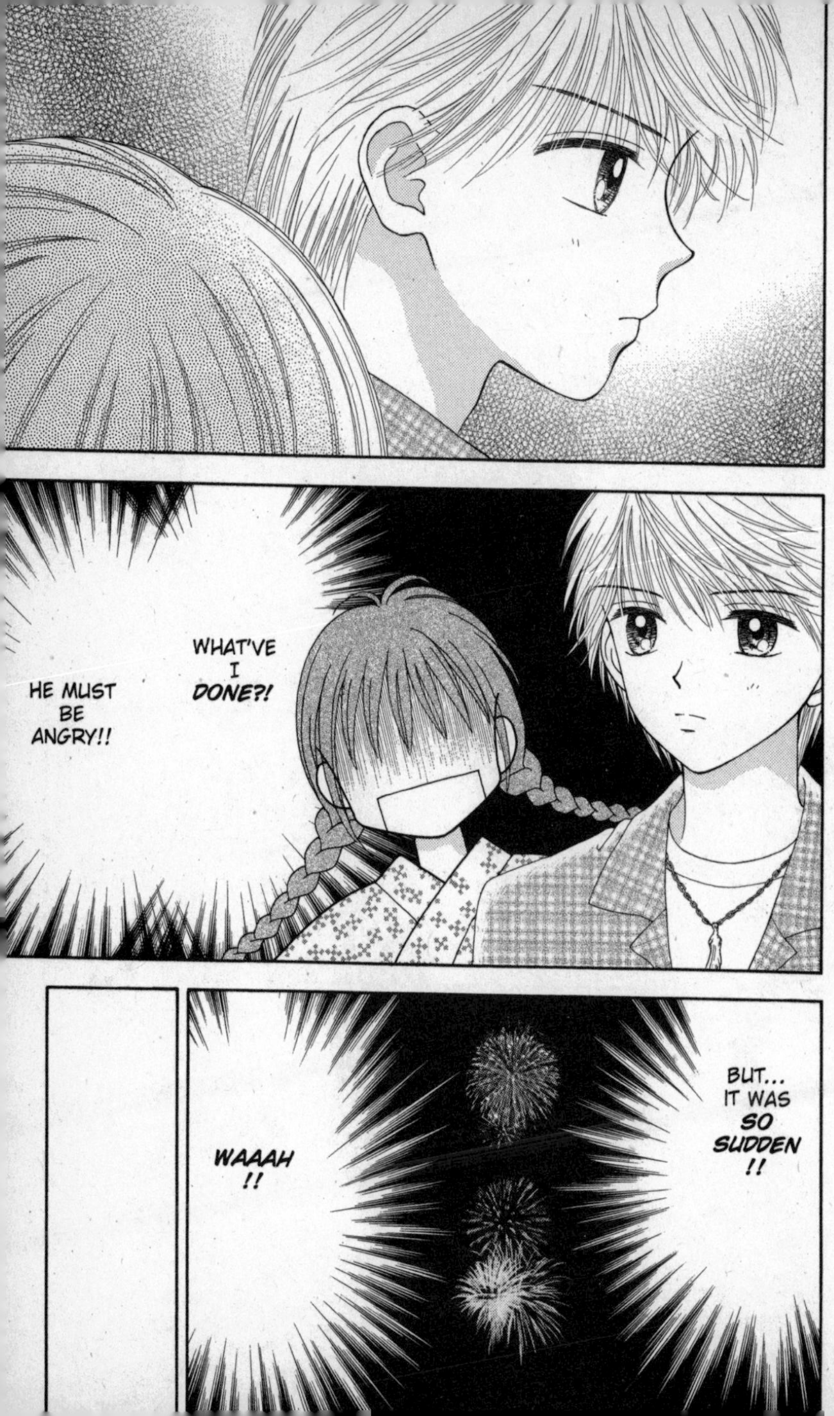
WHAT'VE I DONE?!
HE MUST BE ANGRY!!
BUT... IT WAS SO SUDDEN!!
WAAAH!!

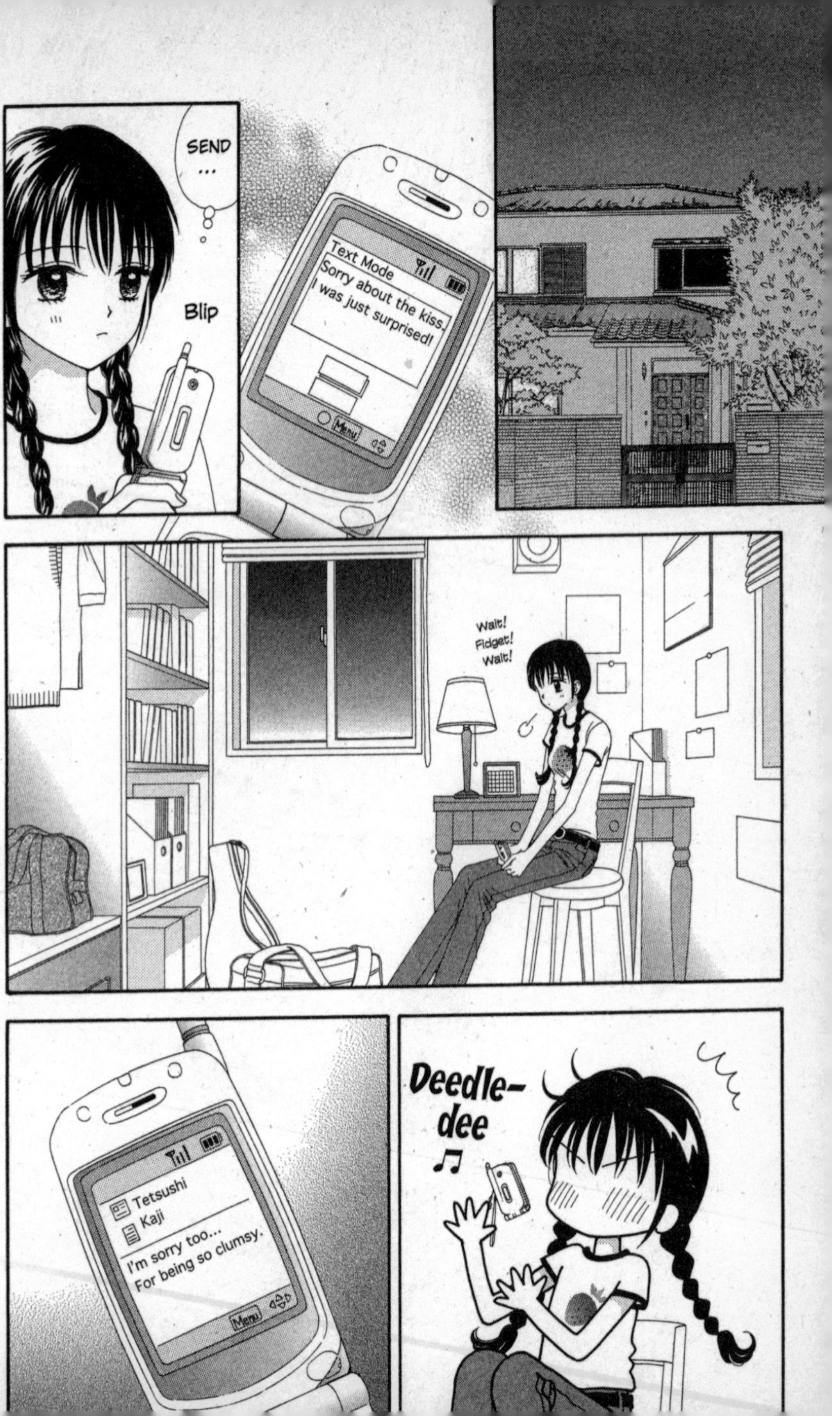

Text Mode
Sorry about the kiss.
I was just surprised!
Menu
SEND ...
Blip
Wait! Fidget! Wait!
Deedle-dee ♫
Tetsushi
Kaji
I'm sorry too...
For being so clumsy.
Menu

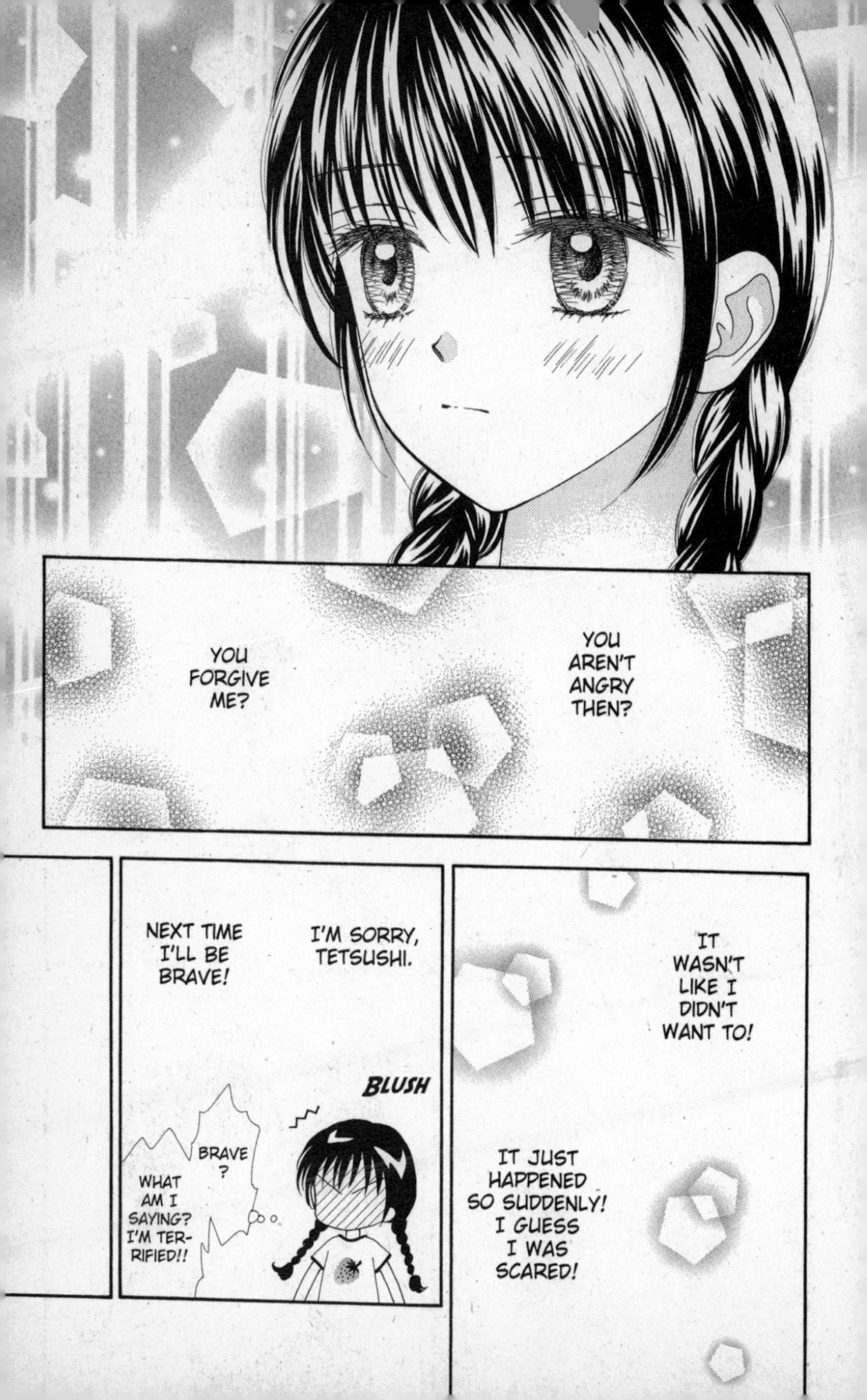
YOU AREN'T ANGRY THEN?
YOU FORGIVE ME?
IT WASN'T LIKE I DIDN'T WANT TO!
IT JUST HAPPENED SO SUDDENLY! I GUESS I WAS SCARED!
I'M SORRY, TETSUSHI.
NEXT TIME I'LL BE BRAVE!
BLUSH
BRAVE?
WHAT AM I SAYING? I'M TERRIFIED!!

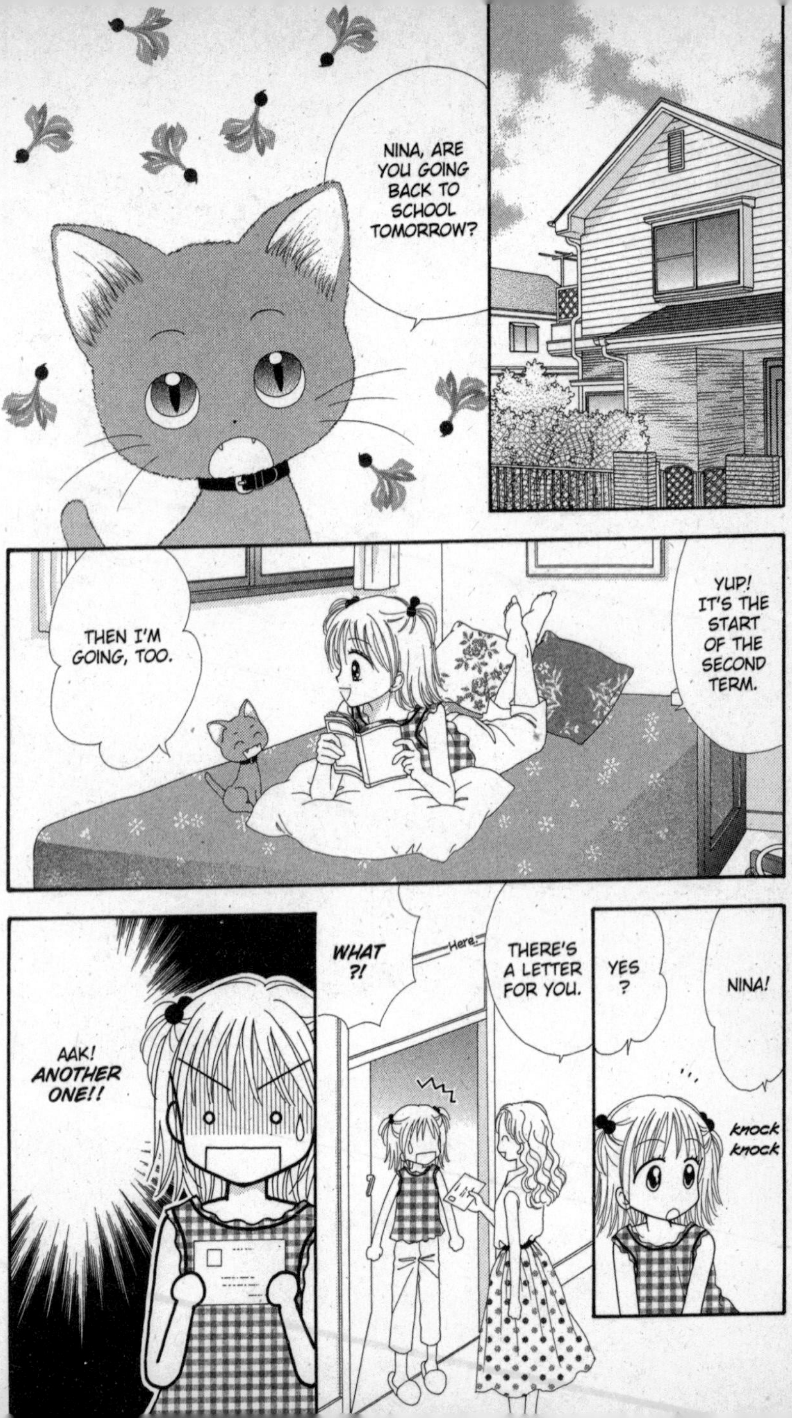
NINA, ARE YOU GOING BACK TO SCHOOL TOMORROW?
YUP! IT'S THE START OF THE SECOND TERM.
THEN I'M GOING, TOO.
NINA!
knock knock
YES?
THERE'S A LETTER FOR YOU.
Here.
WHAT?!
AAK! ANOTHER ONE!!

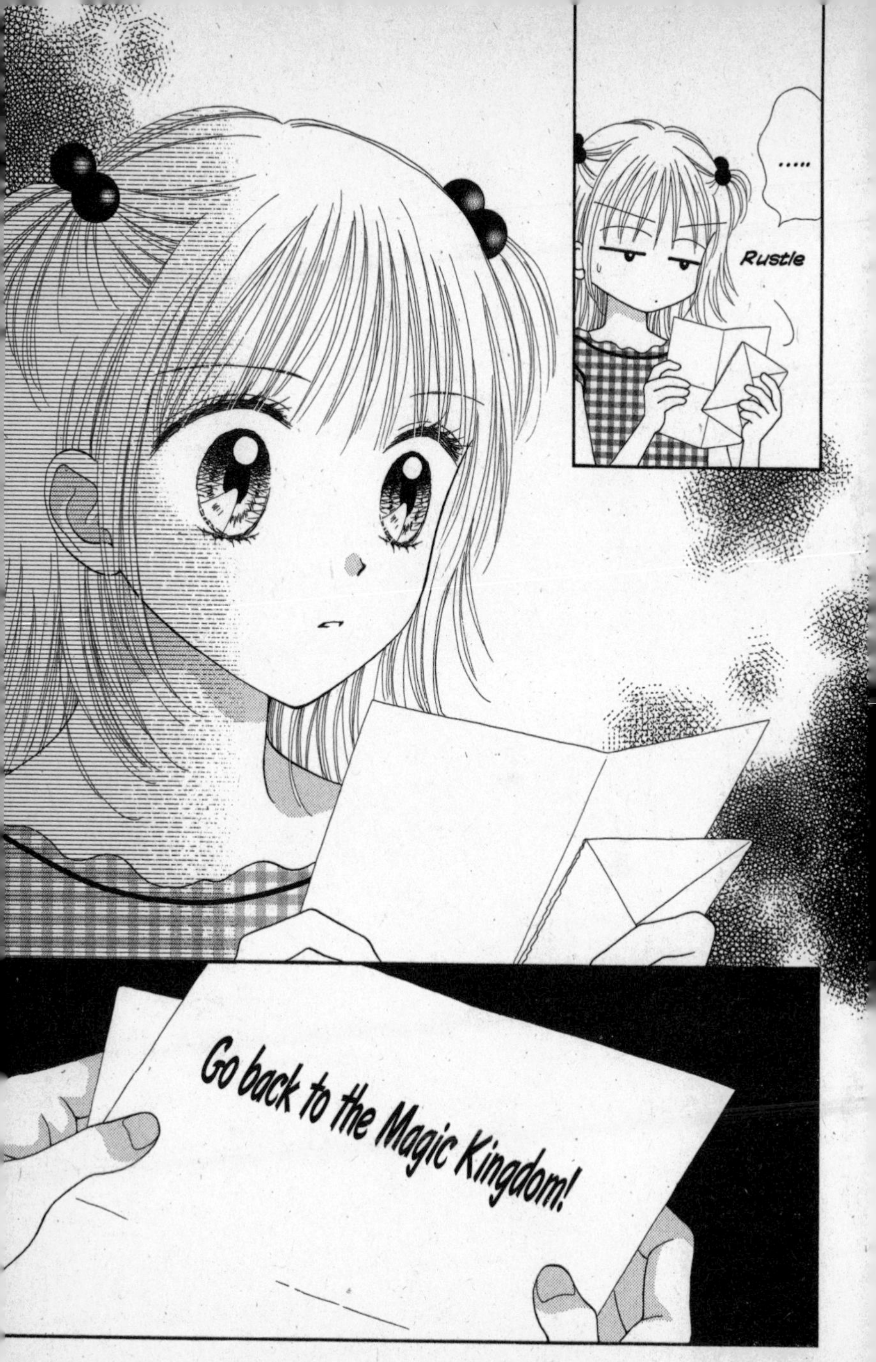
.....
Rustle
Go back to the Magic Kingdom!

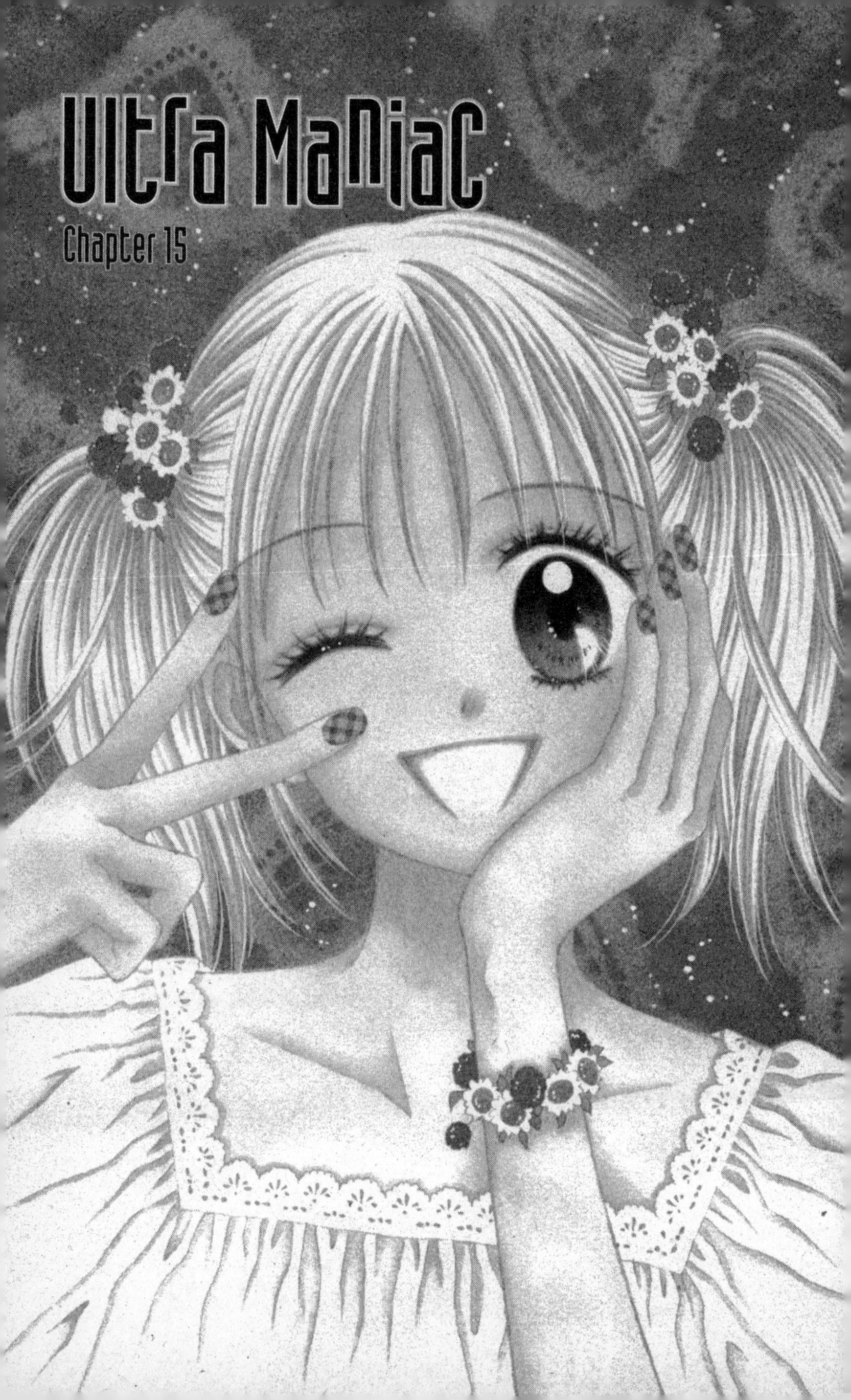
Ultra Maniac
Chapter 15

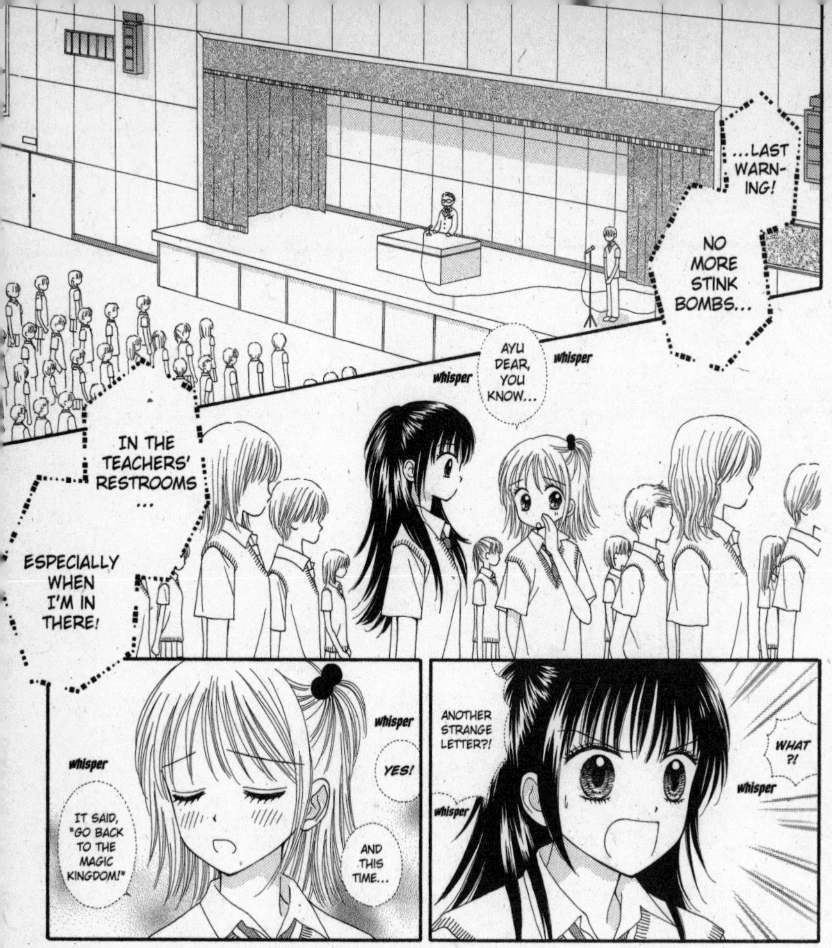
...LAST WARNING!
NO MORE STINK BOMBS...
IN THE TEACHERS' RESTROOMS...
ESPECIALLY WHEN I'M IN THERE!
whisper
AYU DEAR, YOU KNOW...
whisper
WHAT ?!
whisper
ANOTHER STRANGE LETTER?!
whisper
whisper
YES!
AND THIS TIME...
whisper
IT SAID, "GO BACK TO THE MAGIC KINGDOM!"

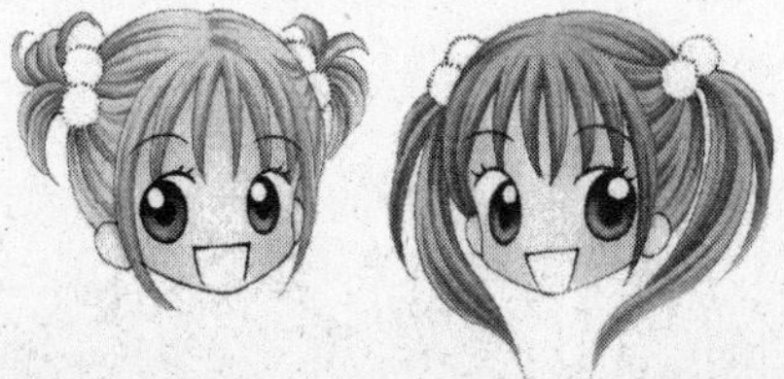

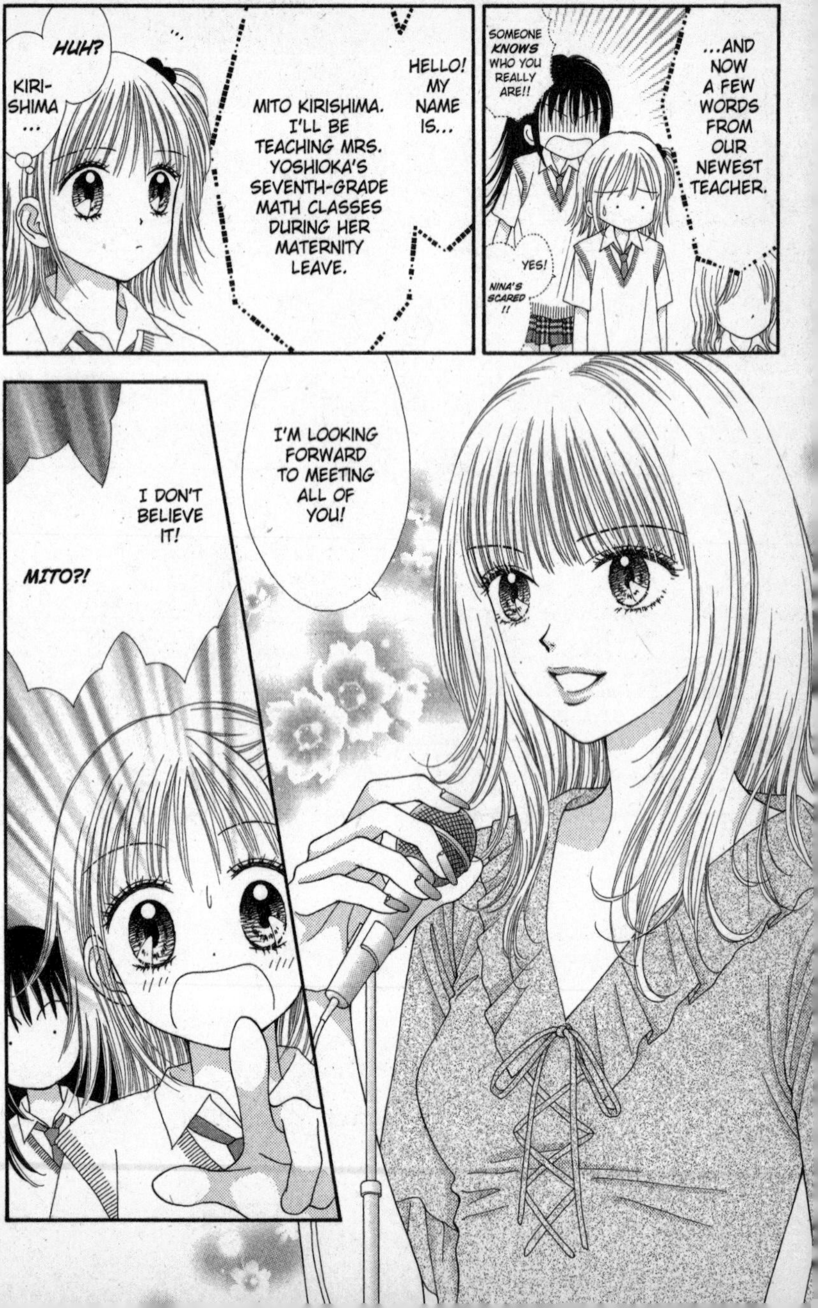
...AND NOW A FEW WORDS FROM OUR NEWEST TEACHER.
SOMEONE KNOWS WHO YOU REALLY ARE!!
YES!
NINA'S SCARED !!
HELLO! MY NAME IS...
MITO KIRISHIMA. I'LL BE TEACHING MRS. YOSHIOKA'S SEVENTH-GRADE MATH CLASSES DURING HER MATERNITY LEAVE.
HUH?
KIRI-SHIMA ...
I'M LOOKING FORWARD TO MEETING ALL OF YOU!
I DON'T BELIEVE IT!
MITO?!

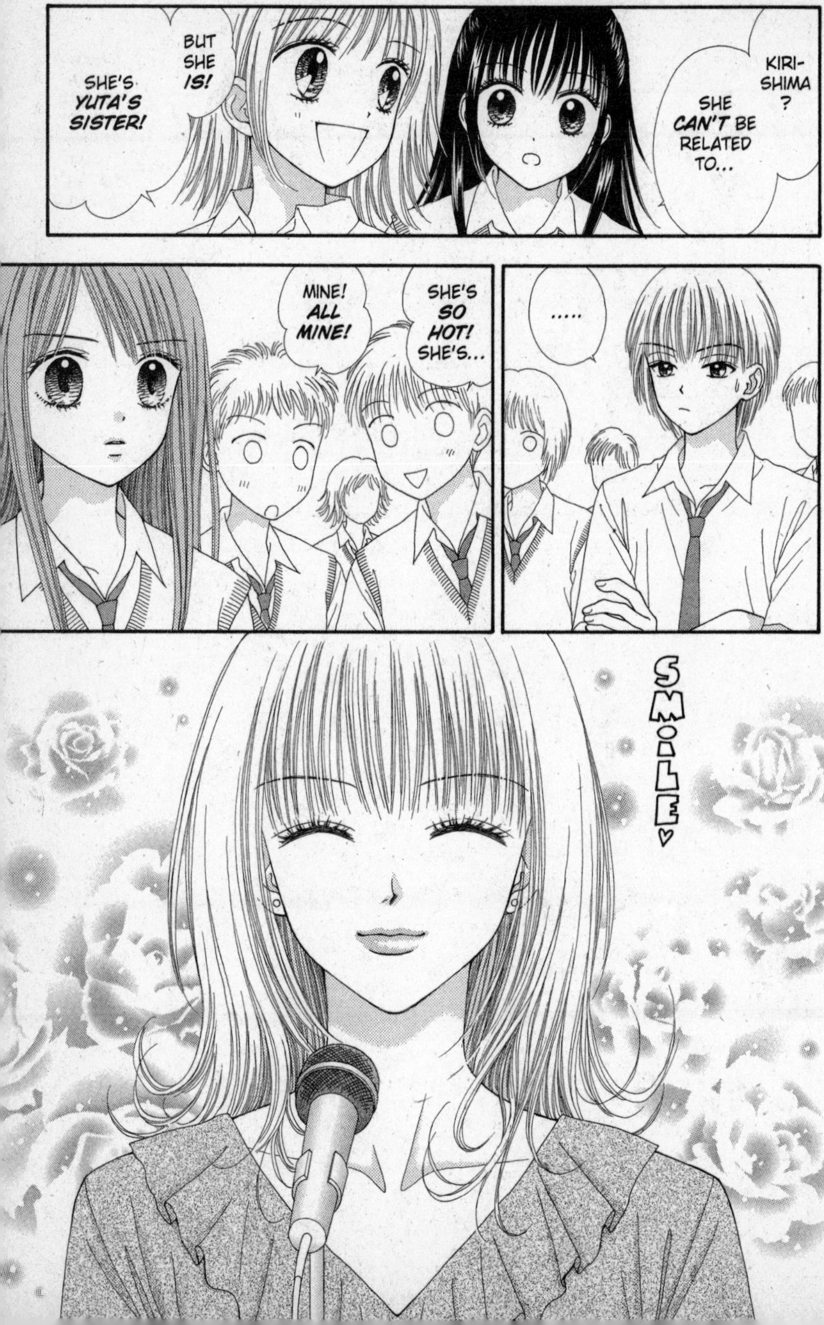
KIRI-SHIMA?
SHE CAN'T BE RELATED TO...
BUT SHE IS!
SHE'S YUTA'S SISTER!
.....
SHE'S SO HOT! SHE'S...
MINE! ALL MINE!
SMILE♥

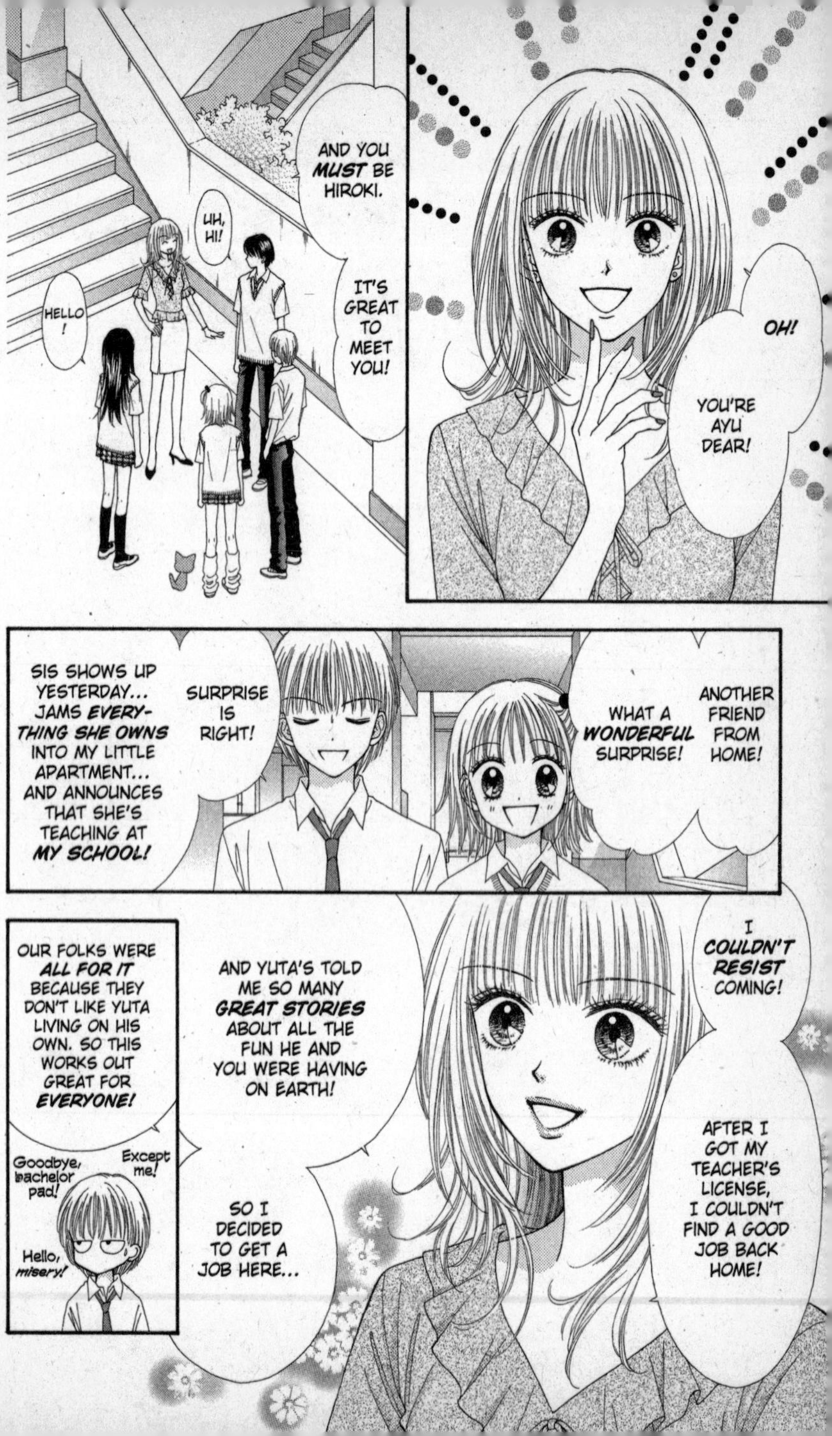
OH!
YOU'RE AYU DEAR!
AND YOU MUST BE HIROKI.
IT'S GREAT TO MEET YOU!
UH, HI!
HELLO!
ANOTHER FRIEND FROM HOME!
WHAT A WONDERFUL SURPRISE!
SURPRISE IS RIGHT!
SIS SHOWS UP YESTERDAY... JAMS EVERYTHING SHE OWNS INTO MY LITTLE APARTMENT... AND ANNOUNCES THAT SHE'S TEACHING AT MY SCHOOL!
I COULDN'T RESIST COMING!
AFTER I GOT MY TEACHER'S LICENSE, I COULDN'T FIND A GOOD JOB BACK HOME!
AND YUTA'S TOLD ME SO MANY GREAT STORIES ABOUT ALL THE FUN HE AND YOU WERE HAVING ON EARTH!
SO I DECIDED TO GET A JOB HERE...
OUR FOLKS WERE ALL FOR IT BECAUSE THEY DON'T LIKE YUTA LIVING ON HIS OWN. SO THIS WORKS OUT GREAT FOR EVERYONE!
Except me!
Goodbye, bachelor pad!
Hello, misery!

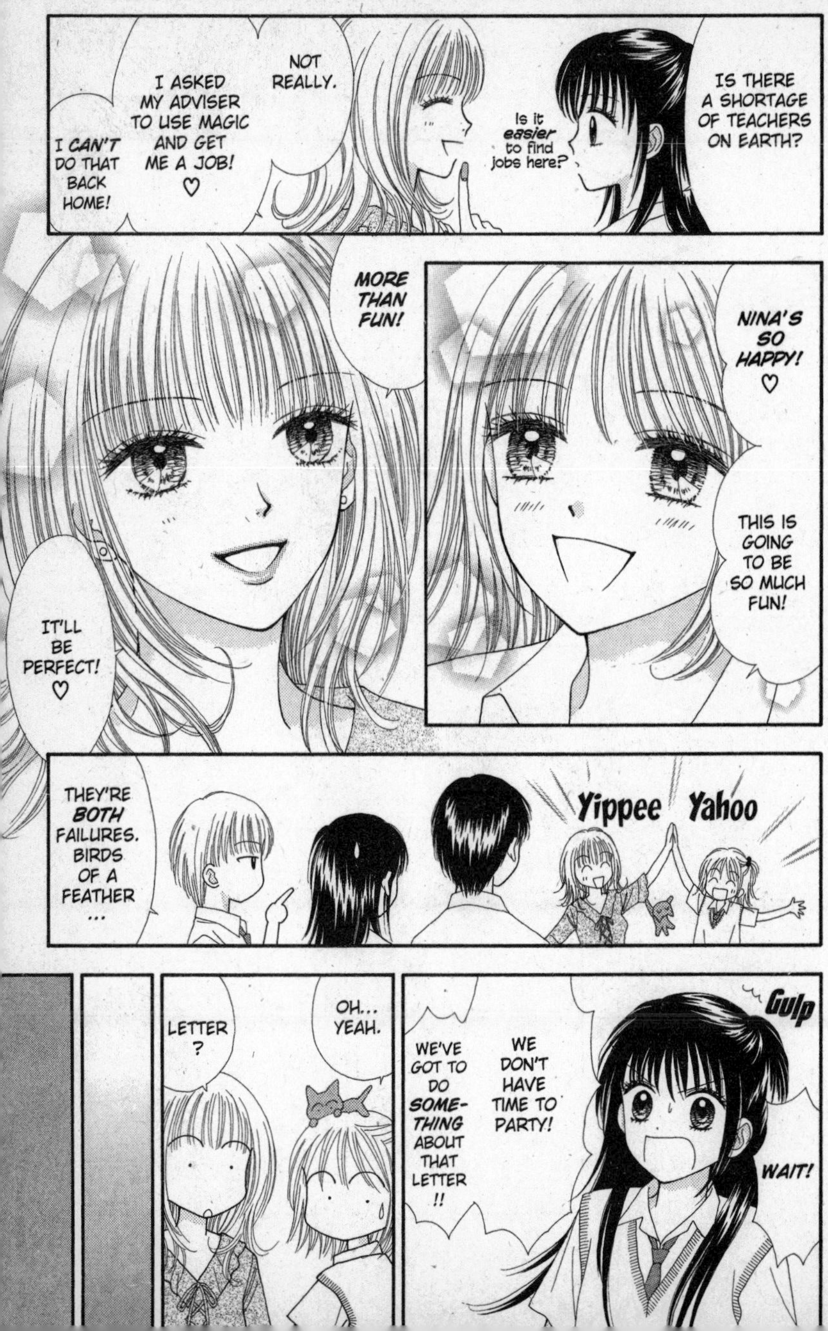
IS THERE A SHORTAGE OF TEACHERS ON EARTH?
Is it easier to find jobs here?
NOT REALLY.
I ASKED MY ADVISER TO USE MAGIC AND GET ME A JOB! ♡
I CAN'T DO THAT BACK HOME!
NINA'S SO HAPPY! ♡
THIS IS GOING TO BE SO MUCH FUN!
MORE THAN FUN!
IT'LL BE PERFECT! ♡
Yippee Yahoo
THEY'RE BOTH FAILURES. BIRDS OF A FEATHER...
Gulp
WAIT!
WE DON'T HAVE TIME TO PARTY!
WE'VE GOT TO DO SOMETHING ABOUT THAT LETTER!!
OH... YEAH.
LETTER?

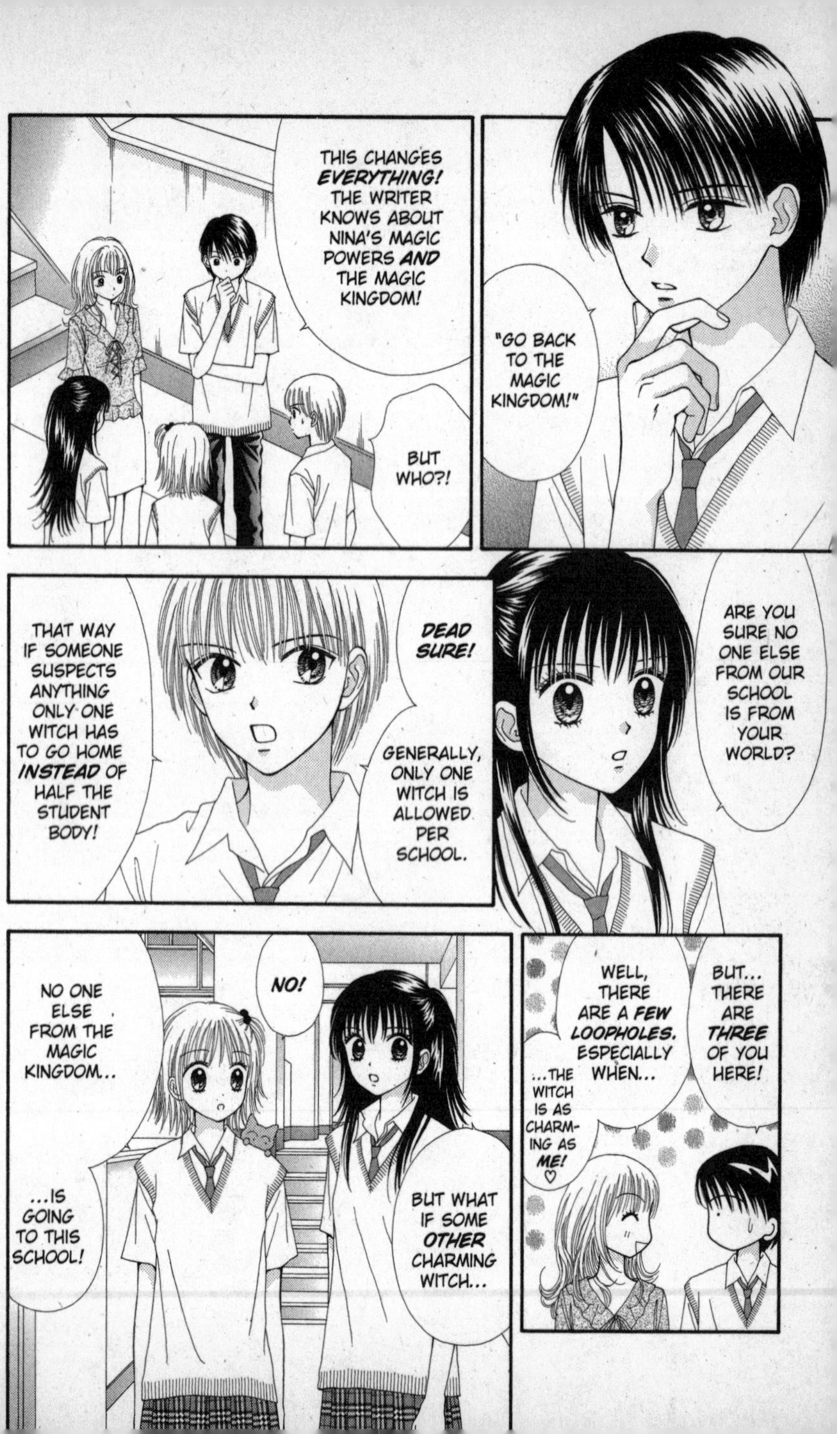
"GO BACK TO THE MAGIC KINGDOM!"
THIS CHANGES EVERYTHING! THE WRITER KNOWS ABOUT NINA'S MAGIC POWERS AND THE MAGIC KINGDOM!
BUT WHO?!
ARE YOU SURE NO ONE ELSE FROM OUR SCHOOL IS FROM YOUR WORLD?
DEAD SURE!
GENERALLY, ONLY ONE WITCH IS ALLOWED PER SCHOOL.
THAT WAY IF SOMEONE SUSPECTS ANYTHING ONLY ONE WITCH HAS TO GO HOME INSTEAD OF HALF THE STUDENT BODY!
BUT... THERE ARE THREE OF YOU HERE!
WELL, THERE ARE A FEW LOOPHOLES. ESPECIALLY WHEN...
...THE WITCH IS AS CHARMING AS ME! ♡
NO!
NO ONE ELSE FROM THE MAGIC KINGDOM...
...IS GOING TO THIS SCHOOL!
BUT WHAT IF SOME OTHER CHARMING WITCH...

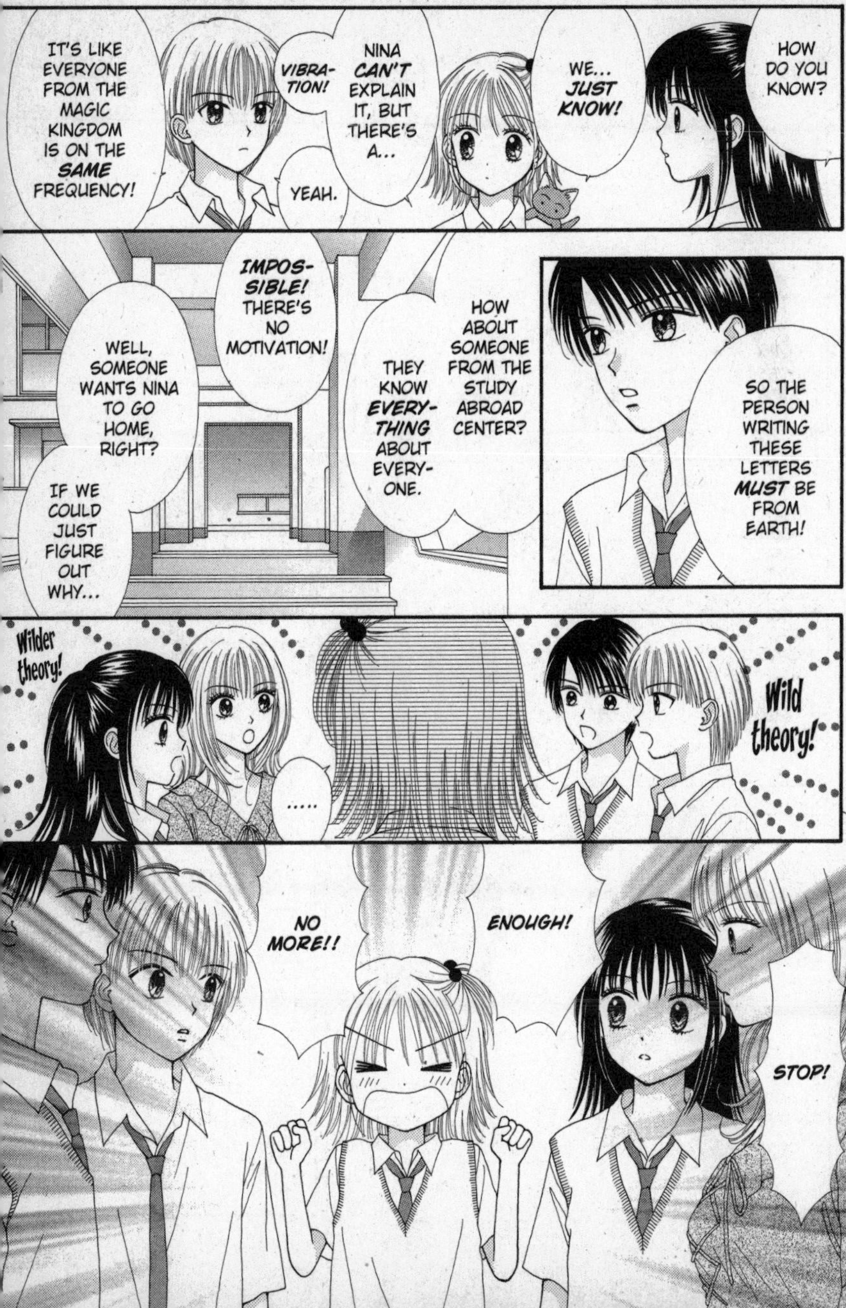
HOW DO YOU KNOW?
WE... JUST KNOW!
NINA CAN'T EXPLAIN IT, BUT THERE'S A...
VIBRATION!
YEAH.
IT'S LIKE EVERYONE FROM THE MAGIC KINGDOM IS ON THE SAME FREQUENCY!
SO THE PERSON WRITING THESE LETTERS MUST BE FROM EARTH!
HOW ABOUT SOMEONE FROM THE STUDY ABROAD CENTER?
THEY KNOW EVERYTHING ABOUT EVERYONE.
IMPOSSIBLE! THERE'S NO MOTIVATION!
WELL, SOMEONE WANTS NINA TO GO HOME, RIGHT?
IF WE COULD JUST FIGURE OUT WHY...
Wild theory!
.....
Wilder theory!
STOP!
ENOUGH!
NO MORE!!

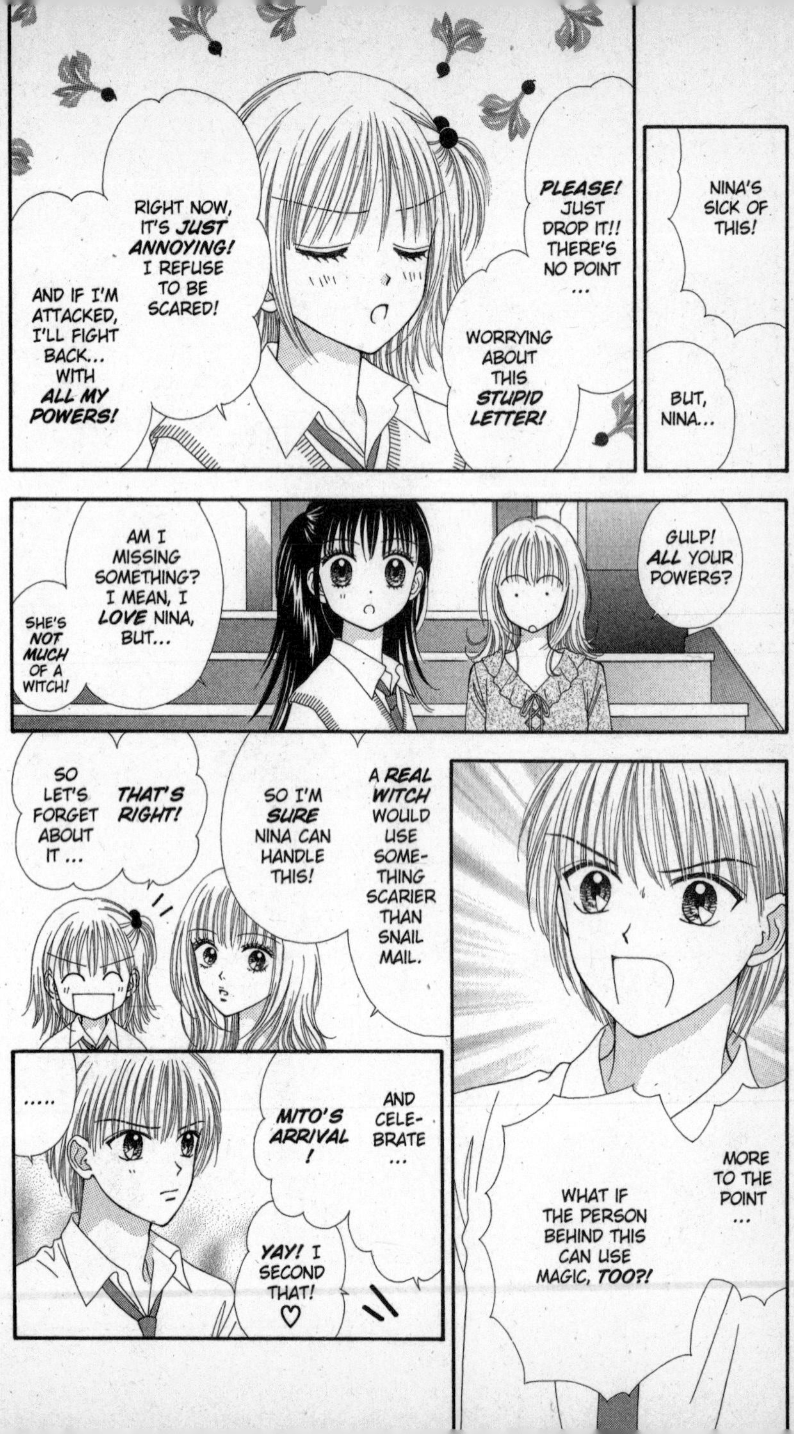

NINA'S SICK OF THIS!
BUT, NINA...
PLEASE! JUST DROP IT!! THERE'S NO POINT ...
WORRYING ABOUT THIS STUPID LETTER!
RIGHT NOW, IT'S JUST ANNOYING! I REFUSE TO BE SCARED!
AND IF I'M ATTACKED, I'LL FIGHT BACK... WITH ALL MY POWERS!
GULP! ALL YOUR POWERS?
AM I MISSING SOMETHING? I MEAN, I LOVE NINA, BUT...
SHE'S NOT MUCH OF A WITCH!
MORE TO THE POINT ...
WHAT IF THE PERSON BEHIND THIS CAN USE MAGIC, TOO?!
A REAL WITCH WOULD USE SOME-THING SCARIER THAN SNAIL MAIL.
SO I'M SURE NINA CAN HANDLE THIS!
THAT'S RIGHT!
SO LET'S FORGET ABOUT IT ...
AND CELE-BRATE ...
MITO'S ARRIVAL!
YAY! I SECOND THAT! ♡
.....

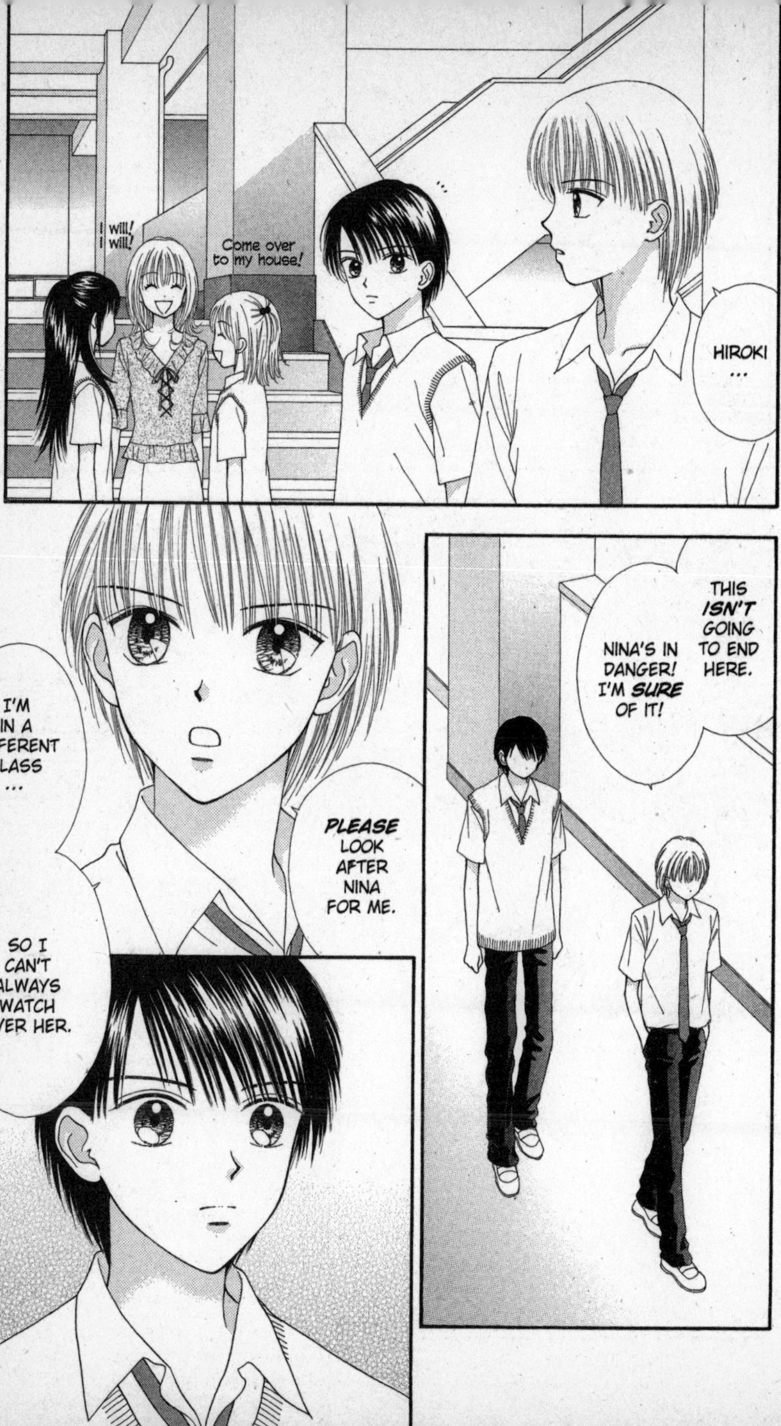
HIROKI ...
...
Come over to my house!
I will! I will!
THIS *ISN'T* GOING TO END HERE.
NINA'S IN DANGER! I'M *SURE* OF IT!
PLEASE LOOK AFTER NINA FOR ME.
I'M IN A DIFFERENT CLASS ...
SO I CAN'T ALWAYS WATCH OVER HER.

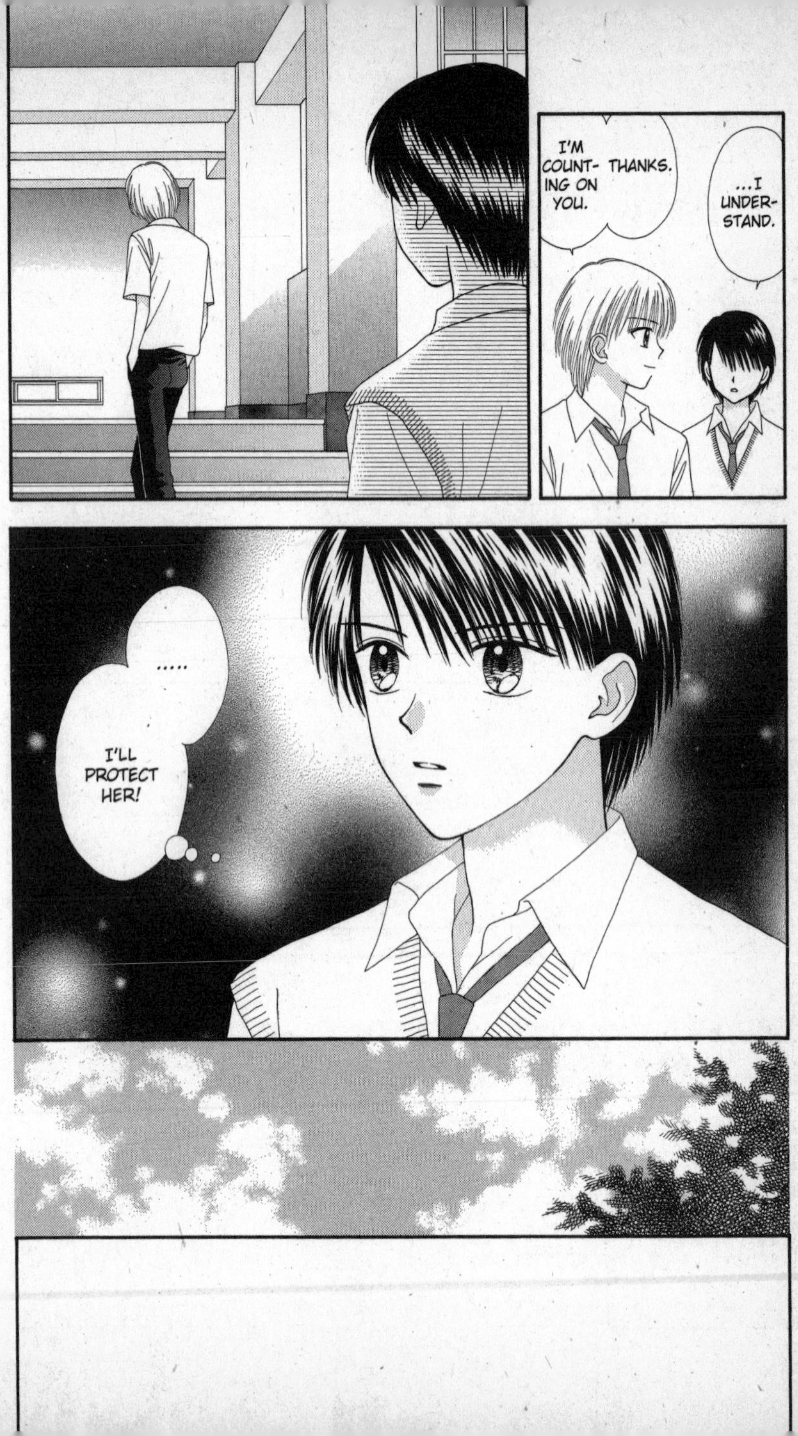
...I UNDERSTAND.
THANKS.
I'M COUNTING ON YOU.
.....
I'LL PROTECT HER!

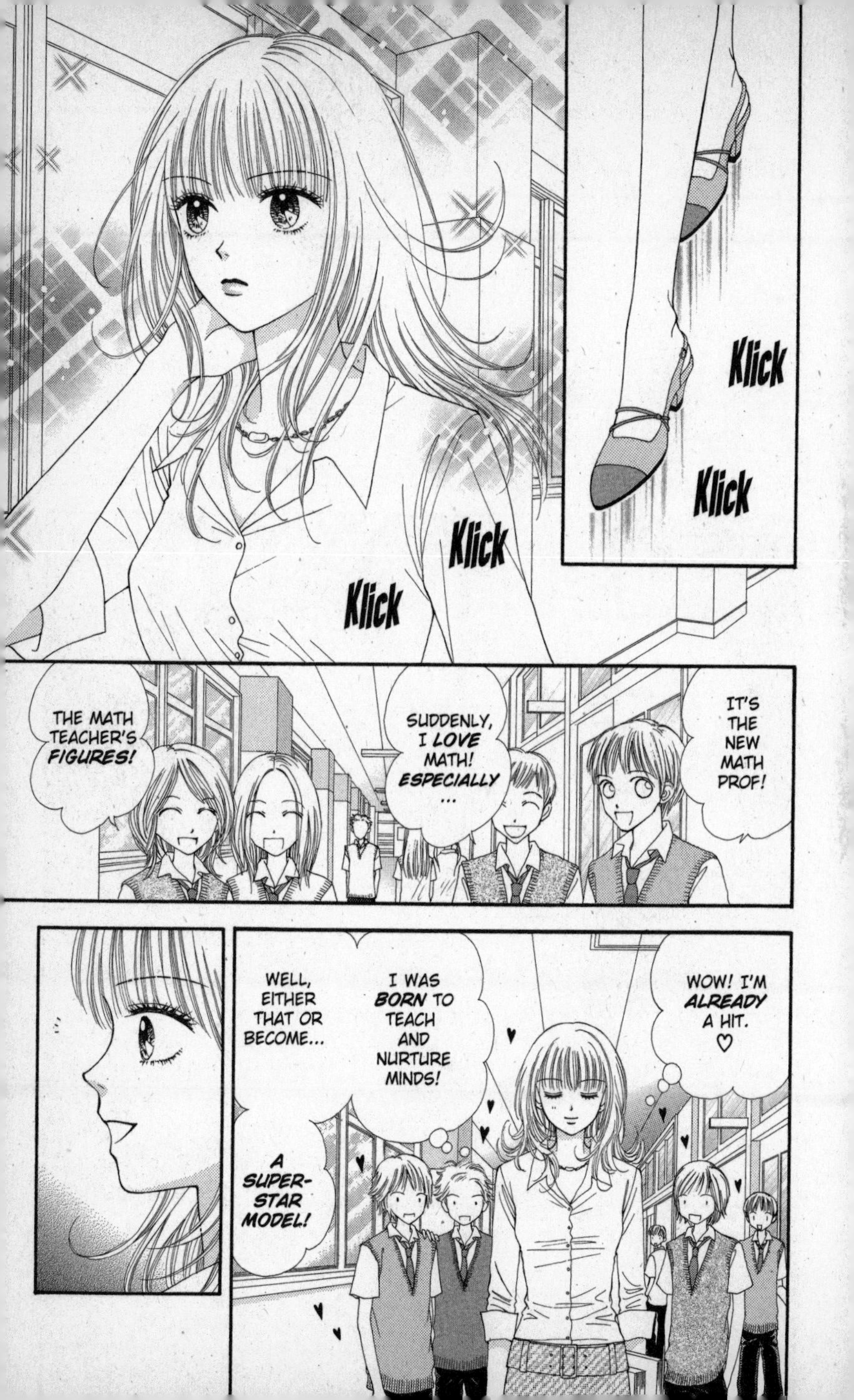
Klick
Klick
Klick
Klick
IT'S THE NEW MATH PROF!
SUDDENLY, I LOVE MATH! ESPECIALLY...
THE MATH TEACHER'S FIGURES!
WOW! I'M ALREADY A HIT. ♡
I WAS BORN TO TEACH AND NURTURE MINDS!
WELL, EITHER THAT OR BECOME...
A SUPER-STAR MODEL!

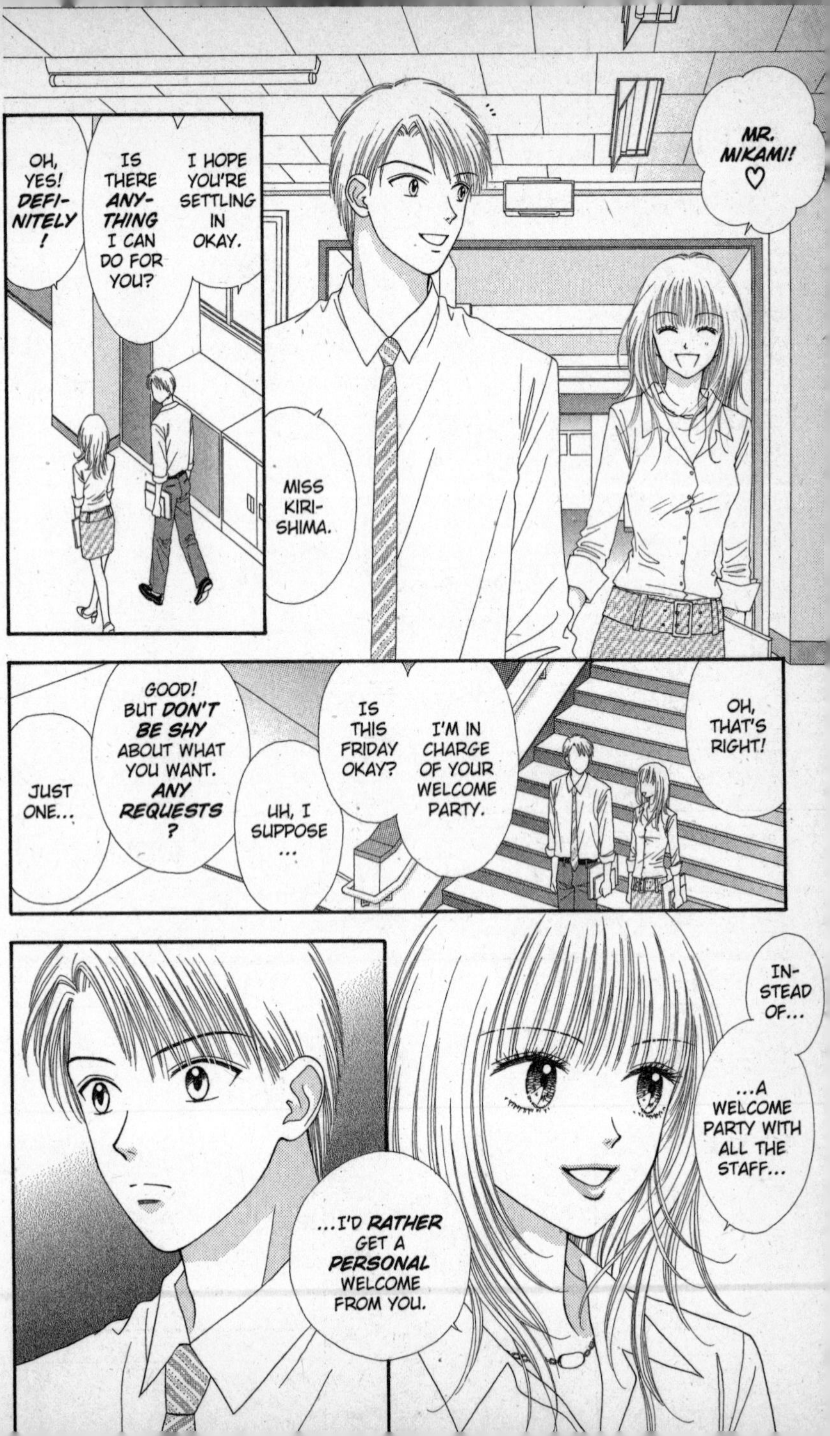
MR. MIKAMI! ♡
MISS KIRI-SHIMA.
I HOPE YOU'RE SETTLING IN OKAY.
IS THERE ANY-THING I CAN DO FOR YOU?
OH, YES! DEFI-NITELY!
OH, THAT'S RIGHT!
I'M IN CHARGE OF YOUR WELCOME PARTY.
IS THIS FRIDAY OKAY?
UH, I SUPPOSE...
GOOD! BUT DON'T BE SHY ABOUT WHAT YOU WANT. ANY REQUESTS?
JUST ONE...
IN-STEAD OF...
...A WELCOME PARTY WITH ALL THE STAFF...
...I'D RATHER GET A PERSONAL WELCOME FROM YOU.

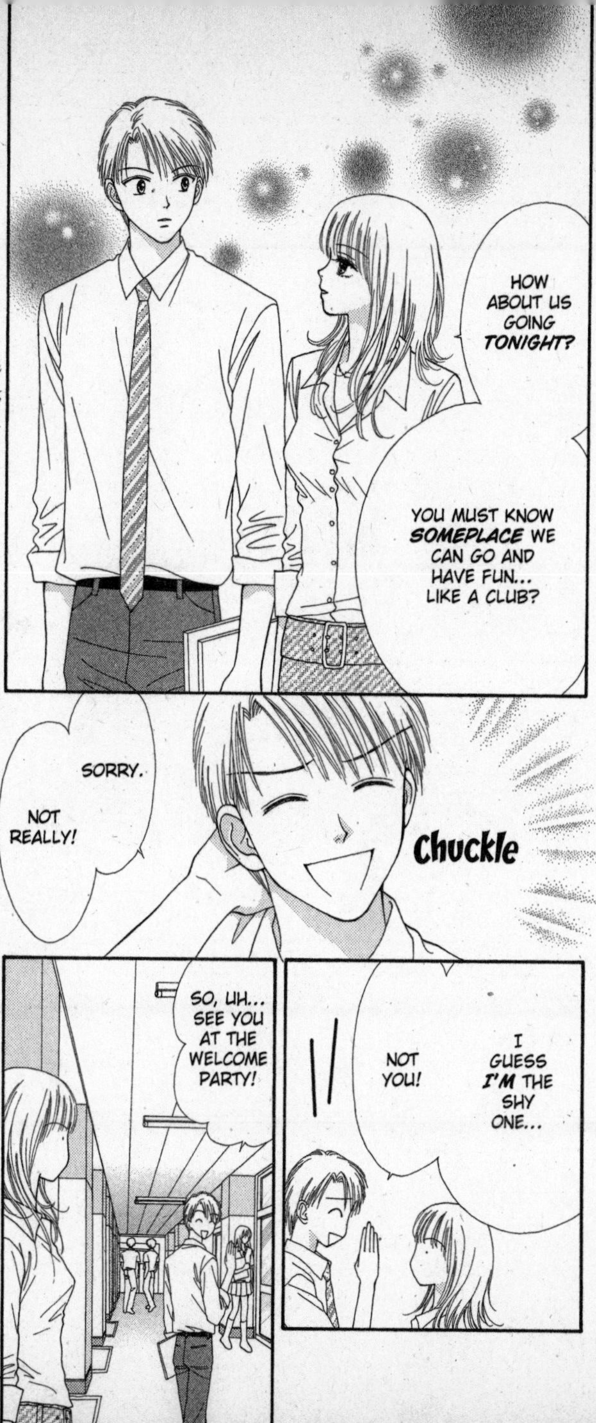
HOW ABOUT US GOING TONIGHT?
YOU MUST KNOW SOMEPLACE WE CAN GO AND HAVE FUN... LIKE A CLUB?
Chuckle
SORRY.
NOT REALLY!
I GUESS I'M THE SHY ONE...
NOT YOU!
SO, UH... SEE YOU AT THE WELCOME PARTY!

FREE TALK 9

So, how was volume three of *Ultra Maniac*?

I'd really like to hear what you think of the series. I'm especially curious about your impressions of the title art pages for each chapter. I had a lot of fun drawing them! (I especially enjoyed dreaming up "Lolita-Goth style" outfits for some of the pages.)

And if you watch the *Ultra Maniac* anime let me know about that, too. The anime is quite different from the manga. For instance, Sayaka and Mito don't show up in the anime, but cute pets (Leo, Shinosuke, and Ayu's pet, Tama) do. The Shojo Beat team is looking forward to hearing your reactions. Write to:

Ultra Maniac
c/o Shojo Beat
VIZ Media
P.O. Box 77010
San Francisco, CA
94107

P.S. See you in volume four!

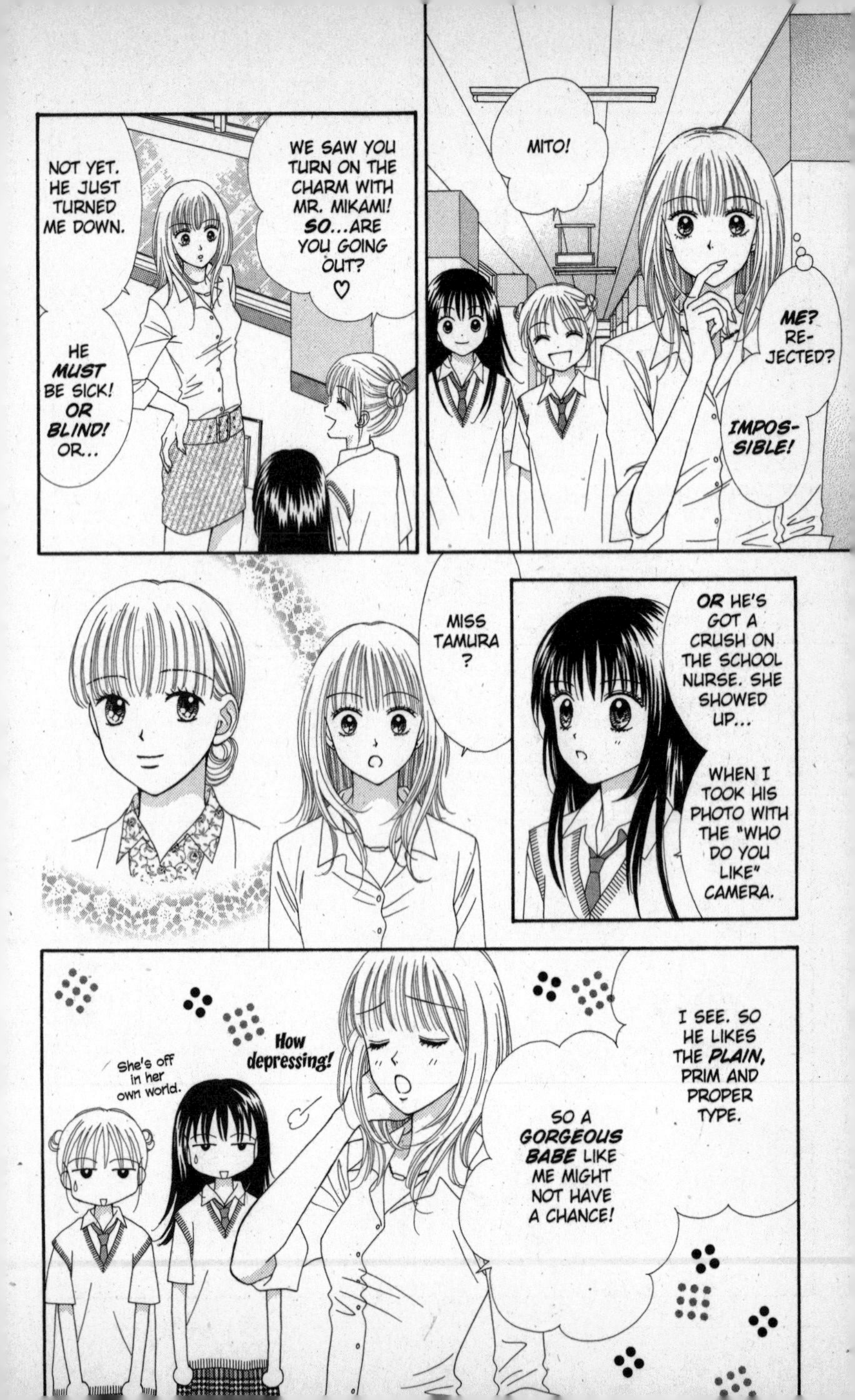
MITO!
ME? REJECTED?
IMPOSSIBLE!
WE SAW YOU TURN ON THE CHARM WITH MR. MIKAMI! SO...ARE YOU GOING OUT? ♡
NOT YET. HE JUST TURNED ME DOWN.
HE MUST BE SICK! OR BLIND! OR...
OR HE'S GOT A CRUSH ON THE SCHOOL NURSE. SHE SHOWED UP...
WHEN I TOOK HIS PHOTO WITH THE "WHO DO YOU LIKE" CAMERA.
MISS TAMURA?
I SEE. SO HE LIKES THE PLAIN, PRIM AND PROPER TYPE.
SO A GORGEOUS BABE LIKE ME MIGHT NOT HAVE A CHANCE!
How depressing!
She's off in her own world.

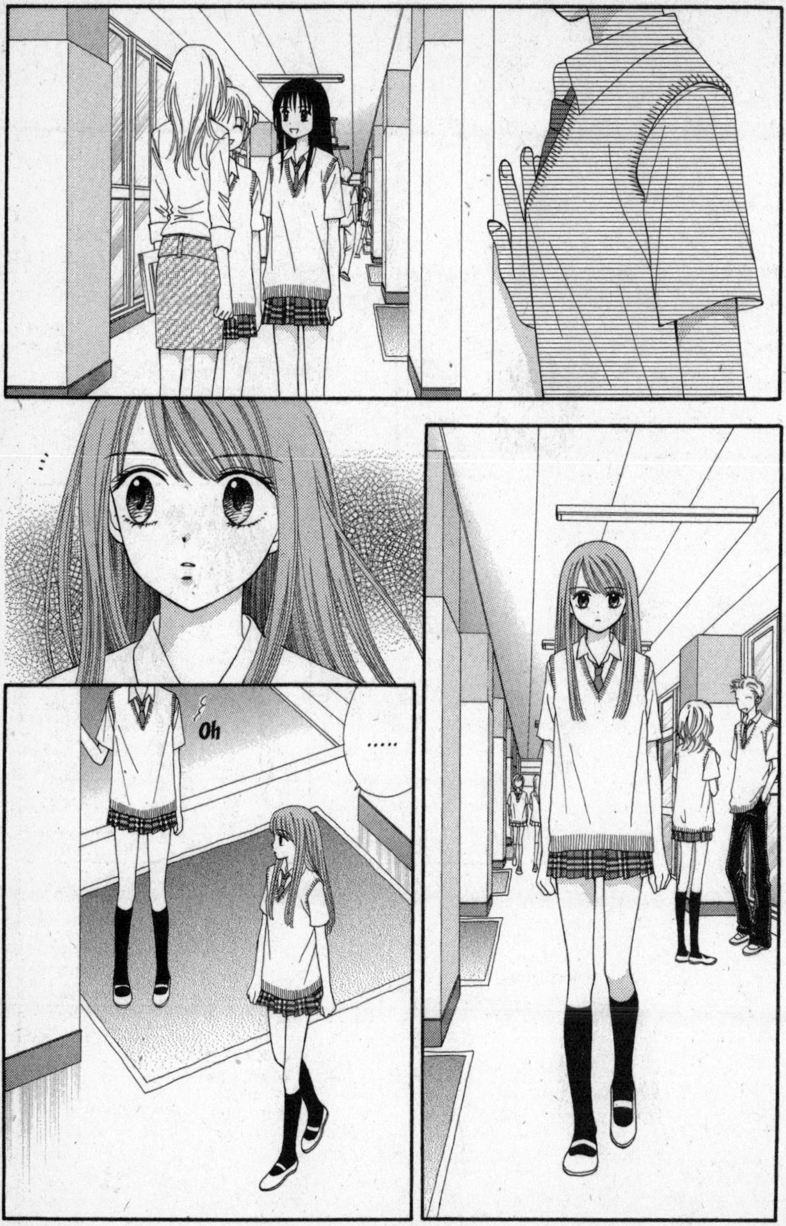
...
......
Oh

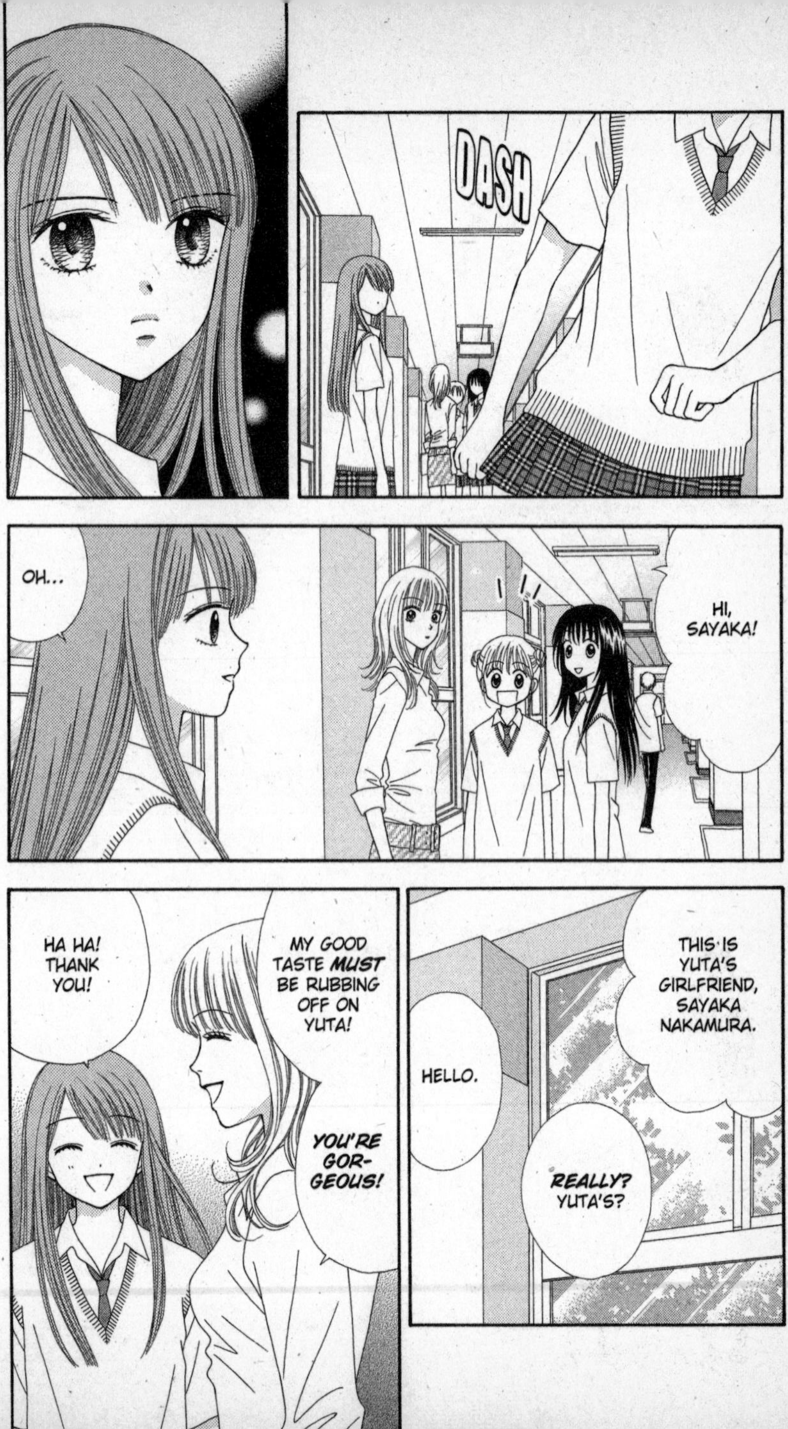
DASH
HI, SAYAKA!
OH...
THIS IS YUTA'S GIRLFRIEND, SAYAKA NAKAMURA.
HELLO.
REALLY? YUTA'S?
MY GOOD TASTE *MUST* BE RUBBING OFF ON YUTA!
HA HA! THANK YOU!
YOU'RE GOR-GEOUS!

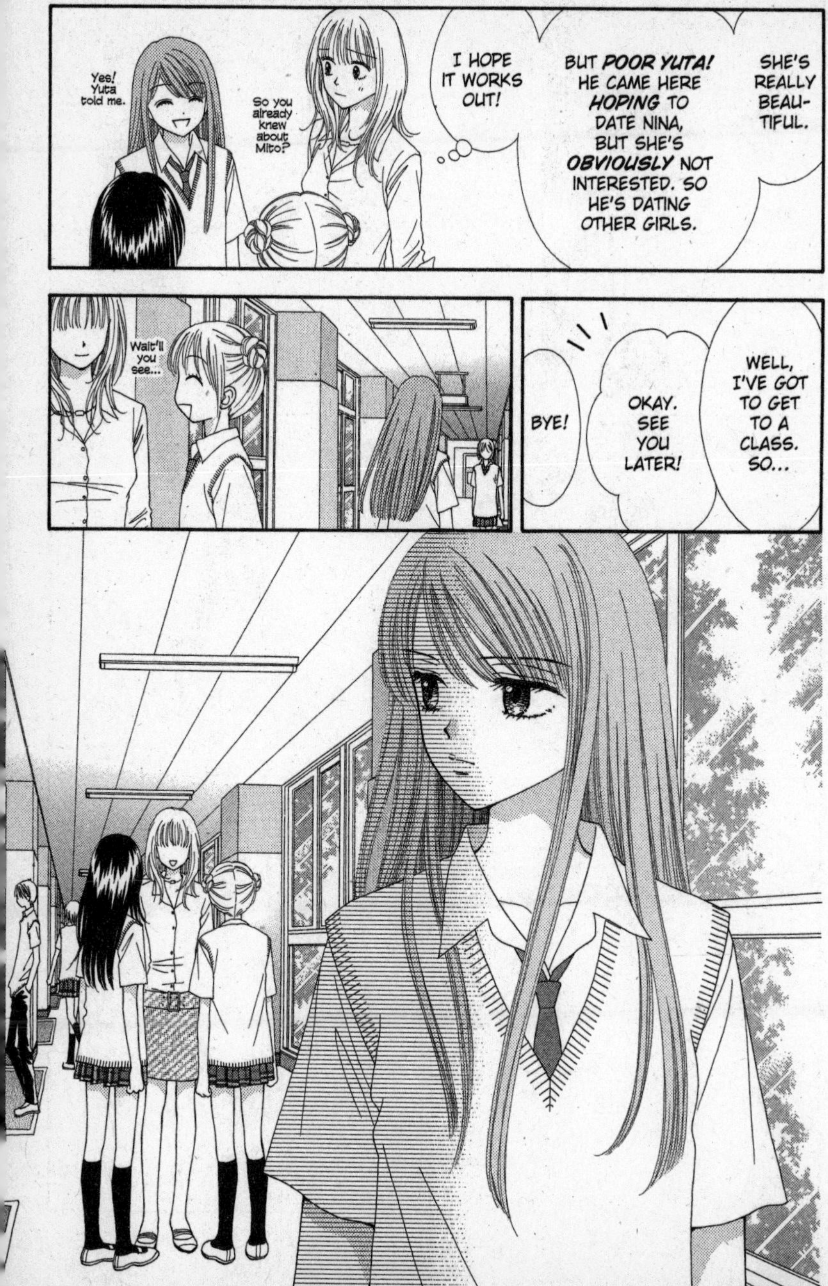
SHE'S REALLY BEAU-TIFUL.
BUT **POOR YUTA!** HE CAME HERE **HOPING** TO DATE NINA, BUT SHE'S **OBVIOUSLY** NOT INTERESTED. SO HE'S DATING OTHER GIRLS.
I HOPE IT WORKS OUT!
So you already knew about Mito?
Yes! Yuta told me.
WELL, I'VE GOT TO GET TO A CLASS. SO...
OKAY. SEE YOU LATER!
BYE!
Wait'll you see...

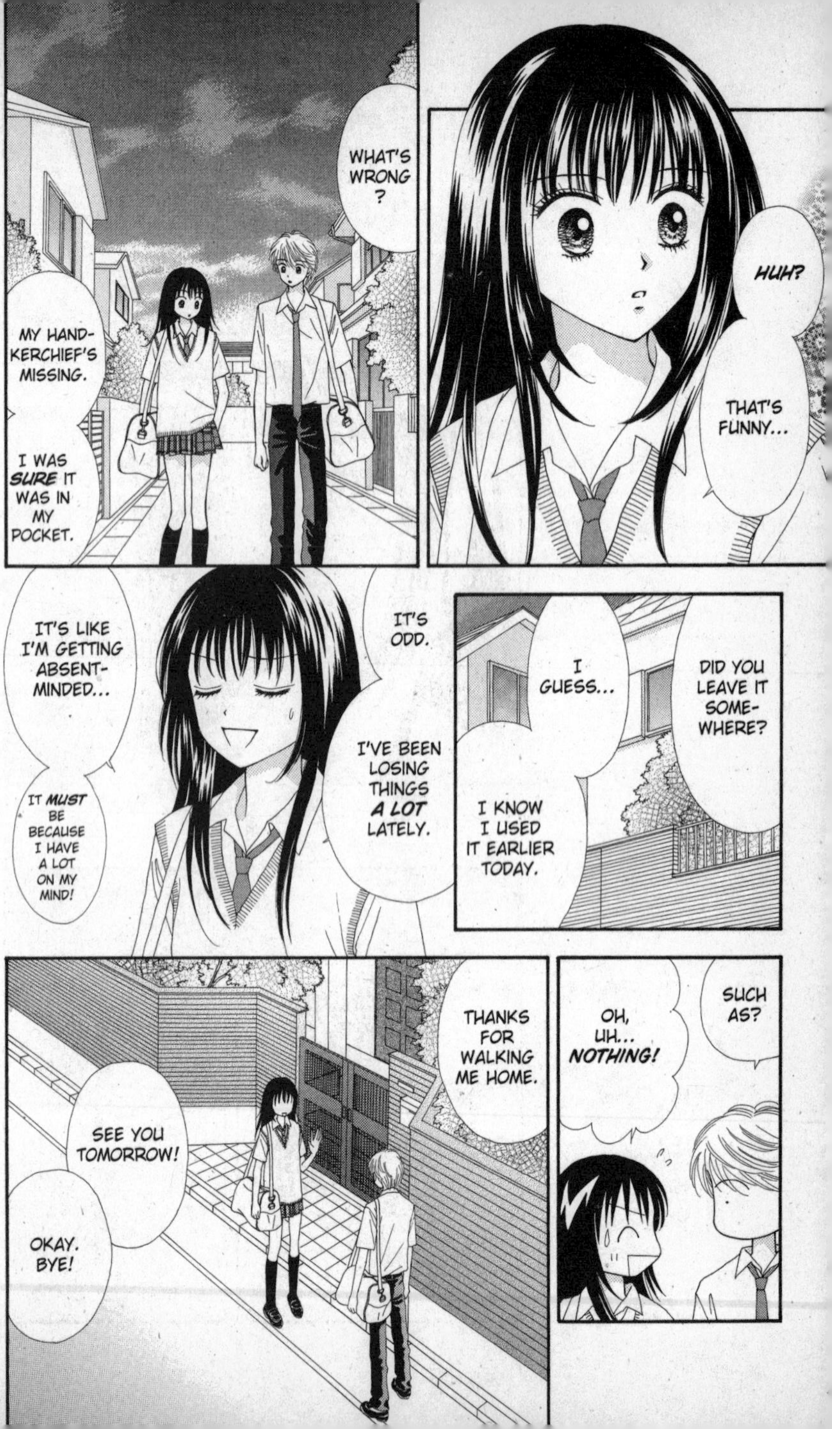
HUH?
THAT'S FUNNY...
WHAT'S WRONG?
MY HANDKERCHIEF'S MISSING.
I WAS *SURE* IT WAS IN MY POCKET.
DID YOU LEAVE IT SOMEWHERE?
I GUESS...
I KNOW I USED IT EARLIER TODAY.
IT'S ODD.
I'VE BEEN LOSING THINGS *A LOT* LATELY.
IT'S LIKE I'M GETTING ABSENT-MINDED...
IT *MUST* BE BECAUSE I HAVE A LOT ON MY MIND!
SUCH AS?
OH, UH... *NOTHING!*
THANKS FOR WALKING ME HOME.
SEE YOU TOMORROW!
OKAY. BYE!

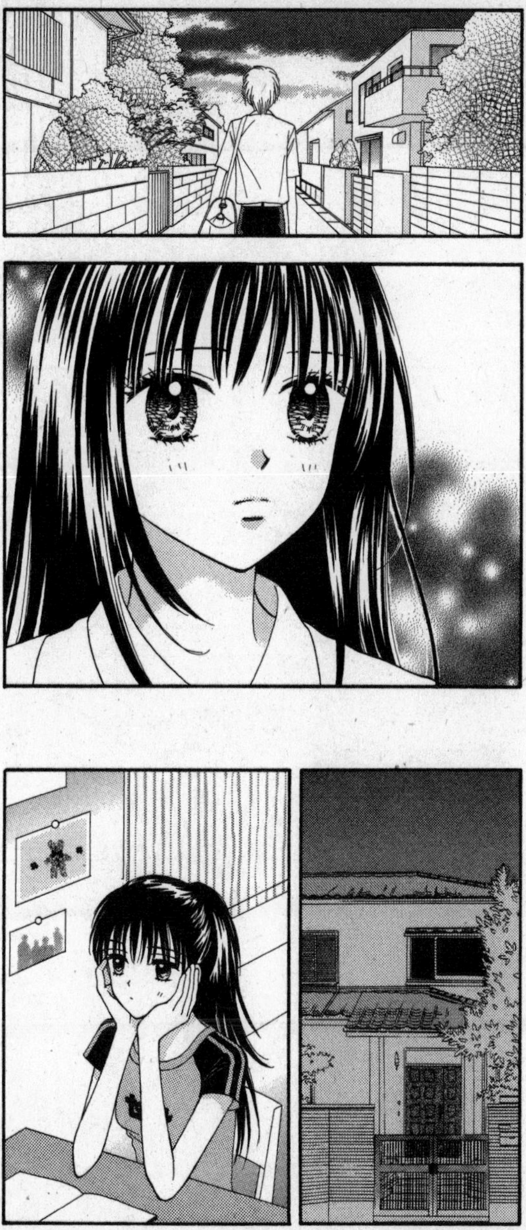

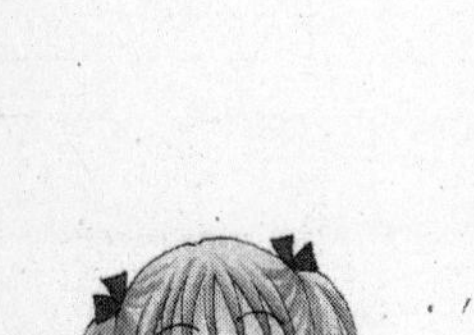

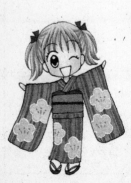

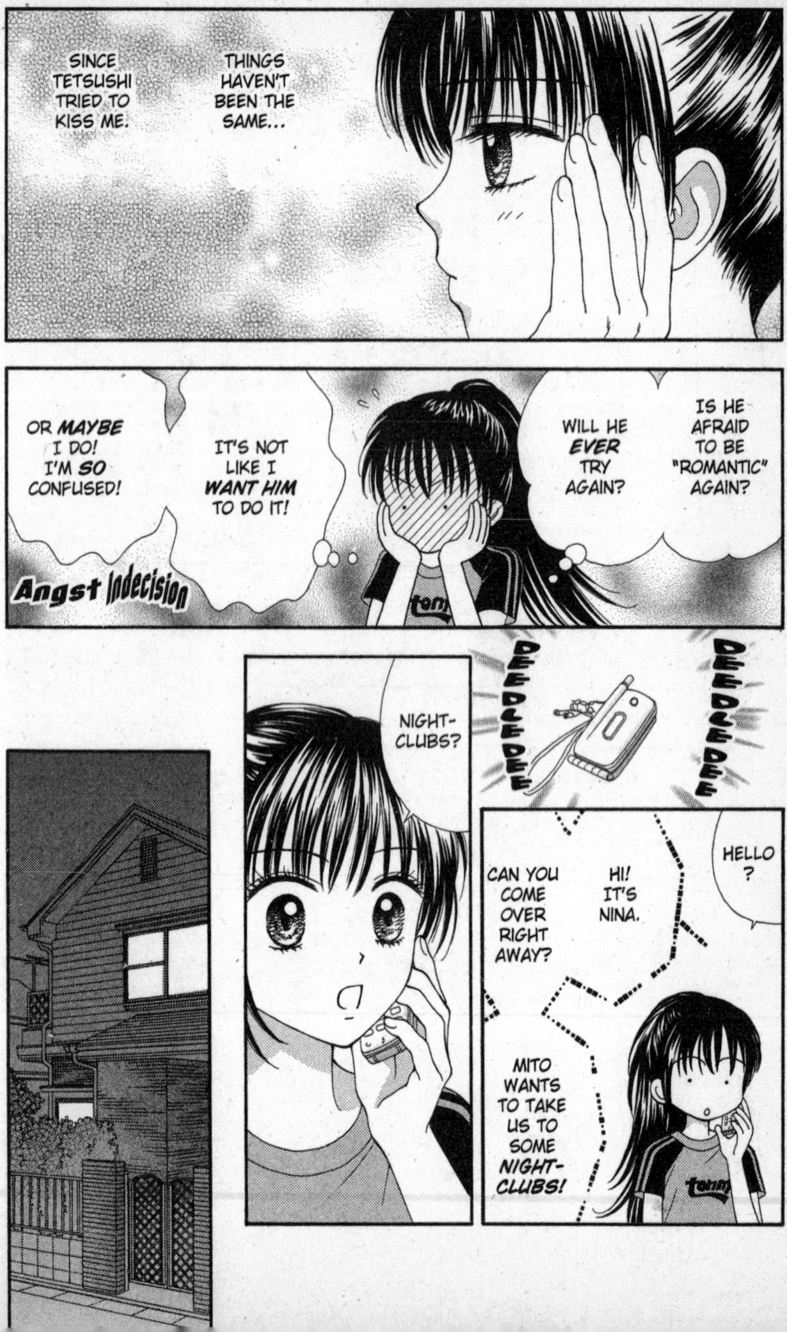
THINGS HAVEN'T BEEN THE SAME...
SINCE TETSUSHI TRIED TO KISS ME.
IS HE AFRAID TO BE "ROMANTIC" AGAIN?
WILL HE EVER TRY AGAIN?
IT'S NOT LIKE I WANT HIM TO DO IT!
OR MAYBE I DO! I'M SO CONFUSED!
Angst Indecision
DEEDLE DEE
DEEDLE DEE
HELLO?
HI! IT'S NINA.
CAN YOU COME OVER RIGHT AWAY?
MITO WANTS TO TAKE US TO SOME NIGHT-CLUBS!
NIGHT-CLUBS?

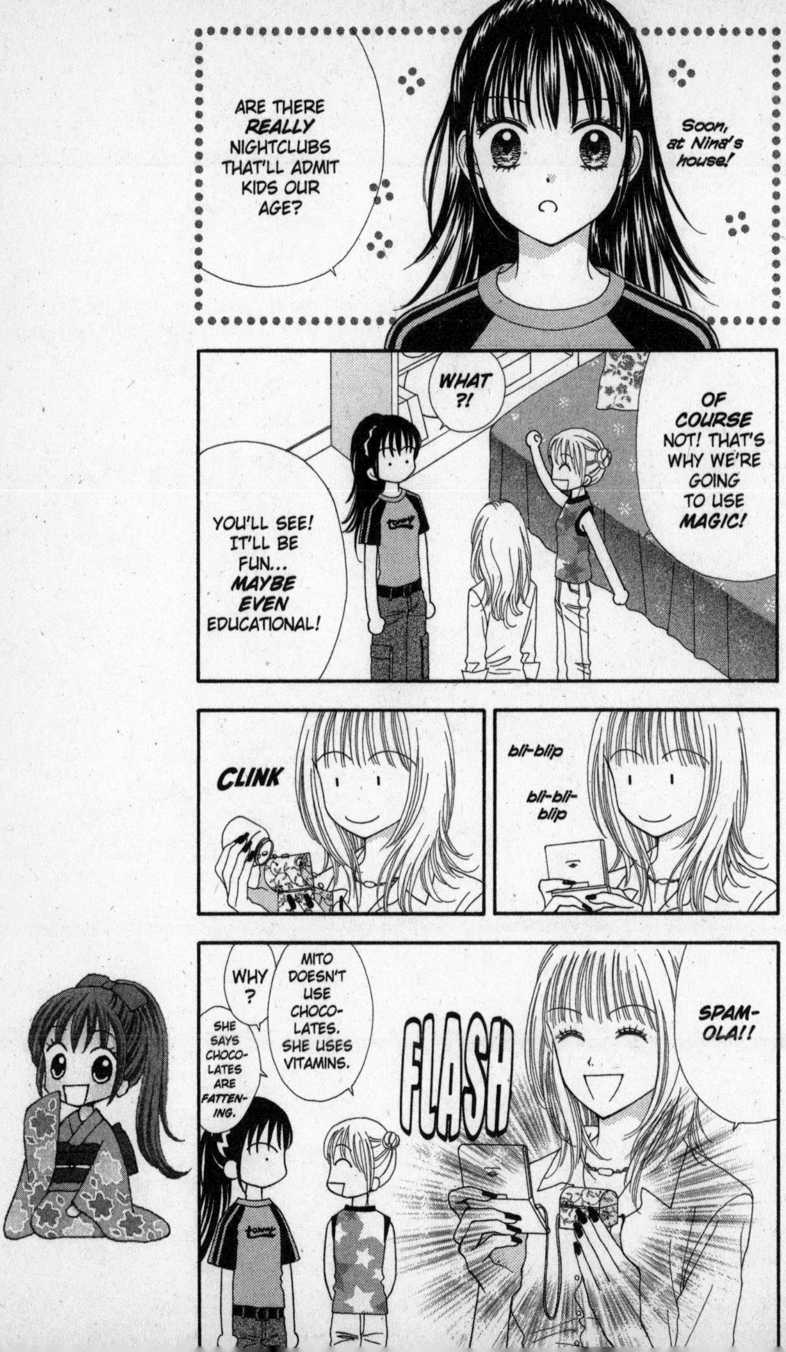
Soon, at Nina's house!
ARE THERE REALLY NIGHTCLUBS THAT'LL ADMIT KIDS OUR AGE?
OF COURSE NOT! THAT'S WHY WE'RE GOING TO USE MAGIC!
WHAT?!
YOU'LL SEE! IT'LL BE FUN... MAYBE EVEN EDUCATIONAL!
bli-blip
bli-bli-blip
CLINK
SPAM-OLA!!
FLASH
MITO DOESN'T USE CHOCO-LATES. SHE USES VITAMINS.
WHY?
SHE SAYS CHOCO-LATES ARE FATTEN-ING.

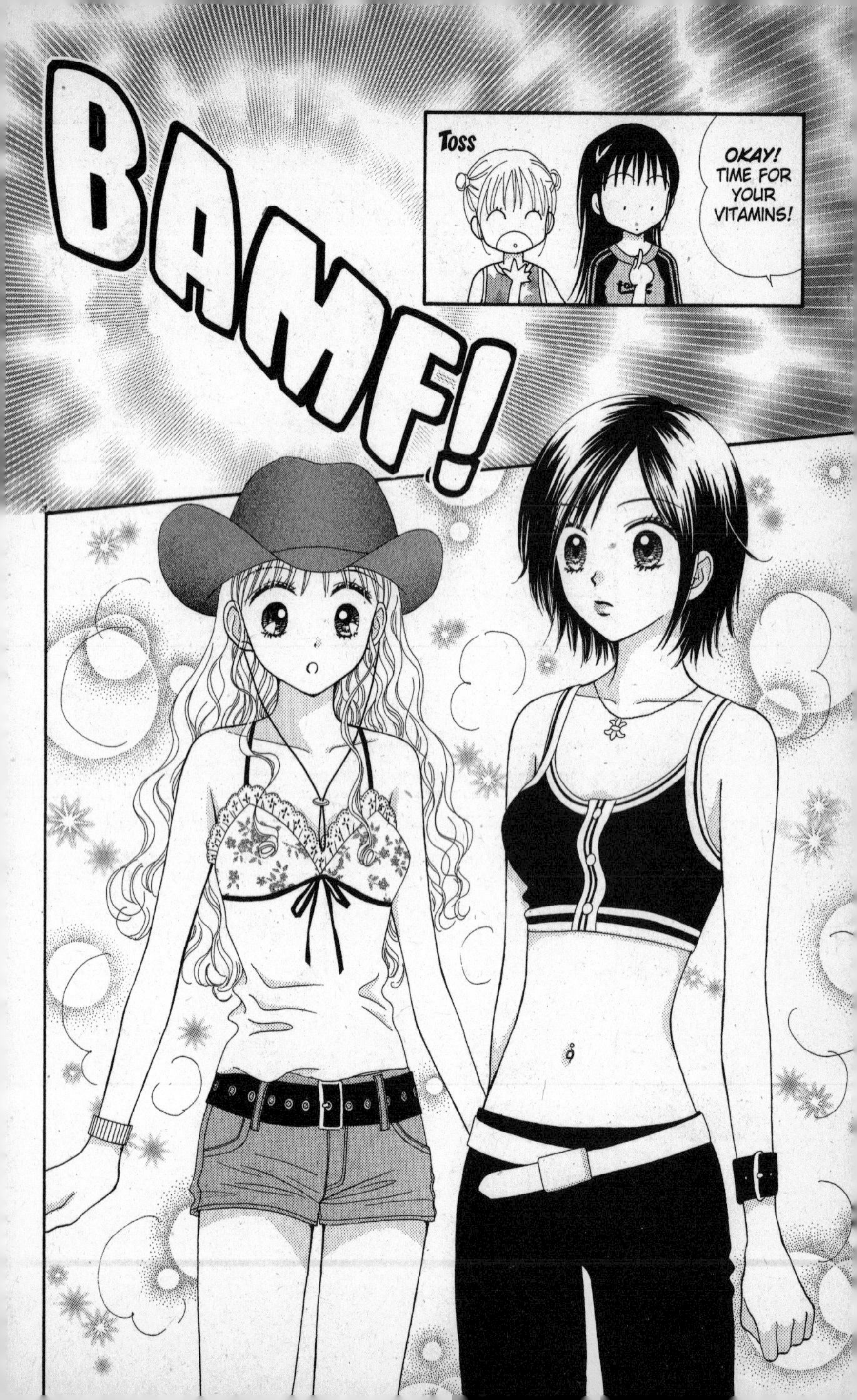
OKAY! TIME FOR YOUR VITAMINS!
Toss
BAMF!

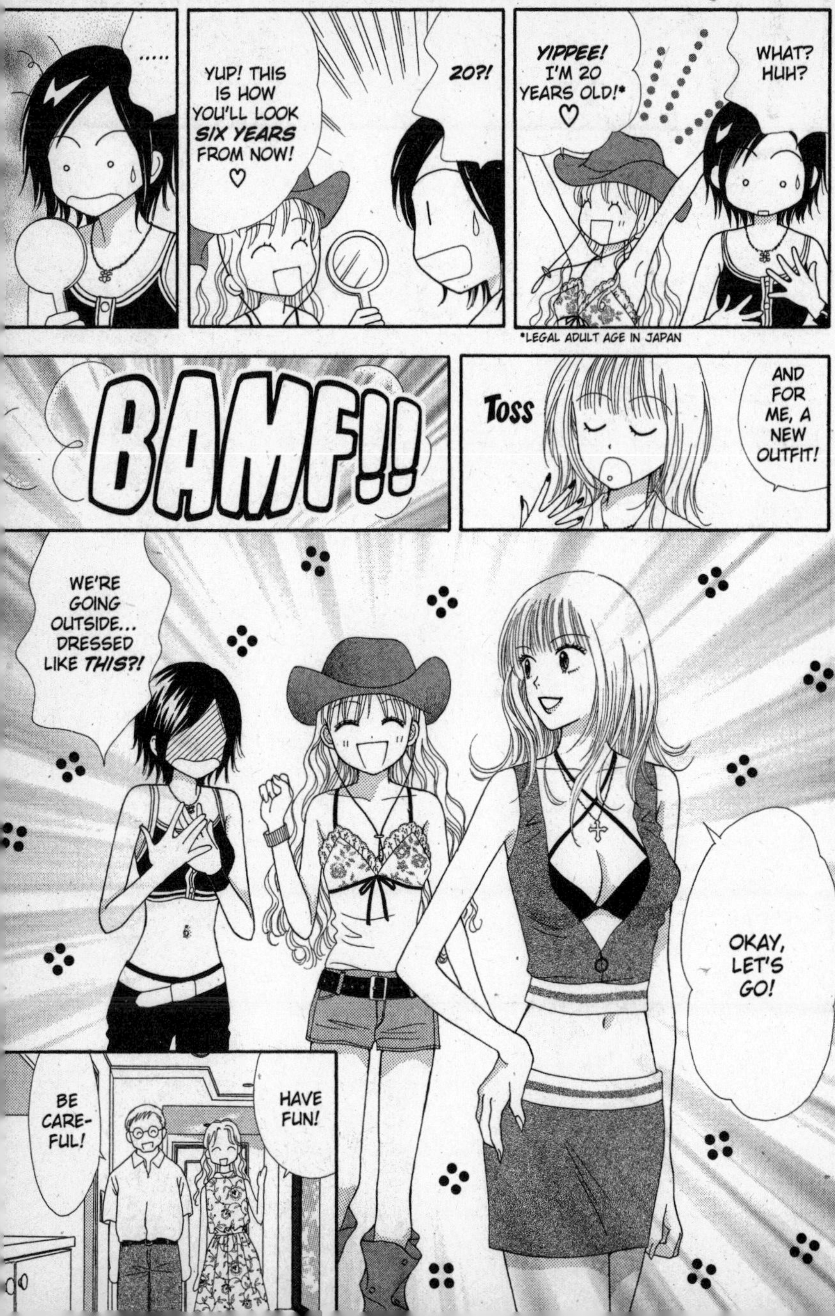
WHAT? HUH?
YIPPEE! I'M 20 YEARS OLD!* ♡
20?!
YUP! THIS IS HOW YOU'LL LOOK SIX YEARS FROM NOW! ♡
.....
AND FOR ME, A NEW OUTFIT!
Toss
BAMF!!
OKAY, LET'S GO!
WE'RE GOING OUTSIDE... DRESSED LIKE THIS?!
HAVE FUN!
BE CARE-FUL!
*LEGAL ADULT AGE IN JAPAN

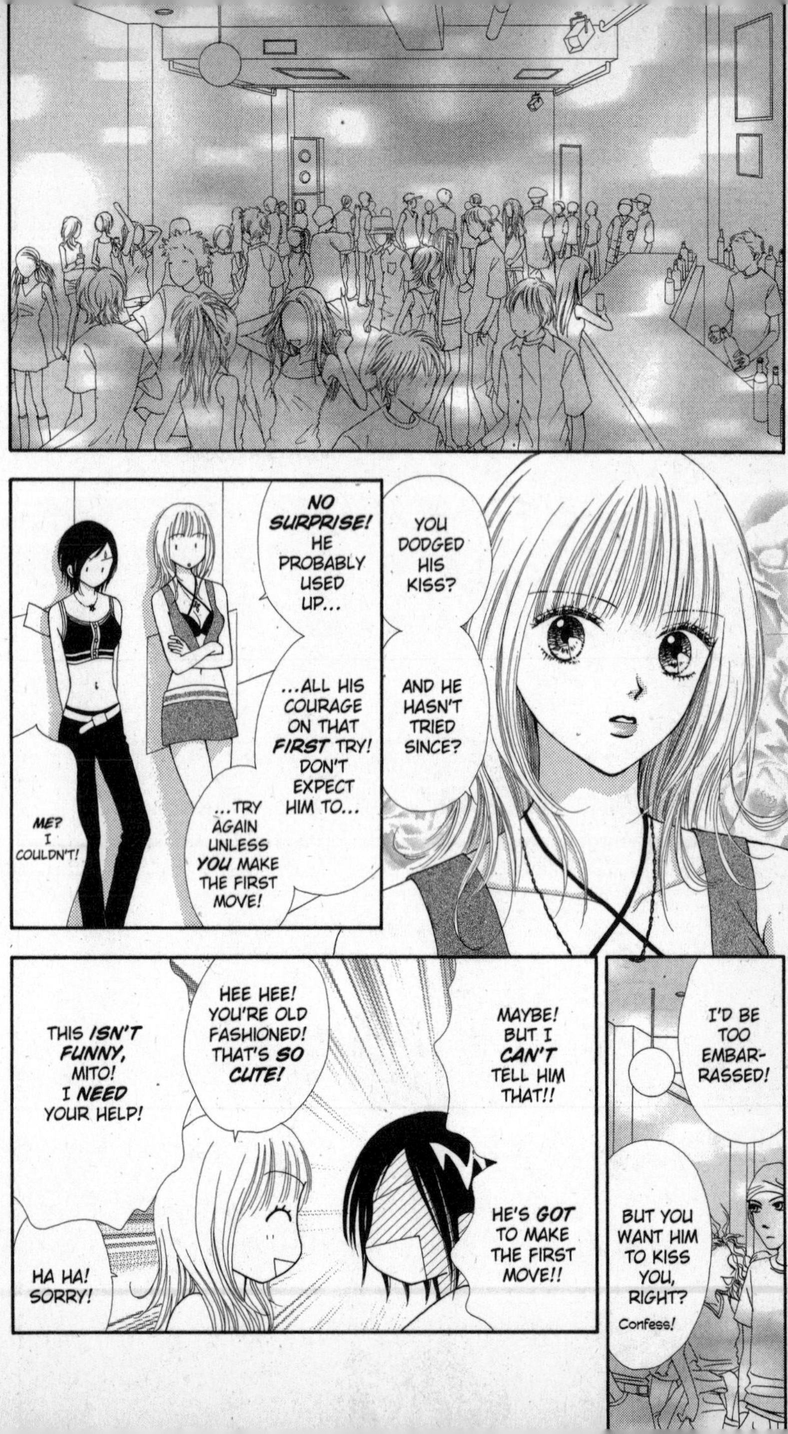
YOU DODGED HIS KISS?
AND HE HASN'T TRIED SINCE?
NO SURPRISE! HE PROBABLY USED UP...
...ALL HIS COURAGE ON THAT FIRST TRY! DON'T EXPECT HIM TO...
...TRY AGAIN UNLESS YOU MAKE THE FIRST MOVE!
ME? I COULDN'T!
I'D BE TOO EMBAR-RASSED!
BUT YOU WANT HIM TO KISS YOU, RIGHT?
Confess!
MAYBE! BUT I CAN'T TELL HIM THAT!!
HEE HEE! YOU'RE OLD FASHIONED! THAT'S SO CUTE!
THIS ISN'T FUNNY, MITO! I NEED YOUR HELP!
HE'S GOT TO MAKE THE FIRST MOVE!!
HA HA! SORRY!

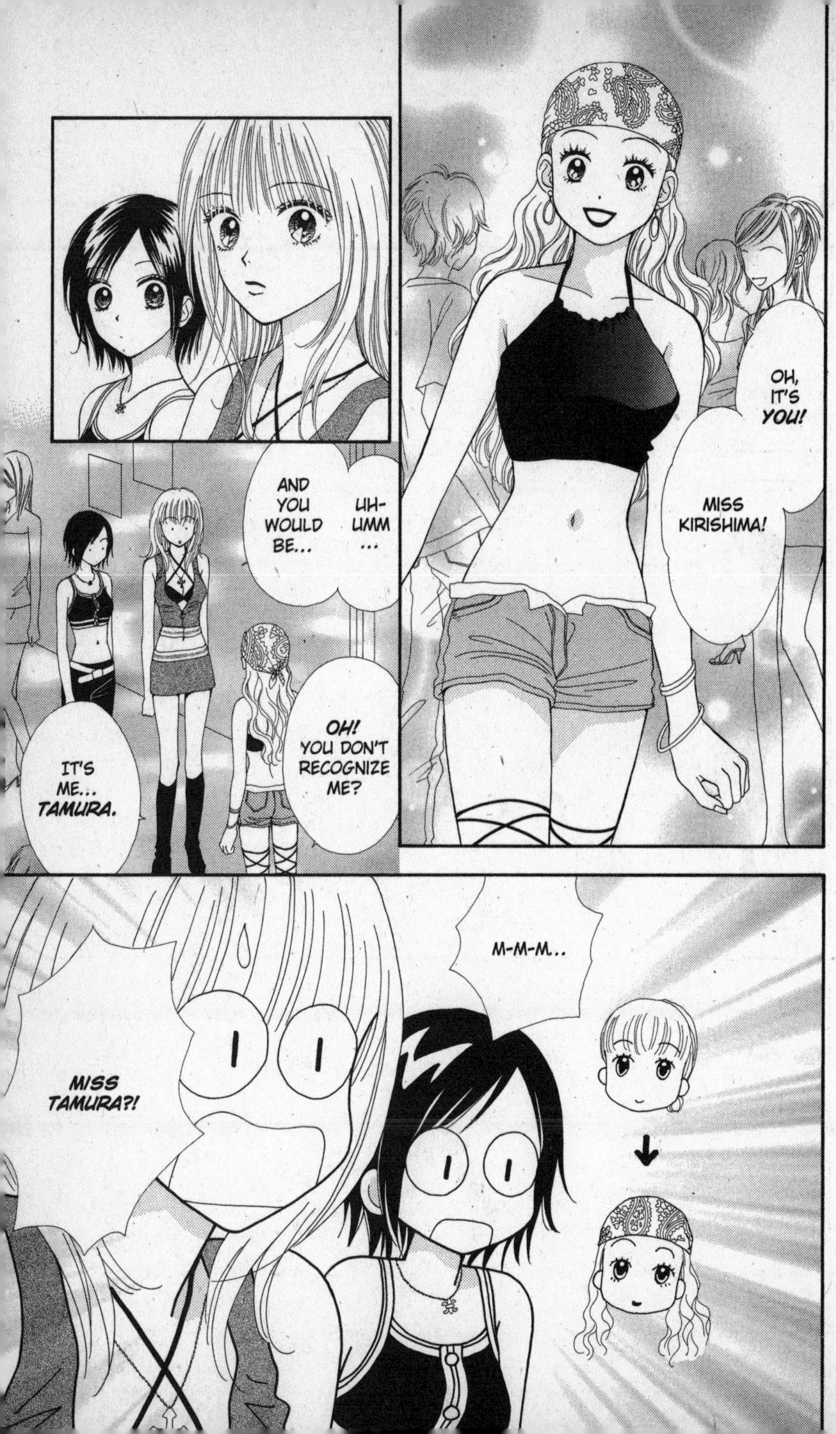
OH, IT'S YOU!
MISS KIRISHIMA!
UH-UMM...
AND YOU WOULD BE...
OH! YOU DON'T RECOGNIZE ME?
IT'S ME... TAMURA.
M-M-M...
MISS TAMURA?!

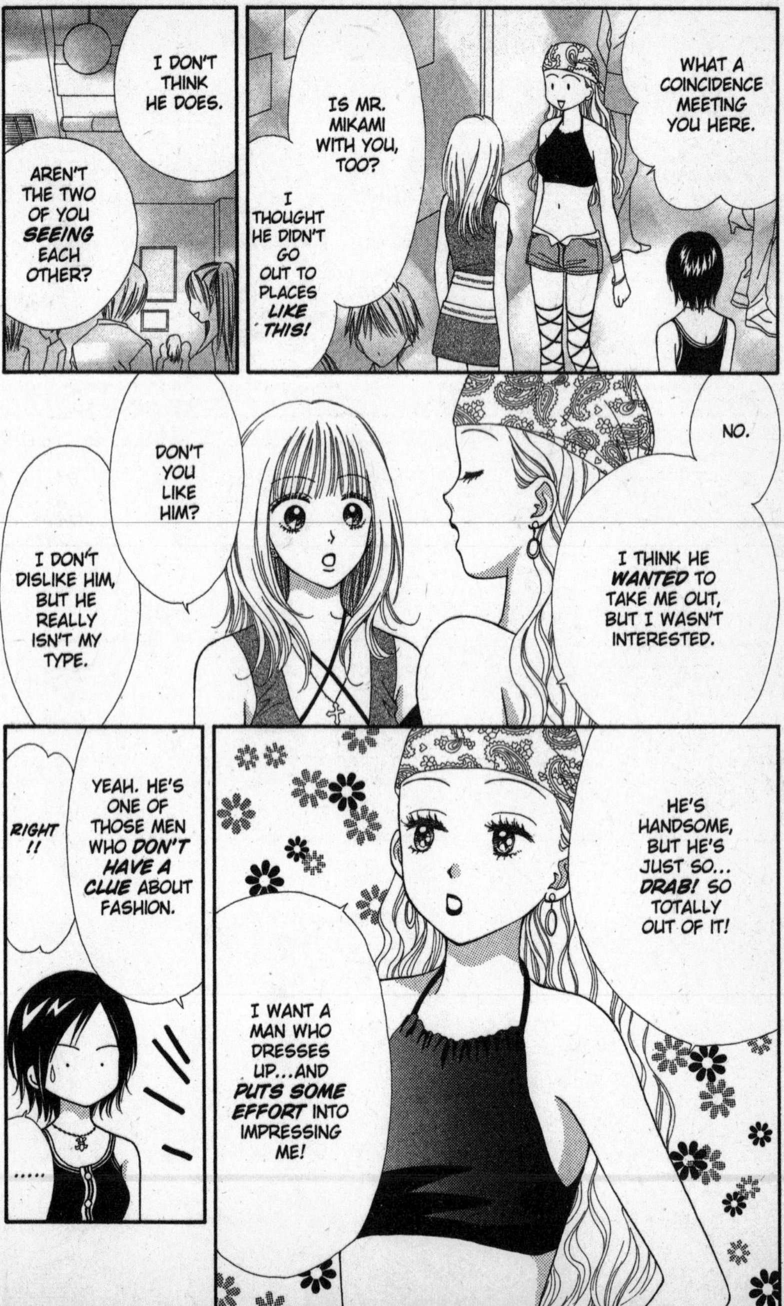
WHAT A COINCIDENCE MEETING YOU HERE.
IS MR. MIKAMI WITH YOU, TOO?
I THOUGHT HE DIDN'T GO OUT TO PLACES LIKE THIS!
I DON'T THINK HE DOES.
AREN'T THE TWO OF YOU SEEING EACH OTHER?
NO.
I THINK HE WANTED TO TAKE ME OUT, BUT I WASN'T INTERESTED.
DON'T YOU LIKE HIM?
I DON'T DISLIKE HIM, BUT HE REALLY ISN'T MY TYPE.
HE'S HANDSOME, BUT HE'S JUST SO... DRAB! SO TOTALLY OUT OF IT!
I WANT A MAN WHO DRESSES UP...AND PUTS SOME EFFORT INTO IMPRESSING ME!
YEAH. HE'S ONE OF THOSE MEN WHO DON'T HAVE A CLUE ABOUT FASHION.
RIGHT!!
.....

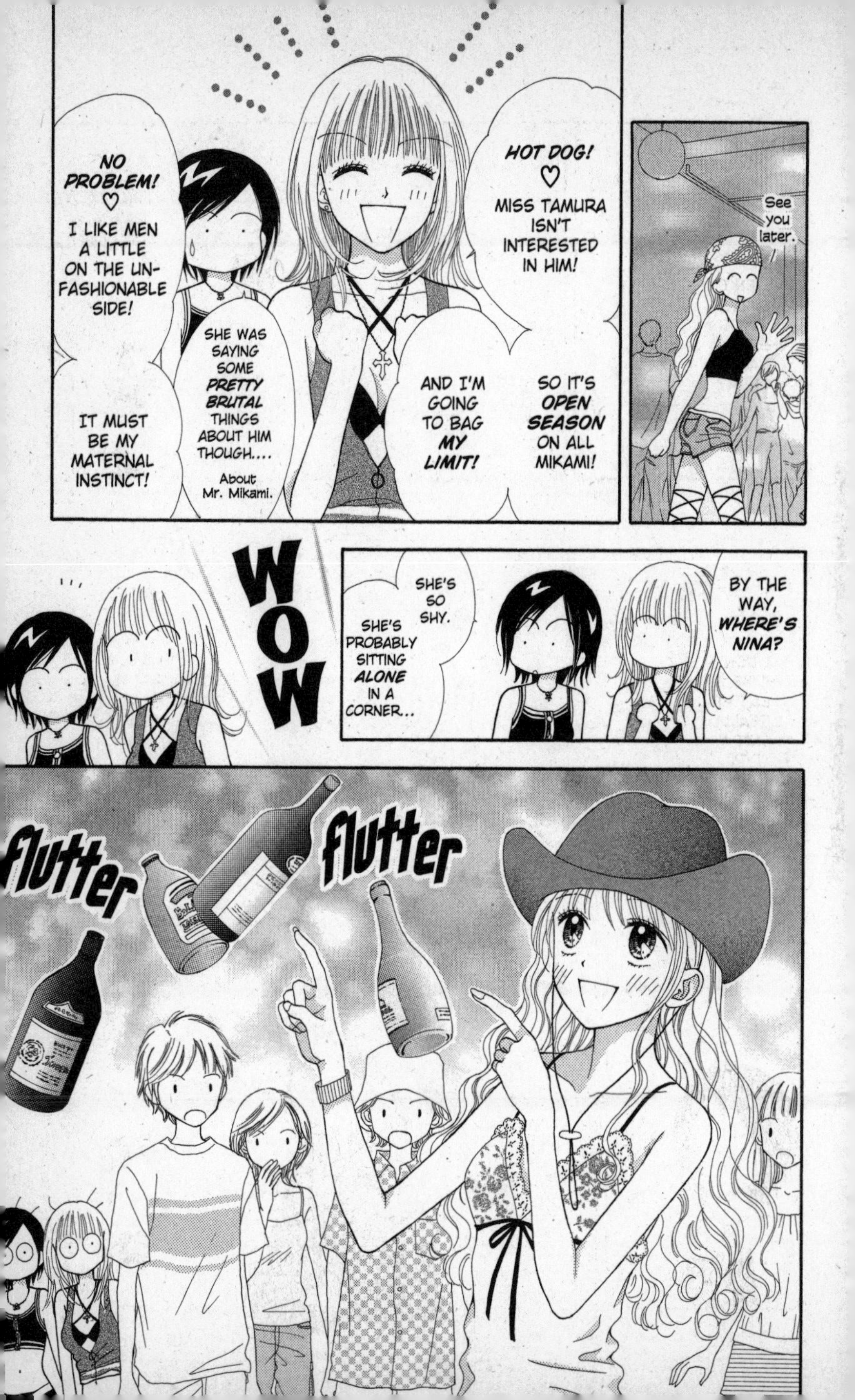
See you later.
HOT DOG! ♡ MISS TAMURA ISN'T INTERESTED IN HIM!
NO PROBLEM! ♡ I LIKE MEN A LITTLE ON THE UN-FASHIONABLE SIDE!
SO IT'S OPEN SEASON ON ALL MIKAMI!
AND I'M GOING TO BAG MY LIMIT!
SHE WAS SAYING SOME PRETTY BRUTAL THINGS ABOUT HIM THOUGH....
About Mr. Mikami.
IT MUST BE MY MATERNAL INSTINCT!
BY THE WAY, WHERE'S NINA?
SHE'S SO SHY.
SHE'S PROBABLY SITTING ALONE IN A CORNER...
WOW
flutter
flutter

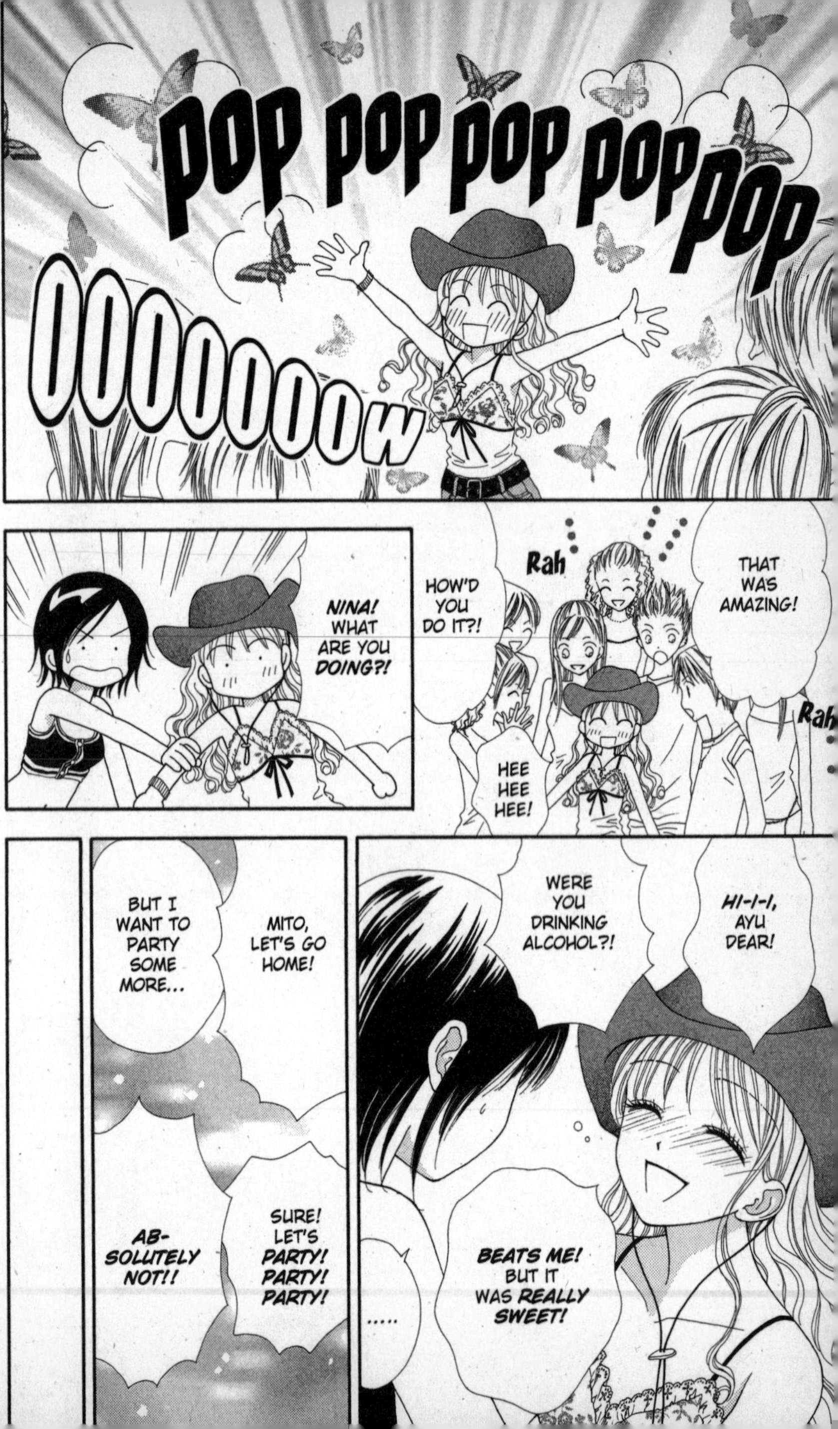
POP POP POP POP POP
OOOOOOOOW
THAT WAS AMAZING!
Rah
Rah
HOW'D YOU DO IT?!
HEE HEE HEE!
NINA! WHAT ARE YOU DOING?!
HI-I-I, AYU DEAR!
WERE YOU DRINKING ALCOHOL?!
BEATS ME! BUT IT WAS REALLY SWEET!
.....
MITO, LET'S GO HOME!
BUT I WANT TO PARTY SOME MORE...
SURE! LET'S PARTY! PARTY! PARTY!
AB-SOLUTELY NOT!!

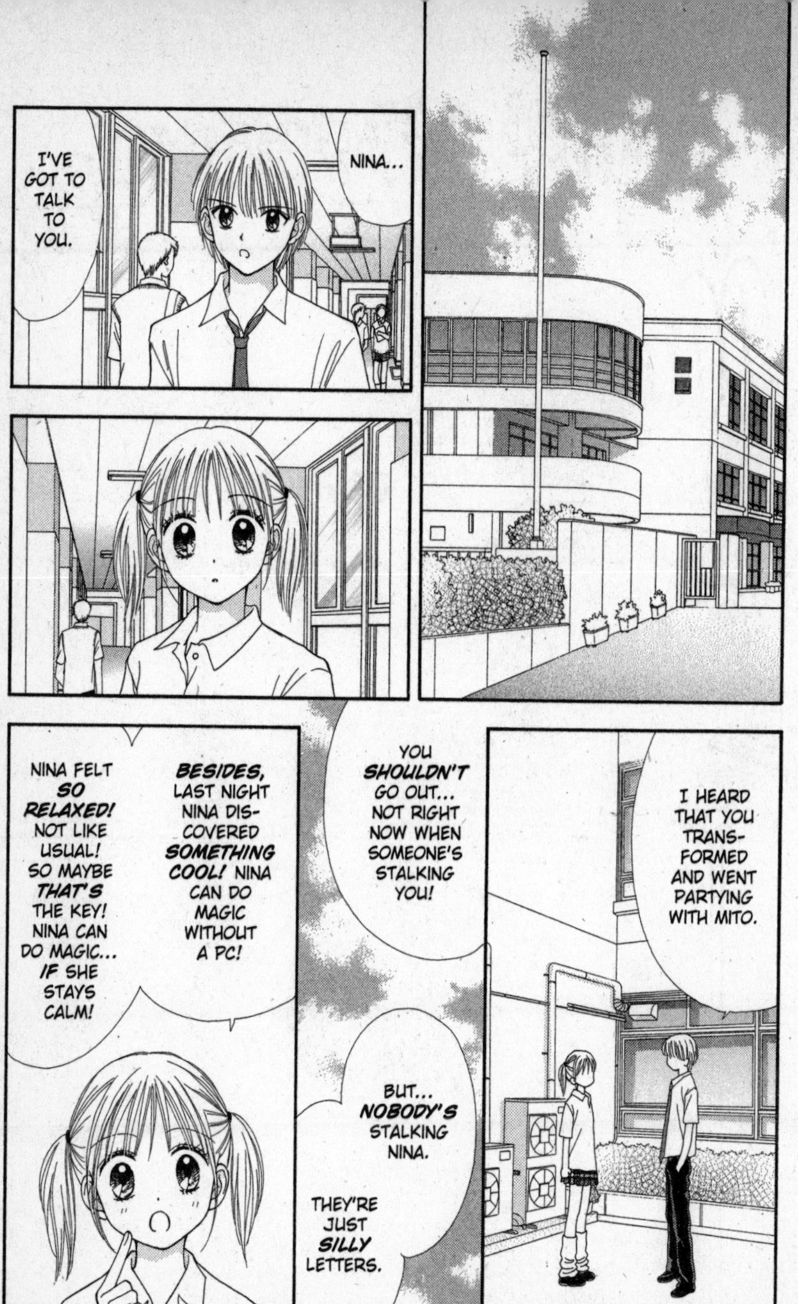
NINA...
I'VE GOT TO TALK TO YOU.
I HEARD THAT YOU TRANSFORMED AND WENT PARTYING WITH MITO.
YOU *SHOULDN'T* GO OUT... NOT RIGHT NOW WHEN SOMEONE'S STALKING YOU!
BUT... *NOBODY'S* STALKING NINA.
THEY'RE JUST *SILLY* LETTERS.
BESIDES, LAST NIGHT NINA DISCOVERED *SOMETHING COOL!* NINA CAN DO MAGIC WITHOUT A PC!
NINA FELT *SO RELAXED!* NOT LIKE USUAL! SO MAYBE *THAT'S* THE KEY! NINA CAN DO MAGIC... *IF* SHE STAYS CALM!

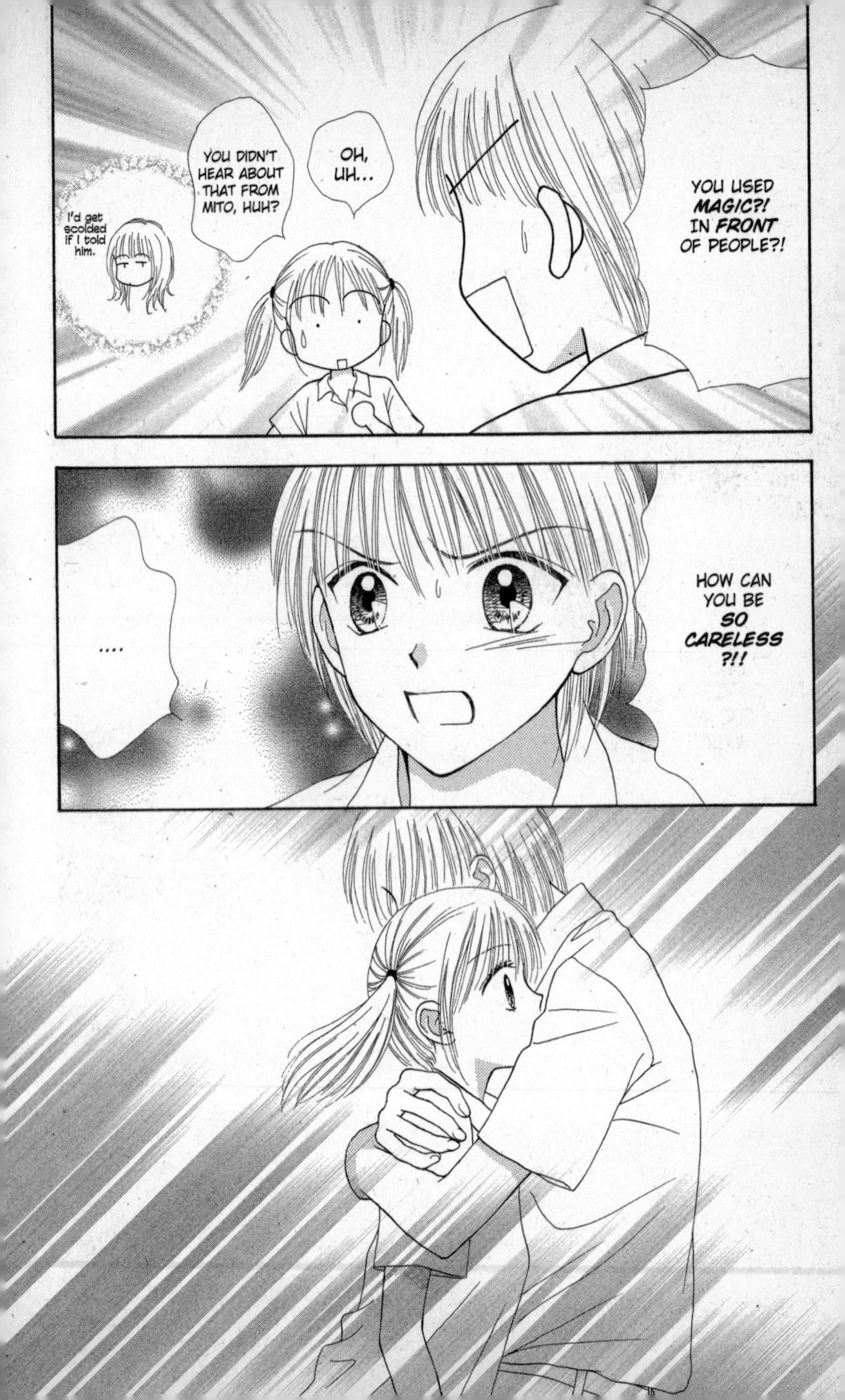
YOU USED MAGIC?! IN FRONT OF PEOPLE?!
OH, UH...
YOU DIDN'T HEAR ABOUT THAT FROM MITO, HUH?
I'd get scolded if I told him.
HOW CAN YOU BE SO CARELESS ?!!
....

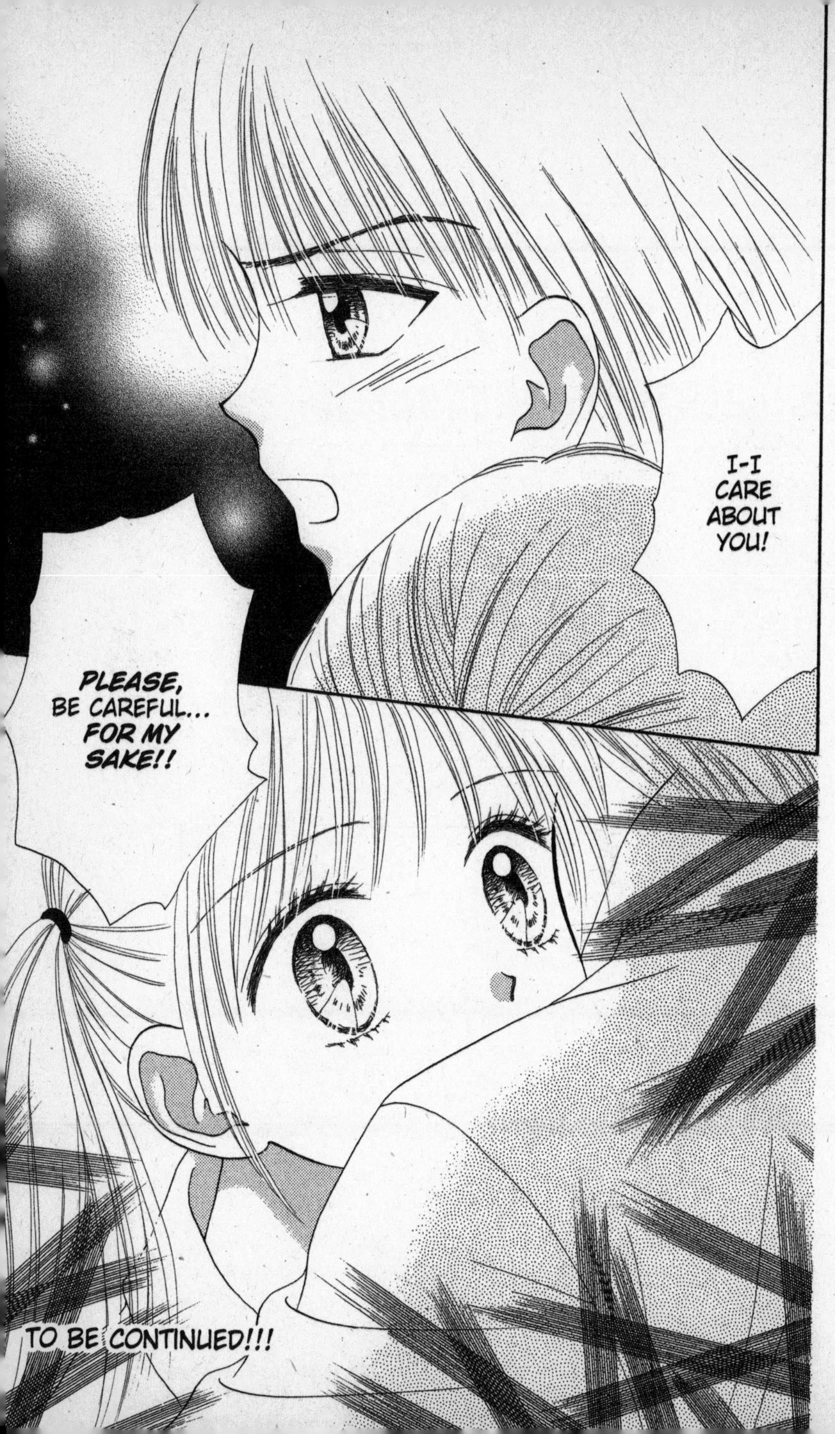
I-I CARE ABOUT YOU!
PLEASE, BE CAREFUL... FOR MY SAKE!!
TO BE CONTINUED!!!

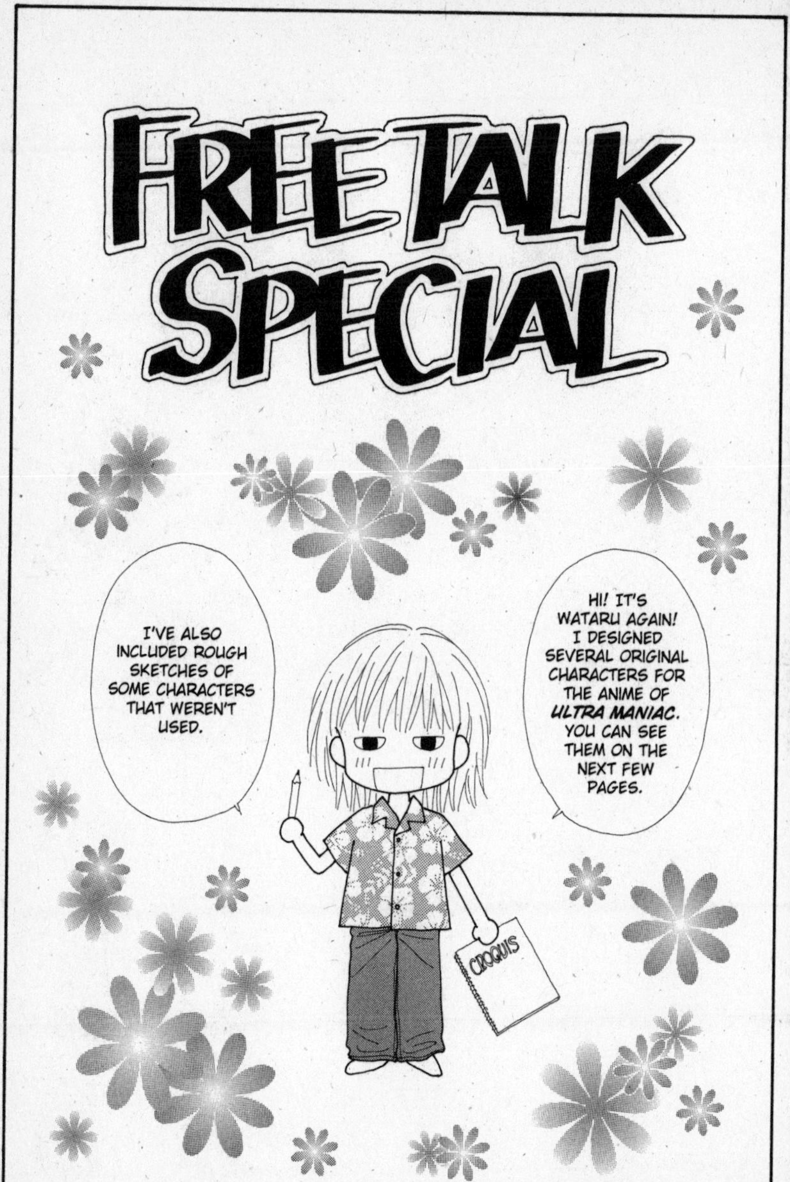
FREE TALK SPECIAL
HI! IT'S WATARU AGAIN! I DESIGNED SEVERAL ORIGINAL CHARACTERS FOR THE ANIME OF *ULTRA MANIAC*. YOU CAN SEE THEM ON THE NEXT FEW PAGES.
I'VE ALSO INCLUDED ROUGH SKETCHES OF SOME CHARACTERS THAT WEREN'T USED.
CROQUIS
2003. May

MAYA ORIHARA (MAYA OPHELIA)

Maya is Nina's rival. Like Nina, she's studying "abroad" from the Magic Kingdom.

At the first brainstorming session, the director asked me if it was okay if to create "a rival." I said it was fine as long as the girl wasn't "all prissy" and said things such as "like, oh my gawd!" I don't like characters that speak that way.

The director said "Yeah, I don't like that type either. We're both on the same page." So I thought it was going to be a character that spoke "normally." But I was surprised when I read the script. Maya talks like a boy! (She doesn't speak crudely. She's more of the "strong, semi-silent type" who rarely says more than few words at a time.)

So I wondered if I should've designed her to look a little less feminine. I only put lashes on the corners of her eyes. But the anime has her with eyelashes from corner to corner, upper and lower eyelids--plus, a very pretty face. Even though she is Nina's rival, she isn't evil or a threat. She isn't even a disagreeable girl.

She's interested in black magic and she's a little different than other girls. She keeps a chameleon as a pet. I thought a pigtail hairstyle would be cute too, like the one on the left page, but it probably won't be used.

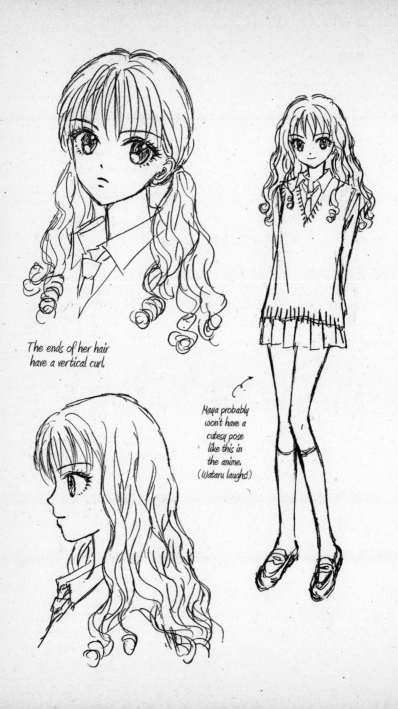

The ends of her hair
have a vertical curl.

Maya probably
won't have a
cutesy pose
like this in
the anime.
(Wataru laughs!)

JUN KAWANAKAJIMA

Never loosens tie.

Short

Small sweater.

Slightly short pants legs.

Kawanakajima was originally supposed to be the class president and become "enthralled" with Nina and chase her around after seeing her in her magic costume.

I was asked to design him so that he wasn't "a pretty boy, but he wasn't a complete nerd or fat" either. But when I drew a generic face that was a little on the skinny side and appeared pretty intelligent, the producer (Naomi Sato) told me that "this is too pretty boy (bishonen.) Unlike shojo manga, anime can't have just beautiful characters." So I redesigned him.

Afterward, though, I said "a class president should have some sort of charisma" otherwise he'd never get elected president. So they made him a class secretary. Up until Chapter 15, rather than being enthralled by Nina, he chases after Nina to expose her as a witch. I gave him the name of Jun Kawanakajima.

Maya's name was probably dreamed up by a member of the anime staff—possibly script series coordinator Miho Maruo.

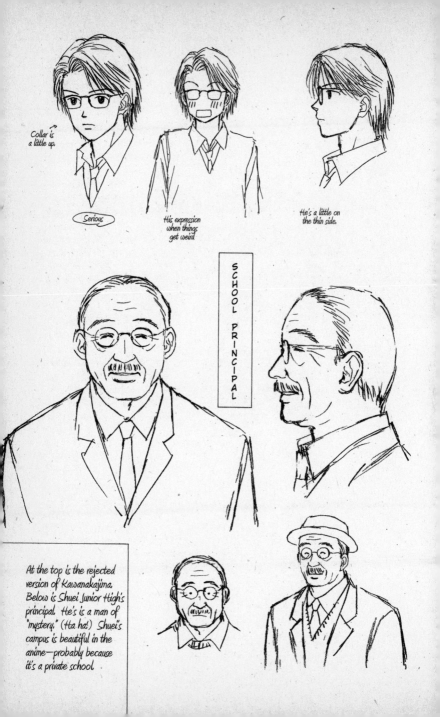

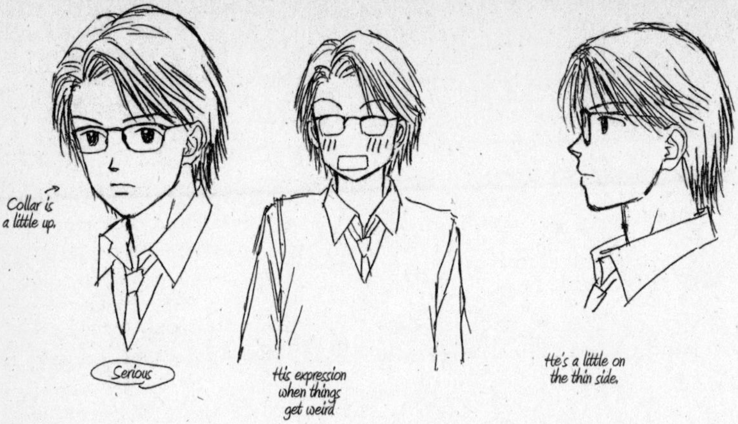
He's a little on the thin side.
His expression when things get weird
Collar is a little up.
Serious

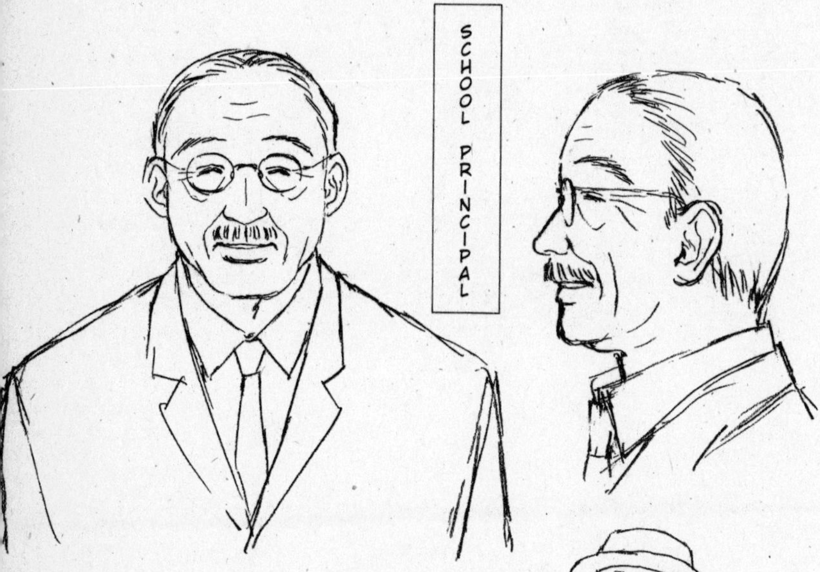
SCHOOL PRINCIPAL

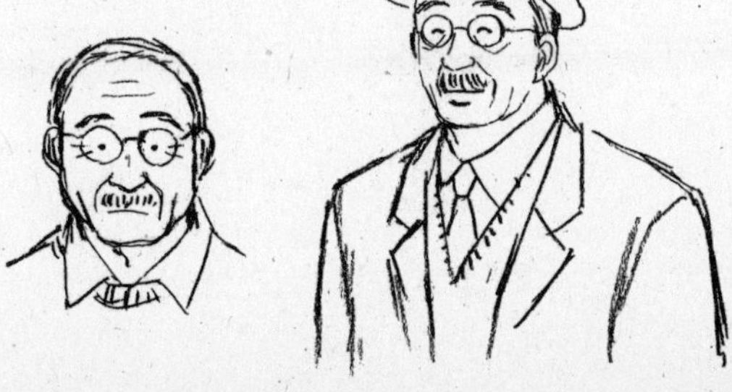

At the top is the rejected version of Kawanakajima. Below is Shuei Junior High's principal. He's is a man of "mystery." (Ha ha!) Shuei's campus is beautiful in the anime—probably because it's a private school.

NINA'S GRANDFATHER

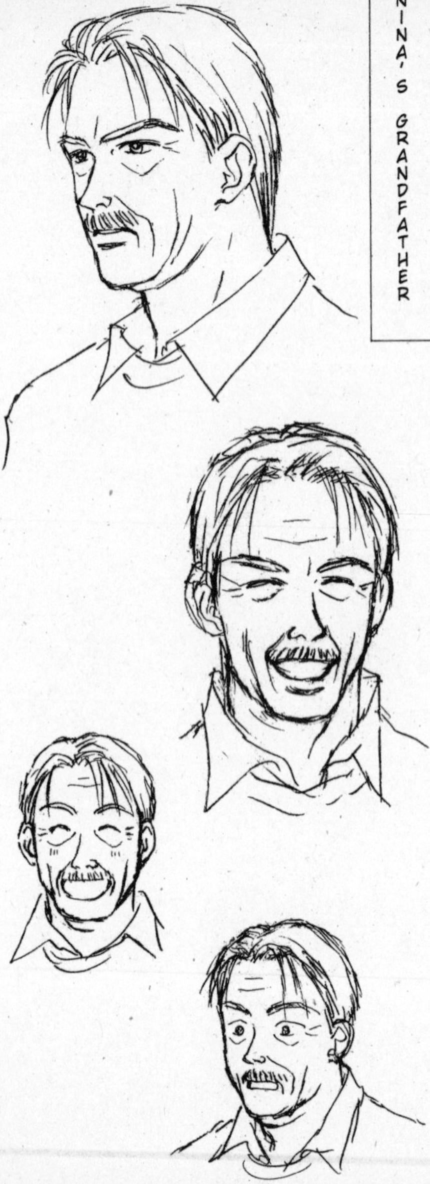

I've drawn old men and women before, but this is the first time I've drawn a grandfather. It turned out to be a lot of fun. I was pretty happy that I had drawn a nice masculine character, but the producer told me that "it didn't fit the image."

No one had told me how he should look. So I drew him the way I wanted. But the anime staff apparently wanted a "short, bald, white-fluffy-mustached" old man for comic relief. (Kinda like the old man from *Yawara!*) So I tried redrawing him with a variety of funny expressions, but the design was still nixed.

Unlike Kawanakajima, this character was related to the main character. So I had an image in my mind of how he should look and I couldn't bring myself to redesign him. In the end, the character designer (Miho Shimokasa) had to introduce a new grandfather that would work for comic relief.

But then something unexpected happened. My version of the grandfather got used after all!

Apparently the president of Ashi Productions said "the creator went to the trouble of creating the character. So use that one." I was happy to hear it, but I felt bad that Miho Shimokasa had to do everything twice.

On the next page you can see Nina's Magic School's uniform. Normally, I like drawing clothes that you can actually see in stores. So when I'm asked to design fantasy clothing it's a lot more work. On top of that, there were detailed requests like 1) a long flared skirt; 2) puff sleeves; 3) frills, but not like an apron; 4) an unusual hat. . . and so forth. So it was even more difficult.

After I finished designing everything, I got a shock. It turns out that the producer actually wanted fancy designs with lots of detail. That's why I was asked to do the designs instead of an anime artist. When most animators create clothing, they make simple designs that are easy to reproduce. Of course, I was thinking, "It's anime—so I can't make this too detailed." So I ended up designing along very simple lines. If I'd have known what the producer wanted, I would have drawn something a lot more detailed.

I was also asked to design a number of outfits for Ayu and Nina, but I didn't have enough time. So apparently the animator copied a number of outfits from the side graphics and title graphics from the books.

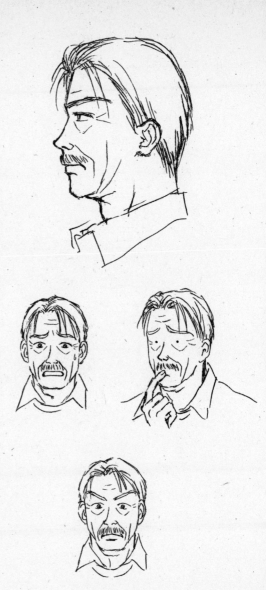

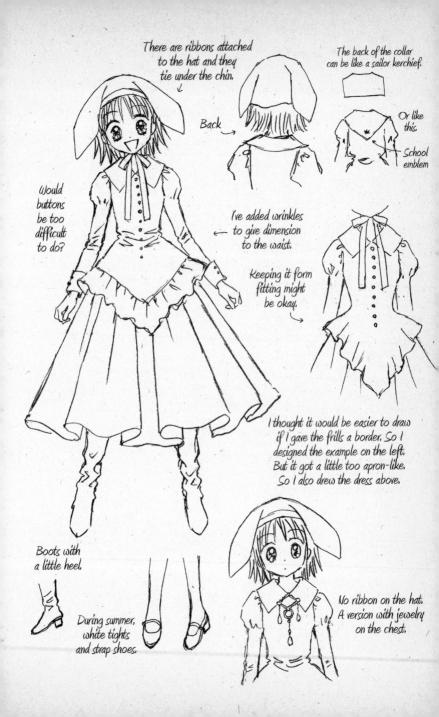

There are ribbons attached to the hat and they tie under the chin.

The back of the collar can be like a sailor kerchief.

Back

Or like this

School emblem

Would buttons be too difficult to do?

I've added wrinkles to give dimension to the waist.

Keeping it form fitting might be okay.

I thought it would be easier to draw if I gave the frills a border. So I designed the example on the left. But it got a little too apron-like. So I also drew the dress above.

Boots with a little heel.

During summer, white tights and strap shoes.

No ribbon on the hat. A version with jewelry on the chest.

Personally, I liked the design on the right and created a lot of detail. I thought that maybe it'd be bad to have just one design, so I created the one on the left as a bonus. For some reason, the one on the left was the animator's favorite.

I wonder why. Maybe it didn't look enough like a "uniform."

But the other design wasn't used without changes. In the anime, the shape of the hat is completely different. There's also a big ribbon on the back of the waist. And the silhouette of the skirt is slightly different.

The uniform I put on Maya on the two-page spread is similar. According to the anime scripts, Maya modified her uniform herself and wears it that way. Its form and color are completely different from Nina's. (Maya's uniform was not designed by me.)

I have no idea why they have to do a costume change every time they use magic. (Ha ha!) I think it's because it's fun.

This type of design, too.

⌐ A beret.
A big one.

NINA'S PARENTS

Since the grandfather is in the anime, I thought the parents might be needed, too. So I drew them. Apparently, though, they won't be used.

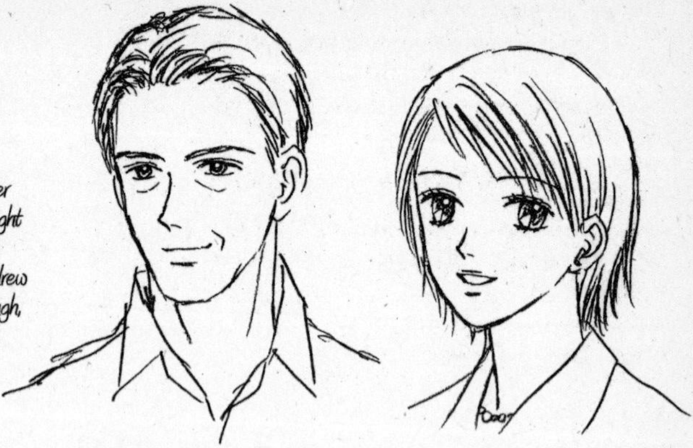

Grandfather is paternal

HOST FAMILY PARENTS

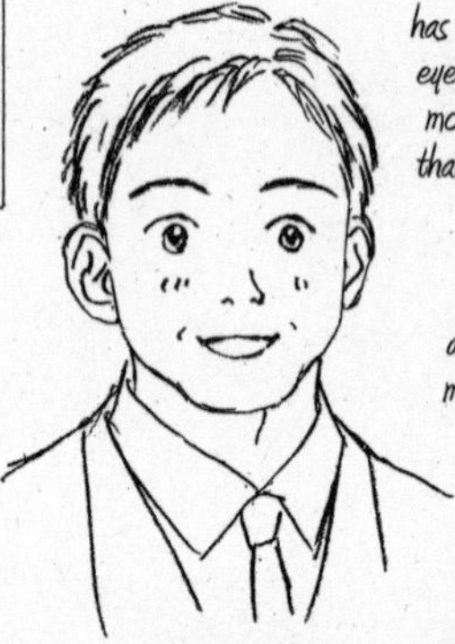

The mom in the anime has top and bottom eyelids and is a lot more fresh-faced than in the manga.

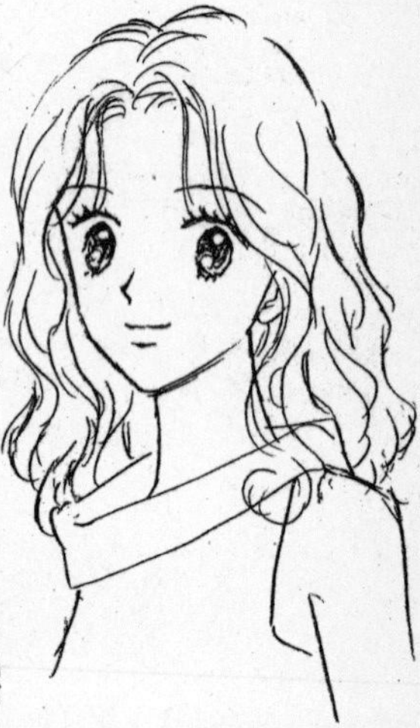

The dad is also different from the manga and doesn't wear glasses (since the principal wears glasses).

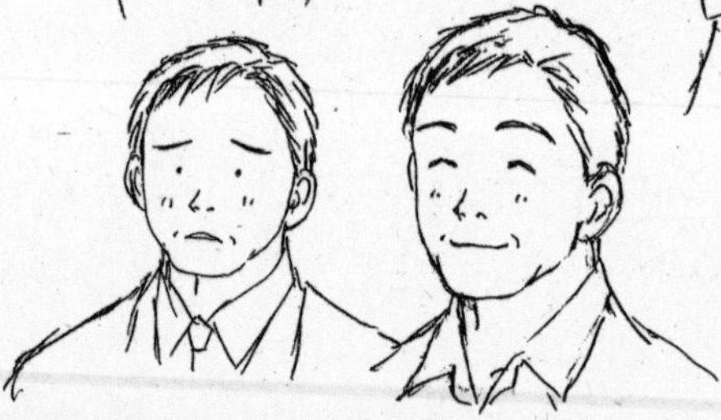

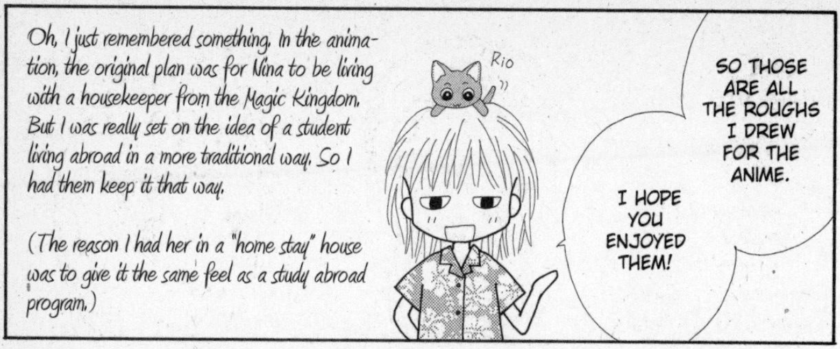
SO THOSE ARE ALL THE ROUGHS I DREW FOR THE ANIME.
I HOPE YOU ENJOYED THEM!
Rio
Oh, I just remembered something. In the animation, the original plan was for Nina to be living with a housekeeper from the Magic Kingdom. But I was really set on the idea of a student living abroad in a more traditional way. So I had them keep it that way.
(The reason I had her in a "home stay" house was to give it the same feel as a study abroad program.)

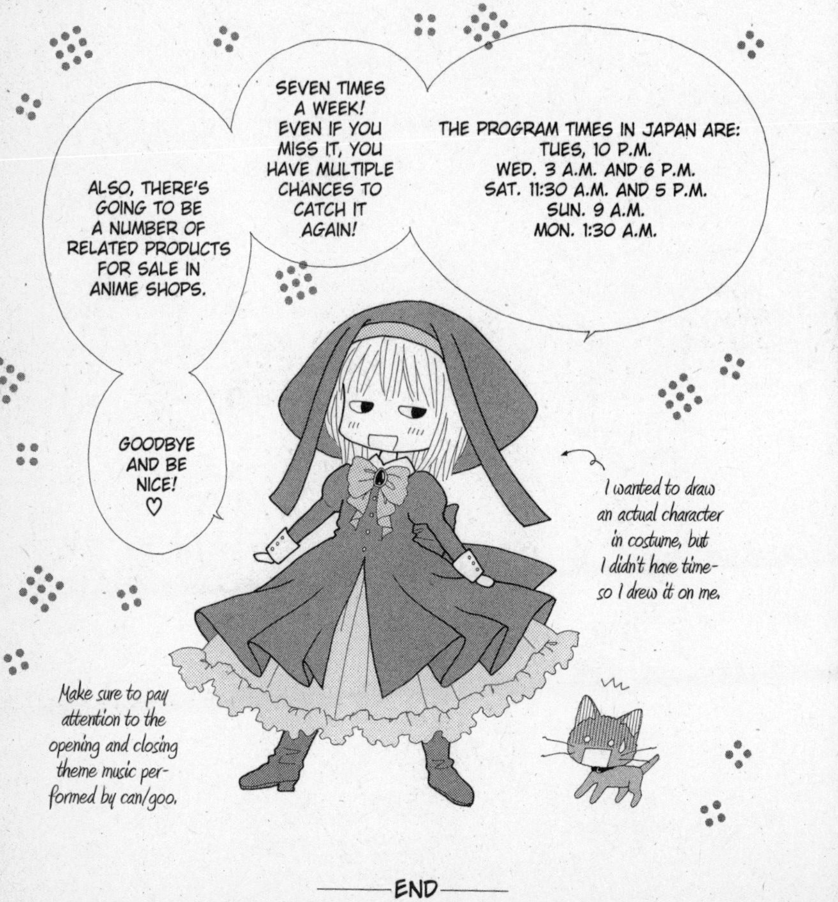
THE PROGRAM TIMES IN JAPAN ARE: TUES. 10 P.M. WED. 3 A.M. AND 6 P.M. SAT. 11:30 A.M. AND 5 P.M. SUN. 9 A.M. MON. 1:30 A.M.
SEVEN TIMES A WEEK! EVEN IF YOU MISS IT, YOU HAVE MULTIPLE CHANCES TO CATCH IT AGAIN!
ALSO, THERE'S GOING TO BE A NUMBER OF RELATED PRODUCTS FOR SALE IN ANIME SHOPS.
GOODBYE AND BE NICE! ♡
I wanted to draw an actual character in costume, but I didn't have time- so I drew it on me.
Make sure to pay attention to the opening and closing theme music performed by can/goo.

—END—

Wataru Yoshizumi

Comments

Yoshizumi Wataru writes: "The story in this volume takes place before and after summer vacation, but readers first saw it in the middle of winter— so I wrote it wistfully remembering summer. Illustrations and cut scene graphics are predominantly wintery and in line with the season."

Bio

Wataru Yoshizumi hails from Tokyo and made her manga debut in 1984 with *Radical Romance* in *Ribon Original* magazine. The artist has since produced a string of fan-favorite titles, including *Quartet Game*, *Handsome na Kanojo* (Handsome Girl), *Marmalade Boy*, and *Random Walk*. *Ultra Maniac*, a magical screwball comedy, is only the second time her work has been available in the U.S. Many of her titles, however, are available throughout Asia and Europe. Yoshizumi loves to travel and is keen on making original accessories out of beads.

ULTRA MANIAC VOL. 3

The Shojo Beat Manga Edition

STORY AND ART BY
WATARU YOSHIZUMI

English Adaptation/John Lustig
Translation/Koji Goto
Touch-up Art & Lettering/Elizabeth Watasin
Cover & Graphic Design/Izumi Evers
Editor/Eric Searleman

Managing Editor/Megan Bates
Editorial Director/Elizabeth Kawasaki
VP & Editor in Chief/Yumi Hoashi
Sr. Director of Acquisitions/Rika Inouye
Sr. VP of Marketing/Liza Coppola
Exec. VP of Sales & Marketing/John Easum
Publisher/Hyoe Narita

Printed in the U.S.A.

Published by VIZ Media, LLC
P.O. Box 77010
San Francisco, CA 94107

Shojo Beat Manga Edition
10 9 8 7 6 5 4 3 2
First printing, October 2005
Second printing, November 2006

store.viz.com

PARENTAL ADVISORY
ULTRA MANIAC is rated A and is suitable for readers of all ages.

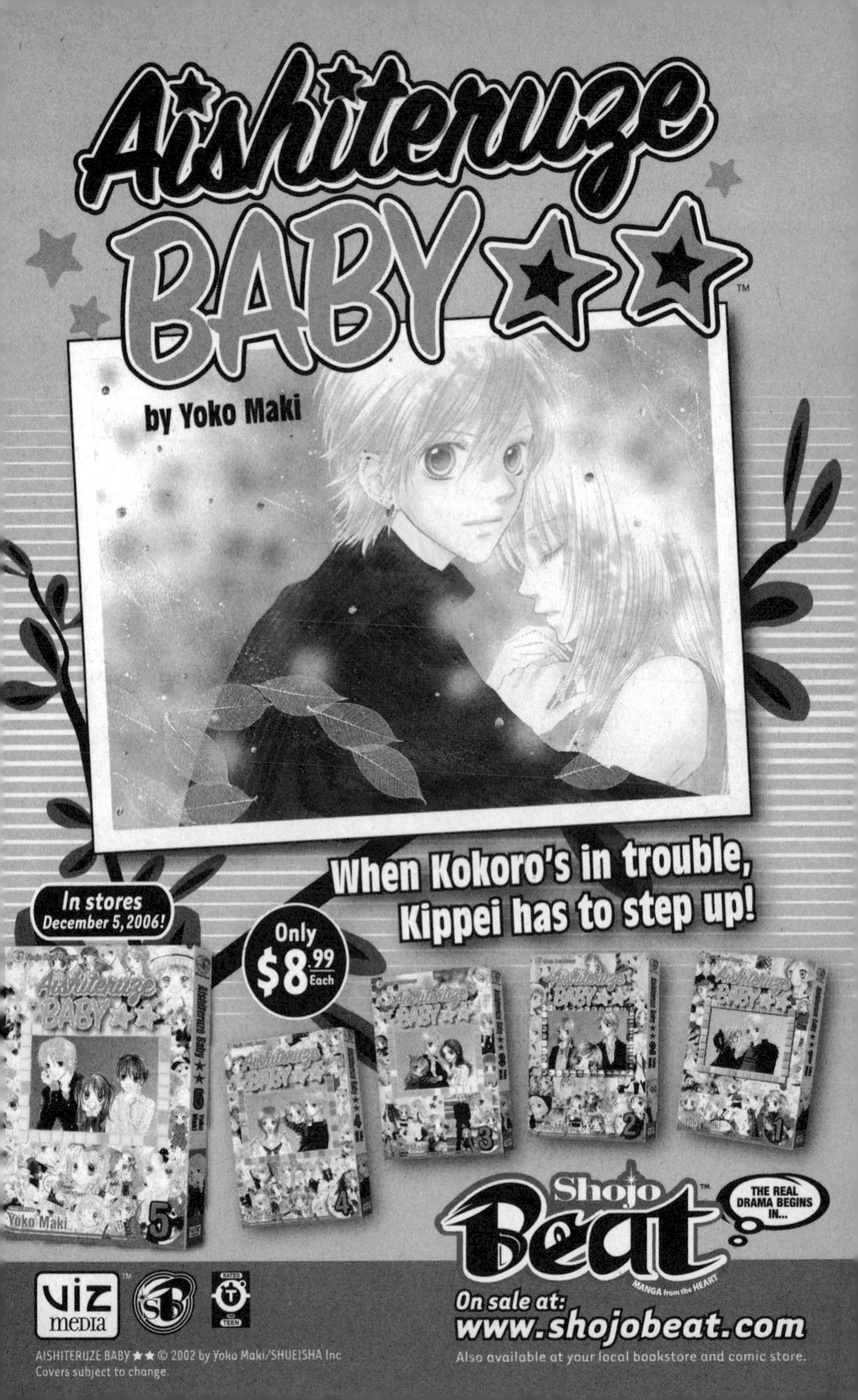
Aishiteruze BABY ★★™
by Yoko Maki
When Kokoro's in trouble, Kippei has to step up!
In stores December 5, 2006!
Only $8.99 Each
Yoko Maki
Shojo Beat™
THE REAL DRAMA BEGINS IN...
MANGA from the HEART
On sale at:
www.shojobeat.com
Also available at your local bookstore and comic store.
viz media
RATED T TEEN
AISHITERUZE BABY ★★ © 2002 by Yoko Maki/SHUEISHA Inc.
Covers subject to change.

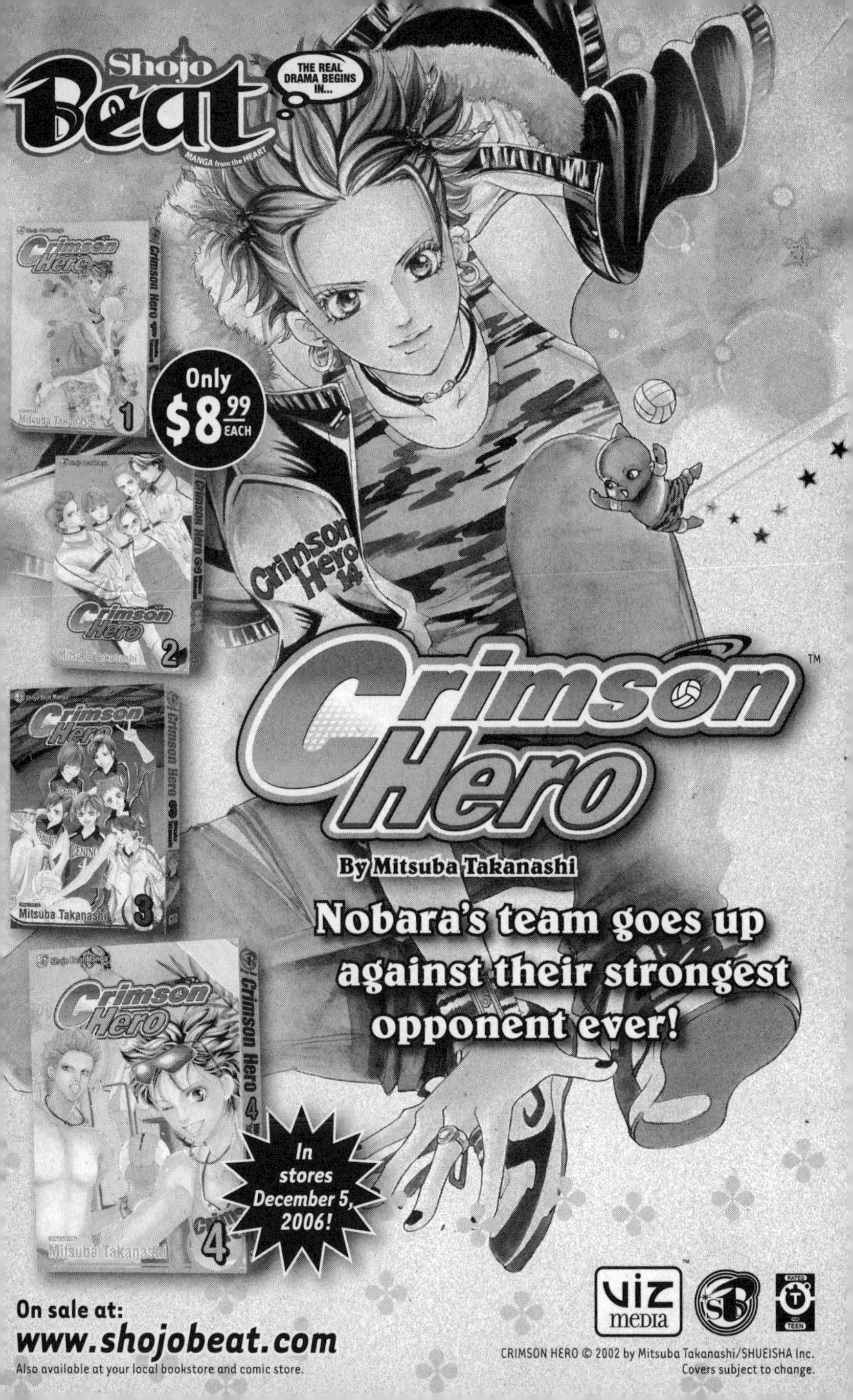
Shojo Beat
MANGA from the HEART
THE REAL DRAMA BEGINS IN...
Only $8.99 EACH
Crimson Hero
By Mitsuba Takanashi
Nobara's team goes up against their strongest opponent ever!
In stores December 5, 2006!
On sale at:
www.shojobeat.com
Also available at your local bookstore and comic store.
viz media
CRIMSON HERO © 2002 by Mitsuba Takanashi/SHUEISHA Inc.
Covers subject to change.